ADAPTING THE ARTHURIAN LEGENDS FOR CHILDREN

ESSAYS ON ARTHURIAN JUVENILIA

STUDIES IN ARTHURIAN AND COURTLY CULTURES

The dynamic field of Arthurian Studies is the subject for this book series, *Studies in Arthurian and Courtly Cultures*, which explores the great variety of literary and cultural expression inspired by the lore of King Arthur, the Round Table, and the Grail. In forms that range from medieval chronicles to popular films, from chivalric romances to contemporary comics, from magic realism to feminist fantasy—and from the sixth through the twenty-first centuries— few literary subjects provide such fertile ground for cultural elaboration. Including works in literary criticism, cultural studies, and history, *Studies in Arthurian and Courtly Cultures* high- lights the most significant new Arthurian Studies.

Bonnie Wheeler, *Southern Methodist University*
Series Editor

ADAPTING THE ARTHURIAN LEGENDS FOR CHILDREN

ESSAYS ON ARTHURIAN JUVENILIA

Edited by

Barbara Tepa Lupack

ADAPTING THE ARTHURIAN LEGENDS FOR CHILDREN
© Barbara Tepa Lupack, 2004

First published 2004 by
PALGRAVE MACMILLAN™
175 Fifth Avenue, New York, N.Y. 10010 and
Houndmills, Basingstoke, Hampshire, England RG21 6XS
Companies and representatives throughout the world

PALGRAVE MACMILLAN is the global academic imprint of the Palgrave Macmillan division of St. Martin's Press, LLC and of Palgrave Macmillan Ltd. Macmillan® is a registered trademark in the United States, United Kingdom and other countries. Palgrave is a registered trademark in the European Union and other countries.

ISBN 1–4039–6296–0 hardback

Library of Congress Cataloging-in-Publication Data
    Adapting the Arthurian legends for children: essays on Arthurian juvenilia / edited by Barbara Tepa Lupack.
        p. cm.—(Arthurian studies; 1)
    Includes bibliographical references and index.
    ISBN 1–4039–6296–0
        1. Arthurian romances—Adaptations—History and criticism.
    2. Children's literature, English—History and criticism. 3. Children's literature, American—History and criticism. I. Lupack, Barbara Tepa II. Arthurian studies (Palgrave Macmillan (Firm)); 1

    PR408.A7A66 2004
    823.009'351—dc21   2003044241

A catalogue record for this book is available from the British Library.

Design by Newgen Imaging Systems (P) Ltd., Chennai, India.

First edition: January, 2004
10 9 8 7 6 5 4 3 2 1

Printed in the United States of America.

For
Raymond H. Thompson
and
Roger Simpson

pioneers in modern Arthurian studies,
esteemed colleagues,
and, above all, cherished friends

and,
as always,
for Al

TABLE OF CONTENTS

ACKNOWLEDGMENTS

This volume was very much a collaborative effort. I am grateful to Bonnie Wheeler, Editor of *Arthuriana* and General Editor of the "Studies in Arthurian and Courtly Cultures" series at Palgrave Macmillan, whose support has been unflagging and whose editorial judgments have been both skillful and sound.

At Palgrave Macmillan, former Senior Editor Kristi Long encouraged the project in its early stages; Vice President Michael Flamini saw the manuscript to fruition. I thank them both. Palgrave Editorial Assistant Matthew Ashford lent much logistical and technical help. At Newgen Imaging, Mukesh V. S. and his staff guided the manuscript through production. I also thank the colleagues and readers who read individual essays or reviewed the manuscript as a whole and who offered valuable suggestions for its improvement.

Many colleagues and friends offered great encouragement and support and, through their works, helped to shape some of my own ideas. I am especially grateful to Kevin Harty, Lissy Sklar, Don Hoffman, Dan Nastali, and Ray Thompson. In preparing my essay for this volume, I referred often to their pioneering studies on Arthurian cinema, literature, and popular culture. Bert Olton's *Arthurian Legends on Film and Television* also provided useful information. *The New Arthurian Encyclopedia* (with supplements), edited by Norris Lacy and others, served as an excellent reference. And Ray Thompson's *Taliesin's Successors: Interviews with Authors of Modern Arthurian Literature* was also a wonderful resource.

At the University of Rochester, Russell Peck, John H. Deane Professor of Rhetoric and English Literature, was generous with advice and assistance, especially with some of the photography. At the University's Robbins Library, Rose Paprocki and Anne Zanzucchi offered moral and technical support, particularly in the preparation of cover and text images.

The contributors to this volume were as gracious as they were knowledgeable. Their insights and expertise gave me a new appreciation of various aspects of children's Arthuriana, and I thank each of them—Andrew Lynch, Judith Kellogg, Lissy Sklar, Cindy Vitto, Ray Thompson, Charlotte Spivack, Dan Nastali, Alan Lupack, Jerry Reel, and Michael Torregrossa—for making this project such a pleasant experience.

And, as always, I am thankful to Alan Lupack, whose judgments I value beyond measure and who is in every respect my best and most cherished resource.

LIST OF ILLUSTRATIONS

INTRODUCTION

Barbara Tepa Lupack

English and American children in the nineteenth and twentieth centuries learned about King Arthur in a variety of ways: through the numerous retellings of Malory and versions of Tennyson for young people; through the host of illustrated volumes to which the late Arthurian Revival gave rise; through picture books, which took both familiar and innovative approaches to the Arthurian stories; through youth groups for boys (and eventually for girls), which were run by schools and churches; through traditional rhymes, songs, original recordings, and rock albums; through school operas, theater pieces, pantomimes, and similar entertainments geared especially to younger audiences; through other forms of Arthurian drama and poetry; through toys, games, and advertising, which brought the legends not just into the culture but also into the home itself; through comics and cartoons; through films, miniseries, and television shows, which made the Arthurian characters tangible and accessible; through juvenile fiction sequences and series; through contemporary feminist recastings of the legends; and through the many multimedia reworkings of perennial favorites, such as the stories of Sir Gawain and the Green Knight and the Connecticut Yankee. By exploring these and other aspects of Arthurian juvenilia, the twelve essays in *Adapting the Arthurian Legends for Children* illustrate both the protean nature and the continuing appeal of the Arthurian legends.

The purpose of *Adapting the Arthurian Legends for Children* is to offer a comprehensive overview of the widely divergent genres in which children's Arthuriana has been treated and to demonstrate to Arthurian scholars and enthusiasts, medievalists, students of British and American culture, and general readers the scope of Arthurian juvenilia, especially in the nineteenth and twentieth centuries, in both high and popular culture. The volume, within a largely Anglo-American context, examines a wide variety of media and analyzes representative individual works. It shows not only how medieval and post-medieval Arthurian texts have been retold and reinterpreted but also how those reinterpretations provide important clues to understanding the original texts as well. In particular, the volume reveals how each adaptation and each adapter—whether by retelling Malory as a model of conduct or as a political adventure, by bowdlerizing the graphic violence committed by Hank Martin in Twain's classic novel, by deemphasizing religion in contemporary versions of *Sir Gawain and the Green Knight*, by democratizing the British chivalric tradition to make it compatible with American ideals in American youth groups and in popular children's literature, or by giving prominence to the legends' female characters in cartoons, films, and other modern media—provides vital insights into the culture and illustrates the ways that the age-old Arthurian stories have been modified, popularized, or otherwise repackaged for contemporary audiences and tastes.

Of the countless writers and artists who have been fascinated and inspired by the Arthurian legends over the years, many first became acquainted with the story as youngsters. In fact, as Jane Yolen noted in an interview with Raymond H. Thompson, "We sometimes forget that most of us come upon the Arthurian legend when we're children." The Arthurian story, she explained, "works whatever age you are. When you're young, you respond to the story of the fellowship and the great deeds. . . . [As you get older] you begin thinking about the romance, and the tragedy, and the beauty," and "you find different things in the legend." But "I think it's really important to remember how almost all of us who came to this story came to it first as children, and grew up with it."[1]

Tennessee Williams, for instance, wrote his "first literary piece" when he was twelve years old; his teacher had assigned the class to pick out a subject for a theme, and Tennessee "chose the Lady of Shalott, drifting down the river on a boat. He read the theme in front of the class," and it had a very good reception. "From that time on," Williams realized, "I knew I was going to be a writer."[2] And, indeed, in a number of his best plays, the image of the Lady of Shalott recurs, usually in the character of the woman who is willing to sacrifice everything for love, often with tragic consequences—one of the hallmarks of Williams's drama.

Novelist Thomas Berger recalled that, as a boy, he "preferred the pleasure of the imagination to those of experience"[3] and read incessantly. He mentions with great fondness his "own boyhood King Arthur. . .the works of one Elizabeth Lodor Merchant," a gift from his father at Christmas, 1931.[4] He later described his own popular novel *Arthur Rex* (1978) as essentially his "memory of that childish version [of *Le Morte d'Arthur*]" as edited and expanded according to his outlandish fantasies (and even some of the droll experiences he has had in the years since).[5] On another occasion, Berger expressed a similar sentiment: "I chose to make my contribution to the [Arthurian] theme," he wrote, "because I had always adored the Arthurian stories as a child, and in my career I sooner or later strive to give permanency to each of my childhood fantasies."[6]

Another important American novelist, Walker Percy, also acknowledged drawing on recollections of his boyhood Arthurian readings while writing his best known novel *Lancelot* (1978). Percy's vision of his protagonist, Lancelot Andrews Lamar, was based in part on "the great picture of Lancelot and Turquine" in *The Boy's King Arthur*, one of the first books he ever read. "The provenance of my Lancelot," he wrote, "is *The Boys King Arthur* [sic] and most importantly the marvellous illustrations—most especially the one of Lancelot bloodied up in his chain mail and leaning on his broadsword and saying to Sir Turquine, who has just said to him, what manner of man are you to have fought me for hours:'I am Sir Lancelot du Lake'—etc."[7] In fact, Percy's reinterpretation—or perhaps his misremembering—of the stories of Lancelot from his childhood became central to Percy's fictional retelling, in which he casts Lancelot and Percival, Lancelot's confessor and friend in the novel, as co-equal achievers of the Grail (though certainly by opposite means).[8] T. S. Eliot had a similar strong Arthurian memory from his childhood: he wrote that a juvenile version of Malory "was in my hands when I was a child of eleven or twelve. It was then, and perhaps has always been, my favorite book."[9]

Not only male authors were influenced by their childhood Arthurian readings; numerous women writers were inspired as well. Catherine Christian, at age eighty, remembered that she first became acquainted with the Arthurian legend when she was five years old; from that time on, she was "fascinated by, and increasingly involved in the story of Arthur, myself. The more research I did, the more I found myself drawn back to the historical setting, and the more interested I became in the intricate comparison between fact and legend."[10] Jane Yolen told Raymond H. Thompson, "one of the first stories that I ever remember reading was the Arthurian story. I read it in *The Book of Wonder*, an encyclopedia belonging to my parents,. . .when I was about seven or eight years old." She recalled that "the Arthurian story just absolutely transfixed me, and I believed that it was the greatest and most wonderful story that was ever told. Then over the years I read all the Arthurian things that children read: Howard Pyle, T. H. White, and all the others. Because it had 'been written,' it didn't occur to me, until my writing career was well advanced, to attempt what I felt was already the greatest story that had ever been told."[11] Rosemary Sutcliff recalled that "Amongst the rather odd collection of books that I was reared on were stories of Arthurian legends," particularly "what we might call the Malory version." As a teenager, she read Tennyson and "loved him. . .but I don't think I would put him down as an Arthurian scholar." Only later, when she was eighteen or nineteen, did she discover the historical side of the legend, aspects of which she later integrated into her own Arthurian work.[12] And while Susan Cooper does not remember specific titles, she supposes that "I must have done [reading of Arthurian stories for younger people] because I knew the legends," a knowledge that she developed further during her later study at Oxford.[13]

Even writers not normally associated with the Arthurian tradition were often deeply influenced by it, especially by their childhood experiences of it. For instance, as a boy, F. Scott Fitzgerald, who was fascinated with medievalism, including the Arthurian myth and the romance of chivalry, read *Scottish Chiefs*, *Ivanhoe*, and action-based historical stories for young men; and by high school he progressed to the works of Tennyson, Chesterton, and Twain. Fitzgerald's earliest writings, according to his *Ledger* entry for June, 1909, included an imitation of *Ivanhoe* called "Elavo" and a "complicated story of some knights," both unfinished.[14] Those early works anticipated his best known work, *The Great Gatsby*, about Jay Gatsby, a contemporary knight errant who had "committed himself to the following of a grail"[15] in his quest for the love of Daisy Buchanan, and other works, including "O Russet Witch!" (about a clerk named Merlin and his ungrateful son Arthur), which incorporated Arthurian characters and images. Reportedly, among Fitzgerald's final projects was a novel—never completed—to be set entirely in medieval times. Fitzgerald passed his interests on to his young daughter Scottie, who recalled the charts of the Middle Ages and the "Histomaps" that hung on the walls of his workroom in their home in Baltimore and his collections of miniature soldiers, "which he deployed on marches around our Christmas trees"; and Scottie herself played "Knights of the Round Table" with paper dolls that had been elaborately painted by her mother Zelda—"coats-of-mail of Galahad and Lancelot. . .[and other] proud members" of the court of King Arthur—in a doll's house described by Fitzgerald in one of his short stories, "Outside the Cabinet-Maker's."[16]

Like his contemporary and sometime friend F. Scott Fitzgerald, Ernest Hemingway modeled his heroes upon romantic, chivalric notions of himself that began in his boyhood. As Michael S. Reynolds demonstrates, much of Hemingway's adolescent reading—*Old English Ballads*, Chaucer, *The Fairie Queene*, and Tennyson's *Idylls of the King*—had as its focus one particular hero: the medieval knight.[17] In his later work, Hemingway continued to be intrigued by numerous aspects of the medieval and Arthurian story, particularly the myth of the wounded Fisher King, whose health is tied to the fertility of the land; and he incorporated details of that aspect of the Arthurian legends into several of his works, especially in a number of the stories of *In Our Time* and in his novel *The Sun Also Rises*, which transformed the war-wounded protagonist Jake Barnes into a contemporary Fisher King.

John Steinbeck, another renowned American novelist, also drew extensively on Arthurian themes and images. "The story cycle of King Arthur and his knights, particularly in the Malory version," he recalled, "has been my passion since my ninth birthday, when I was given a copy of the 'Morte d'Arthur.' Then my little sister, Mary, and I became knight and squire, and we even used the archaic and obsolete Middle English words as a secret language."[18] From that childhood version of Malory, Steinbeck also developed the essential theme of his own fiction: "my sense of right and wrong, my feeling of noblesse oblige, and any thought I may have against the oppressor and for the oppressed."[19] Malory thus helped to shape all of Steinbeck's novels, from those like *The Grapes of Wrath*, which treat the oppressed (though not in an explicitly Arthurian way), to those like *Cup of Gold*, *Tortilla Flat*, and *Sweet Thursday*, which use the Grail quest or reflect other specific Arthurian images and influences—and, of course, his own retelling in *The Acts of King Arthur and His Noble Knights*, an incomplete work that was published posthumously.

It was not only writers who were deeply influenced by their boyhood experiences of the legends. The brief tenure of John F. Kennedy as the thirty-fifth president of the United States has become synonymous with "Camelot" (even though the actual identification between Kennedy and Camelot first occurred soon after JFK's death, when Jacqueline Bouvier Kennedy urged her friend, reporter and historian Theodore H. White, to label her late husband's historical myth in specifically Arthurian terms). But Kennedy's mother, Rose Kennedy, was pleased by the Arthurian association, which she felt was both accurate and appropriate: she recalled Jack "in his boyhood reading and rereading his copy of *King Arthur and the Round Table*."[20] And famed aviator Charles Lindbergh, in his *Autobiography of Values*, equated the bravery of the heroic twentieth-century "knights of the air" with the "chivalry and daring" of King Arthur's knights whom he recalled from his childhood tales.[21]

Adapting the Arthurian Legends for Children confirms the extent to which the stories of King Arthur have influenced both high and popular culture. The twelve essays in the volume survey the numerous ways and the various media in which those stories have been retold or reinterpreted. Andrew Lynch, for instance, in his pivotal essay "*Le Morte Darthur* for Children: Malory's Third Tradition," offers an important historical examination of Malory retellings and adaptations for children, which constitute a kind of "third tradition of cultural dialogue with *Le Morte Darthur*, in parallel with the traditions of its critical receptions and of neo-Arthurian literature and film, yet frequently interacting with it." Lynch traces the contexts, the developments, the outcomes, and some of the ideological implications of this third tradition of Malory; and he details many of the phases—history, spiritual ideal, model of conduct, political adventure, psychological study, myth and fantasy—that Malory versions for children have undergone over the years.

Judith L. Kellogg, in "Text, Image, and Swords of Empowerment in Recent Arthurian Picture Books," stresses the importance of storytelling in identity formation and offers a sophisticated analysis of why and how the Arthurian stories influence young readers. After distinguishing picture books from illustrated books and describing the text–image dialectic in Arthurian tales, she focuses on a key element in many children's stories— the sword—and shows how verbal and pictorial images not only reshape social expectations and cultural concerns but also reveal the "complexity of rituals and pathways that each new generation must learn to negotiate."

Elizabeth S. Sklar, in "The Case of the Disappearing Text: *Connecticut Yankee* for Kids," offers an excellent overview of the variety of editions and adaptations of Mark Twain's *Connecticut Yankee in King Arthur's Court*, which she suggests is a protean and highly exploitable work. Sklar's lively, well-argued, and comprehensive study details the editors' and retellers' adaptive strategies and analyzes their implications for understanding Twain's work and our attitudes toward it.

Cindy L. Vitto, in her provocative essay "Deceptive Simplicity: Children's Versions of *Sir Gawain and the Green Knight*," examines some important modern versions of the Gawain story for children. After looking specifically at the omissions in the story (especially regarding misogyny, religion, and hunting) and the evidence those omissions offer of cultural shifts, Vitto concludes that analysis of such recent works offers surprising insights into the medieval work itself and helps to explain its ongoing popularity.

Raymond H. Thompson, in "The Sense of Place in Arthurian Fiction for Younger Readers," treats the complex facets of this narrative element. He considers the way settings in medieval romance differ from those of Arthurian novels and demonstrates how modern Arthurian fiction creates a credible physical and cultural setting through such devices as the journey. Using two excellent extended examples of how authors like T. H. White and Rosemary Sutcliff skillfully create a sense of place in order to develop character and theme, Thompson suggests a valuable new perspective on juvenile Arthurian fiction.

Charlotte Spivack, in "Susan Cooper's 'The Dark Is Rising,' " identifies the Arthurian themes, characters, and motifs in the novels that comprise the popular series, "The Dark Is Rising." By examining those five novels within the context of fantasy fiction, particularly juvenile fantasy fiction by women writers, Spivack also defines Cooper's place in the Arthurian canon. An excellent complement to Spivack's essay is Raymond H. Thompson's "Interview with Susan Cooper," in which Cooper discusses the importance of the Arthurian tradition and its reverberations within her own fiction.

Dan Nastali, in "Swords, Grails, and Bag-Puddings: A Survey of Children's Poetry and Plays," covers a wealth of fascinating material. In his overview of poetry and plays from the sixteenth century to the present, Nastali treats works both familiar and obscure—from Lowell's ubiquitous *Vision of Sir Launfal* and Tennyson's *Idylls of the King* to "lost" ballads and verses in popular children's periodicals, from early pantomimes and theatrical entertainments to twentieth-century summer plays and regional children's productions—and sheds light into some "curious and lesser-known corners of the Arthurian tradition."

Alan Lupack's "Arthurian Youth Groups in America: The Americanization of Knighthood" is a perceptive analysis of how the Arthurian legends were adapted to the idealizing and democratic values of clubs for young people in the United States. He shows how groups like Forbush's Knights of King Arthur were designed to channel boys' tendencies to form gangs, while the Queens of Avalon and other girls' groups promoted certain ideals of womanhood. Lupack's essay, which provides valuable cultural insights, also examines some of the contemporary juvenile literary works that promoted these moral and democratic values.

Jerome V. Reel, Jr., in "Good King Arthur: Arthurian Music for Children," observes that music is among the most interesting and diverse forms of Arthurian popular culture for young people. He considers a variety of those musical forms, from nursery rhymes and familiar children's songs like "Good King Arthur" to theater pieces, school operas, and rock operas, and shows how each corresponds to or reflects social trends and developments. Reel also provides much useful information on the librettos and the printing history of many Arthurian songs and musical productions.

Michael A. Torregrossa, in "Once and Future Kings: The Return of King Arthur in the Comics," explores a genre of Arthurian studies that has received little serious or sustained scholarly attention. Focusing on Arthur's return through reenactment, invocation, and substitution, Torregrossa reviews numerous works, from Hal Foster's long-running *Prince Valiant* to Rick Veitch's new *Aquaman* series. He argues that Arthurian comic books demonstrate both the evolution of the legend and the assimilation of Arthur into popular culture, especially youth culture.

Barbara Tepa Lupack, in "Camelot on Camera: The Arthurian Legends and Children's Film," surveys cinematic retellings for children, from the various adaptations of *Connecticut Yankee* (perhaps the most American reworking of Arthurian material) to films that reverse Twain's motif and introduce Arthurian characters into modern times; from adaptations of familiar and popular literary works to innovative treatments that democratize or feminize the Arthurian stories; from cartoons and animated feature films to television shows and miniseries. Lupack concludes that, like many earlier forms of Arthuriana for children, films can entertain, instruct, and edify their young viewers.

The essays in *Adapting the Arthurian Legends for Children* offer the first comprehensive overview and analysis of Arthurian juvenilia in the nineteenth and twentieth centuries. They reveal the ways that the Arthurian stories have been retold, reworked, and even remythologized for contemporary readers, viewers, and listeners. Most importantly, perhaps, they demonstrate the enduring appeal of the Arthurian legends and leave us to speculate on the new ways that children will encounter King Arthur in the years to come.

Notes

1. Raymond H. Thompson, "Interview with Jane Yolen," *Taliesin's Successors: Interviews with Authors of Modern Arthurian Literature* (1999) <http://www.lib. rochester.edu/camelot/intrvws/yolen.htm>.
2. Dakin Williams and Shepherd Mead, *Tennessee Williams: An Intimate Biography* (New York: Arbor House, 1983), p. 23.
3. Douglas Hughes, "Thomas Berger's Elan: An Interview," *Confrontation* 12 (Summer 1976): 24 [23–29].
4. Brooks Landon, *Thomas Berger* (New York: Twayne, 1989), pp. 6–7.
5. As stated on the dust jacket of the first edition of *Arthur Rex* (New York: Delacorte Press, 1978).
6. Thomas Berger, Letter to Alan Lupack, December 8, 1980.
7. Letters from Walker Percy to Alan Lupack, the first undated, the second dated February 14, 1987.
8. Letter from Walker Percy to Alan Lupack, February 14, 1987. In that same letter Percy asks, parenthetically: "Did I dream it or is there not in fact a legend which holds that only Lancelot and Percival saw the Grail?"
9. Barry Gaines, *Sir Thomas Malory: An Anecdotal Bibliography of Editions, 1485–1985* (New York: AMS Press, 1990), p. 55. Gaines suggests that the version of Malory to which Eliot referred is Charles Morris's *King Arthur* (1908), the twenty-third volume of "The Historical Tales: The Romance of Reality," a copy of which—inscribed with the young Eliot's signature—is in the collection of Harvard's Houghton Library.
10. Catherine Christian, Letter to Alan Lupack, April 30, 1981.
11. Raymond H. Thompson, "Interview with Jane Yolen." Yolen also recalls reading Tennyson, in particular "a wonderful illustrated version of his poetry" that included "the Lady of Shalott," when she "was nine or ten." In that same interview, Yolen notes that her Arthurian writing ("oddly," Yolen suggests) began with the short story "The Gwynhfar," which grew into a book of stories. And, eventually, some of those stories became novels—e.g., *The Dragon's Boy.*
12. Raymond H. Thompson, "Interview with Rosemary Sutcliff," *Taliesin's Successors: Interviews with Authors of Modern Arthurian Literature* (1999) <http://www.lib.rochester.edu/camelot/intrvws/sutcliff.htm>.
13. Raymond H. Thompson, "An Interview," in Susan Cooper, *Dreams and Wishes: Essays on Writing for Children* (New York: McElderry/Simon &

Schuster, 1996), pp. 186–97, and reprinted electronically in "Interview with Susan Cooper," *Taliesin's Successors: Interviews with Authors of Modern Arthurian Literature* (1999) <http://www.lib.rochester.edu/ camelot/intrvws/cooper. htm>. That interview is published in full in this volume.

14. Matthew J. Bruccoli, *Some Sort of Epic Grandeur: The Life of F. Scott Fitzgerald* (New York: Harcourt Brace Jovanovich, 1981), pp. 20, 28; John Kuehl, ed., *The Apprentice Fiction of F. Scott Fitzgerald: 1909–1917* (New Brunswick: Rutgers University Press, 1965), p. 17.

15. F. Scott Fitzgerald, *The Great Gatsby* (1925; rpt. New York: Scribner's, 1953), p. 149.

16. Scottie Fitzgerald Smith, in Matthew J. Bruccoli, *Some Sort of Epic Grandeur*, pp. 496, 262; F. Scott Fitzgerald and Zelda Fitzgerald, *Bits of Paradise: 21 Uncollected Stories by F. Scott Fitzgerald and Zelda Fitzgerald*, selected by Scottie Fitzgerald Smith and Matthew Bruccoli, with a foreword by Scottie Fitzgerald Smith (London: The Bodley Head, 1973), p. 3. In the poignant story "Outside the Cabinet-Maker's," written when the Fitzgeralds were living at Ellersie in Wilmington and Scottie was six (and published in *Bits of Paradise*), a father buys an expensive doll's house for his young daughter. Though he knows it is only a costly piece of cabinet-making and not a fairy's castle, he imagines for her mysteries "whose luster and texture he could never see or touch any more himself" (p. 140).

17. Michael S. Reynolds, in *Hemingway's Reading, 1901–1940: An Inventory* (Princeton: Princeton University Press, 1981), p. 26, posits that critics have largely ignored the element of "the medieval knight" in Hemingway's work because the chivalric influence, while pervasive, "will not be found on the fiction's surface."

18. Gaines, *Sir Thomas Malory: An Anecdotal Bibliography of Editions, 1485–1985*, pp. 119–20.

19. John Steinbeck, *The Acts of King Arthur and His Noble Knights*, ed. Chase Horton (New York: Farrar, Straus and Giroux), p. 4.

20. Rose Fitzgerald Kennedy, *Times to Remember* (New York: Doubleday, 1974), p. 12, as cited in W. Nicholas Knight, " 'Lancer': Myth-Making and the Kennedy Camelot," *Avalon to Camelot* 2.1 (1986): 29 [26–31].

21. Charles A. Lindbergh, *Autobiography of Values*, intro. by Reeve Lindbergh (New York: Harcourt, Brace, Jovanovich/A Harvest HBJ Book), p. 62.

CHAPTER 1

LE MORTE DARTHUR FOR CHILDREN: MALORY'S THIRD TRADITION

Andrew Lynch

Malory's *Le Morte Darthur* is a book for adult readers, but one that most of them will already have encountered in a version for children. This was not always the case. Before the mid-Victorian period, there was a juvenile Arthurian literature in the form of short histories, chapbook romances, ballads, *Jack the Giant-Killer*, and *Tom Thumb*, but it did not involve Malory, whom young people had to read straight or not at all. J. T. Knowles's *Story of King Arthur* (1862) is usually seen as beginning adaptations of the *Morte* for young readers, a category which has since grown very large. Malory's book remains today, as it was for Tennyson,[1] a notable link between youth and age, still perhaps one of the few narratives that people might encounter in some form throughout their whole reading lives. But since the mid-nineteenth century there has been a troubled double apprehension of the *Morte*: that it is somehow particularly suitable for children yet can only be made so by strenuous adaptation. It has been a text both loved and feared, deeply entrusted and distrusted with cultural labor. Through our double compulsion to give the story to children yet to change it radically for that purpose, Malory sets a revealing test for each generation, each writer, who adapts and retells him.

The test is the more intense since *Le Morte Darthur* (unlike the vaguer category of "Arthurianism") cannot be considered timeless and infinitely malleable material. It is a singular and obsessive text, and has often proved tellingly resistant to its new employments, even to the most enthusiastic reappropriations. The result has been a fascinating and long-running contest between originals[2] and retellings in which, despite Malory's "classic" status, the patterns of change often betray how much rewriters have found the venerable book problematical or simply uncommercial. Conversely, for those readers who know it, the *Morte* continues to "write back" to its adapters for children, as it did to Tennyson, spotlighting their own foibles, assumptions, and preoccupations. The steady stream for the children's market has thus created a third tradition of cultural dialogue with *Le Morte Darthur*, in parallel with the traditions of its critical reception and of neo-Arthurian literature and film, yet frequently interacting with them. Moreover, like those other bodies of work, this one has long since become self-referential and semi-autonomous, often responding to other adaptations as much as to the *Morte* itself. In what follows, I attempt to trace the contexts, the development, the outcomes, and some of the ideological implications of this third tradition of Malory.

There have been so many children's versions of various kinds that this study can make no pretense of completeness. Largely concentrating on the print tradition, I give only a guide to the main characteristics, noting trends and offering some more extended comments on what seem the most important exemplars. Basically, the two strategies of revision are abridgment and retelling. Adapters always have to decide what to keep and what to cut, for no children's versions except those of Howard Pyle have approached Malory in length. They must also decide what elements in the *Morte* they especially want to preserve—the general *fabula*, the specific order of narrative events, or the actual words. That will determine whether they attempt a retelling, an adaptation, or a selection. The five main varieties can be described as: (1) Abridged, censored, and glossed editions for children, with mainly original text; (2) Abridged, censored, and glossed editions for children, but more modernized and altered in diction; (3) Books selecting Malory stories, but mainly retold for children; (4) Books selecting Malory stories retold for children, but with significant new events alongside or replacing Malory's; (5) New works for children with some significant relation to the original *Morte*. These are not the only kinds of children's Malory, but they cover the main trends of adaptation since 1862. The final category—new works—is the one most scanted here, for reasons of space.[3]

I have chosen to treat the material diachronically. Even though this means that sometimes rather disparate books are discussed together, it better allows for the analysis of cultural history. One of the problems of contemporary medievalist studies generally is that we have established all too strong an idea of the Middle Ages as reconstructed between 1800 and 1914, but become progressively vaguer and more purely descriptive on the subject as we approach the present. Everyone knows, rather too glibly, that the nineteenth century used Malory to underwrite nation and empire, chivalry and the gentleman. No comparably strong notions have yet emerged from the twentieth century's *Mortes*, partly because more recent neo-medievalism has not had the prestige of Scott, Tennyson, and the Pre-Raphaelites. Looking at the continuing Malory tradition within children's literature is a limited but concentrated test of continuity and change, a way to articulate important ideological differences within nineteenth-century medievalism and to see if more has happened since then than a faint or ironized echo.

My study is divided into four rough periods: 1485–1861; 1862–1913; 1914–70; 1971–2001. I start in 1485 because the process of censoring, repackaging, and moralizing the text has been going on since Caxton, Wynkyn de Worde, and the 1634 edition. It was no giant step in 1862 to Knowles's offer of a better *Morte* for youth than Malory had provided himself. The chronological divisions suggested here should not be given too much importance, since there has always been a strong continuity in the tradition, with numerous versions reprinted and commercially repackaged over many years. Knowles's, for example, had nine editions from 1862 to 1912, and has been reissued as late as 1995. Ideological eras are a lot harder to establish than changes in publishing "look." One observes overlapping parallel developments of fairly long duration rather than sudden paradigm shifts. "Victorian" censorship of Malory for children lasted long into the twentieth century and is not finished yet. The common notion that chivalric idealism lapsed markedly after the Great War is disputed by printings of Sidney Lanier's *The Boy's King Arthur* in 1880 and 1920; U. Waldo Cutler's *Tales from Malory* in 1911, 1929, and 1933 (revised); Henry Gilbert's *King Arthur's Knights: The Tales Retold for Boys and Girls* in 1911, 1933, and 1934; and five editions of Beatrice Clay's *Stories of King Arthur* from 1901 to 1927.[4] Howard Pyle's series still remains in print as a "classic." World War II was no absolute watershed either. Cecily Rutley's very Tennysonian *Stories of King Arthur's Knights* appeared in 1929 and 1951; Enid Blyton's versions in 1930, 1950, and 1963; Stuart Campbell's in 1933, 1935, 1938, 1941 (twice), and 1964. Roger Lancelyn Green's book (1953) and Rosemary Sutcliff's trilogy (1981) have both been reissued as recently as 1999. Such longevity is as noticeable as change in the tradition. It seems that a good or distinctive product can survive up to fifty years or more, especially with an updated format. It remains to be seen which of the spate of large-format, color-illustrated books of the 1980s and 1990s will last, what new emphases will appear, and how important Malory's text will be in their production.

I should point out also that though "the *event* of children's literature lies in the chemistry of a child's encounter with it,"[5] my comparative survey is necessarily from an adult reader's perspective. I am interested in the traffic between these adaptations and their original, and their relation to each other and to broader cultural changes, things child readers will mainly ignore: "for any book children encounter, the availability of pre-texts and intertexts is rather random."[6] So my discussion is not a window onto childhood (except insofar as reading may create the real condition of childhood) but an adult's investigation of textual "childness," as Peter Hollindale calls it—"shared ground, though differently experienced and understood, between child and adult."

> For the adult, childness is composed of the grown-up's memories of childhood, of meaningful continuity between child and adult self, of the varied behaviour associated with being a child, and the sense of what is appropriate behaviour for a given age, of behavioural standards. . . .This compound of cultural and personal attitudes is articulated in a text of children's literature.[7]

This is not objective territory. Because so many people have first read Malory's stories when young, and delighted as grown-ups in telling them again to children, cultural consciousness of *Le Morte Darthur* has become richly invested with adult "childness," what we remember and imagine about childhood. Simultaneously, thanks to its idealist nineteenth-century revivers, the *Morte* itself, seen as the first chapter of children's literature in English, has come to stand for the beginning, the childhood of British culture. Adaptations of Malory for children are a marketplace where linked ideologies of childness and of the British medieval are displayed and negotiated, but also private places of memory where adult writers and readers ponder the structures of their development and connect their lives. Each will guard a special third tradition.

Before the Age of Retellings: 1485–1861

Malory did not write for children. His book makes no concessions to a young audience and never interpellates its audience as young. Where he discriminates, he appeals to the experience of age—smiling at Gareth and Lyonet's indiscreet assignation (205/25–27),[8] explaining La Cote Male Tayle's greenness on horseback (287/3–13), and frequently stressing the value of long continuance, "olde jantylnes and olde servyse" (649/5). When he suggests an audience, it is gentle and adult—"all jantyllmen that beryth olde armys" (232/15–16), "ye all Englysshemen" (708/34), or "all jentyllmen and jentyllwymmen that redeth this book" (726/14–15). Nevertheless, the *Morte* may have always been "children's literature" in the limited sense that what we would call children, or at least adolescents, probably knew it too, like Sidney's "tale that holdeth children from play, and old men from the chimney corner."[9] It is easy to imagine bright children rapt in reading or hearing someone read the stories, wondering, like Gareth, if they could ever withstand a proved knight (181/25) and following Launcelot as devotedly as young Elayne and Lavayne of Ascolat: "she doth as I do, for sythen I saw first my lorde sir Launcelot I cowde never departe from hym" (639/13–14). Malory's younger contemporary readers, perhaps especially those whose families considered themselves "gentle," must have found it easy to relate to this gripping romance in plain language, which had no competition from any children's books written for pleasure. As a vernacular narrative, it was open to the literate of all ages. Roger Ascham's famous denunciation shows how successfully he thought Malory had appealed to youth of both sexes:

> Yet I know, when Gods Bible was banished the Court, and *Morte Arthure* receiued into the Princes chamber. What toyes, the dayly readyng of such a booke, may worke in the will of a yong ientleman, or a yong mayde, that liueth welthelie and idlelie, wise men can iudge, and honest men do pitie.[10]

The margin of *The Scholemaster* (1571) erupts into pointing hands around this passage. Other early assessments of Malory's effect on the young were obviously more positive. The *Morte* has been tentatively linked to the household culture of Edward IV, where the squires were expected after supper to be "talking of chronicles of kings and other policies."[11] Caxton, as was his habit, advertised the book as good "doctryne" for future life and simply advised readers, both men and women, to "Doo after the good and leve the evyl."[12] Whether or not Malory's stories were actually treated as exemplars for youth, many of them feature aspiring male youths, determined to make good in the adult world. With a few exceptions, the *Morte* is not much concerned with its heroes as children, but it returns repeatedly to their transition from youth to proven knighthood, often involving the assistance of experienced older figures like Governal or Launcelot. For the most part, youth and age cooperate willingly. So young Ywain explains his choice of an elderly guide: "I am yongest and waykest of you bothe, therefore lette me have the eldyst damesell, for she hath sene much and can beste helpe me when I have nede" (98/1–3). These are all success stories. In the early days at Camelot, Tor, sponsored by Arthur and Merlin, does wonderfully in his first quest, setting a pattern for Gareth and La Cote Male Tayle later on. Arthur, Tristram, Alexander the Orphan, Galahad, along with lesser protégés like Gryflet, Hebes, and Lavayne, are followed from childhood or youth into their lives as knights. This preferred narrative shows how completely Malory's culture understands young people in terms of their future roles in maturity. Noble youth is spent in expectation, training, and hero-worship of knights. Prince Tristram, of course, has a noble tutor and gets a seven-year French education in "the langage and nurture and dedis of armys," excelling in music and hunting (231/43–232/4), but the supposed churls Tor and Beaumains seem able to train themselves—Gareth may have learned at home in Orkney, but Malory does not say how young Tor is otherwise ready to become a knight. His cowherd stepfather explains that "allwey he woll be shotynge, or castynge dartes, and glad for to se batayles and to beholde knyghtes. And allwayes day and nyght he desyrith of me to be made knyght" (61/27–29). Gareth disguised as Beaumains is similar: "ever whan he saw ony justyng of knyghtes, that wolde he se and he myght. . . .And where there were ony mastryes doynge, thereat wolde he be, and there myght none caste barre nother stone to hym by two yardys" (179/9–15).The common emphasis on masculine emulation makes Galahad's rearing in a nunnery and his initial self-distancing from Launcelot and other knights more distinctive, but even he is brought to court by "a good olde man and an awnciente" attended by "twenty noble squyers" and commends himself to "my grauntesyre, kynge Pelles, and unto my lorde kynge Pecchere" (518–19). Malory's children, like his women, are not expected to have legitimate interests independent of the male adult power group, and they seem impatient to join it. A child able to read the *Morte* in its own era would have found little difference from an adult in its basic ideological impact. This medieval version of the child as father of the man was a feature that Romantic, Victorian, and Edwardian adapters would find very congenial to their own times. It has faded considerably over the last fifty years, as the rationale for children's literature has moved from instruction toward entertainment.

In the centuries following 1485, Arthur's doubtful historicity, a minor issue for Caxton, became a major one, weakening one aspect of his literary appeal. At the same time, the medieval fictions about him came to seem old-fashioned. The edition of 1634 had to apologize that "In many places fables and fictions are inserted, which may be a blemish to what is true in his history." It appealed to readers' patriotism, asking them to lay aside contempt for the "errors of our ancestors" for the sake of "the immortal name and fame of our victorious Arthur."[13] It also assured them that, although this was "the best form and manner of writing and speech, that was in use in those times," the text had been censored.

> In many places this volume is corrected (not in language, but in phrase); for here and there, King Arthur, or one of his knights, were declared, in their communications, to swear prophane, and use superstitious speeches, all (or the most part) of which is either amended, or quite left out. . .so that, as it is now, it may pass for a famous piece of antiquity, revived almost from the gulph of oblivion, and renewed for the pleasure and profit of present and future times.[14]

The 1634 preface suggests a potential connection among the unrefined virtues of Arthur, the "plain and simple" speech of Malory, and the bright childhood of the British nation, which would be developed enthusiastically by later readers. But by the time children's literature began in earnest in the mid-eighteenth century, there had been no further edition of the *Morte*. King Arthur, in a version very unlike Malory's, featured in children's histories rather than in their fiction. He now had increasingly less credence as a real figure than in the adult popular histories of the previous age. Nathaniel Crouch's *The History of the Nine Worthies of the World* (1687) argued that just as it would be "infidelity" and "atheism" to doubt the truth of Joshua or David, so it would be "incredulity and ingratitude" to reject Arthur, despite the accretion of incredible stories around his name.[15] By the eighteenth century this was changing. Newbery's *A New History of England* (1763), dedicated "To the Young Gentlemen and Ladies of Great Britain and Ireland," maintained the old distinction between true British hero and the creature of "romances,"[16] but in 1764, Oliver Goldsmith firmly relegated Arthur to political fiction and to futility:

> At such a time as this a Christian hero was wanted to vindicate the rights of Christianity, and probably, merely for this reason, fiction has supplied us with a Christian hero. The British Champion is said to have worsted the Saxons in twelve different engagements, yet, notwithstanding all his victories, and whatever his prowess might have performed, it did not serve to rescue his country from its new persecutors.[17]

Arthur seems to have largely vanished from juvenile histories by the nineteenth century and is no longer in books of "Worthies,"[18] but for a long while the space vacated was not supplied by juvenile Arthurian fiction. *Le Morte Darthur* continued to be "King Arthur," and tattered copies of the 1634 edition were still devoured by children. As a schoolboy, Robert Southey "possessed a wretchedly imperfect copy, and there was no book, except the Fairy Queen, which I perused so often, or with such deep contentment."[19] The *Morte* must have been light reading to those painfully learning Latin and Greek. On the crest of the medievalist revival and the growth of Romanticism, reissues by Walker and Edwards in 1816 and by Southey in 1817 not only made it newly available "as a book for boys"[20] but showed it had also become more praiseworthy in contemporary critical terms. The Walker edition freely admitted that Malory was not history, but added that "its merit, as a fiction, is very great. It gives the general reader an excellent idea of what romances of chivalry actually were; it is also written in pure English, and many of the wild adventures which it contains, are told with a simplicity bordering upon the sublime."[21] The potentially negative eighteenth-century connotations of "wild adventures," echoing the definition of "romance" in Johnson's *Dictionary*,[22] are redeemed by reference to the cult of simplicity and the sublime, while "pure English" suggests an influence for both national and moral integrity. The value of the Arthurian story had changed from educational fact to imaginative resource.

Belief that the *Morte* in the original could be given to young readers persisted longer than is sometimes acknowledged. It perhaps explains why new editions and selected versions of Malory kept pace at first with out-right retellings. So much has been written about Victorian censorship for children that it is interesting to note the attitudes of a staunch defender of Malory throughout her life, the best-selling novelist Charlotte M. Yonge (1823–1901).[23] In Yonge's *The Heir of Redclyffe* (1853), the hero Guy Morville is cast in opposition to his worthy but overbearing cousin Philip. Masculine role modeling is a major issue. The eighteen-year-old Guy dis-misses Sir Charles Grandison as a prig and names Sir Galahad (Malory's rather than Tennyson's) as his favorite character in fiction. In their ensuing discussion of Malory, Philip's attitude reflects learned condescension—he is a classical scholar—and greater moral calculation. His accusation of "sameness" in Malory is typical of nineteenth-century criticism.[24] Guy, the true "heir" of England's chivalric past, is a champion of religious idealism:

> "What! Don't you know the Morte D'Arthur? I thought every one did! Don't you, Philip?"
>
> "I once looked into it. It is very curious, in classical English; but it is a book no one could read through."
>
> "Oh!" cried Guy indignantly; then, "but you only looked into it. If you had lived with its two fat volumes, you could not help delighting in it. It was my boating book for at least three summers."
>
> "That accounts for it," said Philip; "a book so studied in boyhood acquires a charm apart from its actual merit."
>
> "But it has actual merit. The depth, the mystery, the allegory—the beautiful characters of some of the knights."
>
> "You look through the medium of your imagination," said Philip; "but you must pardon others for seeing a great sameness of character and adventure, and for disapproving of the strange mixture of religion and romance."[25]

As in Kenelm Digby's view of chivalry, Yonge makes the fervor of innocent boyhood the beginning of adult greatness—Guy has "lived with" the *Morte* rather than frigidly "looked into it," and even while swotting his Greek for Oxford makes "a little refreshing return afterwards to the books which had been the delight of younger days."[26] He is likened throughout to a young Galahad, through his slight figure and stature, his modeling for a portrait of the knight, and the "boyish epic about King Arthur" he has written. Guy inherits a fierce temper from the Morvilles; his battles to subdue it are his own version of chivalric virtue. Like Galahad, he is the youth whose conduct redeems the sins of his ancestors, in this case a grandfather who has recklessly practiced duelling. Like Galahad also, he is the youth who cures the effects of sin in others, then dies the perfect death. Guy learns to overcome his passion for revenge when Philip wrongly accuses him of vice and dies at twenty-one, after heroically nursing his cousin through illness. With early death common and with salvation at stake, Yonge required children to be morally and intellectually challenged by literature, and missed the days when they could read only adult books: "real power was cultivated, and the memory provided with substantial stories, at the time when it was most retentive."[27] Now, she complains, children "are interdicted from the study of that which would stretch their minds lest they should meet with anything objectionable."[28] In Yonge's view, the struggle of young readers with a challenging book is a version of the romance hero's own formative aspiration to higher things and struggle against vice. Its importance overrides censoring caution:

> Bring children as soon as possible to stretch up to books above them, provided those books are noble and good. Do not give up such books on account of passages on which it would be inconvenient to be questioned on. If the child is in the habit of meeting things without comprehension it will pass such matters unheeded with the rest. . . .The only things to put out of its way are things that *nobody* should read, certainly not its mother.[29]

Yonge's scenario sounds comically gendered, but she mentions the "mother," I think, mainly as the parent likely to be choosing books for children in the family. The whole family's literature should be carefully selected, not with a view to avoiding all delicate subjects and mention of vice, but in an informed and conscientious way. Adults and future adults are expected to avoid literature that endangers their particular temperaments or situations. Guy Morville,[30] for example, has avoided Byron, "For who could have told where the mastery might have been in the period of fearful conflict with his passions, if he had been feeding his imagination with the contemplation of revenge, dark hatred and malice, and identifying himself with Byron's brooding and lowering heroes?"[31] Malory apparently fitted perfectly into Yonge's scenario. Boys, she argued, "should have heroism and nobleness kept before their eyes; and learn to despise all that is untruthful or cowardly, and to respect womanhood";[32] it is rather like a modern version of the Pentecost oath of Camelot.[33] Like Malory again, and like Spenser, whom she frequently cites, Yonge always sees youth as in

preparation for adulthood. Childhood reading is an essential part of the
maturing process, the equivalent of young Tor's and Gareth's looking on
at battles and tournaments, and always anticipates further reading. She
recommended C. H. Hanson's *Stories of the Days of King Arthur* (1882),
a broad-based Arthurian compilation, mainly as a precursor to the great
originals:

> Hardly to be called historical, but with the grand outlines of Sir T. Malory's
> great romance, and with excellent illustrations by Gustave Doré. Desirable as
> giving the genuine English heroic tale, noble in itself, and furnishing
> allusions. It is intended to prepare the way for Malory and Tennyson, and
> there is little said of the Quest of the Holy Grail.[34]

For Yonge, reading Hanson is a step on the "way," a quest that will lead children through the delight of the "noble" tale on to the "depth, the mystery,
the allegory" of the *Morte* in its own words, complemented, not replaced,
by Tennyson.

Shortly before the phase of adapted Malories began in the 1860s, Yonge
involved the *Morte* freely in the finest Arthurian children's story of her century, *The History of Sir Thomas Thumb* (1855). Tom Thumb (also discussed by
Dan Nastali in chapter 8 in this volume) had been a chapbook subject in
prose and verse since the earlier sixteenth century, always with adventures
that included residence at Arthur's court, but never Malorian. Henry
Fielding, in the 1730s, had turned it into mock-tragedy and political satire.
Yonge found these versions impoverished and offensive. She set out to
redeem the story in the form of a fairy tale, "free from the former offences
against good taste." Her scholarly notes provide "some of the choice
passages of English fairy poetry" and "give a few sketches from the
romances of King Arthur's Court, often a subject of much youthful curiosity, not easily gratified."[35] Besides Malory, there is reference to Geoffrey of
Monmouth, Old French romances, the stanzaic *Morte Arthure*, Scots ballads
("True Thomas"), and Percy's *Reliques*, together with Spenser, Shakespeare,
Arnold, and Tennyson. (This meant, inevitably, a class promotion for
juvenile Arthuriana from the cottage chapbook to the nursery culture of
privileged homes.[36]) Half-imp, half-human by birth, like Merlin, Yonge's
Tom has to battle the temptation of retreat to the fairy world regularly proposed to him by Queen Mab and Robin Goodfellow. He is taken into
fairyland by Mab, after receiving a wound from Mordred, and lives in
melancholy pleasure there but returns when Arthur's trumpet is heard at
the Last Battle, in time to find his enemy dead and Arthur dying. The story
moves at this point into Malory's majestic words, with Tennysonian notes
strengthened by illustrations of Arthur's barge departing for Avalon and the

last sight of Excalibur.[37] Yonge employs Tom's unique blend of age and youth, experience and innocence, to make this a fable of growth towards moral maturity, the child's responsibility for the adult it becomes. After the battle, Tom lives on to embody the ideals inherited from the departed king. He returns to fight spiders in the deserted halls of Camelot (see figure 1.1) and dies there, refusing Puck's last offer of escape: " 'Away, tempter!' cried the little knight. 'Better honourable death as a Christian than such life as thine.' "[38] The religious allegory of Yonge's *Tom Thumb* bridges the fairy tale and the hitherto adult Arthurian romance tradition, making the child and adult genres interact and deeply identify. In the brilliant illustrations of Jemima Blackburn, Tom is made larger than the fairies yet smaller than Puck, his adult would-be corrupter. Tom's young face wears an expression of near-tragic consciousness, while Mab and the fairy world are strongly sexualized, building on Yonge's references to Spenser's Bower of Bliss and *A Midsummer Night's Dream*, and even with a hint of Bosch's Garden of Earthly Delights. Yet fairy sensuousness is infantilizing, as in Spenser, for it enslaves the mind and prevents the exercise of will in duty. Tom's return to Arthur saves his soul. By analogy, Yonge's return to Malory as a source signals her recovery of almost-forgotten chivalric virtues from the literary past.

Debra Mancoff has stressed the deficiencies of Galahad, the "bright boy knight," in Victorian eyes:

> He would obtain the Grail, but he would never know a woman. He would never lead a household and he would never lead other men. In short, to the Victorian mind, Galahad would never be a man. In stark contrast, Arthur's manly form and mature countenance assured his audience that he—like them—would follow a natural cycle of life.[39]

1.1   Tom Thumb dies defending the deserted halls of Camelot in Charlotte Yonge's *The History of Sir Thomas Thumb* (1855), illustrated by Jemima Blackburn.

Her assessment is truer for the late Victorian period but rather underrates the positive effect of Tennyson's "Sir Galahad" written in 1834, published in 1842, which dominated early Victorian imagination.[40] Members of the Pre-Raphaelite Brotherhood were expected to know it by heart. Despite the sentiments of some later paintings and illustrations, and Tennyson's eventual critique in "The Holy Grail" (1869) and elsewhere,[41] the twenty-five-year-old's poem shows Galahad's idealism as vigorous and effective, serving a man for life. Young Tennyson's hero is a fiercer fighter than any other knight, just as in Malory,[42] where at fifteen he defeats all opponents, even Launcelot. The famous "good blade" that "carves the casques of men" is directly Malorian: "But at the last by aventure he [Galahad] cam by sir Gawayne and smote hym so sore that he clave hys helme and the coyff of iron unto the hede, that sir Gawayne felle to the erthe; but the stroke was so grete that hit slented downe and kutte the horse sholdir in too" (578/3–18). Tennyson's link between Galahad's chastity and his knightly prowess—"My strength is as the strength of ten / Because my heart is pure"—is also Malory's: "Sir Galahad is a mayde and synned never, and that ys the cause he shall enchyve where he goth that ye nor none suche shall never attayne" (535/3–11). In following Malory, the early Tennyson credited youth with a strength and passion capable of dedication to the highest service, the "mightier transports" of religious faith. Yonge obviously learned from both exemplars. With their authors' confidence in the *Morte* behind them, "Sir Galahad," Guy Morville, and Tom Thumb all display the perfected strength of Christian manhood, triumphing in life and looking bravely beyond death to the ultimate "prize." This too is like Malory's Galahad: "Com forthe, the servaunte of Jesu Cryste, and thou shalt se that thou hast much desired to se" (606/25–26). The socially deficient, "ever-naïve" adolescent pictured by Mancoff misrepresents the strong vision that the early Victorians derived from Malory. Only after 1860 did many lose faith in the original *Morte* as a bridge from youth to maturity and require new versions, specially delimited for children.

Revision and Dilution: 1862–1913

The explosion after 1860 of Malory adaptations, mainly for children, is a remarkable development. There is no simple explanation for it. The factors included: "increasing awareness of multiple versions of Arthurian legends,"[43] encouraging revision—there are numerous nineteenth-century versions mixing Malory with tales from the *Mabinogion* or Chrétien de Troyes, Robert de Boron, Icelandic sagas, *The High History of the Holy Grail*, and Spenser; greater censorship and the associated belief that there should be a separate literature for children as a "class," and for the poorer class as a kind of social children;[44] publishers' competition in the growing market for affordable children's fiction, often aiming at readers less literate than Southey and Guy Morville; the very strong influence of Tennyson; widespread disappointment with the original *Morte* as over-long, monotonous, and too much devoted to fighting;[45] above all, the belief that Malory was now especially boys' literature. Clearly, most of these causes were interrelated. They fed on the benign association of chivalric fiction with youth by Kenelm Digby, the early Tennyson, Yonge, and others.[46] These writers had raised rather misleading expectations of a half-symbolic, spiritual idealism in the *Morte*, which others could not so easily find in its complex mass of narratives. Despite the later assertion that "children took them [these stories] over and made them their own...forced their elders, indeed,...to revise and recast them in suitable form,"[47] the first children's retellings follow contemporary adult taste and correspond well with prevailing adult criticisms of narrative sameness and shapelessness in the original.

Taylor and Brewer suggest that "Malory did not need to be translated: his fifteenth-century prose was sufficiently close to modern English, to the language of the Prayer Book and the Bible, to allow him to be read without difficulty in the nineteenth century."[48] This may well have been true, especially if we discount younger children, and there was new access to Malory through Wright's edition (1858) of the 1634 print, and Conybeare's revised abridgment (1868). But the contemporary evidence about children's reception is mixed. Knowles (1862) suggested that the *Morte* was too old-fashioned for children: "in our time it has disappeared from the popular literature and the boys' bookshelves...[because] since the days of cheap books, it has never been modernised or adapted for general circulation."[49] Contradicting him, an anonymous reteller of 1878 asserted that the earlier nineteenth-century vogue continued:

> ...the spell works to this day; boys fall upon the volumes still wherever they may fall in their way, and sit absorbed in them as did their forefathers. They tell you more of Sir Bagdemagus and King Pellinore in a week, than they can of Hector and Diomed at the end of a school half-year. The taste is a genuine one on their part, wholly independent of Mr Tennyson and his fellow-poets, explain it how we will. . . . To the schoolboy the tale is one of infinite delight and wonder, and to those of mature age the exploits of Arthur have something akin to the interest aroused by the inimitable "Punch" among the modern exhibitions.[50]

Why then make a new version? Evidently this retelling is for adults, given its Tennysonian touches—Launcelot is sent to bring Guinevere to Arthur (though at Morgan's instigation); and the Queen muses that "The King is

too spotless pure—too high above me."[51] Those whom Malory reminded
of Punch and Judy could read this instead:

> Her voice had a severe and commanding expression, her dark eyes glowed
> with revengeful fire, and every fibre of her ravishing form quivered through
> the robe of spotless white in which she was apparelled; a golden carcanet,
> studded with gems, encircled her fair brow, and her raven locks floated wildly
> upon the evening breeze.[52]

The nature of the adaptation shows where the *Morte* did not satisfy
mid-Victorian popular adult taste. First, its plot and thematics were not
Tennyson's, which were dominating medievalist imagination, especially
with the prominence they gave to female characters. This soon passed
directly into children's versions. Mancoff's comment that "Women had
little place in these books [Victorian children's Arthurian literature]"[53] is
quite misleading. In adaptations, retellings, and their illustrations, figures
such as Guinevere, the Lady of the Lake, Morgan, Vivien (often in place of
Malory's Nimue), Lynette, and the two Elaines featured very prominently,
and non-Malorian characters like Enid and the "Lady of the Fountain"
were frequently added. Female characters became far more important than
in the original, which is not to suggest that they were empowered beyond
traditional gender roles. The change may be the result of a readership of
girls as well as boys[54] and the growing number of female adapters, starting
in 1881 with "Your Loving Granny" (*Six Ballads About King Arthur*); but
Tennyson's *Idylls of the King* are the main cause. Early versions like Knowles,
Ranking (1871), Hanson (1882), and Farrington (1888) were openly influenced by it in their emphases and selections. Farrington, for instance, builds
her courtship of Arthur and Guinevere on Tennyson, not Malory; her
Gareth marries Lynette, not Lyones; her "Fair Maid" story is strongly
focused through Elaine and includes Tennyson's invention of the tourna-
ment diamonds; and this section and the "Death of King Arthur" are
framed by Tennyson quotations. Greene (1901) was really an Arthurian
"Tales from Tennyson," and Mary MacGregor's *Stories of King Arthur's
Knights* (1905) had for contents: "Geraint and Enid; Lancelot and Elaine;
Pelleas and Ettarde; Gareth and Lynette; Sir Galahad and the Sacred Cup;
The Death of King Arthur."

Second, Malory's style was nothing like historical romance as influenced
by Sir Walter Scott—full of character effects, learned "colour," and
Shakespearean metaphor—nor like the lush descriptiveness of Edward
Bulwer-Lytton. To many, Malory's prose seemed repetitive and undeveloped,
a barrier to modern taste. The perceived necessity to make "modernised"
"children's King Arthurs" barely concealed (as sometimes still happens)

a similar hostility to the actual medieval text, a condescending distaste: only a child could really like (or a medieval "child" have written) such stuff. Hanson, one of the most favorable of early adapters, refers only to "preserv[ing] as much of Malory's quaint style as is consistent with perfect clearness."[55] Morris's modernized version (1892) called the original "not easy or attractive reading, to other than special students of literature."[56] The most tolerant attitude saw it as "free and childish language." "It is not only the words that are childish, but the mood, the quality of the story-teller's imagination is something like a child's. He sees things in vivid, simple pictures." This was from an editor of actual Malory selections for schools.[57] Those who wanted youth to read the medieval original commonly associated its paratactic prose, romance events, and episodic narrative structure with childish taste, in a much weakened form of early Victorian chivalric idealism:

> He writes with the simple straightforwardness of a child, he accepted the improbable with a child's unquestioning faith; like a child he was not only fond of repetition and the enumeration of high-sounding names, but he linked his sentences together with such words as "and" and "so," or "for" and "then." He loved forests and their enchantments, marvellous combats, and fantastic adventures; and he was perturbed by nothing, however irrational.[58]

Thanks to the repetition of such opinions, Malory never gained Chaucer's adult and honorary modern status in the early days of "English Literature," even though in narrative terms, of course, he is not at all simple to adapt. Every scene sets the new writer many subtle problems, and many a modernized version loses energy to cope with them after the first few pages. In the initial sword-drawing, for instance—why has Arthur's parentage been disguised? How will that reflect on Igrayne? Does Ector know that Arthur is King? How deceptive, and for how long, is Sir Kay? How will Arthur take the news? Above all, how will they speak? In practice, the *Morte*'s style was often too simple for Victorian and Edwardian taste, even with a young audience in mind. When Kay asks Arthur to fetch him a sword, he says only "I wyll wel" (8/20). These are Arthur's first words, unbeatably positive and direct.[59] In Blackie and Son's version of 1910, "prepared specially for school children," they conform to an idea of "medieval" eloquence: "Right gladly will I do that. . . .Haste you on with our father. I will return to the town with all speed and will bring you your sword."[60] Both the medievalism and the direction toward children, with its burden of educational responsibility, usually meant, as here, separating the true spirit of medieval chivalry, what Malory *ought* to have written, from his inadequate textual medium.

Third, Malory was either direct or silent on sexual matters, never carefully "suggestive." It was adult taste again that required the *Morte* to change in this respect, though the requirement was often projected onto the needs of a young audience. (Interestingly, Knowles's original edition was soon revised "for a larger public than that of boys only."[61]) Censorship became an important factor, evidently a selling point, since adapters always drew attention to it in their prefaces. They wanted readers to be assured that their "King Arthur" would do the cultural work specified by Tennyson, and that it could be freely given as a present or prize. Knowles (1862) "endeavoured. . .to follow the rules laid down in the 'Idylls of the King'. . .for the preservation of a lofty original ideal"; Conybeare (1868) cut "coarse passages"; Hanson (1882) cut "occasional allusions and episodes which make them unfit to be placed in the hands of juvenile readers." Frith's modernized and abridged edition (1884)

> found it necessary to expunge, and, in one instance at least, to alter the relationship of the characters as given in the old romance. . . . We will not more particularly specify the places in which such alterations have been made. Those who are already well acquainted with the history of King Arthur will not need to search, and those who have not already read the romance will not miss the portions left out.[62]

Frith seems concerned that a list of excisions would be used as a pornographic index to the original. This is all far from Charlotte Yonge's confidence in the child reader. The new attitude meant widespread intervention, because Malory is frank about the existence of sexual passion and makes it a strong motive force, yet has his own reticence too, so censorship could never simply be a matter of cutting a few "sex scenes" to hide the love intrigue. Frith (like many other censors) makes Launcelot marry Elayne of Corbenic—a far worse disloyalty to Guinevere than sleeping with her by mistake;[63] without the love motive, he must suddenly introduce an "enchantment" that drives Launcelot mad, and vague "plots" "laid against the Queen," and he has to exchange Ector's famous lament at Launcelot's death, which refers to "the trewest lover, of a synful man, that ever loved woman" (725/20–21), for a disingenuous evasion: "When he awaked it was hard for any tongue to tell the lament he made for his brother."[64] It was not hard for Malory at this great moment, only for Frith in his self-imposed predicament. This was a typical trade-off of narrative power for unimpeachable content. Farrington has similar trouble with continuity, allowing Launcelot and Guinevere to repent a guilty love which she has not actually brought herself to narrate. Leonora Blanche Lang (1902)[65] was far more skilled at censorship. She gives just enough of Merlin's conversation with Arthur to tell readers who his parents were, without raising further questions, and to predict the mischief to be caused by Mordred, without revealing Arthur as the father. Unlike others who removed the sexual intrigue, she supplied a substitute. Violence, rather than sex, is the besetting sin of her Camelot, and ceasing to kill is Lancelot's way to "forsake sin" in her Grail Quest.[66] There are enough hints, building on Tennyson's story of the courtship, that Guenevere loves Lancelot too much, to make Agrawaine's plot credible and to motivate her final repentance, but not enough to convict them of deep wrong.

Mrs. Lang's version shows how much the *Morte* can be changed in its events without quite losing Malory's effect. She found a plain, clear language that was not Malory but a good modern correlative. Here is her version of Arthur's speech when he draws the sword:

> "If I am King," he said at last, "ask what you will, and I shall not fail you. For to you, and to my lady and mother, I owe more than to anyone in the world, for she loved me and treated me as her son."[67]

This lacks the urgency of the original, with its play of emotions as Arthur moves from son to monarch:

> "Els were I to blame," said Arthur, "for ye are the man in the world that I am most beholdyng to, and my good lady and moder your wyf that as wel as her owne hath fostred me and kepte. And yf ever hit be Goddes will that I be kynge as ye say, ye shall desyre of me what I may doo and I shalle not faille yow. God forbede I shold faille yow." (9/28–30)

Nevertheless, few rewriters did as well.[68] Since nearly half of Malory is in direct speech, their more typical method of abridgment into summary third-person narration distanced readers from the action and intruded the narrator more, so that the "vigour and valour"[69] Frith prized in the original was diluted. There was often no concern to maintain consistency with Malorian style. Farrington has a Guinevere with "eyes as blue as the summer skies; her hair so gold-bright as to have stolen rays from the sun."[70] There was also very little humor. The King Arthur stage shows of the period are occasionally funny to read and show knowledge of Malory as well as Tennyson, but they are adult "burlesque extravaganzas" rather than children's pantomimes.[71]

Despite more worries about character consistency than Malory had shown—Gawain troubled readers from Southey to Howard Pyle[72]—his abridgers often left out the situational touches that make a scene in the *Morte* distinctive. For instance, although young Tor's achievement of knighthood was a favorite event in children's versions, these were more purely fixated on the issue of class promotion than the original; they never included Tor's touching reaction—that Merlin dishonors his peasant mother by revealing King Pellinore as the real father—or showed Malory's concern for the feelings of Aries the cowherd. Blandness of style and incident resulting from censorship and abridgment accompanied over-idealization of character: "the gentle Percival, the patient Gareth, the brave Gawaine, the peerless Launcelot, the merry Dinadan, the pure knight Galahad. All these strongly contrast the treachery and the wickedness of Queen Morgan Le Fay."[73] Gareth's impatient love for Lyones, Gawain's murderous vengefulness, Lancelot's disloyalty to Arthur are all forgotten here. Exemplary characters were supposed to be Malory's strength, in the absence of enthusiasm for his style and narrative structure, but they really became a serious weakness. The *Idylls* had become the "adult" version of the story, but retellers for children were unwilling to acknowledge the flaws that had made the *Morte*'s heroes and heroines interesting to Tennyson or to Morris and Swinburne. Instead they treated them like the stock figures of contemporary juvenile fiction and often made them just as dull.

From about 1890 to the Great War, with the exception of some good school editions (W. E. Mead, Clarence Griffin Child, R. F. Bate), Malory for children became more a matter of retelling than of selection and adaptation. While the adult reader was catered for by new editions of the *Morte* itself and there were still substantial adaptations like Lang's, Clay's, and Cutler's, many children's versions became more childish, often aimed at younger readers, more open to girls, and even more distant from the original.[74] Edwardson (1899) changed Malory's names into "easy" ones for children; MacGregor's book—"Told to the Children" and dedicated "To Marie Winifred"—included a very young Gareth: "Gareth was a little prince. His home was an old grey castle, and there were great mountains all round the castle. . . .Gareth had no little boys or girls to play with, for there were no houses near his mountain home. But Gareth was happy all day long."[75] Away from home, he finds it hard being a servant: "as Gareth's mother had taught her little prince daintily, he did not like their rough ways; and at night he slept in a shed with dirty kitchen-boys."[76] To MacGregor, boyhood is morally superior to dangerous maturity. Lancelot hears Galahad sing Tennyson's song, " 'My strength is as the strength of ten / Because my heart is pure.' And the great knight wished he were a boy again, and he could sing that song too."[77] Why Lancelot wishes so is rather unclear, since his wrongdoing is barely visible. Arthur goes to France only because "a false knight with his followers was laying waste the country across the sea."[78] Originally Tennysonian emphases have disciplined this version to the point where it cannot actually repeat Tennyson's story.

With the cohesive elements of Malory's plot subdued by censorship, late Victorian and Edwardian children's adaptations tended to become collections of unconnected "tales," with a remote ending for the king in old age, rather as in the Robin Hood tradition. This accompanied an emphasis on stories and illustrations of youth. The Blackie edition of 1910 contains, for example, Arthur drawing the sword, La Cotte Mal Taille, Gareth, and Galahad before a brief "Passing of Arthur," suddenly introduced: "The quarrel between King Arthur and Sir Lancelot became so bitter that Sir Lancelot left King Arthur's court and went to France, taking with him all his followers."[79] In Dorothy Senior's version, *The King Who Never Died*, chapter headings divided up the stories as separate fables: "The Knight Who Lost His Temper" (Balin); "The Knight Who Served in the Kitchen." ("The Knight Whose Armour Didn't Squeak" was not far off![80]) Since the main goal of most adaptations after 1880 was to illustrate an idealized and exemplary "chivalry,"[81] Malory's narratives often lost both their integrity and their special status in children's versions. Sidney Lanier kept *The Boy's King Arthur* in a separate volume from his "Boy's" Froissart, *Mabinogion*, and Percy's *Reliques*, but Hanson, Farrington, Edwardson (1899), Greene, Lang, MacGregor, and *The Children's King Arthur* (1909) mixed Malory with a wide variety of other Arthurian, romance, and heroic material. To give one example, Lang's *The Book of Romance* (1902) also contained stories of Roland, Diarmid, Robin Hood, Wayland, William Short Nose, and Grettir.

It is not surprising that in the face of such fragmentation of the narrative, Tennysonian thematics, and general distaste for Malorian style, along with the huge growth of specialist children's literature, some feared that the *Morte* itself would be lost to children. Clarence Griffin Child in 1904 defiantly brought out a school edition of some early "books" (Merlin, Balin)—thinking it "better to give a somewhat extended portion of Malory rather than a series of fragments culled here and there." He spoke for "those who know the earlier versions" and who "cannot repress a certain impatience at times as regards Tennyson's alterations of the stories and his modernization of their intention, the symbolic, or, to use his own term, 'parabolic' significance he gave them." Above all, he stressed the different nature of Malory's prose and what it required of the young reader:

> he must not expect to have the vitalizing elements of the narrative forced upon him and emphasized after the modern manner, so that he cannot miss them, however dense or indifferent he may be. He must pause to let each simple, picture-making phrase deliver its full message.[82]

Child was mainly right, but in the minority, and against the tide of taste. Intense competition from a vastly expanded modern children's literature was inevitably changing the market for old favorites like Malory. Beatrice Clay could even claim that her adaptation of 1905 was needed because "in spite of—perhaps, indeed, because of—the abundance of books for the young, there was a danger of children growing up in complete ignorance of those famous romantic tales that are part of the heritage of the ages."[83] The confidence of the earlier Victorians in *Le Morte Darthur* itself as a guide for youth had changed into support for an increasingly diversified and diluted Arthurian children's literature. The original *Morte* now became more of an adult text in scholarly, popular and "art" editions (e.g., Sommer, Dent, Simmons, Flint), and an English "classic" to be read in schools.

Howard Pyle's self-illustrated Malorian stories, which appeared in four long books from 1903–10, are a special case. Their reputation has often been very high,[84] and they remain in print, but they have also consistently been criticized for clumsy archaism and verbosity.[85] Pyle can hardly be called an abridger. He often draws out speeches and descriptions to far greater length: eleven words in Malory—"Then wolde he have slayne hym for drede of his wratthe" (25/34)—become one hundred and forty in his version.[86] He goes further than anyone of his time in creating an entire, new textual environment for children out of Malory's material, with additions from other medieval sources, "shaped. . .and adapted. . .from the ancient style in which they were first written so as to fit them to the taste of those who read them today."[87] His highly wrought landscape descriptions attempt a "magic," "Celtic" quality that many still think Malory himself should have—the reprint of 1992 calls Pyle's language "appropriately medieval in flavour," "a magical journey to a far-off time." Pyle also romanticizes his own persona in addresses to the audience, which seem to be modeled on Caxton's Prefaces and, to a lesser extent, on Malory's occasional personal utterances. He virtually presents himself as a second Caxton. Frequent moral applications create an exemplary narrative quite unlike the *Morte*, though in line with contemporary attitudes to it:

> Thus Arthur achieved the adventure of the sword that day and entered unto his birthright of royalty. Wherefore, may God grant His Grace unto you all that ye too may likewise succeed in your undertakings. For any man may be a king in that life in which he is placed if he may draw forth the sword of success from out of the iron of circumstance.[88]

The diffuse narrative discourse suggests many possible influences: the abstract style of the Old French prose romances, which Pyle apparently knew; Caxton's grandiloquent prose; touches of "scripture" language, perhaps from his Quaker background—he always writes "exceedingly" for Malory's "passing(ly)," some antiquarian detail in the manner of Scott;[89] a love of solemnity, often darkening to melancholy; and much outright wordiness—"Thus have I told you of this so that you might know thereof."[90] The biggest virtue Pyle's narrative has is its sheer monologic distinctiveness. If young readers could get used to his ways, he offered a romantic textual "world" in which they could fully immerse themselves.

For all the "extraordinary pleasure"[91] that Pyle claims in his work, his illustrations are somber and static, mainly brooding portrait-studies, and often deeply introverted even when they depict action scenes. Launcelot, whose conduct Pyle carefully monitors at all times—he is never more than Guinevere's "very dear friend"[92]—seems as withdrawn in the pictures as in the text:

> And the mystery of that place [Avalon] entered into the soul of Launcelot, so that thereafter, when he came out thence, he was never like other folk, but always appeared to be in a manner remote and distant from other of his fellow-mortals with whom he dwelt.[93]

Even shown climbing a tree to rescue a lady's falcon, a comic episode from Malory's "Noble Tale," Launcelot sits still and sad, as if apart from his own adventure. (See figure 1.2.) It is tempting to see this melancholia as an outcome of the text's intense self-supervision and sexual inhibition. Isolde lives with Tristram "in all truth and innocence of life," but is shamed back to

1.2   Launcelot rescues a lady's falcon in Howard Pyle's *The Story of the Champions of the Round Table* (1907).

Mark, though not to his bed, by Arthur's question: "Is it better to dwell in honor with sadness or in dishonor with joy?"[94] Like other adapters, Pyle combines Malory's two Elaines (of Corbenic and Astolat) and marries the result to Launcelot, who still desires glory and the queen: "Down, proud spirit, and think not of these things, but of duty."[95] The couple go to Camelot, where Guinevere jealously lodges Elaine in a room next to her own and separately from Launcelot. Elaine falls sick and eventually leaves court before Galahad is born, but Launcelot remains in his unconsummated union with the queen, full of remorse. The effect of the plot changes is to keep Launcelot as much as possible from sexual contact with either woman, as Pyle's Isolde is kept from both Tristram and Mark. Tristram, even after drinking the poison and kissing Isolde, "immediately put her away from him and he left her and went away by himself in much agony of spirit."[96] Like Launcelot and Guinevere, these two only *seem* to be lovers, because of slanderous plots. Bors, similarly, is about to marry and settle down, but the Grail quest draws him away—"For duty lyeth before all the pleasures and all the glories of the world."[97] (Perceval rejects Blanchefleur's advances because of his love for "Yvette," but Yvette dies; he thinks of her "in paradise," with "a great passion of love and longing."[98]) Pyle's eternal vigilance allows little freedom to love between the sexes; he "choose[s] to believe good of such noble souls as they, and not evil of them,"[99] but the emotional price of this high-mindedness is perhaps even higher. Love between brother knights, not to be suspected, is more open: "Sir Tristram sits with Sir Launcelot"[100] shows the two celibate heroes brooding together at a table, their hands joined around a single cup. Perceval feels "a great passion of love for Sir Lamorack, and a great joy in that love." He "loved him with such ardour that he could hardly bear the strength of his love."[101]

Pyle has been called a democrat mainly on the strength of some episodes in which his knights are disguised as laborers,[102] but structurally his politics are as authoritarian and hierarchic as Tennyson's and Malory's. Arthur's kingship is his "birthright";[103] he is bound only by his own conscience; his political actions are naturalized as "duty," like Pyle's own labors, finishing the "work which [he] has set himself to perform";[104] all his enemies are villainized. Gareth's status as Beaumains is basically a disguise: "think you that any kitchen-knave could have fought such a battle as you beheld him fight?"[105] Pyle's Geraint makes the Lord of the Sparrowhawk give up half his estate so that the former negligent earl "may support the style of living befitting his rank."[106] Arthur, perhaps to clear him of marital coldness, is made to exile Guinevere's accuser Mador under the threat of burning, where Malory's Arthur—"sworn unto knyghthode als welle as we be" (614/39)—admits him readily to the fellowship again. Physical force is fully sanctioned. Though the last book concludes with a prayer for universal peace, Pyle was unusual for his period in highlighting and inventing details of battle:

> With that blow the brains of the Knight of the Sparrowhawk swam like water; the strength left his limbs; his thighs trembled and he fell down upon his knees and sought to catch hold of the thighs of Sir Geraint. But Sir Geraint avoided him, and reaching forward, he catched him by the helmet and snatched it from his head.[107]

And he deals out punishments with gusto: "Thus died that wicked man, for as King Arthur drave past him, the evil soul of him quitted his body with a weak noise like to the squealing of a bat, and the world was well rid of him."[108] In such moments Pyle shows a narrative energy and creativity that lift him far above the general run of Malory retellers, but it is a pity that his greatest effort should have gone into literalizing Caxton's vague statement that *Le Morte Darthur* was all "wryton for our doctryne" (xv). This emphasis makes his Arthurian books too uniformly slow, solemn, and decorous, both in style and content. They are casualties of idealism, forfeiting the adventurous pleasures of the original for the sake of making the heroes consistently blameless. In this, for all Pyle's distinctiveness, they typify the trend of late Victorian and Edwardian children's Malories.

From Ideal to Political Adventure: 1914–70

Alfred W. Pollard's abridgment of 1917, with memorable illustrations by Arthur Rackham, heralded a slow change in Malory reception over the next fifty years, as chivalric idealism turned more toward adventure and politics. Like all such previous developments, this one began from adult attitudes and was a trend rather than a sudden new orthodoxy. With real wars at hand, Malory's main subject matter seemed less childishly improbable, and his readers could be interpellated again as lovers of adventure, old or young. Literary chivalry did not die suddenly in the trenches, since its political work was assigned far from the real battlefield. Rather, chivalry was now no longer necessarily a half-symbolic mirror for youth, teaching "that highest type of manhood, the Christian gentleman,"[109] in contexts other than war; it could be enthusiastically reattached to ideas of martial virtue.

The ideological issues emphasized in Malory could also change, from ideals of moral probity to practical courage and group loyalty. Lanier's statement that "A good deal of what is really combat nowadays is not *called* combat"[110] can be contrasted with Pollard's 1917 preface, which highlights the "violence, cruelty and luxury" of the old romances, and speaks of men "carrying their lives in their hands and willing to lay them down lightly rather than break the rules of the game or be faithless to word or friend."[111] This was a move roughly in line with the "Race-Life" theory of human development held by prewar Arthurian Christians like William Forbush, who influenced Robert Baden-Powell.[112] Forbush (discussed further by Alan Lupack in chapter 9 in this volume) had seen Arthurianism as a means of harnessing the natural energies of working-class boys. After the feral state of infancy and the barbarism of early childhood, boys (and through them the still-young American nation) would be led toward adult responsibility by Christian training received in the adolescent years of chivalric adventurousness, *wanderlust*, and gang spirit. Linking Arthurianism to early adolescence, seen as a "stage" of human and civil development, Forbush spoke for a new era of trust in the potential of youth and freer allowance to young imaginations: "If the man is to retain a wholesome heroism it must emerge from the joyous savagery of his own childhood."[113] Children's literature had to adapt:

> It is the picturesque and vivid in biography that attracts attention from a boy. To him life is moving, adventurous, highly-colored. The reflective and the passive moods are not his. . . .[he] awaits with surly suspicion and agonizing self-consciousness the clumsy and blunt way by which his preceptor "makes the application."[114]

Influential wartime and postwar Malories seem to exemplify such attitudes in their overall change from moral *exempla* to exciting action narratives. In Hanson's *Stories of the Days of King Arthur* (1882), Doré's dusky illustrations showed combats at a distance, overshadowed by craggy romantic mountains and turrets. N. C. Wyeth's cover for Lanier's second edition (1920) places a full-color sword combat in the extreme foreground, looming above the viewer who feels almost in danger of being trampled by the excited near horse, mantled in a rich red. (See figure 1.3.) The effect is cinematic, even anticipating Technicolor and CinemaScope. The 1880 text, censored and skillfully abridged from Malory's own words, takes on a very different emphasis in this format, with larger print and pages, better margins, and without the cumbersome chapter divisions and hortatory preface of the first edition. There is less to interpellate its reader as a moral subject and a boy than before; something of the Malorian impression is restored of youth eagerly anticipating its future in adult adventure. This was a Malory who could coexist, at a distance, with the tragic-heroic humanism of Hemingway, Steinbeck, and Faulkner.[115]

Color illustration became normal. Philip Schuyler Allen's retelling of 1924 looks like a response to the new Lanier, with eight color pages. Format and artwork often changed faster than the stories themselves. Elizabeth Lodor Merchant's *King Arthur and His Knights* (Philadelphia, 1928) silently

1.3   N. C. Wyeth's exciting portrait of sword combat appears on the cover of the second edition of Sidney Lanier's classic *The Boy's King Arthur* (1920).

put new illustrations to the text of Blanche Winder's *Stories of King Arthur* (London, 1925), a series of myth-like pageants, dominated by its forty-eight color plates. Merchant changed chapter titles and opening paragraphs, and provided a preface stating the new creed of children's literature: "Action rather than reflection and a childlike directness enchain the attention of young imaginations."[116] Eleanor C. Price's *Adventures of King Arthur* (1931), originally in octavo, was soon reissued in quarto (1933) with a bright color "action" cover and numerous illustrations of combat. It showed some signs of a loosened censorship, with a franker sex-plot, a large role for Morgan, and chapter epigraphs from Swinburne as well as Tennyson. The Reverend J. Crowlesmith, author of "Bible Stories for Young Folk" and "Stories of Missionaries and Martyrs," made a steady, muscular version in 1927, reprinted in 1931, for the cheap children's market. He too felt able to include more of the love story than in prewar times, and consequently the book holds together much better. The religious element is emphasized, but Protestantized. In the Holy Grail section, Lancelot's humiliation at the ruined chapel is retained, but not his confession to the hermit, and Galahad's story ends with the healing of the wounded king, not his direct rapture into heaven. Enid Blyton's *The Knights of the Round Table* (1930) was another competent retelling, with a characteristic authoritarianism and relish for punishments. Her Balin is fully justified in killing the Lady of the Lake: "As soon as he saw her, he rode straight at her and cut off her head, for he knew her to be a witch-woman and very wicked. She had caused his mother's death."[117] Blyton's Galahad is happy to hear that the seven knights of the Castle of Maidens have been killed by Gawain: "That is good news. . . . They will return no more to the castle."[118] In Malory's version, the point of the story is a contrast—Galahad has delivered the maidens without bloodshed, because his "lyvyng ys such that he shall sle no man lyghtly" (535/15–16); his reaction to Gawain's deed is a wry comment on the older knight's bloodthirstiness: "I suppose well" (534/3). The notion of Malory's "simplicity" was often maintained by unsubtle adaptations of this kind. Changing editions of Blyton's book show a typical shift from "nursery" to "adventure" format over a wide period. In 1930, as part of John O'London's Children's Library, the artwork featured a very young, curly-haired girl reading on the cover, a "schoolboy" Arthur drawing the sword (though he mysteriously ages twenty years in a short space), and other youthful knights. In *Tales of Brave Adventure* (1963), as reprinted along with a Robin Hood selection, the illustrations mainly fit the new title.

The Edwardian era had a long Indian summer in children's King Arthurs. Despite the slow changes I have noted, virtually all the prewar emphases reappeared in the interwar period also, and sometimes beyond 1950. The vogue for very young Arthurs continued with John Lee's 1920 adaptation, "Told for the Bairns." Arthur's "boyish form"[119] drawing the sword from the stone is on the cover, and the selections are typically child-oriented, with Tor and Galahad prominent. Paul Creswick's *The Story of the Round Table* (1925) is in a pseudo-archaic style influenced by Pyle and pushes a shallow dualism that links Edwardian moralizing with modern Hollywood " 'action' films": "the old eternal idea of Good warring with

Evil. . . .Faith and Love battling with Doubt and Hate; Hope and Gentleness with Despair and Brute Strength."[120] His heavy emphasis on a unified narrative of moral consequences—"Modred, thou wert the black feather in my soul's wing"[121]—continued later Victorian attitudes and anticipated the critical emphases of the Lumiansky school of Malory critics in the 1950s and 1960s. Abridged and modernized versions continued also, with John Hampden (1930) and Stuart Campbell (1933, 1935, and reprints). Especially given the reissue of numerous prewar editions, noted earlier, the period 1920–45 mainly seems derivative. Books settled down comfortably in publishers' lists with no major new literary intertexts, while at an ever greater cultural distance from the great Victorians, especially Tennyson, who still inspired them.[122] Arthurianism had often been a conservative trend. It was now in danger of becoming fully reactionary, enlisting children in an adult rejection of modernism. Even T. H. White's *The Sword in the Stone* (1937), the keenest reply to late Victorian and Edwardian applications of Arthurian "chivalry" for the young, is often nostalgic for the premodern.[123] That was hardly a "children's Malory" like those discussed here, and too complex a book to deal with in this compass, but it came closest to providing what the post-Victorian children's tradition lacked, a major retelling that was fundamentally hostile to the *Morte's* militarism.

Brian Kennedy Cooke tried to explain the stagnant interwar situation in his anti-Edwardian preface to *King Arthur of Britain* (1946):

> a lamentable fashion arose towards the end of the last century of producing insipid special versions for children, illustrated with two-dimensional dummies in pasteboard armour, which kindly but undiscerning aunts and uncles could pick up without efforts on the Christmas bookstalls. . . .It is to be hoped that we have now outgrown this strange habit of thinking that the story must be bowdlerised and rewritten in a manner compounded of mawkishness and whimsy before it can be presented to a child. . . .the problem is to restore him [Malory] to the position in popular favour that he deserves, when so many people are alienated by the rubbish they were given in youth, or discouraged by the length of the real thing.[124]

Demanding a return to Malory's text as "alone and supreme," Cooke included only two illustrations, "in the style of early English miniatures," and centered the book mainly on adventures concerning Arthur, to avoid overlength and digressiveness. But the "problem" remained, and although Cooke issued several new Malory selections and reprints up until 1961, they did not have the effect he seems to have wished. The postwar years saw no decrease, though an improvement, in retellings for children, and they have dominated abridged editions ever since.

The early 1950s was a vital period in Malory adaptation, probably
because of renewed adult interest in his literary qualities caused by Vinaver's
major edition of 1947, T. H. White's novels, and the rise of new medievalist
fantasies as invigorating intertexts. There was also a greater openness to
influence from popular culture. The recent World War and the Cold War
brought out strong political emphases. Motifs of invasion and national
betrayal were common. Nearly all new versions stressed the need for
supreme power to be used firmly by a central government against its enemies, without and within, to guarantee peace and unity. Roger Lancelyn
Green (1953), Alice M. Hadfield (1953), and Antonia Fraser (1954) made
three distinctive contributions at this time.

Green's *King Arthur and His Knights of the Round Table* is now a standard
version. Mainly based on Malory, it adopted Vinaver's recent model—
"quite separate stories...a certain coherence, but no fixed plot"[125]—to
allow for the incorporation of many other medieval sources. As a devotee
of Andrew Lang, Green believed that "great legends, like the best of the
fairy tales, must be retold from age to age: there is always something new
to be found in them, and each retelling brings them freshly and more
vividly before a new generation."[126] In Green's postwar age, the "something
new" was military and political: "chivalry and right striving against the barbarism and evil which surrounded it,"[127] specifically "the Saxons, who
could never be contented with their savage, unfruitful homes in
Germany."[128] On first drawing the sword (in the Coronation year of 1953),
Green's Arthur pledges himself "to the service of God and my people, to
the righting of wrongs, to the driving-out of evil, to the bringing of peace
and plenty to my land." With this are mixed some fairy-tale elements
(Avalon is peopled by "elves") and a discourse of personal development that
must have helped the implied audience, middle-class children facing high
expectations, identify with the characters. Arthur and the knights are always
learning or not learning important lessons for life—Green had formerly
been a schoolmaster—and "the darkness" awaits failure. Unlike most earlier
didacts, Green has a sympathy for Malory's style, which lets him bring out
tactfully the exemplary patterns and comparisons of conduct already in the
narrative. In sections such as "Balyn and Balan," he keeps the directness and
steady emotional affect of the original. He is necessarily more explicit
sometimes in condensing events, but also manages to combine select
phrases and scattered information into new sentences that match the
original in consistency and poise: " 'Go home to Northumberland,' he said,
'and tell them what has chanced. I myself shall ride in search of King Ryon
and slay him, or die in the attempt: for if I slay Ryon, then surely King
Arthur will be my friend again.' "[129] Although events are much contracted,
Green's prose makes them seem paced like Malory's, with an impression of
narrative fullness and room for many stories within the overall framework.

Space is made by combination and telescoping of events—the two Elaine episodes are told together, and the combat with Melliagraunce leads "that same evening" to the assignation between Lancelot and Guinevere, which Mordred surprises. International politics aside, Green's "certain coherence" is based on the love story, presented in terms of sexual temptation which matches both Tennyson's "little rift within the lute" and the religious views of his friend C. S. Lewis: "the powers of evil seeking now more and more desperately to find some tiny loophole through which to climb into the stronghold of good, saw it, and set a cunning snare for Launcelot."[130] Green heaps added guilt on Lancelot through new ironies on top of Malory's— it is young Galahad who unknowingly finds his mad father; the healing of Urry fulfills a prediction of "the passing of Logres"[131]—until both plots are joined. The spiritual powers of evil that prevail over Lancelot and Guinevere finally rematerialize in enemy invasion: "For very soon the Saxons had conquered the whole of Britain and the Dark Ages descended upon all the western world."[132] Green's heavy emphasis on moral downfall leading to national disaster is old-fashioned and departs from the *Morte's* own attitudes, but for literary qualities his book stands out above nearly all modern and earlier retellings. In Charlotte Yonge's phrase, it best "prepares the way for Malory and Tennyson."

Alice Hadfield, a noted scholar of Charles Williams, was also old-fashioned in her great reliance on Tennyson but radical in the tone of spiritual warfare she gave to the stories: "It is a religious world, where Jesus Christ is a real Person to the Knights, and His service is as clear and real as that of the King."[133] Merlin is naturally of special interest to her:

> All traffickers in spirits know that they are controlled by the Ruler of Spirits, the Holy Ghost, but Merlin's pride in himself, which betrayed him into Vivien's hands, took from him that reliance on the Holy Spirit which would have cleared his vision. . . .Merlin is sealed up in the earth by his own folly and pride till all spirits come before their Ruler.[134]

Hadfield reads the significance of Lancelot's sin and the Grail in ways that resemble Charles Williams's "spiritual thrillers" and anticipated later critics. In a 1996 essay, Jill Mann[135] would echo the notion that "Galahad was to be the best knight in the world. . .but in bringing him into existence Sir Lancelot lost all that he loved and honoured."[136] Cooke's postwar patriotism had made Arthur central; Hadfield's was based on the Grail itself, as an allegory of the Christian life:

> It is this approach, this appearance of heavenly things, and the failure to behave rightly towards them, that the famous history of Britain under King Arthur is really about. The fighting and the courage, the ladies and love affairs, the King and the knightly vows, are all part of the life which arose out of this.[137]

Her version is also unusual in its incipient pacifism and Christian "doctrine of equality."[138] She envisages a "new quiet intellectual type" of knights: "Thinking and acting rightly were more important to them than fighting. This was very difficult for the older knights to understand."[139] Lancelot finds that "the things his son knew were more important than the quests and battles."[140] The end comes after "the Hallows were misused and withdrew," when "the whole effort faltered through the clog and drag of sin."[141] It is a bold attempt to respiritualize the story, probably unmatched in that vein since Tennyson's time. The major problem is a comic quelling of dramatic effect by over-explication, such as at Lancelot's discovery he has spent the night with Elaine, not Guinevere: "Now he saw that he had broken his vow and lost both his love and the secret of his strength. 'Alas, that I have lived so long,' he said. He seized his sword and would have killed her, but long habits of the good life stopped him."[142] Nevertheless, Hadfield brought children's Malory back into contact with a contemporary literature and pointed the way toward the later growth of fantasy versions.

The young Antonia Fraser's [Pakenham's] *King Arthur and the Knights of the Round Table* (1954) plays unpredictably and amusingly with the usual story, often for suspenseful and romantic effects. Apart from Tennyson and (occasionally) Malory, Fraser's models are taken from popular culture— Georgette Heyer romances, film, low-brow adventure fiction. Dialogue is unashamedly stagey—"Set fire to the Round Table! Never, while I live."[143]—and the style often verges on "True Confessions" parody: "Guenevere found herself looking at the most handsome face in Britain— Sir Lancelot himself. 'Oh, this is the romance of which I dreamt,' she thought to herself."[144] Heroes shout "Take that! And that!" Weapons "thwack!"[145] A Cold War invasion scenario matches the contemporary film of *Prince Valiant*: "So the Vikings had disguised themselves as knights. That was the reason for their mysterious disappearance!"[146] Especially given that the book was reissued as late as 1985, its discourse seems surprisingly racist. Palomides is a lascivious stage blackamoor who blinds his captives and "grin[s] evilly,"[147] and the Grail Quest becomes a Crusades-style recapture of the vessel "from the hands of the enemies of Christ."[148] The conclusion is "Festival of Britain" patriotism: "Today, over a thousand years later, we feel proud to remember that King Arthur and the knights of the Round Table are part of our national heritage."[149] The joking, lighthearted side of the text was complemented when Rebecca Fraser's pictures appeared in the 1970 edition. It was the first time for a good while that a juvenile King Arthur had been well illustrated in the latest style of contemporary children's picture books. This too was an early pointer to subsequent developments, especially after 1980. In hindsight, the instability of Fraser's 1954 text, with its generic diversity, pop pastiche, and blend of "heritage" with satirical elements, showed that "King Arthurs" like Green's and Hadfield's, built on the neo-Tennysonian model, could not be written for very much longer. *Monty Python* was not that far away.

Another Malory print item from popular culture was the book of the 1954 MGM film *Knights of the Round Table*. It showed an interesting cross-influence from the film of Sir Walter Scott's *Ivanhoe* (1952), also starring Robert Taylor, especially in the plot of Guinevere's abduction. If Scott had based some of the abduction of Rowena and Rebecca on the doings of Meleagant in *Le Morte Darthur*, Malory now received them back from him through the movies. The print idiom for the film is "adventure" fiction: "Cantering along on his magnificent charger, Beric, Lancelot's thoughts were all on the adventures that lay ahead. Adventure was meat and drink, to him; he could not live without it."[150] The "Wild West" flavor is brought out further when Beric saves Lancelot by hauling him from a pool of quicksand, in the style of a Roy Rogers film. There is an emphasis on deterrent force—fighting to keep the peace—and unity, "one England," symbolized by the "ring of stones": "If each stone keeps its balance then all will stand forever."[151] (BBC-TV's *Legend of King Arthur* [1979] and John Boorman's *Excalibur* [1981] would employ very similar political symbolism.[152]) Beside Fraser and the MGM book, Barbara Leonie Picard's *Stories of King Arthur and His Knights* (1955) seems a very traditional Malory recounting, with the familiar additions of Gereint, Yvain, and Sir Gawain and the Green Knight. In clear and readable prose, it made a much more reliable introduction to the Arthurian stories, if less sensational.

After the cluster of publications in the earlier 1950s, little of note in juvenile Malories appears until around 1980, although the market was well supplied by reissues. Academic interest in Malory grew strongly during this period, but in children's literature the *Morte* became overshadowed by Tolkien and his successors in medievalist fantasy, and the inventiveness that the earlier postwar Arthurian retellings had shown was diverted into original Arthurian children's fiction.[153] No doubt this was also encouraged by the popular success of T. H. White's books, issued together in 1958 as *The Once and Future King*. Many of the new children's novels were to have a "Romano-British setting,"[154] sometimes inspired by archaeological programs. (For a further discussion of place in Arthurian fiction, see Raymond H. Thompson's essay, chapter 7 in this volume.) Arthur became historicized in a new way, very different from the *Morte*'s conceptions; the story was often refocalized through different characters, and reassessed traditional motives and events. Those writers who adapted Malory himself look rather conservative by comparison. In Mary Cathcart Burns's *Tales of King Arthur* for school use (1961), "the nobles knew that the king would allow no unfairness or cruelty to any of his subjects. He was the friend and protector

of all his people, whatever their station in life."[155] Using Malory and
Tennyson's *Idylls* together, Burns draws modern parallels through suggested
class exercises: "Do you know the names of any knights who are alive
today? Perhaps a knight lives in your town or village?"; "Keep your eyes
open for an idyllic scene." She attempts an effect of national cultural
continuity, in which legendary history validates the contemporary social
order: "The word 'Order' still means 'a company.' Sir Winston Churchill
belongs to two Orders or glorious companies. What are they?"[156] Clifton
Fadiman's *The Story of Young King Arthur* (1962) is similar, mixing historical information about medieval conditions with a ringing endorsement of
concentrated power: "Find us a king, Merlin. Only a strong and wise leader
can defend us against our enemies, and give us happiness again."[157] Around
the period of the Cuban missile crisis, the message of this version was clear,
but Malory's work was no longer necessarily the best means of propagat-
ing it, and indeed national sovereignty and international politics are not
really the main concern of most of the *Morte*, especially in the children's
tradition. Since the big issues were now power and unity rather than
chivalry, courtesy, and knight-errant adventures, the fifth-century war-
leader struggling against the Saxon tide made a better exemplar than
Malory's late-medieval monarch and his knights, and also came a lot closer
to recent war memories. As those memories faded, Merlin, a relatively
minor figure in Malory, began to outrank his king and the premier knights
in interest. Monarchical and aristocratic heroes had slipped further in relevance and mass appeal, and since the *Morte* was now more "adventure" than
a general guide to conduct, its ideals were harder to apply to all walks of
life than they had been early in the century. Traditional conservative
presentations of Malory—whose political attitudes are undisguised by
Tolkien's fantasy and lack easy bourgeois identification—were out of touch
with the demand for greater social and personal freedoms that arose in the
1960s and 1970s. Gandalf or Frodo Baggins could belong on a school
student's bedroom wall in a way that Arthur or Sir Lancelot could not. For
all these reasons, while *Le Morte Darthur* was growing in academic reputation as a literary text, juvenile medievalism seemed to be leaving it behind.

Psychology, Fantasy, Myth, and Fun: 1971–2001

Appearing at an apparent lull in the appeal of *Le Morte Darthur* to adapters
for children, Rosemary Sutcliff's trilogy (1981) is the high point of
Malorian juvenile fiction. Sutcliff had already set stories in the Romano-
British period, with great success, and perhaps for this reason was more
relaxed in her eventual treatment of the *Morte* itself than some other modern Malory revisers have been. Despite her contemporary Celticism, she

was unique in her intimate but independent relation to the original: "I have followed Malory in the main, but I have not followed him slavishly." In this she felt justified by his own way with sources.[158] Readers who know the *Morte* gain an extra pleasure from seeing Sutcliff's mind interact with it— drawing out possible implications, alert to humor, inconsistencies, and cultural differences, supplying motivations, boldly combining different characters and events (as Malory did) for narrative economy. Her model is the humanist psychological novel rather than the episodic romance of adventure, but, like a gifted director of Shakespeare, she knows how to work with the original text to find a modern correlative. Imagining what her characters would have felt, as Malory did in his own terms, she endows them with a self-conscious quality and unconscious motives that the original does not articulate but that might plausibly be latent within it. Malory's Lancelot simply "thought hymself to preve in straunge adventures" (149/17). Hers is full of self-doubt, wounded by Kay's mockery of his ugliness, and tormented by love of the queen.[159] Her Arthur "pray[s], so deep down within him that he was not even aware of it, that nothing would happen that would force him to know" about Lancelot and Guenever.[160] This psychologizes Malory's more political version: "the kynge had a demyng of hit, but he wold nat here thereoff" (674/40–41). Minor characters like Bagdemagus's daughter are given inner life through sudden changes of narrative focus: "And he [Lancelot] rode away, never knowing that the king's daughter stood looking after him with the salt taste of her own tears on his lips."[161] Again, Sutcliff builds this on a technique of Malory's own: "And as sone as he come thydir the daughter of kyng Bagdemagus herd a grete hors trotte on the pavymente, and than she arose and yode to a wyndowe, and there she saw sir Launcelot" (154/24–26). The impression Galahad can give a modern reader of coldness and inhumanity is tactfully conceded and broken down: "And there were times when Galahad left his body behind for good manners' sake, while he went away into the solitude and the desert places within himself. But now Lancelot had learned to let him go; and so the bond between them grew very strong."[162] Strong human bonds are the most important elements in Sutcliff's story. Her Galahad sends his "love" to Lancelot, not an injunction to beware the world, as a final message.[163] Lancelot's Grail confession cannot be complete because "the love between himself and the Queen was not his alone to confess."[164] Because the love plot was now easier to tell to children—her main audience was born in the 1960s—the Grail Quest could be better integrated than in most previous versions, and the ending is understood as Vinaver's "human drama"[165] rather than as punishment for sin. Sutcliff's narrative still coheres around Lancelot's dawning perception that he cannot be both the best knight of the world and the lover of Guinevere,[166] but in a more tolerant spirit than before.

The most Malorian feature in Sutcliff's books is her great liking, even love, for the major characters, especially Lancelot. His final "repentance" and parting with Guinevere is one of many scenes at once sympathetic and perceptively ironized: "He smiled with great gentleness, the old twisted smile.'But always my chief prayers shall be for you, that you shall find peace and your soul's-heal.' 'Pray for your own,' said Guinevere. 'Pray for your own.'"[167] Sutcliff's characters give the same impression as Malory's, that they and their deeds are enough in themselves and do not have to be *for* anything else. But in her books, unlike his, the protagonists' chief qualities emerge against the grain of their practical roles in the story. The first of the trilogy, *The Sword and the Circle*, is marked by contemporary concerns for unity and right rule, but the books mainly lack Malory's depth of invest-ment in his heroes' social and political functions. In Sutcliff, politics makes an intrusion on their realest being; the overarching plot of the *Morte* is used to bring out their humanity under pressure, more than treated as an end in itself. The strongest political impression is of the horror of war, especially in the climactic Last Battle of *The Road to Camlann*, which draws on both Malory and Tennyson for its elevated diction and rhythms. When, at the very conclusion, Sutcliff gives Ector's famous lament for Lancelot in Malory's own words, it is an affectionate homage but also a further sign of the textual fate that has overshadowed her society from the start. Through the old story already told and known, it was always on "the road to Camlann": human weakness would bring about total destruction by war. In the face of disaster, Sutcliff asserts an ideal of stoic gaiety, giving a hint to Marion Zimmer Bradley's appropriation of the story as a model of micro-political inner consciousness:

> Avalon of the Apple Trees is not like to other places. It is a threshold place between the world of men and the Land of the Living. Here we are in the Avalon of mortal men. But there is another Avalon. The King is here, but he is gone beyond the mist.[168]

Is it too fanciful to think of Arthur's retreat to Avalon and the associated shift from confident action to an inner world as finding new meaning in the age of nuclear threat and in the politically and economically weakened Britain of Sutcliff's times? That mood is more evident in Andrew Davies's *The Legend of King Arthur* (1979), also set in a Romano-British society fac-ing its end: Arthur promises "a blessed land, God's kingdom on earth," but only "until the darkness falls again."[169] A traumatized Morgan, furious with Uther for what he has done to her mother, devotes her life to destabilizing the Pendragon regime: "Kill Uther" becomes "Kill Arthur." The plot underlines the cycle of hatred caused by autocratic greed and military violence, and we see the struggle for power slowly annihilating traditional Arthurian idealism. Bors says, despairingly, "I think that God forsook us all long ago. . . .Strength and luck; that's all there is now. Perhaps that's all there ever was."[170] It is the ethos of Tennyson's Last Battle, but now closer to historical circumstances, with the loss of England's empire and the fear of nuclear holocaust.

Davies's book was tied in with his script for a BBC-TV series, another pointer to the growing influence of popular culture on children's Arthurianism. Film, television, and video technology (discussed by Barbara Tepa Lupack in chapter 12 in this volume) have often supplied the recent models, and have wedded themselves in turn to the tradition. Numerous Arthurian role-playing games now exist, some with loose links to the *Morte*,[171] which is treated as a "fantasy" classic.[172] Ellen Kushan's "Choose your own adventure" book, *Knights of the Round Table* (1988), echoes a contemporary existentialist critical response to Malory[173] but uses it to trump tradition. The book is structured so that if the player-persona prefers to finish reading the old tome (presumably a version of the *Morte*) lent by the bookstore owner/enchanter, his story will end immediately, but he *can* choose to go to Camelot and "take the adventure." True adventure, it is implied, lies in choice and divagation, the thrill of personal discovery, and the chance to change the story. In effect, possibilities are limited by the very generic options on offer, no matter which road is taken. Another long-running influence from popular culture is the comic strip, recently used to good effect in *The Final Battle*,[174] a retelling of Malory's last book for slow readers. Marcia Williams (1996) has also given King Arthur her strip-cartoon treatment, in a series which includes his traditional children's literature company (Sinbad, Robin Hood, Greek Myths, *Don Quixote*) but also Shakespeare and Dickens. Interestingly, the fun of Williams's book centers mainly on Malory's familiar episodes of sword-drawing, the granting of Excalibur and Morgan's stealing of it, the establishment of the Round Table, and Lancelot. The combination of Malory's two Elaines into one is now so common that few children are likely to know the older version, but it is something new to make Galahad's begetting part of Lancelot's first quest. For a conclusion, Williams ignores the *Morte*'s sad ending in favor of a Grail Quest freely mixing various traditions. Galahad asks the right questions and so saves Arthur's realm from devastating famine and plague. The climax is "the crowning of a new Grail King and the restoring of Britain's prosperity."[175] The satirical element in the drawings—Merlin appears prominently as a large shaggy cat—is not extended to the overall fable.

There are also recent stage versions (discussed by Dan Nastali in chapter 8 in this volume), including a pantomime by Paul Reakes (1997) and John Chambers's *Tales of King Arthur: A Play* (1996). The increase of magic and fun over adventure in the children's tradition has reawakened some theatrical possibilities. Chambers's play is substantial, a big improvement on the Edwardian "pageants" of Arthur; it is situated in an anti-chivalric tradition of "inner" heroism, which goes back to Milton's "better fortitude." Chambers emphasizes the vulnerability of the young protagonists (the milieu seems adolescent), but also their love and honest idealism. Comic temptation scenes from the *Sir Gawain and the Green Knight* story support the theme of forgiveness for failure. Pacifist and feminist applications comment on the received version. In a way now familiar, the intrigue arises from Merlin's traumatic snatching of Arthur from Igrayne and concerns Morgan's revenge for her mother. Psychology takes causal precedence over Arthur's claim to power through birthright and the Sword in the Stone. Dindrane (Percival's sister has a name here) asks: "Are only men permitted to undertake adventures?"[176] Elaine tells Lancelot, "I have my own fate. My own destiny. It is tied up with my unborn child. Not with you."[177] Kay is a satirical portrait of an insecure braggart, but the real heroes admit fear and doubt. Even Galahad laments the restraints of his own perfection: "I never make choices for myself. I do what is right. I am not half the man my fellow knights are for I don't have dilemmas."[178]

Unlike Chambers, most later adapters of Malory for children have not followed in Sutcliff's psychological vein. Those that do generally reflect the greater importance of Merlin, Morgan, and Mordred in recent neo-Arthurianism. Robin Lister's *The Story of King Arthur* (1988) has a summary style unlike Malory's but mainly follows his incidents. The narrative is focused through Merlin and keeps him prominent throughout, as in many modern versions. Since Merlin does not have a large role in Malory, this usually necessitates also building up the roles of Morgan and Mordred as his opponents. Lister's Morgan, for example, drugs Arthur to make him think that Morgawse is Guinevere. This old device, once used to save Lancelot's fidelity to Guinevere, now saves the king's. (The Holy Grail itself is used to make Lancelot think that Elayne is Guinevere.) By contrast, Lancelot and Guinevere are simply having "a love affair,"[179] which television and film will have made understandable to young readers. That problem has been solved, but if Guinevere is now less culpable, misogynist readings have another potential focus in Morgan. Villainized as a witch by some, she has become the Arthurian feminist *cause célèbre*. In 1913, Beatrice Clay had to apologize for including Morgan at all: "the difficulty of handling this somewhat unpleasant character was so great that, practically, she did not appear in the first edition."[180] Morgan's prominence today is part of a widespread trend to give more of the legend to its female figures, a restoration of the later Victorian feminine emphasis, but in the terms of William Morris rather than Tennyson. In *Women of Camelot*, Mary Hoffman voices each story through the woman who experiences it: "Imagine how I felt! [says Guinevere]. Lancelot was my only comfort and joy. Without him, I was a loveless queen in a childless marriage."[181]

Juvenile versions of the last twenty years (discussed further by Judith L. Kellogg and Cindy L.Vitto in chapters 2 and 4 in this volume) have mainly emphasized magic, myth, legend, and fantasy, and made their appeal through retold "tales" in large format, fully integrated with numerous color illustrations. Illustrators are now as important as authors. James Riordan's *Tales of King Arthur* (1992), with artwork by the influential Victor Ambrus, leans toward the model of "myth and legend." Riordan is another in the vein of Lang, taking Arthurian materials from multiple sources, including Geoffrey of Monmouth and *Gawain*, and augmenting his Malorian sections with the English prose *Merlin*, Swinburne, and Tennyson, and "ideas suggested by Roger Lancelyn Green's excellent book."[182] Ambrus, a noted illustrator of the *Iliad* and other battle stories, puts violence into children's Malory on a more epic scale than previously seen. Riordan's prose style is more subdued but supports the giant illustrations with considerable battle detail. Nudity in the bedroom pictures is another novelty that aligns Malory with contemporary books of myth and legend rather than traditional romance or adventure. Not all recent versions are like this,[183] but it may be that the children's *Morte* is becoming archaic and mythic, rather than humanist and psychological, and that the post-1960s search for motives and inner meaning will become as outmoded as the Edwardian fetish for moral messages. At any rate, what these stories mean to children will certainly be changed by a new graphic technology which can dominate textual imagination. Rodney Matthews's recent artwork for the *Tales of King Arthur and His Knights* by Felicity Brooks and Anna Claybourne (1998) shows a clear affinity with the role-playing, adventure-book, and fantasy-novel genres, and the text has been shaped accordingly:

> "He's just a kitchen boy," put in the damsel hurriedly. But the Green Knight was staring at them in horror and fury.
> "You've done *what?*" he fumed. "You've *killed my brother?* I'll pay you back for that! I'll KILL you. I'll RIP you to PIECES!"[184]

The Victorians played down the *Morte*'s bloodshed to suit their idealization of "chivalry." Now it is a fierce battle narrative again, reflecting the increased level of violence in children's culture generally, but with a more uncertain ideological application than before. Comparison of Doré's artwork in Hanson (1882), N. C. Wyeth's adventurous style for Lanier (1920), and Ambrus's physical and bloody illustrations for Riordan shows an increasing trend toward uncompromising violent affect alongside an increasing dominance of immediate visual image over the text that describes causes and consequences and deals with the human cost. As digital technology spreads rapidly, it is hard to see this trend reversing. We are likely to see a stronger assimilation, probably a subordination, of complex and reflective print content to the norms of the "hot" media. It is hard to know what the stories will be made to mean in this context; one hopes it will not just be another "fantasy" (read "fundamentalist") version of "good against evil."

The most recent children's Arthurianism also reflects the upsurge of scholarship, mythlore, and popular history around Arthurian material. In a reversal of the Enlightenment trend, "King Arthur" is now a historical fifth-century person to many again. The forthcoming Touchstone Pictures (Disney) film will help to cement a similar image in popular culture, and so may Steven Spielberg's projected TV miniseries. Malory's book is not central to this interest but features within its "myths and legends" category as part of the Arthurian "world." At present, it is hard to know whether popular film will invigorate interest in the book, as Tennyson and White did, or relegate it to the past. Children's Arthurianism is being historicized also in a more modest and scholarly way. Kevin Crossley-Holland's *The King Who Was and Will Be* (1998) is a lively gazetteer for the young, with information on places, characters, romances, and various cultural traditions. (It precedes Crossley-Holland's Arthurian fictional trilogy, which is too recent for me to assess here.) Andrea Hopkins's *Chronicles of King Arthur* (1993) is not a children's book, but it provides a model for introducing young readers to more of Malory's original text. Rather than offering yet another modern makeover, Hopkins tells a composite Arthuriad by letting "the voices of the authors [be] heard in their own style, from the wit and precision of Chrétien de Troyes to the stark dignity of Malory."[185] "[T]he most powerful and dramatic" passages, including many from the *Morte*, are given in the original (or translation) and linked by paraphrase and explanatory sections. Box-insets highlight major characters, places, and cultural influences. Illustrations showcase the rich visual tradition from the twelfth century to Beardsley. There is no modern *The Boy's King Arthur* using Malory's own text, and Lanier's concept is obviously old-fashioned; a new book like Hopkins's made specially for children would be an excellent idea.

As directed to the young, Malory has come through many phases since Caxton's time: history, spiritual ideal, model of conduct, political adventure, psychological study, myth and fantasy, and now history again. The children's *Morte* is flourishing, if popular retellings of familiar episodes are any guide. But in the long run, Malory's special value has been in his words, even more than the favorite stories, and certainly more than the "timeless" fable of a man with a large sword. It may be that the words will be better supported as a guest-text in children's historical Arthuriana than in straight

Arthurian children's adaptations, where they risk becoming superfluous to requirements, apart from a few fossil phrases. Will the hostility to the original *Morte* always latent in making "children's King Arthurs" finally silence its voice? And will children's writers no longer pay Malory the kind of attention that generates a distinctive friction with his style and values? Without Malory's strong contribution, as stimulus or irritant, to children's Arthuriana, will it suffer another period of decline, as in Edwardian times? Will *Le Morte Darthur* have to return to "history" for a while before another dominant intertext, another Tennyson or White, maybe even a Spielberg, gives young readers a new purchase on it? The future is impossible to know. (Who could have predicted a mass market for long novels like the *Harry Potter* series?) The third tradition has always been subject to reductive commercial pressures and periods of stagnation, yet unpredictably blessed by gifted lovers of Malory—from Charlotte Yonge to Rosemary Sutcliff and beyond. Adults make children's literature, and given that adult attention to *Le Morte Darthur* continues to grow and popular Arthurianism for all ages is burgeoning, we may yet see the "vigour and valour" of Malory return for the young, whatever it will mean.

Notes

1. See Hallam Tennyson's *Memoir*, 2, p. 128, quoted in Debra N. Mancoff, *The Return of King Arthur: The Legend Through Victorian Eyes* (London: Pavilion Books, 1995), p. 53.
2. The idea of the "original" *Morte* has altered also, with changes to Caxton (1485) by Wynkyn de Worde (1498) and the edition of 1634, and since the discovery of the Winchester manuscript in 1934 and the subsequent editions by Eugène Vinaver. For Caxton's edition, see Carol M. Meale, " 'The Hoole Booke': Editing and the Creation of Meaning in Malory's Text," in Elizabeth Archibald and A. S. G. Edwards, eds., *A Companion to Malory* (Cambridge, UK: D. S. Brewer, 1996), pp. 3–17. For Wynkyn de Worde's influence on visual presentation of the *Morte*, see Kevin Grimm, "Wynkyn de Worde and the Creation of Malory's *Morte Darthur*," in D. Thomas Hanks, Jr. and Jessica G. Brogdon, eds., *The Social and Literary Contexts of Malory's Morte Darthur* (Cambridge, UK: D.S. Brewer, 2000), pp. 134–53.
3. For broader surveys of neo-Arthurian fictions, see Roger Simpson, *Camelot Regained: The Arthurian Revival and Tennyson, 1800–1849* (Cambridge, UK: D. S. Brewer, 1990); Beverly Taylor and Elisabeth Brewer, *The Return of King Arthur* (Cambridge, UK: D. S. Brewer, 1983); Raymond H. Thompson, *The Return from Avalon: A Study of the Arthurian Legend in Modern Fiction* (Westport, CT: Greenwood, 1985); and Alan Lupack and Barbara Tepa Lupack, *King Arthur in America* (Cambridge, UK: D. S. Brewer, 1999).
4. David Matthews, in "Infantilizing the Father: Chaucer Translations and Moral Regulations," *Studies in the Age of Chaucer* 22 (2000): 104–105, notes a similar postwar survival of Chaucer editions for children.

5. Peter Hollindale, *Signs of Childness in Children's Books* (Stroud: Thimble Press, 1997), p. 49.

6. John Stephens, *Language and Ideology in Children's Fiction* (London: Longman, 1992), p. 88.

7. Hollindale, *Signs of Childness in Children's Books*, pp. 47, 49.

8. Eugène Vinaver, ed., *Malory: Works* (London: Oxford University Press, 1971). All subsequent page and line references to Malory's original text are to this edition and will be cited in the text.

9. Philip Sidney, *A Defence of Poesy*, ed. J. A. Van Dorsten (Oxford: Oxford University Press, 1966), p. 40. See Hollindale, *Signs of Childness in Children's Books*, p. 28: "Children's literature does not denote a text but a reading event. Whenever a successful voluntary transaction takes place between any text and any one child, that text is for the moment 'children's literature.'"

10. Roger Ascham, *The Scholemaster* (London: John Daye, 1571), p. 28.

11. Richard Barber, "Malory's *Le Morte Darthur* and Court Culture under Edward IV," *Arthurian Literature* XII (1993): 152 [133–55].

12. Vinaver, *Malory: Works*, p. xv.

13. *The History of the Renowned Prince Arthur King of Britain and His Knights of the Round Table* (London: Walker and Edwards, 1816), p. xii.

14. *The History of the Renowned Prince Arthur King of Britain and His Knights of the Round Table*, pp. xi, xii.

15. *The History of the Nine Worthies of the World* (London: Nathaniel Crouch, 1687), p. 147. By the time of the Dublin reprint by Richard Fitzimons in 1775 of the edition by Crouch (1687), this passage had been excised from the preface.

16. *A New History of England from the Invasion of Julius Caesar to the Present Time* (London: J. Newbery, 1763), pp. 35–36.

17. Oliver Goldsmith, *An History of England in a Series of Letters from a Nobleman to His Son* (London: J. Newbery, 1764), pp. 33–34.

18. For example, Charlotte Yonge, *A Book of Worthies* (London: Macmillan, 1869); W. H. Davenport Adams, *Before the Conquest; or, English Worthies in the Old English Period* (Edinburgh: William P. Nimno, 1870).

19. Robert Southey, ed., *The Birth, Lyf and Actes of Kyng Arthur* (London: Longman Hurst, Rees, Orme and Brown, 1817), p. xxviii.

20. Southey, ed., *The Birth, Lyf and Actes of Kyng Arthur*, p. xxviii. For boys' reception of the 1816 edition by Walker, see *Life and Exploits of King Arthur and His Knights of the Round Table: A Legendary Romance* (London: Milner and Co., 1878), p. 12: "A writer in an old edition of Blackwood tells us: 'In one large public school a solitary copy in two disreputable little paper-bound volumes was passed from hand to hand, and literally read to pieces, at all hours, lawful and unlawful.'"

21. *The History of the Renowned Prince Arthur King of Britain and His Knights of the Round Table*, p. viii.

22. See Samuel Johnson, *A Dictionary of the English Language* (London, 1755): "*romance*: a military fable of the middle ages; a tale of wild adventures in love or chivalry."

23. For an account of Charlotte Yonge, see Gillian Avery, *Nineteenth-Century Children: Heroes and Heroines in English Children's Stories, 1780–1900* (London: Hodder and Stoughton, 1965), pp. 104–18.

24. Andrew Lynch, "*Malory Moralisé*: The Disarming of *Le Morte Darthur* 1800–1919," *Arthuriana* 9 (4), 1999: 81–93.

25. Yonge, *The Heir of Redclyffe* (London: John W. Parker and Son, 1853), 1. 176–77.

26. Yonge, *The Heir of Redclyffe*, 1. 358.

27. Charlotte M. Yonge, "Children's Literature of the Last Century," *Macmillan's Magazine*, Vols. 19–21 (July–September 1869), 1. 229.

28. Yonge, "Children's Literature of the Last Century," 3. 449–50.

29. Yonge, "Children's Literature of the Last Century," 3. 456.

30. See Jane Austen, *Persuasion*, chapter 11, for Anne Elliot's advice on reading to melancholy Captain Benwick.

31. Yonge, *The Heir of Redclyffe*, 2. 126.

32. Charlotte M. Yonge, *What Books to Lend and What to Give* (London: National Society's Depository, 1887), p. 6.

33. See Vinaver, p. 75: "never to do outerage nothir morthir, and allwayes to fle treson, and to gyff mercy unto him that askith mercy, . . .and allwayes to do ladyes, damesels, and jantilwomen and wydowes socour."

34. Yonge, *What Books to Lend and What to Give*, p. 57.

35. Charlotte Yonge, *The History of Sir Tom Thumb*, ill. "J. B." (Edinburgh: Thomas Constable and Co., 1855), pp. iii, iv.

36. See Gillian Avery, *Behold the Child: American Children and their Books, 1621–1923*, p. 123, for the distinction.

37. Yonge seems even to anticipate Tennyson, whose *Enid and Nimue: The True and the False* was not published until 1857. Her Merlin warns: "Choose the true, not the false. Beware of fairy glitter. Die rather bravely as mortal man than live vainly as weary elf."

38. Yonge, *The History of Sir Thomas Thumb*, p. 87.

39. Mancoff, *The Return of King Arthur: The Legend through Victorian Eyes*, p. 56.

40. Alfred, Lord Tennyson, *The Poems of Tennyson*, ed. Christopher Ricks (2nd edn.; Harlow: Longman, 1986), No. 234.

41. Mancoff, *The Return of King Arthur: The Legend through Victorian Eyes*, pp. 121–23.

42. Vinaver, 521/13–17; 530/29–36; 533–36.

43. Taylor and Brewer, *The Return of King Arthur*, p. 22.

44. Yonge, *A Book of Worthies*, p. 450; Matthews, "Infantilizing the Father," pp. 93–99.

45. Lynch, "*Malory Moralisé*: The Disarming of *Le Morte Darthur* 1800–1919," pp. 82–83.

46. See, e.g., Dinah Craik Mulock, *Avillion and Other Tales* (London: Smith Elder and Co., 1853), p. 59: "Far higher than a dull life of perpetual selfish bliss, is that state of being which consists of temptation and triumph, struggle and victory, endurance and repose." Later, Sidney Lanier found Malory "singularly exemplary and instructive." See Lupack and Lupack, p. 79.

47. Henry Steele Commager, Preface to the first edition (1953) of Cornelia Meigs et al., *A Critical History of Children's Literature* (Rev. edn.; London: Macmillan, 1969), p. xi.

48. Taylor and Brewer, *The Return of King Arthur*, p. 2.

49. J. T. Knowles, *The Story of King Arthur and His Knights of the Round Table* (3rd edn.; London: Strahan and Co., 1868), p. 1.

50. *Life and Exploits of King Arthur and His Knights of the Round Table*, p. 12.

51. *Life and Exploits of King Arthur and His Knights of the Round Table*, pp. 103, 202.

52. *Life and Exploits of King Arthur and His Knights of the Round Table*, p. 25.

53. Mancoff, *The Return of King Arthur: The Legend through Victorian Eyes*, p. 110.

54. Yonge, *What Books to Lend and What to Give*, p. 13, considered that boys' books "may be read by girls also, but most boys will not read girls' books."

55. C. H. Hanson, *Stories of the Days of King Arthur* (London: Nelson and Sons, 1882), p. v.

56. Charles Morris, Introduction, *King Arthur and the Knights of the Round Table* (London: W. W. Gibbings, 1892). In his revised edition of *Stories of King Arthur and His Knights* in 1933, p. xv, U. Waldo Cutler spoke of "the quaintness of the fifteenth-century English, a language rather difficult for modern readers."

57. Dorothy M. Macardle, *Selections from Le Morte Darthur of Sir Thomas Malory* (London: Macmillan, 1917), p. xi.

58. H. Wragg, ed., *Selections from Malory* (Oxford: Clarendon Press, 1912), p. 13, "for use in middle and senior forms."

59. Roger Lancelyn Green, *King Arthur and His Knights of the Round Table* (London: Penguin, 1953; reissued, 1994), p. 6, renders them as "Certainly I will."

60. *King Arthur and His Knights*, pp. 3, 9.

61. J. T. Knowles, *The Legends of King Arthur and His Knights of the Round Table*, 3rd edn., p. vii.

62. Henry Frith, *King Arthur and the Knights of the Round Table* (London: George Routledge and Sons, 1884), p. iii.

63. The marriage with Elaine is also a major problem for Pyle to explain, since he has claimed (in *The Story of the Champions of the Round Table* [London: George Newnes, 1905], p. 23) that Launcelot "never had for dame any other lady except the lady Guinevere." Janet Macdonald Clark, in *Legends of King Arthur and His Knights* (London: Ernest Nister, 1914), pp. 188–89, ingeniously solved both problems by having Launcelot drugged, so that he "forgot all about King Arthur; and it seemed to him that Elaine was Guinevere, and that she was still at home in her father's castle, and that she was going to be married to him." Several versions since have done similarly.

64. Frith, *King Arthur and the Knights of the Round Table*, p. 405.

65. *The Book of Romance* (London: Longman Green and Co., 1902), though published as by Andrew Lang, is apparently the work of his wife Leonora Blanche Lang. See p. ix. The Grettir story was adapted from William Morris by another writer.

66. Lang, *The Book of Romance*, p. 87.

67. Lang, *The Book of Romance*, p. 3.

68. Howard Pyle, *The Story of King Arthur and His Knights* [London: George Newnes, 1903], p. 25, is very stagey in this scene: "Then, when Arthur heard that saying of his father's, he cried out in a very loud and vehement voice, 'Woe! Woe! Woe!'—saying that word three times. And Sir Ector said, 'Arthur, why art thou so woeful?' And Arthur said, 'Because I have lost my father, for I would rather have my father than be a king!' " Stuart Campbell, in *Stories of King Arthur* (London: Collins, 1933), p. 21, is stuffy: " 'If I am indeed king,' he told Sir Hector, 'I shall never forget my gratitude to you, and to the lady whom I have always believed to be my mother. Whatever you ask of me, I will not fail to give it to you.' "

69. Frith, *King Arthur and the Knights of the Round Table*, p. iv.

70. Margaret Vere Farrington, *Tales of King Arthur and the Knights of the Round Table* (New York: G. P. Putnam's Sons, 1888; rpt. 1899), p. 25.

71. See, e.g., William Brough, *King Arthur, or the Days and Knights of the Round Table* (London: Thomas Hailes Lacy, 1864). For the distinction, see Raymond Mander and Joe Mitchenson, *Pantomime: A Story in Pictures* (London: Peter Davies, 1973).

72. See Southey, p. xv; Pyle, *The Story of King Arthur and His Knights*, p. 279; Meigs, pp. 281–82. Pyle's Gawain has not *really* killed Lamorack, and his liaison with Ettarde is only the result of "enchantment."

73. Farrington, *Tales of King Arthur and the Knights of the Round Table*, pp. 7–8.

74. On the near-contemporary "infantilization" of Chaucer in modernized versions, see Matthews, "Infantilizing the Father."

75. Mary MacGregor, *Stories of King Arthur's Knights* (London: T. C. and E. C. Jack, 1905), p. 61.

76. MacGregor, *Stories of King Arthur's Knights*, p. 67.

77. MacGregor, *Stories of King Arthur's Knights*, p. 88.

78. MacGregor, *Stories of King Arthur's Knights*, p. 107.

79. The Blackie edition of *King Arthur and His Knights* (London: Blackie and Sons, 1910), p. 119.

80. A. A. Milne, *Now We Are Six* (London: Methuen, 1927).

81. Frances Nimmo Greene, *Legends of King Arthur and His Court* (Boston: Ginn and Co., 1901), p. vii.

82. Clarence Griffin Child, ed., *The Book of Merlin, The Book of Sir Balin, from Malory's King Arthur* (London: Harrap, 1904), pp. xii–xiii.

83. Beatrice Clay, *Stories of King Arthur and His Round Table* (London: Ernest Nister, n.d. [1905]), p. viii.

84. See Meigs, pp. 281–84; Lupack and Lupack, pp. 80–92.

85. See Meigs, p. 281; John Rowe Townsend, *Written for Children: An Outline of English-Language Children's Literature* (6th edn.; London: Bodley Head, 1995), p. 83. For a new analysis, see Julie Nelson Couch, "Howard Pyle's Story of King Arthur and His Knights," *Arthuriana* 13.2 (2003): 38–53.

86. Pyle, *The Story of King Arthur and His Knights*, pp. 58–59.

87. Howard Pyle, *The Story of the Grail and the Passing of Arthur* (London: Charles Scribner's Sons, 1910), p. iv.

88. Pyle, *The Story of King Arthur and His Knights*, p. 35.
89. For example, the tournament in Pyle (*The Story of King Arthur and His Knights*, pp. 13–16) seems to draw on Scott's *Ivanhoe*, chapter 12.
90. Pyle, *The Story of the Grail and the Passing of Arthur*, p. 130.
91. Pyle, *The Story of King Arthur and His Knights*, p. vi.
92. Pyle, *The Story of the Champions of the Round Table*, p. 23.
93. Pyle, *The Story of the Champions of the Round Table*, p. 9.
94. Pyle, *The Story of the Champions of the Round Table*, p. 255.
95. Howard Pyle, *The Story of Sir Launcelot and His Companions* (London: Chapman and Hills, 1907), p. 97.
96. Pyle, *The Story of the Champions of the Round Table*, p. 181.
97. Pyle, *The Story of the Grail and the Passing of Arthur*, p. 127.
98. Pyle, *The Story of the Grail and the Passing of Arthur*, p. 127.
99. Pyle, *The Story of the Champions of the Round Table*, p. 24.
100. Pyle, *The Story of the Champions of the Round Table*, p. 160.
101. Pyle, *The Story of the Champions of the Round Table*, pp. 282, 285.
102. Lupack and Lupack, *King Arthur in America*, pp. 84–87.
103. Pyle, *The Story of King Arthur and His Knights*, p. 35.
104. Pyle, *The Story of King Arthur and His Knights*, p. 97.
105. Pyle, *The Story of Sir Launcelot and His Companions*, p. 96.
106. Pyle, *The Story of the Grail and the Passing of Arthur*, p. 22.
107. Pyle, *The Story of the Grail and the Passing of Arthur*, p. 20.
108. Pyle, *The Story of King Arthur and His Knights*, p. 129.
109. U. Waldo Cutler, *Stories of King Arthur and His Knights* (London: George G. Harrap, 1905; rev. edn, 1933), p. xix.
110. Sidney Lanier, ed., *The Boy's Froissart* (New York: C. Scribner's Sons, 1879), p. viii.
111. Alfred W. Pollard, ed., *The Romance of King Arthur and the Knights of the Round Table*, ill. Arthur Rackham (London: Macmillan, 1917), p. vii.
112. Victor Watson, ed., *The Cambridge Guide to Children's Books in English* (Cambridge: Cambridge University Press, 2001), p. 402. Considering Pollard's edition as a book strictly for adults, his statement is regressive by Forbush's standards. See William Forbush, *The Boy Problem* (6th edn., New York: Westminster Press, 1907), p. 21: "Loyalty is a much overestimated virtue. It means little more than organized selfishness." For full reference to Forbush's work, see Lupack and Lupack, pp. 60–68. See also Alan Lupack's essay, chapter 9 in this volume.
113. Forbush, *The Boy Problem*, p. 18.
114. Forbush, *The Boy Problem*, p. 110.
115. Lupack and Lupack, *King Arthur in America*, pp. 135–209.
116. Elizabeth Lodor Merchant, *King Arthur and His Knights* (Philadelphia: J. C. Winston, 1928), p. xv.
117. Enid Blyton, *Tales of Brave Adventure* (London: George Newnes, 1930), p. 109.
118. Blyton, p. 161.

119. John Lea, *Tales of King Arthur and the Round Table* (London: S.W. Partridge, 1920), p. 23.

120. Paul Creswick, *The Story of the Round Table* (New York: American Book Co., 1925), p. 1.

121. Creswick, *The Story of the Round Table*, p. 402.

122. See, e.g., *Stories* (1935). The frontispiece, "Lady Making a Shield," is in fact an unrecognized picture of Tennyson's "lily maid" Elaine, making a cover for Lancelot's shield; the narrative emphases are heavily Tennysonian.

123. The same applies more strongly to Arthur Machen, *The Secret Glory* (London: Martin Secker, 1922).

124. Brian Kennedy Cooke, *King Arthur of Britain* (Leicester: Edmund Ward, 1946), p. 8.

125. Green, *King Arthur and His Knights of the Round Table*, p. ix.

126. Green, *King Arthur and His Knights of the Round Table*, p. xii.

127. Green, *King Arthur and His Knights of the Round Table*, p. ix.

128. Green, *King Arthur and His Knights of the Round Table*, p. 4.

129. Green, *King Arthur and His Knights of the Round Table*, p. 27.

130. Green, *King Arthur and His Knights of the Round Table*, p. 216.

131. Green, *King Arthur and His Knights of the Round Table*, p. 295.

132. Green, *King Arthur and His Knights of the Round Table*, p. 327.

133. Alice M. Hadfield, *King Arthur and the Round Table* (London: Dent, 1953), p. vi.

134. Hadfield, *King Arthur and the Round Table*, pp. 101–102.

135. Jill Mann, "Malory and the Grail Legend," in Elizabeth Archibald and A. S. G. Edwards, eds., *A Companion to Malory*, p. 217.

136. Hadfield, *King Arthur and the Round Table*, p. 110.

137. Hadfield, *King Arthur and the Round Table*, pp. 114–115.

138. Hadfield, *King Arthur and the Round Table*, p. 200.

139. Hadfield, *King Arthur and the Round Table*, pp. 145–46.

140. Hadfield, *King Arthur and the Round Table*, p. 147.

141. Hadfield, *King Arthur and the Round Table*, p. 203.

142. Hadfield, *King Arthur and the Round Table*, p. 109.

143. Antonia Fraser, *King Arthur and the Knights of the Round Table* (London: Sidgwick and Jackson, 1970), p. 171.

144. Fraser, *King Arthur and the Knights of the Round Table*, p. 42.

145. Fraser, *King Arthur and the Knights of the Round Table*, pp. 57, 101.

146. Fraser, *King Arthur and the Knights of the Round Table*, p. 67.

147. Fraser, *King Arthur and the Knights of the Round Table*, p. 106.

148. Fraser, *King Arthur and the Knights of the Round Table*, p. 136.

149. Fraser, *King Arthur and the Knights of the Round Table*, p. 192.

150. MGM, *Knights of the Round Table* (London: Ward Lock, 1955), p. 19.

151. MGM, *Knights of the Round Table*, p. 16.

152. See Andrew Davies, *The Legend of King Arthur* (London: Armada, 1979), p. 34: "Sometimes the only way to root out evil is with the sword."

153. For example, by Rosemary Sutcliff and Mary Stewart.

154. Taylor and Brewer, *The Return of King Arthur*, p. 290.

155. Mary Cathcart Burns, *Tales of King Arthur* (London: Longmans, 1961), p. 6.
156. Burns, *Tales of King Arthur*, pp. 61–64.
157. Clifton Fadiman, *The Story of Young King Arthur* (London: Frederick Muller, 1962), pp. 6–7.
158. Rosemary Sutcliff, *The Sword and the Circle* (London: Bodley Head, 1981), p. 8. Sutcliff was echoing Green, p. x, and so indirectly under Vinaver's influence.
159. Sutcliff, *The Sword and the Circle*, pp. 85–89.
160. Rosemary Sutcliff, *The Light Beyond the Forest* (London: Bodley Head, 1981), p. 26.
161. Sutcliff, *The Sword and the Circle*, p. 97.
162. Sutcliff, *The Light Beyond the Forest*, p. 127.
163. Sutcliff, *The Light Beyond the Forest*, p. 145.
164. Sutcliff, *The Light Beyond the Forest*, p. 49.
165. Vinaver, p. ix.
166. Sutcliff, *The Light Beyond the Forest*, p. 43.
167. Rosemary Sutcliff, *The Road to Camlann* (London: Bodley Head, 1981), p. 135.
168. Sutcliff, *The Road to Camlann*, p. 137.
169. Davies, *The Legend of King Arthur*, p. 25.
170. Davies, *The Legend of King Arthur*, p. 104.
171. See, e.g., those on <http://www.gamersattic.com/roleplaying/kapendragon.htm> (accessed June 2002).
172. William Thompson, review, at <http://www.sfsite.com/home114.htm> (accessed June 2002): "the first novel of fantasy."
173. Jill Mann, " 'Taking the Adventure': Malory and the *Suite du Merlin*," in D. S. Brewer and T. Takamiya, eds., *Aspects of Malory*, pp. 71–91.
174. Steve Barlow and Steve Skidmore, *The Final Battle: The Death of King Arthur* (Oxford: Ginn and Company, 1999).
175. Marcia Williams, *King Arthur and the Knights of the Round Table* (London: Walker, 1996), p. 22.
176. John Chambers, *Tales of King Arthur: A Play* (New York: Samuel French, 1996), p. 53.
177. Chambers, *Tales of King Arthur: A Play*, p. 40.
178. Chambers, *Tales of King Arthur: A Play*, p. 59.
179. Robin Lister, *The Story of King Arthur* (London: Kingfisher Books, 1988), pp. 94–95.
180. Clay, pp. vii–viii.
181. Mary Hoffman, *Women of Camelot* (London: Frances Lincoln, 2000), p. 58.
182. James Riordan, *Tales of King Arthur* (London: Hamlyn, 1992), p. 124.
183. E.g., Linda Yeatman, *King Arthur and the Knights of the Round Table* (London: Heinemann, 1991); Peter Oliver, *The Sword in the Stone* (Newcastle: Brimax Books, 1993); Tom Crawford, *The Story of King Arthur* (New York: Dover, 1994).
184. Felicity Brooks and Anna Claybourne, *Tales of King Arthur and His Knights* (London: Usborne, 1998), p. 136.

185. Andrea Hopkins, *Chronicles of King Arthur* (London: Collins and Brown, 1993), p. 9.

Select Bibliography of Malory for Children

Allen, Philip Schuyler. *King Arthur and His Knights*. Chicago: Rand McNally and Co., 1924.

Barlow, Steve and Steve Skidmore. *The Final Battle: The Death of King Arthur*. Oxford: Ginn and Co., 1999.

Bate, R. F., ed. *Stories of King Arthur: From Malory and Tennyson*. London: George Bell and Sons, 1907.

Blyton, Enid. *Tales of Brave Adventure*. London: Dean, 1963. Arthurian sections originally published as *The Knights of the Round Table*. London: George Newnes, 1930.

Brooks, Felicity and Anna Claybourne. *Tales of King Arthur and His Knights*. London: Usborne, 1998.

Burns, Mary Cathcart. *Tales of King Arthur*. London: Longmans, 1961.

Campbell, Stuart. *King Arthur and His Knights*. London: Collins, 1933.

———. *Stories of King Arthur*. London: Collins, 1935.

Chambers, John. *Tales of King Arthur: A Play*. New York: Samuel French, 1996.

Child, Clarence Griffin, ed. *The Book of Merlin, The Book of Sir Balin, from Malory's King Arthur*. London: Harrap, 1904.

The Children's King Arthur. London: Henry Froude and Hodder and Stoughton, 1909.

Clark, Janet Macdonald. *Legends of King Arthur and His Knights*. London: Ernest Nister, 1914.

Clay, Beatrice. *Stories from King Arthur and His Round Table*. Ill. Dora Curtis. New York: E. P. Dutton, n.d. [1905].

Conybeare, Edward. *La Morte D'Arthur: The History of King Arthur*. London: J. R. Moxon, 1868.

Cooke, Brian Kennedy. *King Arthur of Britain*. Leicester: Edmund Ward, 1946.

Crawford, Tom. *The Story of King Arthur*. New York: Dover, 1994.

Creswick, Paul. *The Story of the Round Table*. New York: American Book Company, 1925.

Crossley-Holland, Kevin. *The King Who Was and Will Be*. London: Orion, 1998.

Crowlesmith, Rev. J. *Stories of King Arthur and His Knights*. London: Goodship House, 1927.

Cutler, U. Waldo. *Stories of King Arthur and His Knights*. London: George G. Harrap, 1905; rev. edn. 1933.

Davies, Andrew. *The Legend of King Arthur*. London: Armada, 1979.

Edwardson, E. *The Courteous Knight and Other Tales Borrowed from Spenser and Malory*. Edinburgh: T. Nelson and Sons, 1899.

Fadiman, Clifton. *The Story of Young King Arthur*. London: Frederick Muller, 1962.

Farrington, Margaret Vere. *Tales of King Arthur and the Knights of the Round Table*. New York: G. P. Putnam's Sons, 1888; rpt. 1899.

Fielding, Henry. *Tom Thumb: A Tragedy*. London: J. Roberts, 1730; *The Tragedy of Tragedies*. London: J. Roberts, 1731.

Fraser [Pakenham], Antonia. *King Arthur and the Knights of the Round Table*. London: Heirloom Library, 1954.

Fraser, Antonia. *King Arthur and the Knights of the Round Table*. London: Sidgwick and Jackson, 1970.

Frith, Henry. *King Arthur and His Knights of the Round Table*. London: George Routledge and Sons, 1884.

Green, Roger Lancelyn. *King Arthur and His Knights of the Round Table*. London: Penguin, 1953; reissued 1994.

Greene, Frances Nimmo. *Legends of King Arthur and His Court*. Boston: Ginn and Co., 1901.

Hadfield, Alice M. *King Arthur and the Round Table*. London: Dent, 1953.

Hampden, John, ed. *"Knights of the Round Table" Taken from "Le Morte d'Arthur" by Sir Thomas Malory*. London: T. Nelson and Sons, 1930.

Hanson, C. H. *Stories of the Days of King Arthur*. London: Nelson and Sons, 1882.

Hoffman, Mary. *Women of Camelot*. London: Frances Lincoln, 2000.

Hopkins, Andrea. *Chronicles of King Arthur*. London: Collins and Brown, 1993.

Johnson, Richard. *The History of Tom Thumb*. London, 1621; *Tom Thumb, His Life and Death*. London, 1630.

King Arthur and His Knights. London: Blackie and Sons, 1910.

Knowles, J. T. *The Story of King Arthur and His Knights of the Round Table*. London: Griffith and Farrar, 1862.

——. *The Legends of King Arthur and His Knights of the Round Table*. 3rd edn. London: Strahan and Co., 1868.

Kushan, Ellen. *Knights of the Round Table*. Toronto: Bantam, 1988.

Lang, Andrew. *The Book of Romance*. London: Longman Green and Co., 1902.

——. *Tales from King Arthur and the Round Table*. Ill. H. J. Ford. London: Longman, Green and Co., 1905.

Lanier, Sidney, ed. *The Boy's King Arthur*. London: Sampson Low, Marston, Searle and Rivington, 1880.

——, ed. *The Boy's King Arthur*. Ill. N. C. Wyeth. New York: C. Scribner's Sons, 1920.

Lea, John. *Tales of King Arthur and the Round Table*. London: S. W. Partridge, 1920.

Life and Exploits of King Arthur and His Knights of the Round Table: A Legendary Romance. London: Milner and Co., 1878.

Lister, Robin. *The Story of King Arthur*. London: Kingfisher Books, 1988.

Macardle, Dorothy M. *Selections from Le Morte Darthur of Sir Thomas Malory*. London: Macmillan, 1917.

MacGregor, Mary. *Stories of King Arthur's Knights*. London: T. C. and E. C. Jack, 1905.

Malory, Sir Thomas. *Le Morte d'Arthur*. London: Dent, New York: Dutton, 1906.

Martin, A. T., ed. *Selections from Malory's Le Morte Darthur*. London: Macmillan, 1896.

Mead, W. E. *Selections from Sir Thomas Malory's Le Morte Darthur*. Boston: Ginn and Co., 1897.

Merchant, Elizabeth Lodor. *King Arthur and His Knights*. Philadelphia: J. C. Winston, 1928.

MGM. *Knights of the Round Table*. London: Ward Lock, 1955.

Morris, Charles. *King Arthur and the Knights of the Round Table*. London: W.W. Gibbings, 1892.

Oliver, Peter. *The Sword in the Stone*. Newmarket: Brimax Books, 1993.

Picard, Barbara Leonie. *Stories of King Arthur and His Knights*. London: Oxford University Press, 1955.

Pollard, Alfred W., ed. *The Romance of King Arthur and the Knights of the Round Table*. Ill. Arthur Rackham. London: Macmillan, 1917.

Price, Eleanor C. *Adventures of King Arthur*. London: J. Coker, 1931; rev. 1933.

Pyle, Howard. *The Story of the Champions of the Round Table*. London: George Newnes, 1905.

——. *The Story of the Grail and the Passing of Arthur*. London: Charles Scribner's Sons, 1910; rpt. New York: Dover, 1992

——. *The Story of King Arthur and His Knights*. London: George Newnes, 1903.

——. *The Story of Sir Launcelot and His Companions*. London: Chapman and Hall, 1907.

Ranking, B. Montgomerie. *The Prose Stories of The Idylls of the King*. London: J. C. Hotten, 1871.

Reakes, Paul. *King Arthur: A Pantomime Adventure in Camelot*. London: Samuel French, 1997.

Riordan, James. *Tales of King Arthur*. London: Hamlyn, 1992.

Rutley, Cecily. *Stories of King Arthur's Knights*. London: Religious Tract Society, 1929; new edn., London: Lutterworth Press, 1951.

Senior, Dorothy. *The King Who Never Died*. London: Adam and Charles Black, 1910.

Six Ballads about King Arthur. London: Kegan, Paul, Trench and Co., 1881.

Stories from King Arthur. London: Oxford University Press, 1935.

Sutcliff, Rosemary. *The Light Beyond the Forest*. London: Bodley Head, 1981.

——. *The Road to Camlann*. London: Bodley Head, 1981.

——. *The Sword and the Circle*. London: Bodley Head, 1981.

Williams, Marcia. *King Arthur and the Knights of the Round Table*. London: Walker, 1996.

Winder, Blanche. *Stories of King Arthur*. London: Ward Lock, 1925.

Wragg, H., ed. *Selections from Malory*. Oxford: Clarendon Press, 1912.

Yeatman, Linda. *King Arthur and the Knights of the Round Table*. London: Heinemann, 1991.

Yonge, Charlotte M. *The History of Sir Thomas Thumb*. Ill. "J. B." [Jemima Blackburn]. Edinburgh: Thomas Constable and Co., 1855.

CHAPTER 2

TEXT, IMAGE, AND SWORDS OF EMPOWERMENT
IN RECENT ARTHURIAN PICTURE BOOKS

Judith L. Kellogg

According to Newbery Award-winning author Patricia MacLachlan, the pervasive question that underlies many of the different questions children ask her is "How do we learn to be adults?" The answer, she responds, is that "We take and model our behavior from those we admire and if we are lucky enough to have heroes, we model our behavior after them."[1] For many children, King Arthur is one of these formative heroes, suggesting how inseparable cultural history often is from personal history. Many children develop a fascination with Arthurian tradition very early in life through picture books. Thus it is especially important to understand not just *what* this rich lore teaches children but *how* the stories that carry the special legacy of cultural tradition shape the next generation. Of particular interest here is the doubleness of the storytelling in picture books, the words and images telling parallel stories whose complete meaning is ultimately understood in the interaction between the two media. In this dynamic interaction, Arthur emerges with many faces, from humble communal leader, to teenage idol, to bewildered boy-king, to name just a few, and thus a model for very different interpretations of what constitutes the heroic. This discussion will look generally at why stories are so important in the formation of a child's personal and cultural identity and then specifically at a number of recent Arthurian picture books that take a variety of approaches to this rich lore. Such sampling will provide a prelude to a more extended examination of episodes wrapped around the motif of Arthur's acquisition of his swords, the one he pulls from the stone (or, in some versions, the anvil), and Excalibur, received from the Lady of the Lake. These swords are key emblems of Arthur's power and empowerment at many levels—political, personal, physical, magical, and mythic—and therefore appropriate narrative focal points for examining the transmission of cultural values and their relationship to shaping personal identity. Such analysis also reveals how the text–image dialectic in Arthurian tales functions to create a unique storytelling form, with rich ideological implications.

Walter Fisher points to the inseparability of our humanity from storytelling. He identifies humankind as "Homo narrans," for "all forms of communication need to be seen fundamentally as stories—symbolic interpretations of aspects of the world occurring in time and shaped by history, culture, and character."[2] Although all communication is narrative, certain stories become paradigms through which a new generation learns to negotiate the world and which it uses to develop a sense of identity. As Fisher further postulates, "the world as we know it is a set of stories that must be chosen among in order for us to live a life in process of continual re-creation."[3] Anthony Appiah also theorizes the importance of stories in identity formation as he explores the relationship between large collective categories, such as gender, ethnicity, and nationality, and the "individual and authentic self."[4] As Appiah says, "We make up selves from a tool kit of options made available by our culture and society," and we conceptualize this emerging self in narrative form, so that "collective identities, in short, provide what we might call scripts: narratives that people can use in shaping their life plan, and in telling their life stories."[5]

The stories that children encounter play a vital role in determining the "scripts" they will carry into adult life. And, although stories carry many kinds of scripts, those that showcase cultural heroes have a special resonance because they carry the authority of inherited tradition. The Victorians knew this when they resurrected Arthurian heroes as role models for raising "civilized" gentlemen who would go out and build an empire.[6] Though notions of heroes have changed in different periods, these figures still reflect what a culture deems worthy of emulation. Because picture books provide most children the earliest literary access to heroic "scripting," they can play a particularly significant role in providing ways for a child to learn to negotiate the intersections between public, communal domains and the private, individual world.

In picture books, storytelling takes a unique form. A sequence of pictures has its own narrative structure and tells its own story. The pictures can be a more indelible medium than the text for a young child. After all, a child can pick up and "read" a picture book without knowing the words at all. But it is in "the complexity of interplay between picture-meaning and text-meaning," as Phillip Pullman has observed, that we find "the greatest storytelling discovery of the twentieth century: namely, counterpoint."[7] As Peter Hunt points out, the complex relationship between the verbal and visual allows words to "add to, contradict, expand, echo, or interpret the pictures—and vice versa."[8] This is a fundamentally different function than that of the traditional illustration.[9] An illustration has its own complex relationship to the text. It can simply encapsulate a particularly engaging moment of the narrative; it can certainly be interpretive; and it may also provide a "gloss," directing the reader how to approach a particular text. But the text can still stand alone without any illustrations. By contrast, the images in a successful picture book are inseparable from the narrative and exploit the visual to add layers of meaning not possible with just a simple text or image alone. A good picture-book artist will create and develop dynamic story possibilities beyond the text, the synthesis of word and image rapturously described by Maurice Sendak as a unique entity, "mixed and beaten and smoothed into a picture-book form that has something resembling the lush, immediate beauty of music and all its deep, unanalyzable mystery."[10]

Although few (if any) of the picture books in this study measure up to Sendak's inspired standard, many are nevertheless memorable. A rapid overview of particularly interesting picture-book retellings offers a sampling of the ways that images add resonances not possible in words alone. Although all of these retellings are highly pictorial, a few are on the cusp between picture book and illustrated text. Yet all contain rich visual material and maintain a continuous narrative thread parallel to the text, thus providing the counterpoint that Pullman describes.

Although most of the picture books described here have been published in the last twenty years, an exceptionally interesting earlier example, *Knights of the Round Table* by Emma Gelders Sterne and Barbara Lindsay, with remarkable illustrations by Gustaf Tenggren,[11] suggests how the illustrations play such an intriguing cultural role in the experience of the narrative. Tenggren's fluid and sinewy illustrations not only tell the Arthurian story but also utilize painting styles and compositional motifs borrowed explicitly from great masters. El Greco is dominant, and some of the more horrific scenes are quite Goya-esque. Influences of other European masters and of famous paintings are interlaced throughout and suggest that, in spite of King Arthur's medieval origins, he can wear faces and represent attitudes that span Western history. Yet this transhistorical interplay of styles in the end produces its own unique version, decidedly modern in its look, and illustrates the way every retelling in fact updates Arthurian material, which of necessity is being filtered through layers of older sources.

With certain retellings, this intertwining of the past is highly studied. For example, some of the best illustrators have obviously looked at illuminated manuscripts. Two exquisite examples of those are *Sir Gawain and the Green Knight* (also discussed in this volume by Cindy L. Vitto) and

Sir Gawain and the Loathly Lady, written by Selina Hastings and illustrated by Juan Wijngaard.[12] Each page is framed in medieval patterns, and the illustrations incorporate rich medieval motifs, particularly in the clothing and furnishings. Like Wijngaard, other illustrators borrow compositional elements from medieval renderings. Both Alan Baker's illustrations for Robin Lister's *Legend of King Arthur* and Hudson Talbott's illustrations for several of his own works (discussed at length later in this essay) depict battle and tournament scenes that combine the excitement and energy of realistic horses with the symmetry and balance of stylized medieval renditions. As in medieval illuminations, the love of ritualistic pageantry, heraldry, and sumptuous costumes is apparent in many fine recent depictions, which suggest the ways in which Arthurian legend can provide continuity with the past while still addressing current concerns.

Jamichael Henterly's illustrations for Robert San Souci's *Young Arthur*[13] use medieval visual motifs effectively, with selected pages textured to look like parchment and framed by intricate and colorful Celtic motifs reminiscent of the *Book of Kells*. The illustrations point to a post-Roman world rather than to the more romantic, chivalric world of later renditions. Although the periodization may not be strictly accurate, the attempt to recreate an older Arthurian backdrop is evident in the fact that the knights wear chain mail rather than shining armor and the castle interior is constructed of uneven stones and massive wood beams. The title page features a Stonehenge-like circle, and Arthur, after he is crowned in London, must be crowned a second time as King of Wales. Henterly's illustrations for Robert San Souci's *Young Guinevere*[14] also pick up the Celtic visual motifs, pairing Guinevere's story aesthetically with young Arthur's. Although several pages in *Young Guinevere* contain the Celtic manuscript-like framing, more often the border decoration approximates medieval embroideries, loosely in the style of the Bayeaux Tapestry (anachronistic, but visually charming). All these decorative details provide visual historical contextualization, allowing the child an almost tactile experience of the narrative world, a reaching back to touch a lost past, that the text on its own does not offer.

San Souci's *Young Lancelot*[15] completes the future love triangle that will be so destructive to the Round Table. As with the British Arthur and Roman Guinevere, San Souci identifies the ethnic background of his young French hero, suggesting the ways "diversity" was experienced in early Britain. Visually, the work meshes with the others in its Celtic stylistic influences. The three works also interrelate in their suggestive depictions of character. Although San Souci hints at future trouble in *Young Guinevere* when Merlin cautions Arthur not to marry the young woman who has so captivated him, he does not identify the interpersonal complications but does develop character traits that subtly anticipate the later problems.

If Arthur is appealing but somewhat one dimensional in his dedication to "nobility, justice and wisdom," Lancelot is developed as more complex and conflicted. Knowing even as a youth that he is the best of all knights, he is cold and aloof. But he sheds his arrogance when he is psychologically humbled in the Perilous Chapel. As his foster mother, the Lady of the Lake, has told him, he must become a knight with two hearts: "One should be hard as a diamond when battling cruelty and injustice. The other should be soft as warm wax to respond to goodness and gentleness." The two hearts not only describe the profile of a balanced chivalric knight but also foreshadow Lancelot's divided loyalties, the hard knight-in-arms serving Arthur and the tender man vulnerable to the passionate love offered by the beautiful but impetuous Guinevere.

In the trilogy as developed by San Souci, Guinevere is created as a distinct character, which raises an important issue faced not just in picture books but also by Arthurian tradition generally. Although the tradition may have developed from a mythic base with strong female figures, as it is passed down, it is not particularly kind to women. As Maureen Fries observed, Arthurian women "are essentially ancillary to the male actors of that literary tradition, and must therefore be considered in relation to the male heroic roles they complement or defy."[16] John Stephens and Robyn McCallum add that "modern retellers have made little headway against the endemic connections between female virtue and passive submissiveness on the one hand, and wickedness and female agency on the other."[17] However, a child's picture book gives the author freedom to invent stories that predate the moral lapses of Guinevere's later experience. In *Young Guinevere*, both the text and images show a lively and independent adolescent who defies her father to sneak "farther than hunters and woodcutters dared" into the woods, where she confronts a dragon. Her "courage, strong will, and a certain impulsiveness," traits admirable in a girl raised in contemporary society, are also the same traits that suggest why later, as an adult, she may have dared to transgress in her affair with Lancelot. *Young Guinevere* moves in new directions by giving Guinevere a story of her own and also a strong voice. In this version, although she does accept Arthur from a sense of duty, she is given the choice to make.[18] The cover image typifies Guinevere's characterization. It shows a determined, simply dressed young woman, armed with bow and arrows, alone in the forest. Her beautiful green eyes look confidently straight at the audience.

Another work that explores new territory by examining women's roles in a children's book is Mary Hoffman's *Women of Camelot: Queens and Enchantresses at the Court of King Arthur*.[19] Seven women—Igrayne, Guinevere, Nimue, Lyonet, Morgan, Lady Ragnell, and Elaine of Corbenic—tell, in their own voices, stories that are familiar from the male perspective. The illustrations by Christina Balit are dramatic and stylized, with the figures having strongly defined contours reminiscent of Beardsley, but vividly colored and heavily layered in contrasting patterns. The most unusual of these illustrations in a children's book is the sexually charged representation of Guinevere peering in on a surprised Elaine, in bed with a sleeping Lancelot.[20] Visually, this is quite a stunning rendition, with the perspective configured so that Lancelot's sleeping head is centered exactly between Guinevere and Elaine, his passivity contrasted with the highly charged glares between the two women. The large swatch of white empty page to one side of the figures suggests the silence that buffers this intensely passionate private moment from the court world outside.

Another rendition of the Elaine–Lancelot–Guinevere triangle demonstrates the difficulty of this part of the story for children's writers and suggests a possible reason why Lancelot is not represented as much in recent children's versions of the story as he was in nineteenth- and early twentieth-century renditions, where his sexual lapses were subsumed under his role as the perfect gentleman-knight. Hudson Talbott, who is quite innovative in addressing tough political implications in the Arthurian stories, simply avoids the sexual complications of the story by neatly wiping them out in *Lancelot*.[21] Rather than allowing Guinevere to complicate his life, Lancelot marries Elaine, and the birth of Galahad offers a "they-lived-happily-ever-after" kind of ending. Clearly, the mundane domestic ending degenerates from the mysterious beginning, full of mythic possibilities. Lancelot, whom Talbott depicts as raised by the Lady of the Lake, arrives at Arthur's court to fulfill the prophecy of "a passionate young hero [who] would come one day and change their world forever." In this version, the ethereal otherworldliness often associated with Galahad is displaced onto the young Lancelot, who "seemed to possess both the grace of an angel and the intensity of a panther." Later, he falls in love with Guinevere, but though so intense that it drives him to madness, it is love from afar. As in Malory, he is cured by the Grail; but then, having come to his senses, he marries Elaine. The later images are in marked contrast to the unsettling drama of many of the earlier scenes, from the fiery slaughter and devastation on the first page, to the two-page spread of Lancelot overcoming a towering dragon, to the dark forest scene, with a shaggy, bloody, and nearly naked Lancelot struggling with his madness. But the compelling, stark, and thought-provoking images of the body of this work dissolve in the last two scenes into pink-dominated pastels and sentimental, romantic settings. The ending shows a delightful cordial "family" gathering of two aristocratic couples in a flower-filled garden setting, Lancelot and Elaine arm-in-arm showing off their bouncing Galahad, and King Arthur, in an avuncular mode, touching the baby. Guinevere stands beside him, her distanced, solemn stare hinting at trouble. The wonderful visual touch is Merlin in the background, never mentioned in the text, peering out at the reader with a wise but worried gaze, as if quietly to imply that the story does not stop here.

That Talbott's version of the Lancelot story oversimplifies the resolution of the complex issues that the story sets up well is surprising, given that Talbott is so adept elsewhere in interweaving exploration of dark consequences of even well-intentioned human actions. In *King Arthur and the Round Table*,[22] for instance, he looks with an unsentimental eye at a ruler's responsibilities. In that work, after battling Saxon invaders, a bleeding young Arthur reckons with the consequences of bringing order to his unruly kingdom as he wanders "through the battlefield alone to see for himself what his victory had cost in human life. Once-glorious knights and humble foot soldiers, old friends and sworn enemies—all lay together now." The graphic visual quality of the carnage is startling in a children's book, although ultimately it is meant to convey a stark anti-war message.[23] In a similar manner, Robin Lister's *Legend of King Arthur*, ably illustrated by Alan Baker,[24] does not shy away from some of the more troubling aspects of the story and its intense psychological moments. Lister even includes the detail that when Arthur confronts a vicious giant at the isle of Mont Saint Michel, he happens upon the giant's meal preparation and finds "skewered on each spit, the butchered carcasses of four small children. . .slowly roasting in the flames."[25] The reader is spared the visual representation of that scene, but elsewhere, unsettling images abound. For instance, after Lancelot has tragically killed Sir Gareth and Sir Gaheris while rescuing Guinevere from being burned at the stake, Baker depicts in a grisly close-up the agonized faces of the dead brothers, lying fallen in grass and shrubbery. Jane Curry notes that "violence. . .is not only an important factor in the appeal the tales have for children, but has always been acceptable. Even the primmest of versions can glory in smiting and skewering."[26] But here, in the personalization of some of these images, we see an attempt to use violence provocatively, to incite awareness of its consequences.

Aside from presenting graphic aspects of cruelty, death, and tragedy, Baker's images afford the story an increased emotional resonance and show a complexity of character not often probed in children's retellings. In this version, Morgan le Fey plays the malevolent psychic who tells Merlin about Lancelot and Guinevere's future liaison. In the illustration, Baker captures Merlin's terrible angst as he looks into Arthur's future. The magician stands helplessly before a crystal ball, his head cradled between his hands, isolated in his inability to affect the fatal consequences of misguided human passion.[27] Baker's rendition of Guinevere is quite remarkable as well. Whereas in many versions Guinevere is wispy or insignificant, Baker's illustrations allow her a fuller range of emotions than we usually associate with her. Often relegated to the role of the woman who allows Arthur and, later, Lancelot, to demonstrate their prowess, or more tragically, reduced to a figure instrumental in precipitating the fall of Camelot, Guinevere in one of Baker's illustrations has just driven Lancelot from court after hearing that he has fathered Galahad. Quickly she becomes "sick with sorrow" bitterly regretting "her jealous anger."[28] Baker focuses on the pain, humanity, and vulnerability acknowledged in her tearful face, unidealized and distorted in agony by her concern for Lancelot.

This array of examples thus demonstrates a number of functions performed by images. They create a distinct contextual tone with the setting and decorative motifs; they probe complexities of character; and they maintain a parallel but distinct narrative thread. Several other works whose illustrations effectively perform all these functions deserve mention here. Trina Schart Hyman's images for Margaret Hodges's *The Kitchen Knight*[29] are highly successful in conveying an independent, fast-paced, engaging narrative thread. Full of richly colored detail, the images are filled with vitally individualized representations of even background characters. The visual rhythms are beautifully paced to complement the action, with dark and somber tones interspersed with both red dominated action scenes and quieter pastel sequences. And certain illustrations even insert a smaller framed image of a close-up face, which lends psychological depth to the larger visual narrative perspective.

Two depictions of Merlin's childhood are interesting to view as a pair since they tell essentially the same story from very different perspectives, both of which are successful. Jane Yolen's *Merlin and the Dragons*[30] has Merlin as an old man telling his story to the boy Arthur, who has awakened with nightmares. As Yolen does so wonderfully, she does not simply recount a story but also consciously explores the power of story to transform. Li Ming's exquisite images capture not only the powerful otherworldly energy of battling dragons but also the wonder of the experience of storytelling, in the close-ups of Arthur's totally engaged, awestruck face and Merlin's intent gaze as he both reaches into the past and transfers his knowledge to a boy who has just learned the responsibilities that weigh upon the son of Uther Pendragon. In another work, Robert San Souci's *Young Merlin*,[31] Daniel Horne's illustrations, which coincidentally use a palette of vibrant earthy colors very similar to Ming's, show a more whimsical, self-ironic, almost elf-like Merlin, appropriate to his depiction as "a fey little boy, who laughed a great deal but never cried." (By contrast, Yolen's young Merlin has "a mouth that rarely smiled. He was troubled by dreams, sleeping and waking.") San Souci's story takes Merlin chronologically up to the battle in which Uther Pendragon's brother Aurelius is killed in the civil unrest following Vortigern's treachery. Horne's final image of Merlin, despairing over his beloved Aurelius's dead body, is a sharp contrast to the first image in the work, of a playful and giggling boy Merlin, hiding behind a tomb from a nun who is calling him to prayer.

As with the paired depictions of Merlin, two versions of Chrétien de Troyes's *Yvain* also suggest how the interplay of text and image can draw very different implications from the same source. Gerald McDermott's *The Knight of the Lion* and John Howe's *The Knight with the Lion: The Story of Yvain*[32] (each illustrated by the author) follow Chrétien's basic story line. After defeating a mysterious knight at a marvelous fountain, Arthur's young knight Yvain falls in love and marries the man's widow, Laudine. But then he foolishly loses her when he is lured back to the chivalric life at Arthur's court, and consequently he descends into madness. Regaining his sanity, through the agency of his clever friend Lunete he is reunited with Laudine, but only after reestablishing his heroic reputation. Along the way back to his wife, he earns the trust of his regal companion, the lion who is emblematic of Yvain's nobility of spirit.

Gerald McDermott uses the story to explore the mythic pattern of the hero's journey. He identifies the magic fountain specifically as the Fountain of Life and returns significant events to this location to mark the stages of Yvain's transformation. The story is told from Yvain's point of view, the dramatic range of styles recreating the constantly shifting emotional state of the young hero. The work opens with a stately poetic retrospective overview that invokes the archetypal quality of Yvain's experience. Yvain states: "I am the fugitive from the Garden of Desire, / I am defiant in the face of Death, / I am the victor and the vanquished. / . . .I am the Wild Man on the moor, / I am the queller of demons and ogres, / I am the mate of the fiery-maned beast." Elsewhere, the tone moves from sensuous, to lyrical, to raw and visceral. Throughout, the specificity of the textual detail contrasts with the evocative, fluid, highly stylized black-and-white illustrations, the illustrations working to reflect the emotional overtones more than to capture or comment upon the narrative action. Two very different passages illustrate this dynamic interplay of the textual and the visual. In an early sequence, when Yvain, excited by the possibility of a great adventure, first travels to the Fountain of Life, the text plays on the sensuous details. Yvain rides "through brambles and bushy oak. There is birdsong, the rustle of leaves, and the smell of thornberry crushed underfoot. I trot past unfurling ferns, lichen-covered rocks, circles of mushrooms in the cool earth." In contrast to the concreteness of the text, the accompanying images show patterned, twisted squiggles representing the forest, with a small mounted Yvain springing between two trees. The abstract quality of the images invites the reader to superimpose imaginatively the richly textured description and thus to internalize Yvain's state of mind at that moment, as he excitedly anticipates life's possibilities. In another sequence full of carefully wrought detail (but in a starkly different emotional register), Yvain loses his sanity after being rejected by his wife. His descent into madness is described in all its disturbing physicality and grotesqueness as Yvain narrates: "Bleeding and drooling I crawl through the dead leaves. I chew on roots, I vomit in streams." But the paired visual image is almost surreal, with a naked Yvain set within a thorny and writhing landscape that represents his own tormented psyche, the pain being a prelude to his subsequent "rebirth." By this mix of concrete text and expressionistic image, McDermott manages to draw wide-ranging implications from Yvain's personalized emotional experience.

McDermott's version showcases what he calls in his Author's Note the "dark power of the story" by developing the symbolic pattern of the hero's journey. By contrast, although his story is indeed full of engaging fantastic elements, John Howe offers a more straightforward, third-person narration that is meant, as he says in his Author's Note, to show that the preoccupations of Chrétien's "heroes are often ours today—keeping promises, being brave when it really matters, learning how to speak one's feelings. These are daily challenges we all face." In Howe's illustrations, the key players are young and gorgeous, and the white lion particularly elegant. His use of perspective is especially imaginative and striking; he achieves an almost three-dimensional quality that dramatically engages the reader in the action. In one scene, for example, a horse charges directly into the face of the reader. In another, with the composition decentered and skewed, we find ourselves awkwardly peering through ceiling beams and voyeuristically viewing the funeral of Laudine's first husband. These wild and dizzying scenes are interspersed with quieter, more distanced views set in lush surroundings, so that we have the modulated rhythm of a successful action movie, with the "moral" being less important than a lively and well-paced story line. So, in their retellings and accompanying visual representations, McDermott and Howe show the malleability of Arthurian material by creating from a common source two very different narratives, one a mythic journey of transformation from boyhood to manhood, the other an exciting adventure story with a happy romantic ending.

Two other works deserve brief mention here. Although perhaps better described as heavily illustrated texts rather than as picture books, Molly Perham's *King Arthur and the Legends of Camelot*, illustrated by Julek Heller, and James Riordan's *King Arthur*, illustrated by Victor G. Ambrus,[33] are both quite masterful. Heller's depictions capture equally well high narrative action and detailed, psychologically probing facial portraiture. The often gnarly and dense background settings reinforce the aura of a mysterious world of serious consequence. Victor Ambrus's illustrations highlight a very different aspect of the story. His illustrations show heavily sketched, highly detailed figures, sometimes bordering on cartoons. Ambrus only minimally renders background, and his figures are often filled in with bright, free-flowing colors. The effect is to focus on the primary human action, often in an intensely kinetic fashion, the figures seeming to burst from the page. These illustrations, which work well with the text, are an imaginative reworking of original material that emphasizes the human interaction within the stories.

This brief overview of the interplay between image and text reveals the unique qualities that visual elements can add to a story. Pictures tell their own stories, sometimes even in ways that pull against the text. One good example of this tension is found in Michael Morpurgo's *Arthur: High King of Britain*.[34] Morpurgo's work reads like a script for a Hollywood action hero, presented as the sensitive tough guy who does the violence he must do and does it well, but is saddened and made wiser by the necessity. The boy-king Arthur recalls his victories over Anglo-Saxon invaders:

> My army was on the march for three years, and I never in all that time doubted our invincibility. Every victory brought us new strength and new support. Each brave man we lost in battle was at once replaced by two, then three, then four, till we were more than twenty thousand strong, battle-hardened and every one of us on a fit horse. . . . There is a swath of red earth all across the West Country to mark the place where we hunted them down and destroyed them.
>
> I take no pride in the blood we spilled, nor any pleasure in it, either. In those three years I saw more savagery than can be good for a man's soul. A terrible anger spurred me on so that I became careless for my own safety. Others called it courage, but I knew it for what it was.[35]

But in the illustration of Arthur as boy-king that is highlighted on the cover of the work as well as the title page, one sees the boy far more than the king. Arthur looks more bewildered than angry, and more frightened than battle-weary. This visual depiction of Arthur invites children to wonder how they would feel if suddenly they were told that, by pulling a sword from a stone, they would have to abandon their normal childhood roles and take on the responsibilities of royalty, inspire an army, fight, and kill. Indeed, a hero like Arthur can be an important focal point for asking questions about priorities, values, and relationship to the community.

An engaged relationship with one's community necessarily involves ideological positioning, an aspect implicit in any text or image. To explore the ways recent children's picture books leave differing ideological imprints on youthful readers, we can use as focal point several renditions of Arthur's acquisition of his swords. In fact, Arthur has two swords. The one that he pulls from the stone (or sometimes the anvil) signals his birthright as king. Formerly owned by Uther Pendragon, this sword represents dynastic continuity and worldly authority. Later Arthur acquires the famous Excalibur, given to him by the Lady of the Lake and returned to her upon his death. This sword suggests that Arthur's secular and Christian authority is validated by and built upon older, mythic powers of the Celtic Otherworld. A knight's sword generally is an emblem of his rank and power, but these swords, each with its own mysterious origin, also mark Arthur as one preordained to undertake extraordinary personal and political challenges.[36]

Walt Disney's 1963 film adaptation of T. H. White's *The Sword in the Stone*, which, though not recent, is probably the version of the Arthurian legend most often encountered by children, even today. This animated cartoon and the book that followed fancifully describe the young Arthur's preparation to become king, long before Arthur is aware of his destiny.[37] When Arthur first meets Merlin, the boy tells the bumbling magician that his life's ambition is to be a "knight's squire." Merlin intuits that the boy has some special calling and thus takes a keen interest in him, inspiring him with his belief in education; through his magician's powers to transform, he gives Arthur an insider's view of the workings and hierarchies of the natural world. This experience at transformation will provide a strong foundation for Arthur and give him the ability to accept his major metamorphosis, from humble squire to King of Britain, for he is quite daunted at first by his newfound role as king. In Disney's version, we see the seeds of an introspective, angst-ridden Arthur, who will no doubt need a lot of psychotherapy when he grows up. Visually, Arthur's insecurities are highlighted by his smallness, from our first view of him, dominated by his gigantic stepbrother, Sir Kay, to the end, where we leave him encumbered by an overly large crown that suggests the burdensome and disturbing responsibilities of adult life. Given that the scenes preceding the ending focus on Arthur's legitimization of his regal authority by pulling the sword from the stone, the absence of the sword, the symbol of his power, is striking in these final scenes. But, in fact, Arthur need not worry, for unlike the Arthur of medieval sources, no one contests his position, and his destiny is to "live wonderful adventures as the head of the Knights of the Round Table."[38] In essence, his life is the stuff of fairy tales, as he is assured that he will live happily ever after. Nothing too difficult here for children to digest.

Robert Sabuda's story and illustrations for his *Arthur and the Sword*[39] show how flexibly this story can be adapted to differing ideological concerns. Sabuda remakes the sword-pulling episode to stress the Christian context. On the first page, we learn that the story occurs "at the time of the celebration of Christ's birth," and far more of the story takes place in the church and church courtyard than at the tournament or in the community. The sword is repeatedly called a "holy sword." But the most dramatic Christian thrust comes with the images, all of which are done in the style of intensely colored stained-glass windows. The anvil with the sword is depicted as an altar, and the scene in which Arthur draws the sword shows him behind the altar-like anvil, as a priest officiating at a mass. The whole scene is filled with doves, indicating that the Holy Spirit is attending at this service. The final words in the text, that the sword would be "raising high the country out of darkness, and bringing forth a new world," suggest that a kind of communal conversion accompanies this momentous event. However, the community that will be affected is never depicted. The last image is of the isolated sword, surrounded by vibrant, mandala-like yellow and orange rays on a bright purple background. This glowing ending of triumphant renewal evokes a tone of finality that precludes further exploration of the psychological or political complexities of the moment.

Hudson Talbott, in his *Sword in the Stone*,[40] also caps Arthur's triumph at the end of the narrative on an upbeat note, but in a much more public context and with more provocative overtones. The work closes as Arthur swears to dedicate his own life to the good of his people; he declares, "In your trust I shall find my strength." But his optimism and faith are built on shaky ground. Like Disney's Arthur, he is reluctant to accept authority, not because he is daunted by the task but because of the painful realization that in becoming king he must give up his private life and the only family he has known. Arthur has grown up not knowing about his birthright, and Talbott, in narrating the sequence in which Arthur finds out who his father is, takes full advantage of his innocence. Before the grand, public, ritual pulling of the sword from the stone that identifies Arthur as legitimate king before his people, Arthur first pulls the sword from the stone in the presence only of his stepfather Sir Ector (whom he had believed to be his actual father) and his stepbrother Kay. The act is set in a dark and now empty public square. The painful isolation of the moment is intensified by the fact that a previous illustration has depicted this same square in daylight, bustling with busy crowds of people from all classes, engaged in a myriad of activities. Once young Arthur has shown those closest to him that he can pull the sword from the stone, he has a quiet moment to reflect on the implications of his achievement, the most painful being that he no longer has the luxury of a private life. He sobs, "I don't want to be king. Not if it means losing my father!" But Arthur has no choice. He cannot escape his personal history, even if he is not fully conscious of it. And through this hero, children can also think about the fact that everyone, even a king, at a certain point must necessarily separate from the personal security of family and enter the public world of adulthood. For every child, that public world must be entered in a specific society at a particular moment in history, and Talbott is keenly aware of the resonance of Arthur's historical moment. Preceding this sequence is a remarkable illustration that highlights the interconnectedness of previous and present cultural moments. This particular interweaving of text and image illustrates better than any I know how many layers a visual image can add to the text. Here the full resonance of text and image is completed only by their juxtaposition with each other. In a two-page spread, a pictorial narrative surrounds a text that raises troubling questions about Arthur's public triumph. The text suggests behind-the-scenes manipulation of power by Merlin and the Archbishop, who oversee the public pulling of the sword from the stone. These two men, although from different backgrounds, are united in an agonizing struggle for leadership that has been tearing Britain to pieces since the death of Uther Pendragon. The country is "shattered into dozens of quarreling, petty kingdoms" and thereby made vulnerable to barbarian invasions from the outside. It is this context that brings Merlin and the Archbishop together to stage Arthur's entry into the political scene. Merlin tells the Archbishop, "If I have your leave to use my magic, I shall create an event to bring forth this young heir and prove to the world that he is the true and rightful high king of Britain."

The two facing pages on which the text recounts the two old men hatching their plans are extraordinarily rich visually. Beyond the overt action, the framing images add a haunting cultural dimension, for they not only evoke the emotional intensity of the societal despair described in the text but also encapsulate various layers in the larger development of Arthurian tradition generally. Recall that an historical Arthur, if he in fact existed, would have been a fifth-century post-Roman Celtic leader who fought against the Anglo-Saxon invasion, not the more familiar literary King Arthur, presiding with Queen Guinevere over a glorious, sumptuous court at Camelot and supported by his Knights of the Round Table. A close look at the details of this frame indicates how both of these contexts, that of Arthur's historical origins and that of literary tradition, are implicated.

These disturbing framing images are rendered in black and white (the non-colors of dreams and nightmares, as well as of news photos and old documentaries) punctuated by splashes of orange from the pattern of relentless fires, repeated throughout the scene. Depicted in this frame, families are destroyed, children are butchered, women are carried off, and greed and violence prevail. The savagery is committed not just by the barbarian (i.e., Germanic) invaders, presumably distinguished by their horned, Viking-like helmets, but by those in the armor associated with Arthur's chivalric Britain, as seen elsewhere in the work. Significantly, in this frame, the Germanic invaders and British knights do not fight each other. The aggressors are not presented as adversaries, but rather as two repetitions of a similar violent pattern of behavior from two separate eras, fused in the cultural memory, and articulated in Arthurian legend. (The fire pattern, as well as the dress of one set of peasants, is—I think—meant to evoke the Holocaust as well and to remind the modern reader that our own civilization is not immune to perpetuating such horrific behavior.[41]) The victims within both contexts are simple people, the non-aristocrats who did not create these problems but who suffer the consequences. For these people, "Fear was a constant companion of those who managed to stay alive." Superimposed on this scene is the image of the two concerned old men conversing, their headdress protruding into the scenes of devastation and directing the lines of the composition of this background, just as they themselves are trying to direct the political developments that will end the devastation.

This complex of image and text provides an extraordinary layering of the chaos of the Anglo-Saxon invasion, the period from which Arthurian legend emerged, upon the fictional context of the story as presented here. The merging of the two worlds is further played out fictionally and imagistically in the interaction of the two old men "of different faiths," Merlin representing the Druidic priesthood of the older Celtic world of Arthur's origins, and the Archbishop the later Christianized world of Arthur's emergence as a literary figure. This historical, fictional, and imagistic layering works to suggest how Arthur has come to represent a collective societal need to find a focal point around which to resolve the tensions embedded in any society. In this particular fiction, the societal problems are immense enough that Merlin must step in with his magic to provide that focal point, by facilitating Arthur's pulling the sword from the stone. But the textual and imagistic configuration also makes a sophisticated general statement about the construction of any cultural moment from intersecting historical, political, and social contexts, supported and sustained by the narrative "scripts" a culture tells about itself and passes on to its children.

In orchestrating Arthur's triumph, Merlin is no political slouch. He fully understands the performative aspects necessitated by political power. In this sequence, Arthur, though in fact the legitimate heir, becomes the pawn of the real wielders of power, Merlin and the Archbishop, whose brilliance is to script a performance which neither the key "actor" nor the audience perceives as such. Talbott's rendition fully captures the success of the performance, focusing as it does on the audience as much as on Arthur. In a visually powerful scene, as Arthur approaches the sword in the stone, the focus is not on him but rather on the faces of the people looking straight into his face, reflecting the idea that the "people" over whom Arthur will rule are significant players in this drama. And in fact, these curious and anxious faces are now looking directly at the reader, forcing us to imagine *being* Arthur at this moment. In the next scene, where the perspective has shifted to the crowd watching Arthur draw the sword from the stone, we become an engaged part of that crowd, gazing in wonderment as Arthur succeeds. The next scene, which draws the visual perspective back even further to show the magnitude of the now jubilant crowd, insists on the welcome entry of humility, generosity of spirit, and innocence in this world so badly tainted by arrogance, self-interest, and corruption. The text states that not all voices were united in supporting Arthur, but any dissension gets lost in the visual celebration.

Since the signification of Uther's sword involves the responsibilities and the price of accepting public, political power, its acquisition must be played out on a public stage. However, Arthur's second great sword, Excalibur, more profoundly reflects Arthur's personal, internalized, and even mythic relationship to power. And fittingly, Arthur acquires Excalibur during a more private and introspective moment in his experience. Books by Carol Heyer and by Hudson Talbott,[42] both entitled *Excalibur*, recount this moment. Each follows the same plot line, roughly borrowed from Malory. Arthur, in an ill-advised single combat with a much stronger and more experienced knight, breaks the sword that he had pulled from the stone. Merlin then takes Arthur to an otherworldly realm, where the Lady of the Lake directs him to an intricately beautiful sword offered by a mysterious hand rising from the water. Once re-armed, Arthur chooses not to re-attack the knight who defeated him but instead welcomes him into the fellowship of the Round Table. But for all the similarities in plot line, each author, through the interplay of words and images, tells a very different story.

Heyer's visual style is significant, for it shapes the reader's perception of Arthur. Like Talbott in his *Sword in the Stone*, she is keenly aware of the performative possibilities in Arthur's story, but not from the same political perspective. Heyer's images are overtly theatrical. Her experience as a set designer is apparent in the representations that resemble a beautifully, sometimes hauntingly, staged presentation, with the lighting carefully directed and the sets and backdrops striking. And her Arthur certainly has the "star" quality of a teenage idol. The cover of the book presents a gorgeous, long-haired, bejeweled young man striking the pose of a rock musician holding a guitar (with the guitar replaced by the sword Excalibur). Unlike Talbott's Arthur, who is an unwitting performer, Heyer's Arthur knows he is on center stage.

Heyer's version begins straightforwardly. Arthur learns that a Black Knight is challenging any knight attempting to pass into Camelot, so the young king sets out to "make the entrance to Camelot safe." In the ensuing battle,

Arthur is saved when Merlin puts the obviously stronger adversary to sleep, after which Merlin tells Arthur that he will help him replace the sword he has broken in single combat. By contrast, Talbott's version begins in a more complex fashion, with Arthur in the public realm, leading his army to victory against the invading Saxons. However, Arthur's victory leaves him still wrestling to resolve the tensions between public obligation and private desires, a problem Talbott explored in other contexts in his *Sword in the Stone*. When Arthur laments that, unlike his knights, he cannot embark upon quests, Merlin reminds him that a king's life is not one of quests but of remaining as a stable center of society. "Each of us has a unique destiny. There's much to be gained by understanding your role in life and much to be lost by ignoring it." He later makes explicit Arthur's role, telling him, "A King's duty is to his people, not to his pride." Arthur, however, ignores the magician's advice and slips quietly out of the palace to face the Black Knight alone. Arthur's subsequent defeat can be seen as a punishment for his prideful assertions of private will, and the breaking of his sword reflects the failure of his political will. The sword he gets as a consequence is much more powerful, not just an emblem of secular, political power, but an entity infused with mythic and otherworldly power. Talbott effectively uses visual images to draw the reader into a mythical world so that Arthur's failure and later moral success follow a pattern similar to journeys of other great mythical heroes, who are carried by their actions to the realm of death and symbolic rebirth. (Joseph Campbell's discussion of this pattern is still classic.) By the time Merlin saves Arthur from certain death, the young king is slashed, drenched with blood, and unconscious. As Arthur "writhed in agony" for three days, "fever drove Arthur into the nightmarish realm between life and death," where he "alone had to face the fiery visions burning his mind." In a darkened room, Arthur is shown, his face contorted in his sleep, attacked by fiery dragons and demons, clearly confronting his own mortality. When he recovers (i.e., is reborn), he is "distant and sad," and rides silently with Merlin for days toward the Otherworld. The image shows the two riding their horses through a vast, eerie stretch of water that signifies the boundaries between actual and mythical world.

The dynamics of Heyer's depiction of this episode are quite different. After his defeat by the Black Knight, Arthur is physically unscathed, his deepest wounds being his anger and shame. After Merlin encourages him not to let either victory or defeat ruin him, Arthur laments, "I still feel as though I am nothing," but his "thought returned to his broken sword." He gets his new sword easily, for the Lady of the Lake tells him he deserves it— an important difference from Talbott's Lady of the Lake, who *asks* Arthur whether he deserves it and thus draws out Arthur's commitment to dedicate his life to using Excalibur well. Arthur humbly responds that he will dedicate his life to proving that he does. His first thought after receiving Excalibur is "May I be worthy of you," and Merlin observes the "reverence with which Arthur handled Excalibur." Whereas Talbott's Arthur lets go of his ego after receiving Excalibur, the sword seems to draw out the ego of Heyer's hero, for he reacts to the astounding gift with triumph rather than humility and "imagined how he would feel going into battle, knowing that he could not be killed." Given this reaction, he is right to "wonder if he would be able to use the sword wisely." When he desires to go back and refight the Black Knight, Merlin must remind him that fighting now would bring little honor. Although that interchange is in Malory, Talbott, by contrast, chooses to omit it, suggesting that Arthur has internalized Merlin's lesson of restraint.

In both versions, as in Malory, the Black Knight Pellinore willingly relents his challenge to Arthur's authority and is sworn in as a member of the Round Table. However, this event happens in very different surroundings in the two works. For Heyer's Arthur, it is a private event, happening at night, attended to by Merlin and Bedivere. For Talbott's Arthur, it happens in an open field, where Pellinore comes accompanied by Arthur's men to ask whether he can join his company. Fitting again the general pattern of the hero adventure, this episode in Talbott shows the hero bringing the lessons he has internalized in this confrontation with death back to heal and order the community. The final visual image highlights the commitment to community solidarity, shared with reverence by all of Arthur's gathered knights.

Heyer's rendition also ends with the community reunited, but with quite a different ambiance. Arthur's entourage ends up at a party in a setting that conjures up a medievalized celebrity gathering, at which Arthur continues his center-stage performance, telling the "story of his quest for the mighty Excalibur." The last words of the story recount how Arthur's knights admire "in amazement the beauty of the sword and its magical scabbard," although the sword does not figure at all in the picture.[43] If the last visual image of a picture book in some way sums up the ethos of that work, the reader sees in Talbott's the notion that political power incurs an obligation to serve communal interests, and in Heyer's the assurance that political power perpetuates privilege and the "good life."

This comparison illustrates how different the ideological structures that emerge from the same story can be. The power of Arthurian legend is that it can be told and retold, thus providing comfortable and reassuring cultural continuities. But no two versions ever tell quite the same story. Clearly every retelling is also an act of reinterpretation that, consciously or not, reflects a different facet of the society in which it is created, variations of the communal "script" to be read in both the text and the images. Through this broad view of Arthur's revival in recent picture books, we can better understand the dynamics of the processes by which a dominant set of images can be reinterpreted to mirror back a society's varied and changing cultural expectations and concerns. The verbal and pictorial images in turn reshape these expectations and concerns, thus revealing the complexity of rituals and pathways that each new generation must learn to negotiate. The continuing fascination of young children with Arthurian tradition speaks to the important role in this process played by the heroes encountered early in life.

Notes

1. Patricia MacLachlan, unpublished keynote address for the Tenth Biennial Conference on Literature and Hawaii's Children, "Children's Literature: A Gathering Place," Honolulu, Hawaii, June 15–17, 2000.

2. Walter Fisher, *Human Communication as Narration: Toward a Philosophy of Reason, Value, and Action* (Columbia: University of South Carolina Press, 1987), p. xi.

3. Fisher, *Human Communication as Narration*, p. 65.

4. Anthony Appiah, "Identity, Authenticity, Survival: Multicultural Societies and Social Reproduction," in Amy Gutman, ed., *Multiculturalism: Examining the Politics of Recognition* (Princeton: Princeton University Press, 1994), p. 149 [149–63].

5. Appiah, "Identity, Authenticity, Survival," pp. 155, 159–60.

6. For good discussions of this period, see Debra Mancoff, *The Return of Arthur: The Legend Through Victorian Eyes* (New York: Abrams, 1995), and Mark Girouard, *The Return to Camelot: Chivalry and the English Gentleman* (New Haven: Yale University Press, 1981). Jane Curry, "Children's Reading and Arthurian Tales," in Valerie Lagorio, ed., *King Arthur through the Ages*, Vol. 2 (New York: Garland, 1990), pp. 149–64, includes a brief but succinct overview. Although it does not explicitly treat Arthurian tradition, for useful contextual material, see Joseph Bristow, *Empire Boys: Adventures in A Man's World* (London: HarperCollins, 1991). For a discussion of the way this ethos was translated into American culture, see Jeanne Fox-Friedman, "The Chivalric Order for Children: Arthur's Return in Late Nineteenth- and Early Twentieth-Century America," in Debra Mancoff, ed., *King Arthur's Modern Return* (New York: Garland, 1998), pp. 137–58.

7. Phillip Pullman, "Invisible Pictures," *Signal* 60 (September 1989): 171 [160–86].

8. Peter Hunt, "Criticism and Picture Books," in *Criticism, Theory and Children's Literature* (Oxford: Blackwell, 1991), p. 176 [189–201]. For an overview of various approaches to the text–image relationship, see the introduction to Maria Nikolajeva and Carole Scott's excellent *How Picturebooks Work* (New York: Garland, 2001), pp. 1–28. Other important full-length discussions include Perry Nodelman, *Words About Pictures: The Narrative Art of Children's Picture Books* (Athens: University of Georgia Press, 1988); Joseph H. Schwarcz

and Chava Schwarcz, *The Picture Book Comes of Age* (Chicago: American Library Association, 1991); Jane Doonan, *Looking at Pictures in Picture Books* (Gloucester: Thimble Press, 1993); and Ellen Handler Spitz, *Inside Picture Books* (New Haven: Yale University Press, 1999). W. J. T. Mitchell, *Picture Theory* (Chicago: University of Chicago Press, 1994), though not explicitly focused on picture books, provides a useful context for this discussion; Mitchell takes "iconology well beyond the comparative study of verbal and visual art and into the basic construction of the human subject as being constituted by both language and image" (p. 24). In looking at the relationship between words and pictures, his task is "to replace the predominantly binary theory of that relation with a dialectical picture, the figure of the 'image-text' " (p. 9).

9. Many recent artists have gone to the classic renditions of the past for insight and inspiration. Since one often notices stylistic influences of important illustrators, a brief mention of the most influential is in order. The first important children's version of Malory was J. T. Knowles's *Story of King Arthur and His Knights of the Round Table* (1862), illustrated by G. H. Thomas. A number of subsequent retellings with beautiful illustrations followed. The most important of these are those by Andrew Lang, *The Book of Romance* (1902), illustrated by Henry Justice Ford; Henry Gilbert, *King Arthur's Knights: The Tales Retold for Boys and Girls* (1911), illustrated by Walter Crane; Howard Pyle's four volumes (1903–10), illustrated by the author; Sidney Lanier, *The Boy's King Arthur* (1917), illustrated by N. C. Wyeth; and Alfred Pollard, *The Romance of King Arthur and His Knights of the Round Table* (1917), illustrated by Arthur Rackham. One must also mention the illustrations of Aubrey Beardsley, who, beginning in 1892, offered innovative black-and-white line drawings for a complete version of Malory's *Morte Darthur* published by Dent in 1893–94. Beardsley's bold, stylish, often satirical renditions for the complete version departed dramatically from the chivalric ethos of the text and were hardly appropriate for children. With their erotic suggestiveness and "naughty" depictions of, for instance, clearly hermaphroditic figures, they were even seen as blasphemous by some respectable Victorians. However, an abridged version for young people was published in 1900. Also worthy of note is the Medici Society's four-volume edition of Malory's *Morte Darthur* (1910–11), since the forty-eight elegant watercolors by Sir William Russell Flint are often reproduced. Gustave Doré's dramatic and emotion-filled illustrations for Tennyson's *Idylls of the King* are also influential. For a broader view of Arthurian visual representations, see Muriel Whitaker, *The Legends of King Arthur in Art* (Cambridge, UK: D. S. Brewer, 1990). See also Andrew Lynch's discussion of retellings of Malory for children, in this volume.

10. Maurice Sendak, *Caldecott and Co.: Notes on Books and Pictures* (New York: Farrar, Straus, and Giroux, 1988), p. 172. Sendak picks up the musical analogy again in discussing the "balancing between the text and the pictures. You must not ever be doing the same thing, must not ever be illustrating exactly what you've written. You must leave a space in the text so

that the picture can do the work. Then you must come back with the word, and now the word does it best and the picture beats time" (pp. 185–86).

11. Emma Gelders Sterne and Barbara Lindsay, *Knights of the Round Table*, ill. Gustaf Tenggren (New York: Golden Press, 1962).

12. Selina Hastings, *Sir Gawain and the Green Knight*, ill. Juan Wijngaard (London: Methuen, 1981); Selina Hastings, *Sir Gawain and the Loathly Lady*, ill. Juan Wijngaard (New York: Lothrop, Lee & Shepard, 1985).

13. Robert San Souci, *Young Arthur*, ill. Jamichael Henterly (New York: Doubleday, 1997).

14. Robert San Souci, *Young Guinevere*, ill. Jamichael Henterly (New York: Doubleday, 1993).

15. Robert Sans Souci, *Young Lancelot*, ill. Jamichael Henterly (New York: Doubleday, 1996).

16. Maureen Fries, "Female Heroes, Heroines and Counter-Heroes: Images of Women in Arthurian Tradition," in *Popular Arthurian Traditions*, ed. Sally Slocum (Bowling Green: Bowling Green State University Popular Press, 1992), p. 7 [5–17].

17. John Stephens and Robyn McCallum, *Retelling Stories, Framing Culture: Traditional Story and Metanarratives in Children's Literature* (New York: Garland, 1998), p. 142.

18. Not a picture book, Lynne Pledger's "Gwenhwfar," in *Camelot: A Collection of Original Arthurian Stories*, ed. Jane Yolen (New York: Philomel, 1995), pp. 63–76, is a moving and bleak children's rendition of Guinevere's constricted situation. It concludes with a serving woman telling Gwenhwfar, who desperately wants to stay in the convent where she has been raised, " 'a healthy girl like yourself is as fit as any to be queen.' The carcass of a calf, still hanging in the doorway of the barn, twirled at the end of a rope."

19. Mary Hoffman, *Women of Camelot: Queens and Enchantresses at the Court of King Arthur*, ill. Christina Balit (New York: Abbeville, 2000).

20. Hoffman, *Women of Camelot*, p. 53.

21. Hudson Talbott, *Lancelot* (New York: Morrow, 1999).

22. Hudson Talbott, *King Arthur and the Round Table* (New York: Morrow, 1995).

23. In this mode, although it does not treat Arthur specifically, a sustained critique of the heroic ethos generally is contained in *A Necessary Fantasy?: The Heroic Figure in Children's Popular Culture*, ed. Dudley Jones and Tony Watkins (New York: Garland, 2000).

24. Robin Lister, *The Legend of King Arthur*, ill. Alan Baker (New York: Doubleday, 1988).

25. Lister, *The Legend of King Arthur*, p. 42.

26. Curry, "Children's Reading and Arthurian Tales," p. 157. The fascination with violence does go back to the early children's retellings. If Victorian mores allowed no sex, they had no problem with violence, which no doubt contributed considerably to the allure of the stories for schoolboys. Even the grisly climactic scene in which Mordred and Arthur kill one another inspires several of the more memorable illustrations in the juvenile tradition.

27. Lister, *The Legend of King Arthur*, p. 39.

28. Lister, *The Legend of King Arthur*, p. 67.

29. Margaret Hodges, *The Kitchen Knight*, ill. Trina Schart Hyman (New York: Holiday House, 1990).

30. Jane Yolen, *Merlin and the Dragons*, ill. Li Ming (New York: Dutton, 1995).

31. Robert San Souci, *Young Merlin*, ill. Daniel Horne (New York: Doubleday, 1990).

32. Gerald McDermott, *The Knight of the Lion* (New York: Four Winds, 1979); John Howe, *The Knight with the Lion: The Story of Yvain* (Boston: Little Brown, 1996).

33. Molly Perham, *King Arthur and the Legends of Camelot*, ill. Julek Heller (New York: Viking, 1993); James Riordan, *King Arthur*, ill. Victor G. Ambrus (Oxford: Oxford University Press, 1993).

34. Michael Morpurgo, *Arthur: High King of Britain*, ill. Michael Foreman (San Diego: Harcourt Brace, 1994).

35. Morpurgo, *Arthur: High King of Britain*, pp. 25–26.

36. I have previously discussed several of the works treated in the following section, but with a focus on Merlin, in my essay "The Dynamics of Dumbing: The Case of Merlin," *The Lion and the Unicorn* 17 (1993): 57–72.

37. The book adaptation based on the animated feature is Walt Disney, *The Sword in the Stone* (New York: Mouse Works, 1995).

38. Disney, *The Sword in the Stone*, p. 92.

39. Robert Sabuda, *Arthur and the Sword* (New York: Atheneum, 1995).

40. Hudson Talbott, *The Sword in the Stone* (New York: Morrow, 1991).

41. Another illustration with intriguing transhistorical characteristics is depicted opposite the title page of John Matthews and Bob Stewart's *Legends of King Arthur and His Warriors* (London: Blandford Press, 1987). Reproduced in Stephens and McCallum, p. 137, it shows Merlin, arms outstretched, standing before a backdrop consisting of a collage of multi-ethnic soldiers, spanning time periods from prehistory to the twentieth century.

42. Carol Heyer, *Excalibur* (Nashville: Ideals, 1991); Hudson Talbott, *Excalibur* (New York: Morrow, 1996).

43. This final focus on the materiality of Excalibur fits well with Jack Zipes's theories about the co-option of folk literature by a modern industrial society which places value upon consumerism above all else, creating a belief in people "that the goods they consume and produce actually nourish their potential to develop." See Zipes, *Breaking the Magic Spell: Radical Theories of Folk and Fairy Tales* (New York: Methuen, 1979), p. 98.

CHAPTER 3

THE CASE OF THE DISAPPEARING TEXT: *CONNECTICUT YANKEE* FOR KIDS

Elizabeth S. Sklar

> *Mark Twain's three previous solo novels*—Tom Sawyer, The Prince and the Pauper, *and* Huck Finn—*were published primarily for children. . . . Is* A Connecticut Yankee in King Arthur's Court *intended for children? Is it appropriate for children?*
>
> —Andrew Jay Hoffman[1]

Mark Twain's *A Connecticut Yankee in King Arthur's Court* is arguably the single most visible and widely disseminated individual text in the entire neo-Arthurian canon. Internet searches for the title turn up two hundred and twenty-three hits on the OCLC, more than six hundred on Amazon, and a daunting nine thousand nine hundred and seventy on Google. According to the current *Books in Print*, twenty-seven different editions of *Connecticut Yankee* are immediately available, ranging in price from under $4 for mass-market productions such as the Airmont Classics series or Tor Classics to $60 for the Iowa–California edition. (A reprinted library edition, publisher and editor unspecified, sells for $79.) Vintage editions of the text command considerably more. The Limited Editions Club version (1948), a fancy, high-end production illustrated by Honoré Guilbeau and introduced by Carl Van Doren, typically sells for about $100, while first editions go for anywhere between $200 and $2,000, depending on the condition of the specific copy.

Connecticut Yankee has also proved to be a wondrously protean, infinitely exploitable, and highly marketable text, having been profusely reedited, reduced, amputated, spun-off, ripped-off, and in the extreme reaches of textual bad manners, mauled. Treatments of this book range from the reverential to the downright sassy, flitting from high to popular culture and back again with remarkable agility. Versions of one sort or another appear in every medium imaginable: in standard print texts, illustrated novels, audio-cassette readings, a variety of comic-book and comic-book-like formats, cartoons and animated films, television adaptations, stage versions (including musicals), films,[2] and e-texts, at least one of which is formatted for PalmOS. And it turns up in the most unexpected places, ranging from a 1988 edition of the novel published in Tokyo and a 1987 Russian film version (*Novye prikluchenia janke pri dvore Korola Artura*[3]) to a Spanish animated cartoon adaptation ("Un Yanqui en la corte del Rey Arturo") and a Spanish imprint of the Illustrated Classics comic book version.

Twain's novel has been interpreted in non- or extra-textual media as well. Two movements of Paul Alan Levi's *Mark Twain Suite*, a work for mixed chorus, tenor solo, and orchestra, for example, are based on *Connecticut Yankee* episodes ("The Great Joust: L'Homme Arme" and "The Awful German Language");[4] contemporary artists such as Donato Giancola and Paul Berenson have painted their interpretations thereof;[5] and a 1985 Romanian stamp entitled "Un Yankeu la Curtea Regului Arthur" featured Disney's Goofy as the stake-bound Yankee incanting "*incipea eclipsa mea*" as he points to a partially eclipsed sun.[6] The book has provided the pretext for any number of time-travel films, at least one detective fiction (*A Connecticut Yankee in Criminal Court: A Mark Twain Mystery*),[7] themed costume parties ("Costume-Con [Convention] 2000 Friday Night Social, A Connecticut Yankee in King Arthur's Court. Hear Ye! Hear Ye!"), and numerous spin-off titles, such as *A Contracting Officer in King Arthur's Court* (a thematized legal guide to the contract appeals process, complete with illustrations); *A Connecticut Yankee in Penn's Woods: The Life and Times of Thomas Bennet*; *Connecticut Yankee in the 8th Gurka Rifles: A Burma Memoir*; and *Connecticut Yankee in the Frontier Ozarks: The Writings of Theodore Pease Russel*. The list of *Connecticut Yankee* products could be expanded a hundredfold.

Amidst this welter of *Connecticut Yankee* material is a sizeable body of editions, abridgments, and adaptations in a variety of media specifically targeting a juvenile audience. In the pages that follow, I shall be examining some of these youth-oriented versions of Twain's novel, with a primary emphasis on print texts.[8] But a preliminary caveat is in order: this is not by any means as straightforward an undertaking as it might seem. I shall begin, therefore, by addressing some of the issues that complicate this enterprise.

Problematics

By rights, the study of juvenile versions should be unnecessary, a mere exercise in redundancy, because *A Connecticut Yankee in King Arthur's Court* is popularly and academically regarded as "children's literature" already. It is so categorized, for example, at BookSpot.com and at a University of Calgary website dedicated to "Movies and TV Based on Children's Books." While Amazon more broadly identifies *Connecticut Yankee* as "young adult" fiction, the *School Library Journal* marks it for readers from grade 5 on; likewise the unabridged edition illustrated by Trina Schart Hyman targets children from grades 5 through 8. GradeSaver.com assigns *Connecticut Yankee* to "Grade 7 English," while the Lycos Zone Directory considers it appropriate for students in grades 9–12. In short, *Connecticut Yankee* occupies, and has long occupied, a secure position in secondary and even elementary education curricula.

The assumption that *Connecticut Yankee* is standard juvenile fare creates a number of problems, the first of which, for my purposes, is that it is often difficult to determine which of the many editions, versions, or adaptations intentionally target young audiences, a problem compounded by films, plays, and television productions that bill themselves as "family fare." The situation is further complicated by the fact that, despite the confidence with which *Connecticut Yankee* is purveyed as canonical curricular material (though the reading-level assessments do appear a bit whimsical), the Library of Congress catalog's subject list in the descriptive matter of their holdings on this title only once includes the term "juvenile fiction."[9] Curiously, even versions patently directed to younger readers, such as Ruth T. King's abridged edition, intended for use in high-school English classes, and Joanne Barkan's *A Pup in King Arthur's Court*, which targets a middle-school readership, are not identified by the Library of Congress as juvenile fiction.

While I have chosen, therefore, to confine my discussion to those editions or versions of *Connecticut Yankee* that bear some structural, stylistic, strategic, or material markers implying juvenile audiences, even this is not always a reliable guide. A case in point here is "A Samurai Cat in King Arthur's Court,"[10] which might appear at first to be a youth-friendly companion piece to *A Pup in King Arthur's Court*. However, quite the opposite pertains. Although the Yankee persona, a hefty feline named Miaowara Tomokato, time-travels back to Camelot, and while some traditional Arthurian figures like Lancelot, Gawain, and Mordred do make brief appearances, "Samurai Cat" is more reminiscent of Douglas Adams than of Twain. The story, if indeed it can be called a story at all, is a mind-boggling maelstrom of anachronistic allusion. Such figures as Robert E. Lee, Erich von Stroheim, and Barry Manilow (the last cast as a member of the heathen pantheon along with Woden and Thunor) play walk-on parts, and the reader is bombarded by a firestorm of contemporary and historical references that includes, but does not consist exclusively of, Milton Friedman, the Teamsters, the Pointer Sisters, Dom DeLuise, the Warsaw Pact, protectionism, CNN, the *London Times*, Saducees and Pharacees, and

Sir Laurence Olivier. Mingling with the traditional Arthurian figures are such characters as Sir Freddy Laker and Morgan le Fairchilde. In-jokes run rampant, starting with a gryphon (deceased) named "Merv." The Saxon leader Horsa's son is named Mr. Ed; generously endowed watermaidens try to seduce the protagonist with Reese's Pieces, and Tomokato at one point teams up with Wisconsin Platt ("a middling-sized man very much in need of a shave, wearing a leather coat and a weather-beaten fedora").[11] Factoring in what the film industry coyly labels "language" (Morgan describes herself as a "badass"; there is a discussion of a cinematic close-up of a "baby's butt"; and Mordred uses the "s"-word), blasphemy (a note hanging on a plastic statuette of the Blessed Virgin reads "To Joseph of Arimathea, all the best, Mary"), substance abuse (our hero is offered a hit of cocaine), and some purely bodice-ripper illustrations, the result is a veritable Family Values nightmare.[12]

Another difficulty connected to the classification of *Connecticut Yankee* as juvenile fiction is that it refuses to behave like normal, well-mannered children's literature. In theory, since it is already for young readers, the novel should require no special treatments, adjustments, tweakings, flourishes, or apologies to render it appropriate for youngsters. After all, we do not find such prolific editorial and interpretive interventions in conjunction with, say, *Black Beauty*, the Hardy Boys and Nancy Drew series, Lloyd Alexander's novels, *Harry Potter*, and other classical or neo-classical youth fiction. That *Connecticut Yankee* has been so abundantly readjusted suggests that something is amiss. I would posit that the novel has been seriously misclassified and that this is the ur-problem, responsible for all the others: the uncertainties as to reading-level or grade-appropriateness; the blurred boundaries of audience; the plethora of abridgments, illustrated versions, and other sometimes desperate attempts to fix what is "wrong" with the original. What is wrong, I suggest, is the assumption that *Connecticut Yankee* is children's literature in the first place.

For, despite its curricular canonicity, *Connecticut Yankee* strikes me as eminently unsuited for a juvenile and even for an adolescent readership. Under its playful veneer lurks a bitter, cynical, misanthropic, misogynistic, and often cruel text, offering up a dark vision of human nature and culminating in brutal mass slaughter. Although it is commonly cited as a comic masterpiece, the sources of its whimsy lurk in corners generally unavailable to most adult modern readers, let alone children and adolescents. While the juxtaposition of ancient and modern as a comic device is by now a shopworn film and comic book topos with which most youngsters are familiar, Twain's "modern" has long since become obsolete. The technology is outmoded; even the diseases are out of date. *Connecticut Yankee* is a highly topical and chronologically localized nineteenth-century cultural product, addressing social problems, literary politics, technologies, and issues of national identity virtually meaningless to a generation for most of whose members the Vietnam conflict is ancient history. The competent reader, moreover, is required to possess a special kind of literacy: the satire invokes, and therefore assumes, some audience familiarity with Arthurian literature at large and Malory in particular (not to mention some notion of the historical Middle Ages). And Tennyson needs to be added to this referential admixture as well: with its mercilessly judgmental and patronizing representation of Arthur and his court, *Connecticut Yankee* also constitutes a literary Bronx cheer at Tennyson's high-minded and romanticized representations of the Matter of Arthur (and at the then-fashionable British neo-medievalism in general). Ultimately, the chronological constraints, the passé cultural assumptions, and the range of allusion in *Connecticut Yankee* renders it far more alien to youthful audiences than the most recherché science fiction: the horizon of expectation has gone AWOL.

Additionally, Twain's quirky rhetorical play, with its zany melange of excerpts from Malory, pseudo-medieval dialogue, and nineteenth-century colloquialisms, combined with moments of purposefully rambling and long-winded prose, makes for an impotable stylistic beverage for most readers of any age, especially in this era of quick cuts and short bytes. Indeed, as I shall argue, in the case of adaptations of *Connecticut Yankee* for juvenile audiences, Twain's wayward registration and distinctive prose style are as much a target for tampering as are the alien historical and cultural milieu and the novel's jaundiced view of humanity. Finally, unlike *Tom Sawyer* or *Huckleberry Finn*, *Connecticut Yankee*'s protagonist is a grown man, not a lad—so the point of view, as well as the registration and content, militates against the notion that this is a novel for a juvenile audience. We are left, then, with a most disconcerting paradox: a children's book that is not for children.

The Aurelia Syndrome

Among the collage of pieces collected in Twain's *Celebrated Jumping Frog of Calaveras County* is a grotesquely humorous little arabesque entitled "Aurelia's Unfortunate Young Man." It recounts the woes of a young lady named Aurelia Maria, who is engaged to a gentleman with an unsurpassed gift for self-destruction. The decline of Williamson Breckinridge Caruthers begins with a case of smallpox, which leaves his face "pitted like a waffle-mould and his comeliness gone forever." Then he begins to systematically shed his body parts: walking into a well, he breaks a leg so disastrously that it has to be amputated; then one arm is shot off "by the premature discharge of a Fourth-of-July cannon." Subsequently, he loses an eye to erysipelas, breaks his remaining leg, and finally manages to get himself scalped. What thus remains of Aurelia's erstwhile lover—now a Monty Pythonesque one-eyed, one-armed, pockmarked, legless, and hairless human remnant—bears no resemblance to the man he once was. Fittingly, Caruthers's sorry case history provides the perfect paradigm for what happens to *A Connecticut Yankee in King Arthur's Court* in the hands of those who have undertaken to adjust the novel for juvenile audiences: piece by piece it is disfigured and dismembered, until it would be barely recognizable to its own author. In what follows, I will look at the strategies of adaptation and trace the trajectory of the novel's dismantling, as larger and larger pieces of the original print text are modified, maimed, or lopped off to the point that ultimately Twain's text disappears entirely.

The first stage of this process is actually a kind of prelude, in that it does not entail any textual intervention or adaptive maneuvers beyond enhancement of the material text, that is, unabridged editions of *Connecticut Yankee*, the physical properties of which imply a youthful audience.[13] The earliest of these that I have found is the 1917 Harper edition illustrated by Henry Pitz. Twain's text is left intact, but the volume is adjusted in size, appearance, and layout to appeal to younger readers. It is a fairly large book, measuring 9 × 6 inches, using ten-point type for the text proper and a generous twenty-point for the running head. White space is generous as well, the side margins measuring 1.5 inches, with 1.75 inches at the top and bottom of each page. The length of this volume (four hundred and fifty pages as compared with the two hundred and seventy-two of the Bantam Classic edition, for instance) speaks to the degree that readability was considered an important factor in its production. It contains twelve elegant black-and-white matte full-page illustrations, not including the cover image, which, like the frontispiece, is in color.

The very presence of illustrations is a significant index of intended audience, since visual imagery plays a primary role in all versions of *Connecticut Yankee* for the young,[14] and Pitz's illustrations are particularly interesting for the way in which they re-present the text for juvenile readers. Their Pre-Raphaelite, graceful, painterly style, with its attention to texture, light, and fine detail, stands in striking contrast to the edgy linearity and witty commentary of Daniel Beard's original illustrations, casting a romantic haze over the subject matter as if to cushion youngsters from the shrapnel of the text they purport to illustrate. The settings, figuring, and subject matters of these illustrations reinforce this affect. In seven of the images, counting the frontispiece, landscape is prominent, often dwarfing the human figures therein. No wind, rain, or snow mar these landscapes, which evoke eternal spring with their flower-studded meadows, sun-dappled ponds, and gracious trees in full leaf. By the same token, in the two color images no primary shades are permitted to intrude upon the vernal ambiance.

The choice and representation of human figures is equally interesting with respect to reinterpretation of Twain's text: a process of juvenilization and feminization seems to be taking place. Hank Morgan, who admits to the age of forty in Twain, appears to hover somewhere between adolescence and manhood, while Sandy, whose visual presence here is disproportionate to her fictional role—she is featured in four of the twelve illustrations—is a sweet-faced Pre-Raphaelite lass of about fifteen. Morgan Le Fey is represented as well, sharing Sandy's youthfulness and ethereal beauty. Male authority figures are rare: there is only one image of Merlin, and King Arthur is never represented in full regal array. In fact, there are only two images of Arthur in all, both showing him disguised as a peasant: no crown, robes, or scepters here.

Further, few of the illustrations represent major incidents in the narrative, and those that do pull their punches. The illustration for "The Smallpox Hut," for example, does not show the interior of the hut, nor the victims therein, but rather displays Arthur knocking at its door. The landscape details are foregrounded, and the sun plays benignly on the wall of the hut, betraying no hint of the horror that lies behind the door—indeed, the dwelling's appearance is deceptively inviting. Even more revealing of the bowdlerizing thrust of these illustrations is the final plate in the book. Four-fifths of the picture plane is dominated by the monumental, fully rendered figure of a mounted knight, both man and horse in full tournament panoply (see figure 3.1). The diagonal formed by the knight's shield and his helmet direct the eye to the more faintly rendered viewing stands in the near background, and behind that, a castle atop a hill, seen as through a scrim. Barely visible in the middle ground, sandwiched between the horse's head and the knight's helmet, is a tiny masculine figure (no larger than the foot of the foreground figure) holding his bent right arm about mid-chest level. The viewer can faintly discern, and then only upon intense scrutiny, a rectangular object in this figure's hand. Surprisingly, the caption reads, "I snatched a dragoon revolver out of my holster; there was a flash and a roar." Thus, read as a unit, Pitz's imagery not only resists Twain's narrative but also creates a counter-narrative, one apparently deemed more appropriate to young readers than Twain's text, the fictive landscape of which is littered with filth, poverty, disease, free-range pigs, bicycles, telegraph wires, electrical generators, and the body parts of knights and mangled horses. And so, with these gestures of visual denial, begins the project of textual revision.

Tweaking Twain

The next phase of textual intervention launches the Aurelia Syndrome proper: literary redactions—abridgments and adaptations—that set about dumbing down Twain's text to improve its accessibility for a juvenile audience.[15]

3.1   Henry Pitz's illustration for the Harper edition of *A Connecticut Yankee in King Arthur's Court* (1917) creates a counter-narrative deemed more appropriate to young readers than Twain's text.

This process entails a number of interrelated surgical procedures, ranging from cosmetic alteration to amputation. I shall begin by looking in some detail at the adaptive strategies of two such modified print editions from the middle of the twentieth century: the Globe edition, adapted by Ruth T. King and illustrated by Thomas Fraumeni (1948), and the Whitman edition, illustrated by Frank Nicholas (no adapter listed, 1955). While these are both illustrated texts, the illustrations tend to be incidental flourishes to the textual matter rather than commentaries upon it. These versions target different age groups and vary in the degree of their interventionist maneuvers, but both make use of similar adaptive strategies, the most common of which are excision, conflation, lexical modification, and syntactic streamlining.[16] The general nature of these editorial moves is concisely summarized, if somewhat oversimplified, in the first paragraph of King's brief "Editor's Preface":[17]

> In adapting the text of *A Connecticut Yankee*, every attempt has been made to keep the style and the spirit of the original. The changes have for the most part consisted in substituting words to meet the understanding of the reader with a limited vocabulary, and omitting or abstracting descriptive and philosophical passages which seem too detailed or difficult for such readers.[18]

King's edition (1948), with its uniquely abridged title (*A Connecticut Yankee* on the cover and spine, although the full original title appears on the title page), identifies itself as "adapted" and is intended primarily as a pedagogical edition for high-school classes—King taught at Farragut High School in Chicago; her collaborator is listed as Elsa Wolf, Teacher of English and Journalism, Bowen High School, Chicago; and the book contains some instructional apparatus: "Questions for the Pupil," a chapter-by-chapter list of questions apparently intended as homework assignments, and "Questions for Discussion," which are "designed to stimulate thinking and group discussion."[19] Both appear as end matter. The eleven full-page black-and-white illustrations by Hilton D. King are executed in a bold, minimally textured linear style, captioned with quotations from the text. It is a utilitarian volume, whose size (7.75 × 5.75 inches) and olive-drab cover announce it as a nononsense production suitable for educational purposes.

The Whitman abridgment comes with no editorial or instructional apparatus, but the target age group is readily inferrable. Judging from the book's physical properties—such as its dimensions (8 × 5.5 inches), its glossy illustrated cover, and its font size—the publisher, if not the anonymous editor, envisioned a readership in late childhood and early adolescence: the book has the same look and feel as the original Nancy Drew volumes of a similar vintage. The cover image is a dead-giveaway: a fair-haired, slender but well-muscled adolescent Hank (one assumes), astride a rearing black stallion, six-shooters belted on, felling a fully armed knight with his trusty lasso—a cowboy in tights. The text features twenty-four full-page two-color illustrations, stylistically unremarkable black-and-white plates with alternating taupe and turquoise wash. None is captioned. Additionally, each chapter is headed by a quarter-page illustration. The increased proportion of artwork to text here (more than twice as many illustrations, not counting capital images, as in the King edition) suggests that the book was thus enhanced in order to draw in a voluntary rather than a captive audience.

Since the Whitman/Nicholas abridgment is the less interventionist version of *Connecticut Yankee* of this pair, indeed possibly the least interventionist of all the adapted versions I have examined, it may serve as a good test case for what happens to Twain's original when it is adjusted for juvenile readers.[20] Insofar as fidelity to the original is an applicable concept here at all, the Whitman abridgment reproduces a reasonably high proportion of Twain's text; while there are a considerable number of deletions, lexical intervention is kept to a minimum, and Twain's language is for the most part preserved verbatim in the portions of the text that are used. Even with this relatively mild degree of editorial intervention, however, sizeable portions of the original narrative are omitted: six chapters are eliminated entirely,[21] and others are concatinated or conflated. The Whitman edition anomalously omits the frame narrative, an odd choice for a relatively conservative abridgment, I think, since the frame is historically an essential generic marker for dream fiction.[22]

The Whitman abridgment's general modus operandi may be illustrated by comparing the reduced version to Twain's original in the beginning of "The Eclipse" chapter (Whitman 5, Twain VI).[23] In what follows, plain text represents Twain's original; the italicized words, phrases, or sentences represent those portions of Twain's text retained and incorporated verbatim into the adapted version; and bolded units correspond to emendations or additions. Brackets mark deleted material. The Whitman "Eclipse" chapter begins toward the end of Twain's second paragraph, the first having been elided in its entirety:

But it is a blessed provision of nature that at times like these, as soon as a man's mercury has got down to a certain point there comes a revulsion, and he rallies. Hope springs up, and cheerfulness along with it, and then he is in good shape to do something for himself, if anything can be done. When my rally came, it came with a bound. I said to myself that my eclipse would be sure to save me, and make me the greatest man in the kingdom besides; and straightway my mercury went up to the top of the tube, and my solicitudes all vanished. I was as happy a man as there was in the world. *I was* [even] *impatient for tomorrow to come, I so wanted to gather in that great triumph and be the center of all the nation's wonder and reverence. Besides, in a business way it would be the making of me; I knew that.*

Meantime there was one thing which had got pushed into the background of my mind. That was the half conviction that when the nature of my proposed calamity should be reported to those superstitious people, it would have such an effect that they would want to compromise. So, [B]y *and by* [when] *I heard footsteps* coming, that thought was recalled to me, and I said to myself "As sure as anything, it's the compromise. Well, if it is good, all right, I will accept; but if it isn't, I mean to stand my ground and play my hand for all it is worth."

The door opened, and some men-at-arms appeared. The leader said: "The stake is ready. Come!"

The stake! The strength went out of me, and I almost fell down. It is hard to get one's breath at such a time, such lumps come into one's throat, and such gaspings, but as soon as I could speak I **croaked** : *"But this is a mistake—the execution is tomorrow."*

"Order changed; been set forward a day. Haste thee!"

I was lost. There was no help for me. I was dazed, stupefied, I had no command over myself; I only wandered purposelessly about, like one out of his mind; so the soldiers took hold of me, and pulled me along with them, out of the cell. . .[24]

Although the scarring left by this particular instance of textual surgery is relatively minor, it is representative in many respects, save degree, of what happens in all the texts under consideration here, and it may be useful to examine some of the results of the editorial choices made by the anonymous adaptor of the Whitman version. At the most obvious level, in terms of brute word count, even this modest cannibalization loses a hefty two hundred and seventy-three words, and this from what amounts to a mere two-thirds of a page in the original. Although the abbreviation surely results in improved readability, the gains entail some crucial sacrifices. The primary casualty here is the representation of the protagonist. While some of Hank's grandiosity is retained ("I so wanted to gather in that great triumph and be the center of all the nation's wonder and reverence"), the intensity and extent of his narcissistic fantasy is diminished; suppressed are his certainty that he will become "the greatest man in the kingdom," and the delusional ease with which he transmutes hope into a reality of his own devising (his belief that the approaching footsteps herald the submission of a "compromise" that he is empowered to regally accept or reject at will). Both the humor of the punctured fantasy—the wonderful contrast between his grandiosity and his abject panic when reality strikes—and the irony of Hank's imperial aspirations get lost in the shuffle. Also suppressed is the Ugly American motif that runs throughout Twain's novel, here represented by the omitted remark about "those superstitious people." What we have is the beginning of the transformation of Hank Morgan from a flawed narrator to a trustworthy one, from a borderline personality to a neutralized, conventional, and therefore more socially acceptable "hero."

Clearly, while readability would appear to be the primary conscious criterion for whatever actions are taken against the original text by abridgers and adapters, other agendas are called into play as well, particularly with respect to what gets edited out. This phenomenon is abundantly evident in the Whitman abridger's treatment of the final sections of the novel, "War!"

and "The Battle of the Sandbelt," where the omissions, considerably more extensive than those in the earlier portion of this version, function simultaneously to re-form the protagonist and to literally defuse Twain's apocalyptic conclusion. In "War" (Whitman, chapter 36), verbatim passages alternate with drastic omissions. Gone is the entirety of Clarence's disquisition on the fate of the Arthurian court—Twain's own abridgment of Malory's denouement, which includes the affair of Lancelot and Guinevere (with its unseemly implications of sexuality) and Mordred's treachery (incest and patricide being no fit subject for children), and the hefty chunk of the *Morte Darthur* proffered as "war correspondence"[25]—the most Arthurian portions, in fact, of Twain's novel. Gone as well are almost all references to the Church, a depoliticizing gesture, surely, and one that is not by any means unique to this particular version. And, oddly enough, given the general trend in adaptations to retain the technological spin of the original, gone is the discussion between Hank and Clarence concerning the engineering details of the final preparations for war. In all, approximately two-thirds of the nine pages that constitute the chapter in the Bantam edition have been elided.

Where the suppressions from "War!" appear to combine an agenda of increased narrative efficiency with the desire to shield young readers from any hint of adult sexuality and contentious ideologies, the omissions from "The Battle of the Sandbelt" undertake a wholesale revision of both Twain's denouement and the essential nature of his protagonist. Only four of eleven pages survive the editor's knife in the Whitman abridgment, which reproduces the first part of Twain's chapter verbatim (except for the bowdlerizing excision of Hank's homoerotic observation that his fifty-two lads were "As pretty as girls"[26]), up to the protagonist's detonating the inital dynamite blast prior to the battle proper. Then it falls silent, save for replicating the source text's final paragraphs. Leaping from Hank's opening volley to the very end of Twain's chapter, the abridged portion in question reads:

> In that explosion all our noble civilization-factories went up in the air and disappeared from the earth. It was a pity, but it was necessary. We could not afford to let the enemy turn our own weapons against us.[27]

> *

> Within ten short minutes after we had opened fire, armed resistance was totally annihilated, the campaign was ended, we fifty-four were masters of England![28]

The silent elision of more than six pages here eliminates the entire battle sequence and its horrific consequences: the "homogeneous protoplasm" of men and armor resulting from the initial explosion that makes it impossible to count the dead; the "smell of burning flesh" as human beings are serially electrocuted; the ghastly vision of a "black mass piling itself up beyond the second fence" that resolves into "a solid wall of the dead—a bulwark, a breastwork, of corpses"; the auditory horror ("*There* was a groan you could *hear*! It voiced the death-pang of eleven thousand men").[29] With the suppression of the battle sequence and the concomitant radical temporal dislocation—almost a full day and night of narrative time are conflated, so the battle appears to last only ten minutes—the nightmare surrealism of Twain's climactic episode is converted into an easy, swift, near-bloodless victory for Hank and his "darling fifty-two." Tellingly, the final sentence of the second paragraph just cited, with its appalling statistics—"Twenty-five thousand men lay dead around us"—has been silently excised.

Given the mid-1950s publication date here, it is entirely possible that the impetus for these textually destructive moves, in part at least, is that the residual stench of Hiroshima and the postwar revelations from the Nazi death camps were still too vivid to allow the abridger to handle these eerily prescient images with equanimity. But whatever the case may be in historical terms, the result of these omissions is not only to spare the sensibilities of young readers, but also to radically modify the character of the protagonist by suppressing, along with the gory details of battle, Hank Morgan's descent into Luciferian demagogy. Although some small conscience remains to him in the original—he admits to Clarence that the imminent destruction "seems an awful pity" and confesses that the silence of the mass electrocutions "was very creepy"[30]—in the main he enacts his technological theatrics not only without remorse, but with considerable enthusiasm. Reveling in his own showmanship ("Loud and long continued applause"), Hank admires the effects of his contriving with a series of self-congratulatory remarks. "As to the destruction of life, it was amazing," he allows upon viewing the devastation brought about by his initial detonation, and in the end he is no more compunctious about the vision of "three walls of dead men" than a tourist might be about the Grand Canyon: "Land, what a sight!"[31] For all his democratic platitudes, he callously dehumanizes his victims, mere "ignorant creatures," deficient in all save "mere animal might."[32] (How far is it, after all, from Hank's gleeful declaration "We will kill them all" to Kurtz's "Exterminate the brutes"?) That such textual contortions are required to make the novel's denouement presentable for younger readers speaks eloquently to the issue of *Connecticut Yankee* as "juvenile fiction."

Although Ruth King, like the anonymous adapter of the Whitman version, makes a good-faith effort to preserve as much as she judges appropriate from the original novel, attempting, in her own words, "to keep the style and the spirit of the original" (editorial Preface), her adaptive maneuvers tend to be somewhat more aggressive than those of the Whitman adapter. For starters, twelve chapters are omitted here to Whitman's six.[33]

Perforce, episodic conflation is considerably more frequent in King's adaptation than in the Whitman one, necessitating a fairly high density of paraphrase and plot summary. Additionally, as per her stated objectives, King intervenes at the lexical as well as at the structural and rhetorical levels, "substituting words to meet the understanding of the reader with a limited vocabulary." The result is a translation, from rendered "literary" language into a kind of neutered prose, as in the following excerpt from King's "The Eclipse," where, among other things, Twain's extended mock-heroic metaphor wryly predicated on the most mundane technology is evidently considered too challenging for adolescent readers, and therefore disposable:[34]

> *But* it is a blessed provision of nature that *at times like these, as soon as a* **man gets low enough** [Twain, "man's mercury has got down to a certain point"] *there comes a* **change** [Twain, "revulsion"], *and* **hope springs up** [Twain, "he rallies"], *and cheerfulness along with it, and then he is in good shape to do something for himself, if anything can be done. When my* **hope** [Twain, "rally"] *came, it came with a bound. I said to myself that my eclipse would be sure to save me, and make me the greatest man in the kingdom besides; and straightway* **my fears** *all vanished* [Twain, "my mercury went up to the top of the tube, and my solicitudes all vanished"]. *I was as happy a man as there was in the world. I was even impatient for tomorrow to come, I so wanted to gather in that great triumph and be the center of all the nation's wonder and reverence. Besides, in a business way it would be the making of me; I knew that.*

Other such lexical interventions include "hurry" for "haste thee," "hiding" for "concealment," "brought about" for "wrought," "greatest" for "vastest," "fights" for "shindies," "love" for "penchant," "knights" for "chivalry," and so forth. Lexical substitution extends even to chapter titles.[35] Twain's "The Tournament" becomes "The Challenge" (perhaps invoking a cowboy metaphor), and "The Yankee and the King Travel Incognito" becomes "The Yankee and the King Travel in Disguise." King's modification of the original "Knights of the Table Round" to "Knights of the Round Table" may be a related phenomenon, undoing Twain's deliberately quaint inversion to yield a more familiar syntax.

The textual havoc that even the best-intentioned editorial meddling can wreak is evident in King's treatment of the final episodes of *Connecticut Yankee*, where almost frantic cutting and pasting results in a crazy quilt of Twain snippets, silently and sometimes dramatically emended, loosely threaded together by précis, paraphrase, and plot summary. Into a single eight-page chapter entitled "Three Years Later—War," King tries to cram four chapters from Twain: "Three Years Later," "The Interdict," "War!," and "The Battle of the Sand Belt." The first four pages of King's amalgam are taken pretty much verbatim, with a few elisions, from the first two-and-a-half pages of Twain's

"Three Years Later."[36] The remaining material (a full fifty percent of King's chapter), however, covering three chapters from Twain's original, is preponderantly précis and plot summary, running from the illness of Hello Central, through the subsequent trip to France and the civil war culminating in Arthur's death, to Clarence's preparations for war and the fortification of Merlin's cave, to the final battle and its depressing outcome. Needless to say, King omits even more of the unpleasant battle details and the unpalatable disintegration of Hank's character than does the Whitman abridgment. To the novel's climax are consigned a mere four paragraphs of what amounts to patchwork plagiarism of Twain's original; the following paragraph, for example, consists of two sentences from one page of the original, a single sentence from another, and three short sentences from a third page:

> It was time for the second step...[phrase deleted]. I touched a button...
> [phrase deleted]. In that explosion all our noble [civilization] factories went up
> in the air and disappeared. It was a pity, but it was necessary. We could not afford
> to let the enemy turn our weapons against us. (**Twain** 263–64) I picketed the
> great embankments thrown up around our lines by the dynamite explosion...
> [phrase and sentence transition omitted] and sent an engineer and forty boys
> beyond our lines to the south to turn a mountain brook that was there and
> bring it within our lines...[two phrases omitted] so that I could make [instant]
> use of it in an emergency. (**Twain** 265) We waited a long time...[three sen-
> tences elided]; then we saw a row of black dots appear along the ridge top—
> human heads...[four sentences omitted]. An armed host was taking up
> quarters in the ditch...[three sentences omitted]. I signaled to turn the current
> in the two inner fences. (**Twain** 267)[37]

Although this passage is marginally Twainian at best, at least it still retains some words and sentences actually written by Twain, found somewhere in the original novel, even if not in this particular sequence. In the summary/paraphrase portions, however, Twain's voice is completely silenced, his language replaced by King's own vanilla rhetoric:

> Civil war had broken out with Lancelot and the king on different sides and
> King Arthur had been killed. The church had stepped in and with all the knights
> that were left was determined to defeat us and bring back the old world. It was
> to be a fight between science and tradition with all its old superstitions.[38]

Thus King dispatches with the first five pages of "War!" In passages such as this, where summary and plot précis entirely replace Twain's text, the assault on authorial prerogative further escalates as the adapter commits an act of textual ventriloquism, usurping the narrator's role and appropriating the narrative voice, producing at best a bland concoction that may go down easily enough, but is totally flavorless, and assuredly free of any Twainian contaminants.

The casual manner in which even diligent and well-meaning adapting editors, such as those just discussed, dispense with Twain's rhetoric (in King's words, "descriptive and philosophical passages which seem too detailed or difficult"), with narrative voice, with story elements they deem irrelevant or improper, and with Twain's structural choices—that is, the very features that make the original a "literary classic" in the first place—suggests some interesting underlying assumptions about textuality in general and perhaps about what constitutes authorship or literary property as well. Chief among these assumptions seems to be the notion (encouraged by the booming digestive enterprises such as Cliff Notes) that a work of prose fiction consists principally in its skeletal plot.[39] A natural corollary, then, is that all authorial markers are disposable, so long as the general outline of events is retained. While King's adaptation moves only partially in this direction, some of her chapter title modifications, in addition to her other editorial maneuvers, indicate the premium placed on storyline elements. Although, as noted above, several of her title modifications involve lexical intervention or synonymy, the majority serve to convert allusive (or elusive) chapter titles to plot outline. Thus "Slow Torture" becomes "Ways and Highways," "Defend Thee, Lord" becomes "Sandy and the Boss Meet Adventures," "Marco" is translated into "The Yankee and the King Entertain," and "Dowley's Humiliation" into "The Yankee Argues Too Well."

Crossing the Divide

With its proactive textual intervention, its inclination to replace the original rhetoric with generic prose, and its whittling away at thematics, characterization, and style, King's abridged *Connecticut Yankee* exemplifies the adaptive strategies that are taken to extremes once the boundary between primarily verbal and predominantly visual textualities has been traversed. On the cusp of *Connecticut Yankee* versions that can legitimately be called abridgments and those adaptations that dispense with Twain's text altogether—the graphic novels and comics that are fundamentally illustrated plot outlines—is the 1977 Illustrated Classic edition adapted by Lucia Monfried, who may also be responsible for the illustrations. (No attribution is provided.) Described on the back cover as "a specially adapted version for young readers," this pleasant little book, with its minuscule proportions (5.5 × 4 inches) and abundant illustrations, seems tailor-made for small hands and young attention spans, all its features pointing to a primary-level audience. Print text and visual imagery share equal billing here. The volume consists of two hundred and thirty-four pages, fifty percent of which are given over to illustration, with text and images presented *en face*. With approximately four inches of twelve-point text per story page, and every other page featuring an image, precious little of Twain's novel remains; indeed, Monfried eliminates fifteen of the forty-four chapters from the original, slightly over a third of Twain's text.

Oddly, of the three versions considered thus far, Monfried's adaptation, despite its brevity and the tender age of its target audience, does perhaps the least violence to Twain's novel. Granted, the extent of textual reduction is drastic. The first three and a half pages of "The Eclipse," for example, are reduced to the following:

> When I thought of the eclipse, I was as happy as could be. It would be sure to save me. But not only that. It would be the making of me.
> The morning came. I heard footsteps. The door opened and a guard said to me, "The stake is ready. Come. Haste thee."
> They took me through the maze of underground corridors to the court-yard. There was the stake, and on all sides sat the multitudes.
> As I was being chained to the stake, the crowd was silent. Dread was in their faces. A man knelt to light the fire. A monk began some words in Latin, but stopped suddenly and raised his eyes toward the sky.
> The multitude rose slowly and stared into the sky. I followed their eyes. As sure as guns, there was my eclipse beginning! I struck a grand pose, my arm pointing to the sun and said:
> "Stay where you are. If any man moves—even the king—I will blast him with thunder and strike him with lightning."
> The multitude sank meekly to their seats. I knew I was master of the situation now.[40]

The brief paragraphs (none in the book as a whole is longer than five sentences) and the syntactic transparency—simple subject-verb-object structures with minimal embedding—are obvious markers of a text designed for young readers and auditors. Nonetheless, as it transpires, the majority of the words, phrases, and sentences, here as elsewhere in the book, are in fact Twain's own. What is remarkable here—and again this pertains to the entire adaptation—is the grace with which this drastic textual surgery is executed and the intelligence with which Twain's text is preserved, albeit in miniaturist fashion: the style and voice are consistent throughout, with none of the disconcerting shifts in registration that result from the sometimes gauche cutting and pasting in the King and Whitman abridgments. This is in all respects, visually and rhetorically, an eminently readable little book.

Even within the constraints dictated by the nature of this adaptation, Monfried is surprisingly successful at retaining "the style and spirit of the original" that King touts as one of her own adaptive desiderata—in fact more so, in some ways, than in King's own abridgment. Monfried does not underestimate the capacity of her young audience, keeping the dumbing-down quotient to a minimum. Wherever possible, for example, she retains lexical material that might ordinarily be judged beyond the understanding of her target readership. In the passage cited, we find Twain's "maze of underground corridors," "dread," "multitude," and "sank meekly." She retains the archaic "Haste thee" (for which King substituted "Hurry" for a high school audience), and even when simplifying a Twainian mouthful such as "I was in one of the most grand attitudes I ever struck," Monfried comes as close as possible to the original phrasing (in this case, "I struck a grand pose"). Likewise, she opts for minimal bowdlerization, confronting rather than avoiding (as is often the case with the adaptations geared to a more mature juvenile readership) unpleasant and potentially disturbing issues: Morgan's casual stabbing of her page, the abomination of slavery, the tragic realities of smallpox, Twain's representation of the Church as the villain of the piece, Lancelot's affair with Guinevere, and the fight to the death between Arthur and Mordred are all included here.[41] The degree to which Monfried retains the "spirit of the original" despite distasteful or politically hazardous subject matter is exemplified by her treatment of the slavery episode:

> I took my leave and rushed to the slave quarters. Empty! Everybody gone! Everybody except for one—the slave master. His body had been battered to a pulp. The place looked like there had been a terrible fight.
> I found a man who told me the story.
> "There were sixteen slaves here," he said, "who rose against their master in the night. The slave who was most valuable got free of his bonds by magic, and when the master discovered his loss, he threw himself on the other slaves. They broke his neck and beat him until he was dead."[42]

These grim details are perhaps startling as components of a text aimed for relatively young children, but they *are* faithful to the template. Likewise the execution passage in this episode: "Then the first slave was blindfolded, and the rope was pulled. A noose was placed on the second slave. Then the third was hung. It was dreadful."[43] Above all, Monfried does not flinch at the astounding death toll that attends upon the Yankee's Arthurian adventure: his shooting of Sagramore and nine other knights, the electrocution of the first knight to touch the charged fence, and the body count from Hank's initial blast in the novel's denouement ("Everything exploded with a thunder-crash, and five thousand were blown into the sky").[44] Tellingly, where both the King and the Whitman versions suppress the final death toll, Monfried's conclusion to the penultimate chapter reads, straight from Twain's text, "Twenty-five thousand lay dead around us."[45] Whether or not such material is appropriate for young children may be a matter of debate, but as a representation of Twain's novel, Monfried's adaptation is in many ways truer to the original with respect to plot details, characterization of the protagonist, and tone than either the King or the Whitman abridgments.

Despite their cartoon-like aspect—stylized, dynamic, uncluttered black-and-white drawings—the captioned illustrations are of a piece with the forthright nature of Monfried's adaptation. The image captioned "Smallpox!," for example, shows the interior of the hovel with Hank kneeling beside the dying woman; "Nothing Can Break Arthur's Spirit" represents the king being beaten with a bullwhip by the slavemaster; "The Hanging" features the scaffold, complete with nooses and the masked executioner.[46] In striking contrast to Pitz's illustration of the shooting of Sagramore, the illustration entitled "Hank's New Weapon—A Revolver"[47] foregrounds Hank; the revolver, shown as it discharges, is the focal point of the image, and we see Sagramore about to topple from his horse as the bullet strikes. Monfried's illustrations are neither incidental flourishes, as those in the Whitman and the King abridgments, nor do they create a counter-narrative, as was the case with Pitz's imagery. Rather, they comprise a pictorial parallel with the narrative, an alternate but co-valent visual text: a youngster could conceivably "read" the illustrations in sequence and come away with a fairly good feel for the storyline and the texture of the book.

The Four-Color Yankee

The King, Whitman, and Monfried adaptations of *Connecticut Yankee* amply demonstrate the Aurelia Syndrome in action. In the graphic versions, the project of dismantling Twain is fully realized. The replacement of Twain's rhetoric with vanilla prose that began in the more conservative adaptations as a compensatory device for omissions and compressions becomes the order of the day. The neutralization of the protagonist, Hank's transformation into a generic hero, the first moves toward which were the results of deletion and bowdlerization, receives the finishing touches. The steadily increasing proportion of images to print text—eleven plates in King, twenty-four in the Whitman, one hundred and seventeen in Monfried—culminates in a predominantly visual text, to which the verbal component pays homage. And the assault on the original work's structure that began in the prose adaptations with chapter elision, conflation, and title modification at last batters down the last vestiges of internal boundaries as originally discrete episodes are melded into one continuous narrative.

The graphic versions of *Connecticut Yankee* come in two basic formats: pictorial books and comics.[48] In the pictorial, or biblioform, category are the

Regents Illustrated Classics (1981) version adapted by Elaine Kim, the 1984 AI version (no editorial or artistic attribution), and the 1997 Classics Illustrated reprint published by Acclaim Books, likewise lacking creative attribution. These are slender, easy-reading volumes, all soft-cover, consisting respectively of forty-seven, sixty-one, and forty-seven pages. They are also small books, ranging from 6.5 × 4 inches (AI) to 8.75 × 6 inches (Regents). The illustrations for the AI and the Regents versions are in black and white; the Classics Illustrated version has been recolored by computer. In standard comic book format, versions include the 1945 Classics Comic (reprinted fourteen times through the early 1970s) and the King Classics (1977).

While there is some variety among these versions with respect to proportion of print text to image, and of action or dialogue to narrative, and differences as well in visual representation of the major figures (the fair-haired Hank vs. the Rhett Butler/riverboat gambler Hank, a chastely garbed Sandy vs. the voluptuous blonde Sandy, a dark-haired and -bearded Arthur vs. Arthur the Graybeard), these details are minor compared to the common features dictated by generic demands of a mass-market product. All the graphic versions focus on action as opposed to reflection, foregrounding the visual over the verbal, print text being safely confined within balloons or rectangular boxes (the boxed matter containing narrative or transitional material, such as "I stayed in the Valley of Holiness for awhile. One day. . ." or "Le Fey gave in, and the crowd rushed to the door like a mob").[49] Stylistic differences in visual representation are assuredly more attributable to the trends of the time than to the individual vision of the artists (usually anonymous) and the colorists. All versions promote the deceptive notion that they have been authored by Mark Twain (or, in the case of the AI and Classics Illustrated versions, Samuel Clemens), despite the fact that rarely, if ever, does a single word or phrase of Twain's appear; and, with only one exception,[50] all include a biographical note about Twain, usually at the end of the work.

Of more interest, perhaps, is the bizarre history of textual transmission here, because it demonstrates the degree to which Twain's novel has been not merely appropriated but entirely supplanted. For among the five illustrated adaptations enumerated above, only two—the AI adaptation and the King Classic—are stand-alone versions. The remainder form an almost classical stemma from base text to variant versions. The catch is that the base text is no longer Twain's *A Connecticut Yankee in King Arthur's Court*.

This perverse textual history begins with a surprising disconnect. The original 1945 Classic Comic was published by Gilberton as part of a series of comic book redactions of Great Works, including *Ivanhoe*, *Moby Dick*, *The Three Musketeers*, *The Count of Monte Cristo*, *Gulliver's Travels*, and *A Tale of Two Cities*. The adapters of *Connecticut Yankee* are listed as Ruth A. Roche and Tom Scott, and the artist is identified as Jack Hearne. As already noted, this version saw fourteen reissues, the last in the early 1970s. At some point, the title to the series as a whole changed from "Classic Comics" to "Classics Illustrated." Presumably, however, it did not change hands, as the 1971 issue still identifies Gilberton as the copyright holder, with a copyright date of 1945; and the company slogan, "Featuring Stories by the World's Greatest Authors," appears on the cover of both issues. One might assume, then, that the 1971 printing is simply a reissue of the original, and that is how it is usually represented bibliographically. But this is not the case. Despite the copyright note, the Classics Illustrated version undertakes a complete revamping of the original. Both the graphics and the print material are radically altered. The content is changed as well: for example, whereas in the original Gilberton version Hank's first encounter with Sandy occurs when she comes to court petitioning for the release of her mistress from an ogre, in the Classics Illustrated her petition concerns the Holy Fountain, and the captive princesses episode is eliminated entirely. Even the authorial attribution is modified: where the original was attributed to Mark Twain, the later version lists the author as Samuel L. Clemens.

The textual history becomes even more convoluted in subsequent years, as the silently revised Classics Illustrated version becomes the base text for a different, apparently independent version, The Regents Illustrated Classics *Connecticut Yankee* (1981). Adapted and with an editorial foreword written by Elaine Kim, this biblioform version is intended for instructional use by ESL and reading-challenged students, and comes, like Ruth King's abridgment, with a generous and well-contrived pedagogical apparatus: divided into three major parts, it features a "Getting Started" section at the beginning of each part, with discussion questions, vocabulary list, and glossary, and more apparatus at the end of each section, consisting of "Getting the Main Idea," "Understanding Details," and "Building Vocabulary." It is identified as "Level B—High Beginning" text, "based on a cumulative list of 750 words." Kim's procedure here has something else in common with King's alterations of Twain's text: she adjusts the lexicon and the syntax of the original to suit the anticipated skill level of the target audience. Kim's source text is not Twain, however, but the Classics Illustrated version: the graphics, episodic structure, and sequence of events are identical. Only the language is changed. In this simplification of a simplification, "the world went out" becomes "the world suddenly became dark"; "Get along back to your circus" becomes "Go away, or I'll call the police!" Merlin's assertion regarding the infamous well, "I have done what man could. The mortal does not live who can restore the fountain," translates into "I did everything a man could do. Nobody can save this fountain." In the boxed narrative portions, Kim changes all verb forms to the present tense: "I ran out into the night and threw myself at the dim figure" is revised to "I run out into the dark night and jump on a man." Kim's procedure is undoubtedly unimpeachable, given her pedagogical objectives. But that her source is a comic book version of Twain rather than the original novel gives one pause: in the world of traditional print culture, this is tantamount to plagiarism. The publisher makes no acknowledgment whatsoever of the actual source text; nor are the illustrator and the original adapter listed.

The latest recension of the 1971 base text is the 1997 Classics Illustrated *Connecticut Yankee*, now published by Acclaim Books. Although the graphics and text remain unchanged from the exemplar, this reprinting has undergone considerable transformation with respect to physical properties and generics. No longer in standard comic book format, the Acclaim edition has become bibiloform, with a glossy cover the trendy graphics of which are jarringly unrelated to those of the conservative, 1970s interior art, although the latter has been visually enhanced through computer recolorization. Disowning its comic-book genealogy, it is now offered as a "lively study guide" (according to the back cover). Even the original slogan, "Featuring Stories by the World's Greatest Authors," has changed: this is now "Your Doorway to the Classics." No mention is made of either the original Gilberton publication or the 1971 version of which this is a faithful reprint: the copyright is now owned by the Frawley Corporation. Additionally, Acclaim holds the copyright to "All new material and compilation"—a puzzling claim on the face of it, given the unaltered state of graphics and text. What enables the publisher to make this claim, apparently, is the addition of an attractively printed and informative fifteen-page essay by Andrew Jay Hoffman, which covers such topics as "The Author," "The Characters," "The Plot," and "Themes," with sidebars on Twain's politics, the publishing history of *Connecticut Yankee*, and an intriguing insertion entitled "King Arthur in the Court of Kamehameha IV," concerning Twain's original plans for this story. And so, with a mere reduction in size, the addition of a glossy cover, and the attachment of an instructive essay, a graphic publication originally designed for entertainment has become a short-cut to academic success with the work of an author and a text that have, for all practical purposes, altogether vanished.

Going to the Dogs

Given the longstanding curricular establishment and the unchallenged canonicity of *Connecticut Yankee*, it is not surprising to find a didactic component in adaptations with a specific pedagogical agenda, such as Ruth King's high school text, or even in the Regent's ESL/slow-reader version. That a tarted-up comic book such as the 1997 Acclaim adaptation should also feature a didactic component is, on the other hand, rather startling.

It transpires, however, that didactic matter had been easing its way into graphic versions of *Connecticut Yankee* since the original 1945 Gilberton publication, with its end-piece on Mark Twain—a practice continued, as noted, by all but one of the subsequent graphic versions, regardless of provenance. The 1971 Classics Illustrated initiates what will become an escalating didactic trend by exhorting the reader, immediately following the final story frame, "NOW THAT YOU HAVE READ THE CLASSICS ILLUS-TRATED EDITION, DON'T MISS THE ADDED ENJOYMENT OF READING THE ORIGINAL, OBTAINABLE AT YOUR SCHOOL OR PUBLIC LIBRARY." The use of the Classics Illustrated version for pedagogical purposes in the Regents Classic and the extensive academic appendix to the 1997 Acclaim revamping of the same text are merely logical extensions of this practice. While marketing considerations were most likely the primary impetus for these didactic accretions, I suspect that another phenomenon is at work here as well, which I would describe as the Guilt Factor—a gesture of expiation for tampering with canonicity, an apology for messing with a "Classic." It is surely not irrelevant that all the graphic adaptations of *Connecticut Yankee* appear in series with "Classic" in the title: Classic Comics, Classics Illustrated, King Classics, Regents Illustrated Classics, Pocket Classics (the AI edition). And it is probably not accidental either that the didactic machinery in pictorial narratives was first set a-whirring in the early 1970s, the decade of "Why Johnny Can't Read."

The workings of the Guilt Factor are abundantly manifest in Joanne Barkan's novel, *A Pup in King Arthur's Court* (1998), the most recent literary adaptation of Twain's work. *Pup*, described by the publisher as "Inspired by *A Connecticut Yankee in King Arthur's Court* by Mark Twain," is an entry in the popular "The Adventures of Wishbone" series, the protagonist of which is a Jack Russell terrier who experiences time travel to the world of timeless classics: the series includes such titles, variously authored, as *The Prince and the Pooch*, *Robinhound Crusoe*, *Hunchdog of Notre Dame*, *Muttketeer!*, and *Moby Dog*. *A Pup in King Arthur's Court*, featuring six handsome full-page and twelve smaller black-and-white drawings by Arvis Stewart, targets a middle-school audience.

The principal plot of Barkan's novel involves two sixth-graders, Joe Talbot and his sidekick Dave, who start a rival sports newspaper because they feel that the eighth-graders in charge of sports news at Sequoyan Middle School unfairly marginalize soccer. In the process they seriously alienate the eighth-grade editors of the *Sports Report*, Anna and Ryan, because through their superior computer skills Joe and Dave have produced a more popular product. In the end, the foursome engages in productive negotiation and mature conflict resolution, ending class warfare and restoring harmony on the journalistic front at Sequoyan.

Interlaced with this story is the Twainoid subplot, in which Joe's dog, Wishbone, imagines himself as Hank Morgan, journeying mentally to Camelot where he becomes a canine version of the Yankee. The novel's narrative loops back and forth between main plot and subplot, gradually increasing the number of contiguous *Connecticut Yankee* episodes until, by the end, the principal pretext and the subplot appear to have exchanged positions. The relationship between the two story strands at all points, however, is vexed, the transitions between plot and subplot both awkward and artificial. The interface is accomplished typographically rather than rhetorically, with visually disruptive bolded transitional material of the "meanwhile-back-at-the-ranch" variety:

> **A first-rate report on the soccer playoffs, one that uses the latest in computer graphics—that is a brilliant idea.**
> **Meanwhile, someone else desperately needs a brilliant idea—Hank Morgan. In his prison cell, he's just heard that he's been sentenced to death.**[51]

The parallels between the two plots, moreover, are tenuous at best, depending in large part, as the back cover prose boasts, on the celebration of "New technology over old ideas"—or in a transitional moment within the text, **"Three cheers for modern inventions."**[52] Ironically, Barkan's decision to preserve as much of Twain's original language as possible (albeit in the modified form that characterized the King and Whitman adaptations) makes for an even more uncomfortable fit between the principal narrative and the *Yankee* sequences.

Detracting still further from narrative momentum and surface cohesion is the novel's didactic turn of mind. While some instructional material appears discretely as end matter—the inevitable Twain biography and a three-paragraph section on the genesis and thematics of Twain's novel—much of the didactic matter invades the story proper.[53] After seeing his human friend struck on the head during a soccer match, Wishbone thinks, "*I'm sure I've come across something like this before. What was it?. . .Aha! I've got it! I'm thinking of Hank Morgan.*" This in turn triggers a didactic excursus:

> **Hank Morgan is the hero of a terrific novel called *A Connecticut Yankee in King Arthur's Court*. Hank gets clobbered on the head during a fight. He's knocked out cold. He wakes up to discover that he's traveled back in time over thirteen hundred years! He's gone all the way back to the sixth century!**
> **The well-loved, nineteenth-century American writer Mark Twain wrote *A Connecticut Yankee in King Arthur's Court*. It was published in**

1889. Twain wrote this novel in the first person—as if Hank Morgan were telling the story himself. The novel begins in the city of Hartford, Connecticut, in the late 1800's.[54]

Immediately thereafter begins the next chapter: "Wishbone pictured Hartford, Connecticut in the year 1885. Horse-drawn carriages clattered up and down the busy cobblestone streets."[55] And so it continues for three paragraphs, an introductory lecture on nineteenth-century urban culture. With more self-assurance than accuracy, like a wannabe Mr. Peabody, Wishbone muses in response to David's comment that the eighth-graders' *Sports Report* "is like something out of the Dark Ages,"

> *Dark Ages? Oh, yeah, the period after the fall of the Roman Empire. The Dark Ages lasted approximately from the year 476 to the year 1000. That includes the time of King Arthur.*[56]

Lexicon is evidently taken to be an issue as well, and transparently masked vocabulary lessons erupt periodically: "I figured that my escort had escaped from an asylum—one of those special hospitals where they cared for the insane—mentally ill—people," or, during Wishbone/Hank's first conversation with Clarence,

> "I am a page," he told me.
> My tail twitched with irritation. *Another patient. This one thinks he's a page—one of those boys who does errands for a king or queen.*[57]

The most dramatic didactic eruption occurs between chapters two and three with the insertion of a three-page vocabulary list (coyly titled "Wishbone's Dictionary for Anyone in the Dark About the Dark Ages"), which includes a further discussion of Dark Ages, obsolete verb forms (doth, hath, 'tis, me thinks), one inflectional ending (-eth), some antiquated expletives (forsooth! marry!), and a host of nouns from "chain mail" to "sundial" and "moat." Whoever compiled this glossary seriously underestimates the knowledge of middle-school children, I suspect, with entries that include "quest," "yonder," "knight," and "dungeon." Why the term "democracy" was included here is anybody's guess. While Barkan and the series editors are to be commended for good intentions and clever contrivance, *A Pup in King Arthur's Court* is an object lesson in the futility of attempting to cajole Twain's novel into a format judged suitable for juvenile consumption.

Coda

If I were forced to select a single twentieth-century version of *Connecticut Yankee* for a youngster in my charge, my choice would not be any of the adaptations discussed here, but rather the 1988 Books of Wonder unabridged edition of Twain's original, brilliantly illustrated by Caldecott medalist Trina Schart Hyman. The gift edition is a beautiful production, sharing with the Pitz edition all the markers of a text aimed at a juvenile audience: with its twelve-point font, ample white space, and russet cloth binding, front cover graced with a gold-embossed illustration, it is an eloquent reminder that bookmaking can still be an art. In addition to eight full-page color illustrations, the volume sports ten rectangular black-and-white drawings, the size and shape of a bookmark, located in the left-hand margin on the first page of each new chapter, functioning rather like rubrication or illuminated capitals in manuscript production to signal textual boundaries. The drawings recur in random distribution, although there is a patterning here as well: the images that appear with the highest frequency correspond to the relative importance of their subjects in the main narrative. In descending order of frequency, the subjects are "The Boss and Sandy," "King Arthur," "Slavery," and "Clarence."[58] The other recurring motifs are "A Bit of Enchantment" (smoke exuding from Hank's helmet), "Merlin," and "Sir Ozana Le Cure Hardy" (featuring the signboard advertising Persimmons's Soap). Additionally, there are two drawings entitled "Hello Central" and one of "The First Newspaper." All have the elegance of a Dürer etching, executed with the distinctive panache characteristic of Hyman's images. Even without the color illustrations, this would be a visually captivating book.

With the illustrations, it is simply stunning. Hyman's images constitute an exhilarating antiphon to the textual matter, responsive to both the tone and texture of Twain's narrative. Executed in a dynamic, in-your-face, linear style, these illustrations hover on the border of comic-book art but never quite cross over, indirect homage, perhaps, to Beard's drawings for the original edition. Using a mannerist palette, Hyman varies the hues according to the setting or mood of the particular incident each illustrates: blues, purples, and burgundies for the twilight "Restoration of the Holy Fountain," browns and olive drab for "In the Smallpox Hut," mustard, reds, and sky-blues for "The Tournament," for example. The human figures dominate the settings and are never subservient to them. The juvenilization of those figures that characterized Pitz's imagery has no place here: Hank Morgan is clearly represented as middle-aged (looking on the dust jacket illustration remarkably like Abraham Lincoln). Visual bowdlerization is nowhere evident. "In the Smallpox Hut," for example, renders the interior of a hovel, with an emaciated woman half-reclining in the foreground tended by an anxious-looking, disheveled man, while Arthur bears in his arms a wasted, obviously moribund young girl. In a similar vein, Hyman's "Morgan Le Fey" features the corpse of Morgan's recently stabbed servant occupying the entire foreground (spilling beyond the picture frame, in fact), a dagger buried in his chest and blood staining his tunic. Morgan—a woman of a certain age with sharp features and sharper claws—casually nudges the corpse with her daintily shod foot as she turns her head to chat with her shocked guests. Hank's expression is one of horrified bemusement, while Sandy looks as if she is about to be ill. Not all of the illustrations, of course, are confrontational. Each reverberates to the incident it represents, and the emotional content is richly varied. If *Connecticut Yankee* were for kids, this would be the edition of choice.

The Right Stuff

Print text and graphic versions of Twain's *Connecticut Yankee* represent but a small portion not only of Yankiana in general, but of the subclass thereof targeting juvenile audiences, for—with a serendipity that Twain himself would surely appreciate—twentieth-century technology has enabled new media to have a field day with the tattered remains of Twain's original. For youngsters we have, for example, a generous array of cartoon spinoffs—the classic and still unsurpassed "Bugs Bunny in King Arthur's Court" (1972); a made-for-television animated *Connecticut Yankee in King Arthur's Court* from 1970, with voiceover by Orson Bean; a segment of Mr. Peabody's "Improbable History" from "The Adventures of Bullwinkle and Rocky" (1961); and, tangential but still related, the "King BJ" episode from the *Beetlejuice* television series, first aired in 1992, and the "King Arthur and the Knights of Justice" cartoon series. In the past decade and a half, the youth film scene has been virtually saturated with cinematic versions of *Connecticut Yankee* (discussed further by Barbara Tepa Lupack in chapter 12 in this volume), ranging from those that purport, however vaguely, to derive from Twain (*A Kid in King Arthur's Court*, Keshia Knight Pulliam's *A Connecticut Yankee in King Arthur's Court*, *Kids of the Round Table*, *A Young Connecticut Yankee in King Arthur's Court*, and *A Knight in Camelot*), to spinoffs that share only the time-travel-to-Camelot motif, such as Disney's *Unidentified Flying Oddball*, *The Excalibur Kid*, and *Johnny Mysto, Boy Wizard*. And on a more traditional front, theatrical redactions for young audiences abound, the best known of which is probably Larry Nestor's *A Connecticut Yankee*, which has appeared as a play as well as a musical (1990). R. Rex Stephenson's adaptation of *Connecticut Yankee*, first performed in 1998, features Merlin as a computer whiz, and other theatrical versions targeting youngsters have recently been mounted by such varied troupes as the Jefferson College Players, the New American Theater Company, and school-age youngsters themselves at Lutheran High School in Indianapolis and the Earle B. Wood Middle School Drama Club in Rockville, Maryland.

The Ballard Institute and Museum of Puppetry has performed an adaptation by Brad Korbesmeyer as well. While this list of non-print versions of *Connecticut Yankee* is by no means exhaustive, it is indicative of the extent to which Twain's story, liberated from the generic constraints of prose fiction and the burden of fidelity to a "classic," has taken on a life of its own. *Connecticut Yankee* has, willy nilly, become a staple of contemporary youth culture. It may no longer be Twain, as Parke Godwin is no longer Malory, but it helps to insure that both the Matter of Arthur and the Yankee himself will continue to circulate as cultural currency for at least another generation to come.

Notes

1. Andrew Jay Hoffman, Study Questions, 1997 rpt. of the Classics Illustrated *Mark Twain, A Connecticut Yankee in King Arthur's Court* (New York: Acclaim Books, n.d.).

2. In his *Camelot Project* filmography at <http://lib.rochester.edu/camelot/cphome.stm>, Kevin Harty lists twelve *Connecticut Yankee* film versions, running from 1920 to 1995. To these must be added the 1998 Whoopi Goldberg vehicle, *A Knight in Camelot*, and a host of tangential films like *The Excalibur Kid* (1998) and *The Black Knight* (2000). (For a discussion of youth-oriented *Connecticut Yankee* films and other Arthurian-themed movies, see the essay by Barbara Tepa Lupack, chapter 12 in this volume.)

3. See Harty filmography for details.

4. Paul Alan Levi, *Mark Twain Suite* (New York: Lawson-Gould; distr. Cherry Lane Music, n.d.)

5. See <http://www.donatoart,com/yankee.html> and <http://www.paulb.com/conyank5.htm>.

6. See <http://mreclipse.com/SENL> and <http://webhome.idirect.com/~kmalicki/stamps85to91.htm>.

7. Peter J. Heck, *A Connecticut Yankee in Criminal Court: A Mark Twain Mystery* (NY: Berkeley Prime Crime, 1996).

8. These include not only versions in standard literary format (i.e., editions, abridgments, or adaptations) but also any kind of text with some printerly/readerly component, including graphic versions and comics. Print versions (aside from multiple unadulterated versions of the original text) actually represent a relatively small proportion of *Connecticut Yankee* products.

9. This for the unabridged edition illustrated by Trina Schart Hyman (New York: William Morrow & Co., 1988). Typically, *Connecticut Yankee* is cross-referenced with Arthurian romances, knights and knighthood, Great Britain, time travel, and fantastic fiction.

10. Mark E. Rogers, *A Samurai Cat in King Arthur's Court* (New York: TOR, 1986).

11. Rogers, *A Samurai Cat*, p. 33.
12. *A Samurai Cat* is equally unsuited to juvenile readers in terms of registration, with its offhand references to such concepts as "mind–body dualism" and stylistic self-indulgences like "there was something both archetypically pulp-adventurish and vaguely archaeological about him."
13. Such complete editions for children seem relatively rare; abridgments and other adjusted texts are much more common.
14. With only a few exceptions, the presence of illustrated material is a reliable index of youth-oriented editions and versions of the novel. Of the "adult" editions I am aware of, only the Limited Editions production and the Reader's Digest abridgment are accompanied by illustrative material. Interestingly, the Reader's Digest edition, though not targeting younger readers, shares some features such as readability markers—comfortable font size and ample white space—with youth editions.
15. Since any abridgment is by its very nature an adaptation of the source text and the line between the two processes is, in any case, fuzzy at best, I am restricting my own use of the term "abridgment" to signify editions that retain a substantial portion of Twain's prose despite omissions and emendations. Both the Whitman (Racine, WI: Whitman Publishing Company, 1955) and the King (New York: Globe Book Company, Inc., 1948) versions that I discuss are abridgments by this criterion. King's version, however, describes itself, not entirely inaccurately, as "adapted."
16. In the comparisons that follow, I shall focus on two episodes from Twain: "The Eclipse" and the final few chapters of the book, "War" and "The Battle of the Sandbelt."
17. That King's is the only such editorial preface in the texts I have examined suggests either that adaptation is such a common practice in children's literature that no explanation is needed or that Twain's novel is considered as public property, and therefore free game for whatever snipping, cutting and pasting, or revising seems necessary at any given moment. The trivializing of secondary authorship in *Connecticut Yankee* abridgments and adaptations is prettily exemplified by the Whitman edition, which contains no editorial attribution at all. Interestingly, not just the Whitman but other editions as well are known by their illustrators rather than by their editors.
18. Ruth King (with Elsa Wolf and Hilton D. King), *A Connecticut Yankee in King Arthur's Court*, ill. Thomas Fraumeni, p. iii.
19. King, *Connecticut Yankee*, 314 ff. and 321 ff.
20. In starting with the Whitman edition of *A Connecticut Yankee in King Arthur's Court*, ill. Nicholas Frank, I am deliberately stepping out of chronological order, since my materials do not conform to a developmental or evolutionary paradigm but rather organize themselves around genre and both generic and source-specific editorial tactics.
21. "Sir Dinadan," "The Beginnings of Civilization," "Sandy's Tale," "Knight-Errantry as a Trade," "A Pitiful Incident," and "Three Years Later." The chapter count here, and in the remaining prose versions, may not be precise

because of blurred narrative boundaries: a common abridgment strategy in all these texts is to briefly paraphrase the material of entire episodes or to conflate material originally kept separate in the original.

22. Although the frame is omitted by some of the less faithful adaptations as well, such as the Classic Comics version(s) and Monfried's drastic abridgment, it is retained not only by Ruth King but also by the AI pictorial edition and the Kings Classics comic.

23. My citations from Twain's original are from *A Connecticut Yankee in King Arthur's Court* (New York: Bantam Classic, 1981).

24. Twain, pp. 26–27; Whitman, p. 37.

25. Twain, pp. 250–54.

26. Twain, p. 263.

27. Whitman, p. 281; Twain, 263–64.

28. Whitman, p. 281; Twain, p. 270.

29. Twain, pp. 269, 270.

30. Twain, pp. 265, 269.

31. Twain, pp. 265, 264, 270.

32. Twain, pp. 265, 266.

33. The deleted chapters are "Sir Dinadan the Humorist," "Merlin's Tower," "Beginnings of Civilization," "Freemen," "Sandy's Tale," "Knight Errantry as a Trade," "The First Newspaper," "Drilling the King," "Sixth-Century Political Economy," "A Pitiful Incident," "An Encounter in the Dark," and "The Interdict."

34. This metaphor is eliminated in the Whitman edition as well.

35. The Whitman abridgment does not tamper with chapter titles.

36. The most interesting omission here is the Yankee's plan to "overthrow the Catholic Church and set up the Protestant faith on its ruins" (pp. 241–42), one of the Yankee's "two schemes." King reduces his mission to "a scheme," and is consistent in avoiding all but a single passing reference to the Church (here "the church," p. 305) thereafter. Given that the Whitman edition treads very delicately here and that most other adaptations avoid the material of "The Interdict" altogether, it looks very much like consensual censorship in the name of political correctness.

37. King, pp. 306–307.

38. King, p. 305.

39. Indeed, those wishing to avail themselves of plot outline and summaries of *Connecticut Yankee* may consult Spark Notes, Cliff Notes, Classic Notes, and MonkeyNotes, or simply go to CheatBooks.com.

40. Lucia Monfried, *A Connecticut Yankee in King Arthur's Court* (New York: Playmore, Inc., 1977), pp. 39–40.

41. Monfried, pp. 72, 171 f., 212 f., 204, 212–214, 209 f.

42. Monfried, p. 172.

43. Monfried, p. 181.

44. Monfried, pp. 194–96, 224, 222.

45. Monfried, p. 228.

46. Monfried, pp. 123, 162, 163, 180.

47. Monfried, p. 195.
48. Only those comic book versions that purport to be authored by Mark Twain (or Samuel L. Clemens) and to represent the original novel are being considered here, such spinoffs and ripoffs as "A Connecticut Ice Cream Man in King Arthur's Court," "The Green Arrow in King Arthur's Court," and the Twainoid *Justice League Europe Annual #2* being, regrettably, beyond the scope of the present essay. I am indebted to Michael Torregrossa ("Camelot 3000 and Beyond: An Annotated History of Arthurian Comic Books," *The Camelot Project* at <http://lib.rochester.edu/camelot/cphome.stm>), Alan Stewart (*Camelot in Four Colors.* <http://camelot4colors.com>), and Rudy Tambone, webmaster of Classics Central (<www.classicscentral.com>), for their generous assistance in serving as pathfinders and tour guides through this relatively alien bibliographical territory. (For a discussion of the return of King Arthur in comic books, see the essay by Michael A. Torregrossa, chapter 11 in this volume.)
49. The illustrated versions do vary considerably in the amount of narrative/transitional material presented, ranging from a minimalist approach in the King Classic and the original Classic Comic to versions consisting of more narrative than dialogue, such as the AI version, which reads like an illustrated Cliff notes. All except the 1945 Classic Comic use first-person narrative.
50. Only the Regents Illustrated *Connecticut Yankee* fails to provide the obligatory Twain biography.
51. Joanne Barkan, *A Pup in King Arthur's Court*, illustrated by Arvis Stewart (Allen, TX: Big Red Chair Books, 1998), p. 45. See also pp. 39, 66, 71, 108, 111, 129, 133. An additional typographical intervention takes the form of a series of paw prints, which precede the bolded transitional material and serve as well to mark passage of time or transitions between episodes in the Yankee-narrative proper.
52. Barkan, *Pup*, p. 108.
53. Barkan, *Pup*, pp. 161, 163.
54. Barkan, *Pup*, pp. 11–12.
55. Barkan, *Pup*, p. 13.
56. Barkan, *Pup*, p. 44.
57. Barkan, *Pup*, pp. 18, 23.
58. Hyman, *A Connecticut Yankee in King Arthur's Court*, pp. 9, 8, 6, 5.

Select Bibliography of *Connecticut Yankee* Versions for Children

Prose Editions and Adaptations

Unabridged and Illustrated Editions of A Connecticut Yankee in King Arthur's Court *(alphabetical by illustrator)*

Ciardiello, Joseph. *A Connecticut Yankee in King Arthur's Court*. Afterword by T. E. D. Klein. *World's Best Reading*. Pleasantville, NY: Reader's Digest Association, Inc., 1984.

Hyman, Trina Schart (ill.). *A Connecticut Yankee in King Arthur's Court*. Afterword by Peter Glassman. Books of Wonder. New York: William Morrow & Co., 1988.

Pitz, Henry. *A Connecticut Yankee in King Arthur's Court*. Gift Edition. New York: Harper & Brothers, 1917.

Adapted/Abridged and Illustrated Editions (alphabetical by author or abridger)

Barkan, Joanne. *A Pup In King Arthur's Court*. "Inspired by *A Connecticut Yankee in King Arthur's Court*." Ill. Arvis Stewart. Allen, TX: Big Red Chair Books (div. of Lyric Publishing), 1998.

King, Ruth T. with Elsa Wolf and Hilton D. King. *A Connecticut Yankee in King Arthur's Court*. Ill. Thomas Fraumeni. New York: Globe Book Company, Inc., 1948.

Monfried, Lucia. *A Connecticut Yankee in King Arthur's Court*. Pocket size, alternating prose and illustrations. Moby Books. New York: Playmore, Inc., 1977.

Nicholas, Frank (ill.). *A Connecticut Yankee in King Arthur's Court*. Abridgment anonymous. Racine, WI: Whitman Publishing Company, 1955.

Graphic Adaptations and Comics

AI (pocket-book format). *A Connecticut Yankee in King Arthur's Court*. West Haven, CT: Academic Industries, Inc., 1984.

A Connecticut Ice Cream Man in King Arthur's Court. *House of Secrets* # 123. DC Comics (September 1974).

Classic Comics No. 24. *A Connecticut Yankee in King Arthur's Court*. 2nd edn. NY: Gilberton Company, 1946. 14th edn., 1971.

Kim, Elaine (adaptation). *A Connecticut Yankee in King Arthur's Court*. Regents Illustrated Classics. New York: Regents Publishing Company, Inc., 1981.

King Classics. *A Connecticut Yankee in King Arthur's Court*. NY: King Features Syndicate, 1977.

Scott, T. (adaptation) and Andrew Jay Hoffman (concluding essay). *A Connecticut Yankee in King Arthur's Court*. Classics Illustrated. New York: Acclaim Books Study Guides, 1997.

The Green Arrow in King Arthur's Court. *Adventure Comics*. No. 268. DC Comics (January 1960).

Films

A Connecticut Yankee in King Arthur's Court. NBC, 1989. Dir. Mel Damski.

The Excalibur Kid. Canarom Productions and Castle Films, 1998. Dir. James Head.

A Kid in King Arthur's Court. Walt Disney Pictures, 1995. Dir. Michael Gottlieb.

Johnny Mysto, Boy Wizard. Paramount (Kushner-Locke and Full Moon Entertainment), 1997. Dir. Jeff Burr.

Unidentified Flying Oddball. Disney, 1979. Dir. Russ Mayberry.

A Young Connecticut Yankee in King Arthur's Court. Filmline International, 1995. Dir. R. L. Thomas.

Other

A *Connecticut Yankee in King Arthur's Court*. NY: Bantam, 1981.

Longo, Dennis. "A Contracting Officer in King Arthur's Court." *Program Manager* (July–August 2001), 30–39.

Nestor, Larry and Tim Kelley. *A Connecticut Yankee: The Musical* (stage adaptation). Denver, Pioneer Drama Service, Inc., 1990.

Rogers, Mark E. *A Samurai Cat in King Arthur's Court*. In *More Adventures of Samurai Cat*. A TOR Book. New York: Tom Doherty Associates, 1986.

Stephenson, R. Rex. *A Connecticut Yankee in King Arthur's Court* (stage adaptation). Venice, FL: Eldridge Publishing, 2000.

CHAPTER 4

DECEPTIVE SIMPLICITY: CHILDREN'S VERSIONS OF *SIR GAWAIN AND THE GREEN KNIGHT*

Cindy L. Vitto

Although the Arthurian legend in particular has attracted many retellings for children, many (if not most) medieval scholars would see little value in such versions. I confess that until recently I fell into the same mold, holding the original as the privileged text and seeing adaptations for children as inherently inferior, perhaps even superfluous. Yet I have come to discover that a surprising tool for tackling the most sophisticated medieval texts is the apparent simplicity of children's versions. As modern authors struggle with the complexities of the text and carve out what is worth retaining versus what should be jettisoned, and as illustrators turn their talents to highlighting the printed word, discerning scholars can trace the cognitive and creative footprints of those writing for children and in so doing come to new realizations.

Perhaps no text in Middle English remains as appealing and simultaneously enigmatic as *Sir Gawain and the Green Knight*, the late fourteenth-century romance written by an anonymous author who, unlike Chaucer, was not associated with the court of London but was evidently associated with a similar courtly milieu in the northwest of England. Because of his West Midlands dialect, much more foreign to us today than Chaucer's dialectical version of Middle English, comparatively few have read the work in its original version; however, most undergraduates taking a course in early British literature encounter *Sir Gawain and the Green Knight* in translation.

Authors and critical readers of children's versions of this work should be aware of many of the large questions with which medieval scholars grapple in their interpretation of *Sir Gawain and the Green Knight*. The *Gawain*-Poet (as he—or perhaps even she—is often called) wrote at least three other extant poems: *Pearl*, *Cleanness*, and *Patience*; a fourth poem, *Saint Erkenwald*, may be by the same author.[1] All of the poems survive in a single manuscript, known as Cotton Nero A.x., currently housed in the British Library. Except for *Sir Gawain and the Green Knight*, all are religious works but with lively dialogue, attention to detail, and thematic depth that help to mark them as the work of the same poet.

Thus perhaps the first interpretive question to arise on reading *Sir Gawain and the Green Knight* is how to place it in context with the author's other works. Does this poem contain elements that, like the others, would make it didactic, spiritually instructive?[2] Or should we regard it as distinct from the others, evidence of the appeal of the Arthurian legend even in the fourteenth century so that a poet primarily interested in Christian narrative (at least, as far as we know) would venture to tell a secular romance?

With no solid answers about how to place *Sir Gawain and the Green Knight* in line with the other poems of Cotton Nero A.x., medieval scholars find themselves faced with a series of additional questions with no easy answers. As we shall see, authors of children's versions must somehow deal with these questions in order to shape their own stories. The most basic and important question is that of theme. Does the poem represent a coming-of-age ritual as Gawain passes his "test" but, having experienced sexual desire and a dread of mortality, must receive a nick to signify his inevitable imperfection? Or is it a poem about the importance of reading signs along the way, signs that Gawain excusably misses? Or does it represent, in the person of Morgan le Fay, a warning about the dangers of powerful, manipulative women? And what about the prominence of excuses in this poem? Gawain exculpates himself by blaming women, but then goes to the opposite extreme by assuming guilt and wearing the green girdle as a sign of humiliation, only to find that Arthur's court has excused him and has adopted the green girdle as a sign of worthiness. Finally, do the references to Troy that frame the poem indicate something about universal values— the inevitable nature of courtly culture, the dangers of women, the desire for glory on the part of warriors, to name just a few possibilities?[3]

Even this brief and necessarily curtailed exposition of the poem's interpretive difficulties should indicate that it might seem unlikely material for children's literature. Yet at least five children's versions of *Sir Gawain and the Green Knight* have been published since 1967, and—even more surprising to those who tend to look down a bit upon the discipline of children's literature—those versions have much to tell us about ways to read the original text. This essay will examine each of these versions to determine the author's "take" on the story of Sir Gawain's encounter with the Green Knight: Constance Hieatt's *Sir Gawain and the Green Knight* (1967), Selina

Hastings's *Sir Gawain and the Green Knight* (1981), a chapter from Neil Philip's *The Tale of Sir Gawain* (1987), a chapter from Michael Morpurgo's *Arthur: High King of Britain* (1994), and Mark Shannon's *Gawain and the Green Knight* (1994).[4] All of these versions, except for Shannon's, appear targeted to readers age ten or older; Shannon's version, with many pictures and large print, is suitable for younger readers, but probably not much younger than seven- or eight-year-olds.

Before we look at each work on its own, an enlightening preliminary exercise is to determine what all of these versions have omitted in the retelling and to attempt a rationale for the omissions. First, none of these works includes the Troy frame or the *"honi soit qui mal y pense"* motto presumably tacked on at the end of the original. A reasonable assumption is that the modern authors consider the Troy frame and the motto of the Order of the Garter irrelevant to the story, especially in light of the fact that most children today would have little or no background to allow them to understand these allusions.[5] Another glaring omission, to a medievalist familiar with the original, is Gawain's diatribe against women at the moment he learns that the Green Knight is actually his hospitable host, who, with his wife as accomplice, set up this test for Gawain under the ultimate direction of Morgan le Fay. Much critical ink has been spent on considering why these lines exist in the poem and what this rancorous passage reveals about the true nature of Gawain, renowned for his courtesy and chivalry toward women (at least within this poem; in other tellings of the Gawain legend—Malory's, for example—Gawain is capable of using women indiscriminately and without compunction).[6] No doubt the children's authors omitted this aspect not only because the passage seems discordant for a hero but also because of the major cultural shift that has taken place in our view of women—or at least in our officially sanctioned view of women. To include this passage in a modern retelling would risk the wrath of editors and of the parents who would buy these books for their children.

Two aspects of the original are not dropped entirely but decidedly downplayed in the children's versions: the attention given to the hunt scenes and to the religious aspects of the original. Hieatt is most faithful to the original by devoting significant space to all three hunts, with the greatest amount of descriptive detail given to the boar and its disconnected head, reminding us of Gawain's own threatened decapitation. Philip also describes the hunt to some extent, with the creative twist that Gawain actually "sees" the hunts played out in shadow form on the wall of his bedroom while he dallies with the lady. He is simultaneously engaged in both hunts, an aspect of the original that in this version is made explicit: "I could not escape her. And yet I remembered my host. How could I not, when

I felt in the air each arrow shiver from his bow, and heard in the space between my ear and brain the cries of the does as they fell."[7] In this version Gawain also dreams of the boar's head, seeing it in tandem with the Green Knight's severed head. Both Morpurgo and Hastings mention the hunts but give no description other than revealing that the host brings home his quarry each night, and in both cases on the first day he arrives with only one deer (a stag in Hastings's version) rather than with the bountiful number of does we find in the original. Finally, because the temptation scene in Shannon's work takes place at night, no hunt at all is involved in his version.

Since the original text does spend much time describing the hunt and also the dressing of the meat, we see here clear evidence of a cultural shift. Today's children are, for the most part, disconnected from the realities of hunting or, sometimes, ignorant even of the fact that the meat in the refrigerator was once a living animal. To include this aspect of the story to the same extent or in the same detail as in the original would create an imbalance for today's young audience, since many children would likely find these details even more horrifying than the impending threat to Gawain's life. The poet's own audience, of course, would have had an intimate understanding and respect of the hunt. For them, the hunt details would confirm Bertilak's nobility, courage, and sense of ritual; in addition, they would probably have had no difficulty seeing Gawain as yet another prey, although one with the chance of escaping death by exercising the higher human virtues.[8]

Another cultural shift is clear when we realize that, besides downplaying the hunt, most of these authors also de-emphasize the religious aspects of the story. Even in the original, of course, Gawain's test is not explicitly a religious but a spiritual one, a test of truth. The principal question on which the plot hangs—will Gawain hold true to his word?—expresses a primary cultural value of the late Middle Ages, a value by which all could be measured but without which no man could truly claim the title of nobility.[9] Around the edges of the original text, though, readers will find ample evidence that courtly life is ordered around religious ritual, and it is this Christian background that is lessened or omitted altogether in the modern versions. Morpurgo and Shannon remove any reference to Gawain's praying or crossing himself before he spots the castle in the distance; in Philip, he prays for shelter to celebrate Christmas; in Hastings, he prays to Mary for shelter because he is so miserably cold and tired of fighting all the monstrous creatures of the forest; in Hieatt, he prays to hear mass on Christmas morning. Only Hastings's version frames Gawain's meeting with the hostess in the context of having heard mass shortly after he arrives at the castle. Hieatt's version does mention that "the lord conducted Gawain to the chapel, since it was Christmas Eve," but the others omit this detail entirely. Thus only Hieatt and Hastings make explicit reference, through the word "mass," to the Catholic faith that the original text takes for granted.

Another interesting omission that in the original text is clearly linked with religion is the symbol of the pentangle, its significance explicated painstakingly in the original in connection with Gawain's innate goodness. The author explains that Gawain shows perfection in his five senses, always emerges victorious in the endeavors of his five fingers, honors the five wounds of Christ, celebrates the five joys of Mary, and demonstrates the five virtues of generosity, brotherly love, clean mind, faultless manners, and compassion. Although the pentangle fades from the reader's attention as the story moves on (as, indeed, its lessons seem to fade from Gawain's attention as well), it remains as a telling backdrop to the temptation scenes and is eventually replaced by the green girdle that Gawain adopts as his new symbol by the end of the poem. The modern versions either jettison the pentangle altogether or drastically downplay its significance. All of them drop the explication of the five points of the star to which the original devotes forty lines in all (lines 625–65).[10] Shannon's Gawain has no pentangle but instead wears as his talisman the elaborately woven sash that Caryn, his beloved, has given him for the journey. Morpurgo does not mention the pentangle directly but does refer once to "the star of Logres on Gawain's shield."[11] Hastings makes a low-key religious association, calling the pentangle a "holy symbol." Philip and Hieatt make the symbolism more understandable in terms of the poem's subsequent events, but both avoid elaborate explanation. In Philip's version, Gawain himself paints the pentangle, an "emblem of perfect truth," on his shield before setting out; in Hieatt's version, the pentangle is labeled as the "sign of perfection," is worn as Gawain's badge on his shield and on his tunic, and is recalled briefly when Gawain returns to court after his ordeal sporting a different badge, the green girdle.

Whereas the children's authors probably omitted the hunt details because the majority of young readers would not be prepared for such graphic details, here the omission of references to religion or to the pentangle probably has a different motivation. A savvy children's author would most likely skirt issues of religion, at least in an adventure story. Although the original audience would have taken Christianity for granted as an essential part of the culture, today's readers have different expectations. If readers recognize this tale as an adventure story, then they might find the teaching of values acceptable, but not the teaching of doctrine. On the other hand, if it is a story designed for a Christian market—and it seems that the tale could easily be retold in such a way as to make it suitable for this niche—then the Christian aspect would have to be further developed than in the original. In any event, it seems clear that the Christian backdrop is not essential for the modern retellings of this tale, although for the original author and audience that backdrop would be inescapable. In no other framework could a truly noble knight like Sir Gawain operate.

The omission or downplaying of the pentangle in the modern versions is less easy to explain, especially given the detailed explication of this sign in the original. Perhaps the children's authors see it as a plot weakness that the original text first emphasizes and then forsakes further mention of this sign. The poet takes such pains to explain the significance of the pentangle that its absence later in the poem becomes conspicuous, indicating Gawain's ever-growing risk of breaching the perfection that he has adopted as his insignia. Alternatively, perhaps the children's authors fear emphasizing the pentangle because of its possible association with black magic, despite its explicitly positive meaning in the text. In any event, it seems that it would be relatively easy—even desirable—to write a children's version in which the pentangle would play a prominent role, but that is not the case in any of the versions examined here.

Having looked at the major elements omitted or downplayed by these five children's authors, we can turn to the opposite consideration and examine what they all include. While avoiding to a large extent the details of the hunt and religious associations, all of the children's versions tackle to some extent the sexual implications of the plot. Hieatt's version is the most low-key in this regard, as the narrator merely remarks upon the kisses the lady offers without commenting on Gawain's reaction. Hastings's version presses the sexual undertones a bit more but throws greater attention upon Gawain's embarrassment and discomfort, although on the third morning the lady's beauty moves him to a different sentiment: "When he saw how lovely she was, and how ardently she gazed at him, he was gravely tempted to betray his trust."

Morpurgo's version is probably most explicit in delineating Gawain's desire, underlined by the repetition of the word "want." On the morning of the first temptation, the narrator tells us, "The trouble was, he didn't want to resist her, even though he knew he should"; on the second morning, "When she offered him two kisses he did not find it at all difficult to accept, and this time the kisses were sweeter and longer than before, kisses he could not forget even if he had wanted to—and he did not want to"; at dinner that evening, "Although Gawain tried to look the other way, he found he did not want to." Finally, on the third day, he explains regretfully to his hostess that "As a man I want to [love you], but as a knight I must not, I cannot." On this morning the lady "stroked his hair and traced his mouth with her finger"; then "she kissed him three times, and so passionately this time that she left Gawain quite breathless, his heart pounding."[12]

In his version, Philip similarly emphasizes Gawain's desire by trying to capture the tantalizing and very physical nature of what happens to the knight. Years later, as Gawain describes the events of the first morning to his squire, those sensations are still vivid: "All my nerves were outside my skin. She was no nearer me than you are now, but I felt her pressing close, so close that when she moved it was a pain to me."[13]

The lady is least alluring, indeed frightening, in Shannon's version, where the temptation occurs only once, in the middle of the night. Lady Bertilak, as the narrator calls her, steals into the guest chamber, her eyes glowing "with a light so pale and enchanting that Gawain wondered if he might be dreaming." She does not offer herself to him directly but instead wants to exchange her magic sash for the one Gawain is already wearing, a handwoven gift from Caryn (his lady in Arthur's court), which he has promised not to remove until his return. Gawain refuses the exchange without hesitation, protesting, "Your offer is kind. But if I do indeed lose my life, it will be with this sash I now wear tied around my waist. I have made my promise." Interestingly, even though Gawain has no difficulty resisting this single temptation offered him, he still receives a nick from the Green Knight, as "a little souvenir of the North Country."

The fact that none of the authors attempt to dodge the temptation and its consequences makes it clear that this is one of the core elements of the poem. Yet the variations evident in the authors' treatment of the temptation scenes make it equally clear that each modern author must settle upon narrative choices at the outset that indicate his or her own "take" on the story. In other words, in adapting the original text each author must decide on theme. In the case of *Sir Gawain and the Green Knight*, critics who have been reading this poem for years—for generations—have yet to agree on the essential meaning, the theme, of the work. This is one reason the poem remains the center of so much critical attention, for it is rich, suggestive, and elusive enough to evade definition. However, the children's authors must somehow embrace a particular theme in order to shape their adaptations for young readers. To uncover the theme(s) chosen by these authors, we must look closely at each version in light of a few key elements: narrative point of view, the reasons why Gawain originally accepts the Green Knight's challenge, the explanation the Green Knight offers at the end, and Gawain's welcome as he returns to Arthur's court. The versions are discussed in the order of their faithfulness to the original text.

Hieatt's version offers no surprises to readers familiar with the original. Told from the omniscient point of view, the story centers on whether Gawain can live up to his badge of the pentangle, the sign of perfection. In Hieatt's version, as in the original, Gawain steps forth to relieve Arthur of the unseemly task of accepting the Green Knight's challenge, since no other knight comes forward. In language that echoes the original, he characterizes himself as "the least of them [the knights]" and proclaims that "my life is worth little. But I am the first to ask." After Gawain's ordeal, the Green Knight explains that Morgan, Gawain's aunt, sent him to test Arthur's knights; so, when Gawain returns to Arthur's court wearing the green silk, he explains it as a sign of having failed the test: "'This is the sign of my shame and untrustworthiness,' he said. 'Because I did not keep one promise, my perfect star is crossed with a knotted green sash. I shall wear it forever.'" Arthur smiles, though, and orders all the knights to wear green sashes to honor Gawain and to show their love for him. Hieatt's version does dodge various complications that the original offers us, such as Gawain's misogynistic outburst, Morgan's intention to kill Guenevere, and the question of whether the court's acceptance of the green sash will ultimately lead to downfall, as can be inferred from the Troy frame. But taken as a whole, it does justice to the original and frames the story in terms of whether Gawain has lived up to the ideal of truth. Thus Hieatt's version simplifies to some extent the original text but keeps the focus squarely on whether Gawain has kept his word, while retaining as well the problematic element of Gawain's self-debasement at the outset and at the close of his adventure. Is Gawain's self-characterization as the least of the knights, and his extreme humiliation at the end of the tale, a true portrayal of how he sees himself and his actions? Or is there a gap between inner reality and outer show? Hieatt, like the original author, does not raise the question directly but allows it to be rather easily inferred by an astute reader. Thus if we agree that the theme of *Sir Gawain and the Green Knight* is the importance of keeping one's word, the hero may not actually live up to this value despite his success from the perspective of the Green Knight and Arthur's court.

Hastings's version is similar to Hieatt's in that it tells the story from the omniscient point of view and has the Green Knight reveal Morgan as the initiator of the test, sending him to test the renown of Arthur's knights. Gawain here, though, is described by the narrator as the youngest of the knights, one who has not had the chance to prove himself, and so this version is basically an initiation story. Although he has apparently failed the test of truth—the Green Knight states bluntly, "You broke your word"—he also tells him: "You have confessed your guilt and now you are as pure as if you had never been at fault." Gawain takes the girdle as a sign to humble himself, to recall his frailty, but Arthur decrees that all shall wear a green girdle as "a badge of the highest honour and purity of heart." Thus both Hieatt and Hastings stake out the imperative of truth as the major idea for their stories; however, in Hastings's version this adventure marks Gawain's experiential entrance into knighthood.

Philip and Morpurgo, though, write versions that depart significantly from the original text. Immediately apparent is the fact that both elect to tell the tale from the first-person point of view. Changing the narrator from omniscient to first-person, of course, leads to a more direct telling of the story but simultaneously calls into question the narrator's reliability or, at the very least, the question of why the character would choose to tell this tale, and to whom.

In Philip's version, Gawain himself is speaking, as an aged knight near the close of the Arthurian saga, to his young squire. As Gawain lies wounded outside Lancelot's besieged castle, he tells the story with the benefit of hindsight and with a sense of the end of Camelot before him. He explains that he took up the Green Knight's challenge "for shame of looking away when the green knight held my eyes." Considering that as he is speaking, he is exhibiting the extreme obstinacy, the perversity of will, that helps to bring about the downfall of Arthur's court, we see that Gawain has come a long way from a moment of youthful cowardice and that perhaps he has spent his entire knighthood proving himself in reaction to that one moment at the outset of his career. Indeed, later in the story Gawain confirms that what happened in this episode of his life has formed the core of his being: "The three days that followed [i.e., the three days of temptation] are the centre of my life, boy. Everything led to them, or from them."[14]

The explanation of why this test is of such importance may lie in the fact that it reveals a dark side of himself. As he reaches the point in his tale when he accepts the sash, he explains to his squire, "I had thought, boy, I could face out all temptation. Perhaps we never really know ourselves until the last extreme."[15] After striking the third blow, the Green Knight makes it clear that Gawain's wound comes from trusting more in magic than in God. Yet if Gawain learned his lesson then and is now trusting in God, it is clear that as he tells this story near the end of his life, he trusts in the vengeful God of the Old Testament, not the merciful one of the New. Once more, then, we come up against the dark side of Gawain, although quite possibly a young reader would not discern the shadow.

The tale ends, however, on an ironic note that no one can miss. Gawain first tells the squire how all the knights swore to wear the green girdle as a sign of his victory, although he saw it as failure. Then, almost as an afterthought, he adds, "It's a strange thought: no doubt Sir Lancelot is wearing just such a sash, even as we speak."[16] The fact that these two best knights of Arthur's court are still wearing the same sash, yet are at war with each other, expresses beautifully the contradictions and cross-purposes at the heart of the Arthurian legend and emphasizes as well the darkness of being at war with one's brother or with one's self. Philip's version contains Jungian undertones that accord well with the original text but add a level of ironic sadness to this version, for the sash links together forever these two warring knights, ying and yang.[17]

The first-person narrative voice, very effective in Philip's text, works for Morpurgo's version as well, although this time it is Arthur's voice we hear, and we are rooted in the present of the narrative. Arthur's words to Gawain as the young knight prepares to accept the Green Knight's challenge stand as a theme for the work: "Things are not always as they seem."[18] This message is certainly clear in the original text, of course, as Gawain (and first-time readers) miss symbolic cues and take signs at their face value. At the end of Morpurgo's version, in a logically literal demonstration of "things are not always as they seem," the Green Knight transforms before Gawain's eyes into his host and then informs him that his "magic" belt is just an ordinary belt after all. He also informs him that his wife, who in this version causes Gawain to ache with desire, was not what she seemed: "You see, she told me everything. I knew every word that passed between you, every look."[19] Interestingly, at the end of the story Gawain offers to his fellow knights tangible evidence—the belt—as proof of his adventure. Although "things are not always as they seem," this ending goes out of its way to remove the symbolism from the belt and instead make use of it as literal proof that Gawain's story is true. Arthur's narrative voice assures us, though, that this tangible proof is superfluous: "He need not have done so, for knowing Gawain as we all did, none of us seated at the Round Table ever doubted a word of his story."[20] Thus Gawain returns to the acclaim of the other knights, but the adventure has reinforced his already-existing reputation for truth rather than serving as his launching point into this ideal. Another twist in this version is that Arthur's knights do not adopt the green girdle as a collective sign, an omission that further emphasizes its use as a literal token of truth and a refusal to assign to it symbolic value. It is almost as if, once Gawain has passed the test of his adventure, he has also passed beyond the ambiguous world of multiple significance. There is no longer any need to rely on symbolic value, and indeed even the tangible value of the belt as a demonstration of narrative truth is deemed gratuitous.

A secondary theme of Morpurgo's version is the extraordinary behavior required of a knight. One essential knightly quality, of course, is courage. Sir Bernlak, as he is called here, tells Gawain that he was sent by Nemue, the Lady of the Lake, to test the courage of Arthur's knights. Nemue does not actually appear in this version, resulting in a simplification of the original, and the use of "Nemue" rather than "Morgan" removes from this adventure much of the undertone of darkness that would be inescapable for readers familiar with the Arthurian legend. When Gawain first accepts the Green Knight's challenge, he does so in order to prove himself, but not for the first time as in Philip's version. He offers his services to Arthur by saying, "I've rested on my laurels long enough. It is time I proved myself fit again to sit around this table." Finally, when his guide suggests that he flee from the Green Chapel, Gawain explains about Arthur's knights: "We may feel afraid, but we do not flinch and we do not run."[21]

Besides exercising courage, a knight must hold to high standards of moral conduct. Gawain is tested to the limit by the lady but, as already noted, makes the necessary distinction between chivalric and primitive behavior: "As a man I want to," he tells the lady on her final visit, "but as a knight I must not, I cannot." He is torn again after having accepted the belt, for in this version he wears it during the final night of dancing and feasting, and its presence torments him. Although he was able to act rightly by resisting the lady's bodily temptations, thereby differentiating between instinctive and knightly behavior, in accepting the belt he makes the same differentiation but the wrong choice. As he lies in bed that night he realizes, "The belt might save his life the next day, but it would not save his honor. All night long he lay in a turmoil of guilt, but he could not bring himself to hand over the belt and give up his only chance of life." The Green Knight himself makes clear that in this version, Gawain's performance as a knight is being tested. As in the original, he excuses Gawain from blame for wishing to save his life and commends him for resisting sexual temptation: "If you had once weakened and dishonored your knighthood, then I tell you, your head would be lying there at my feet, your life's blood pouring out on the grass."[22]

A final distinction of Morpurgo's version is its humor. The Green Knight, for example, calls Arthur's knights a "motley crew," "dunderheads," and "chickens"; as Gawain prepares to strike off the Green Knight's head, he exclaims, "Kneel, you overgrown leek!"[23] In addition, a touch of whimsy appears in the opening paragraph when Arthur mentions his dog, Bercelet, licking its lips in anticipation of Arthur's feast. Because in this version the host is named Sir Bernlak, the dog's name foreshadows the adventure to come and also seems to be a playful combination of "Bercilak" and "Gringolet."

Despite variations and/or omissions, all of these versions remain relatively faithful to the plot and spirit of the original text. The one children's version that departs radically from the original is Mark Shannon's. In this version, Gawain is a young, untried, nervously stuttering knight whom the others mock. His only defender is a young woman named Caryn, at whom he glances for affirmation just before he strikes off the Green Knight's head. The theme of this version is truth in love, for although Gawain accepts the Green Knight's challenge in order to prove himself, his real test is whether he will remain true to his promise to Caryn that he will wear the sash she has woven for him until he returns to her. As mentioned earlier, in this text Lady Bertilak lets herself into Gawain's room at night, just once rather than on three occasions, and offers to exchange her magical crimson sash for his own, embroidered by Caryn with intricate pictures over the course of the year that Gawain waited for his adventure. His temptation, if we can call it that, is momentary: "The dark folds of the sash seemed to stretch and wind before Gawain like a path through a vast wood. But in his mind's eye, Caryn appeared and his heart rose up." Lady Bertilak leaves without protest when he refuses her sash, but she reappears later, at the Green Chapel, to reinforce her husband's comment on Gawain's worthiness.[24] The Green Knight proclaims, "You proved your knightly passion when you accepted our challenge, and your honesty and courage when you kept your promised rendezvous." The lady chimes in, "Most important of all, you were true to the mysteries of your own heart."

In Shannon's version, then, there are no hunts, no prolonged scenes with the lady, no Morgan behind the story's action. There is only Gawain, who must prove himself courageous and true in order to deserve Caryn. The two are bound together as long as Gawain wears the sash she has woven for him. The innocence of these two young lovers stands in stark contrast to the dark powers of Bertilak and his wife, which might explain why, even though he has not failed in any way, Gawain nevertheless receives a nick from the Green Knight's axe. He has brushed up against death and temptation and cannot remain unscathed as he heads "back toward Caryn, King Arthur and home."

If I have been successful in reaching my objective, this brief excursion through five children's versions of *Sir Gawain and the Green Knight* demonstrates the benefit of reading medieval literature through the lens of necessarily simplified adaptations. Readers familiar with the medieval text will be struck even more forcefully by the complexity of the original by comparing it to the "watered down" versions of modern children's authors. At the same time, a critical reading of the children's versions allows us to track and articulate what the authors see as the bare essentials of the original. In this case, all of the children's authors agree that "truth" is the core of this narrative, but they differ in how to define that truth and how to delineate the proof-tests of that truth.

We can also glean valuable insights into both similarities and differences of the late fourteenth-century English cultural landscape and our own. Truth remains a value to be tested and esteemed, and tales of marvels and monsters fascinate us as much now as ever. Yet elements such as details of the hunt and of dressing the meat, the elaborate (and religious) explication of the significance of the pentangle, the unself-conscious Christian backdrop to the action, and the frame of the Trojan War have receded in importance or disappeared altogether, while a modern young audience can readily handle the innuendoes of the lady's forays into Gawain's bedroom.

Finally, and perhaps most important, the number of available children's versions should cause us to ponder just why this story remains so popular—because it tells the story of a young knight's testing, his *rite de passage*? Because it links sex and danger, even death? Because it is at heart a family romance, a retelling of every child's need to break away from home and ultimately return again? Because it upholds the moral value of keeping one's word at any cost, no matter how tempting the alternatives? In fact, the array of modern children's versions indicates that we will never fix the complete truth of *Sir Gawain and the Green Knight* and condense it into a compact, universally agreed-upon package. That is precisely what constitutes the ongoing appeal of the original—and why children's authors will continue to find this a tale worth retelling.

Notes

1. Because the manuscript provides no titles for these poems, the titles are those assigned by later editors. It thus makes an interesting exercise to come up with alternate titles and to consider how different titles can change our views of the works. The most recent critical edition of the poems is Casey Finch's *The Complete Works of the Pearl-Poet* (Berkeley: University of California Press, 1993), with translation by Finch and facing-page Middle English text edited by Malcolm Andrew, Ronald Waldron, and Clifford Peterson. This volume does include *Saint Erkenwald*.

2. Several critics have considered the poet's works as a whole. See, e.g., Lynn Staley Johnson, *The Voice of the Gawain-Poet* (Madison: University of Wisconsin Press, 1984); Sarah Stanbury, *Seeing the Gawain-Poet: Description and the Act of Perception* (Philadelphia: University of Pennsylvania Press, 1991); Robert J. Blanch and Julian M. Wasserman, *From Pearl to Gawain: Forme to Fynisment* (Gainesville: University Press of Florida, 1995); and Sandra Pierson Prior, *The Fayre Formez of the Pearl Poet* (East Lansing: Michigan State University Press, 1996).

3. It is impossible to acknowledge more than a few of the critics who have developed a wide variety of perspectives on *Sir Gawain and the Green Knight*. What follows is a mere sample, for the sake of illustrating the rich variety of critical stances. Christopher Wrigley's "*Sir Gawain and the Green Knight*: The Underlying Myth" (*Studies in Medieval English Romances: Some New Approaches*, ed. Derek Brewer [Cambridge: D. S. Brewer, 1988], pp. 113–28) considers the poem as a demonstration of Gawain's *rite de passage* from boyhood to knighthood, an idea first advanced by Charles Moorman in "Myth and Medieval Literature: *Sir Gawain and the Green Knight*," *Medieval Studies* 18 (1956): 158–72. Ross Arthur's *Medieval Sign Theory and Sir Gawain and the Green Knight* (Tonawanda: University of Toronto Press, 1987) explores the poem as an educational experience for Gawain and the reader as we learn to read crucial signs within the text. Somewhat related, in terms of commodifying signs within the poem, is R. A. Shoaf's *The Poem as Green Girdle: Commercium in Sir Gawain and the Green Knight* (Gainesville: University Press of Florida, 1984). Feminist approaches to the poem abound, but two of the often-cited early articles are Sheila Fisher's "Leaving Women Aside: Women, History, and

Revisionism in *Sir Gawain and the Green Knight*" (in *The Passing of Arthur: New Essays in Arthurian Tradition*, ed. Christopher Baswell and William Sharpe [New York: Garland, 1988], pp. 129–51, and also in *Arthurian Women: A Casebook*, ed. Thelma S. Fenster [New York: Garland, 1996], pp. 77–95), and "Taken Men and Token Women in *Sir Gawain and the Green Knight*" (in *Seeking the Woman in Late Medieval and Renaissance Writings: Essays in Feminist Contextual Criticism*, ed. Sheila Fisher and Janet E. Halley [Knoxville: University of Tennessee Press, 1989], pp. 71–105). Also noteworthy are Ivo Kamps's "Magic, Women, and Incest: The Real Challenges in *Sir Gawain and the Green Knight*," *Exemplaria* 1 (1989): 313–36, and Geraldine Heng's "Feminine Knots and the Other in *Sir Gawain and the Green Knight*," *PMLA* 106 (1991): 500–14. Clare R. Kinney, on the other hand, in "The (Dis)Embodied Hero and the Signs of Manhood in *Sir Gawain and the Green Knight*" (in *Medieval Masculinities*, ed. Clare A. Lees [Minneapolis: University of Minnesota Press, 1994], pp. 47–57) considers what the poem tells us about medieval masculinities, while David Boyd discusses the poem's "queer" undercurrent in "Sodomy, Misogyny, and Displacement: Occluding Queer Desire in *Sir Gawain and the Green Knight*" (*Arthuriana* 8 [1998]: 77–113). Scholars have also fruitfully interpreted the poem in light of medieval history and culture; recent examples include Carl Lindahl, "*Sir Gawain and the Green Knight* and Myth in Its Time," in *Telling Tales: Medieval Narratives and the Folk Tradition*, ed. Francesca Canade Sautman, Diana Conchado, and Giuseppe Carlo Di Scipio (New York: St. Martin's, 1998), pp. 249–67, and Phillipa Hardman, "Gawain's Practice of Piety in *Sir Gawain and the Green Knight*," *Medium Aevum* 68 (1999): 247–67.

4. Following is complete bibliographic information for these five versions: Constance Hieatt, *Sir Gawain and the Green Knight*, ill. Walter Lorraine (New York: Thomas Y. Crowell Company, 1967); Selina Hastings, *Sir Gawain and the Green Knight*, ill. Juan Wijngaard (New York: Lothrop, Lee & Shepard Books, 1981); Neil Philip, *The Tale of Sir Gawain*, ill. Charles Keeping (New York: Philomel Books, 1987) (chapter 4 is entitled "Sir Gawain and the Green Knight"); Michael Morpurgo, *Arthur: High King of Britain,* ill. Michael Foreman (New York: Harcourt Brace, 1994) (chapter 7 is entitled "Gawain and the Green Knight"); Mark Shannon, *Gawain and the Green Knight*, ill. David Shannon (New York: G. P. Putnam's Sons, 1994). Note that only Morpurgo's and Philip's versions include page numbers for citation.

5. For a discussion of the Troy frame, see, e.g., Malcolm Andrew's "The Fall of Troy in *Sir Gawain and the Green Knight* and *Troilus and Criseyde*," in *The European Tragedy of Troilus*, ed. Piero Boitani (Oxford: Clarendon, 1989), pp. 75–93. Leo Carruthers discusses the closing motto and its applicability to the poem in "The Duke of Clarence and the Earls of March: Garter Knights and *Sir Gawain and the Green Knight*" (*Medium Aevum* 70 [2001]: 66–79).

6. For a summary of criticism on this intriguing passage, a critical crux of the poem, see Julian Wasserman and Robert Blanch, "Gawain's Antifeminism: From Gollancz and Tolkien to the Millennium," *Medieval Perspectives* 15.2 (2000): 21–33.

7. Philip, *The Tale of Gawain*, p. 33.

8. Several critics have turned their attention to the hunt scenes in the original text. See, e.g., Henry L. Savage, "The Significance of the Hunting Scenes in *Sir Gawain and the Green Knight*," *Journal of English and Germanic Philology* 27 (1928): 1–15; Peter McClure, "Gawain's *mesure* and the Significance of the Three Hunts in *Sir Gawain and the Green Knight*," *Neophilologus* 57 (1973): 375–87; Gerald Morgan, "The Action of the Hunting and Bedroom Scenes in *Sir Gawain and the Green Knight*," *Medium Aevum* 56 (1987): 200–16; and Anne Rooney, "The Hunts in *Sir Gawain and the Green Knight*," in *A Companion to the Gawain-Poet*, ed. Derek Brewer and Jonathan Gibson (Woodbridge, UK: Boydell and Brewer, 1999), pp. 157–63.

9. See J. Douglas Canfield, *Word as Bond in English Literature from the Middle Ages to the Restoration* (Philadelphia: University of Pennsylvania Press, 1989).

10. I have chosen to use the lines as numbered in a version easily accessible to undergraduate students of the poem, Marie Boroff's translation in *The Norton Anthology of English Literature, Volume I*, 6th edn. (New York: Norton, 1993), pp. 202–54. Scholars of the poem may wish to refer to Casey Finch's *Complete Works of the Pearl Poet* for the text of the original.

11. Morpurgo, *Arthur: High King of Britain*, p. 72.

12. Morpurgo, *Arthur: High King of Britain*, pp. 76–77.

13. Philip, *The Tale of Sir Gawain*, p. 33.

14. Philip, *The Tale of Sir Gawain*, p. 33.

15. Philip, *The Tale of Sir Gawain*, p. 36.

16. Philip, *The Tale of Sir Gawain*, p. 38.

17. Philip's version also provides an interesting twist on the phenomenon of the young and old ladies in the original text. The hostess and her elderly companion, eventually revealed to be Morgan le Fay, are sometimes appraised as two halves of the same person; Heng goes even further to link Guenevere, the Virgin Mary, the hostess, and Morgan (502–03). Thus Philip's device of using the green sash to link together Gawain and Lancelot is a creative twist that may spring from the original text's impulse to link together the women of the narrative.

18. Philip, *The Tale of Sir Gawain*, p. 71.

19. Morpurgo, *Arthur: High King of Britain*, p. 81.

20. Morpurgo, *Arthur: High King of Britain*, p. 81.

21. Morpurgo, *Arthur: High King of Britain*, pp. 71, 78.

22. Morpurgo, *Arthur: High King of Britain*, pp. 76, 77, 81.

23. Morpurgo, *Arthur: High King of Britain*, pp. 71, 72.

24. The lady's presence at the Green Chapel represents, of course, a radical departure from the original narrative, in which the Green Knight invites Gawain to return to the ladies in the castle now that Gawain has "passed" his test. The thought of facing the lady and Morgan leads Gawain into his vitriolic speech about the dangers of women, a speech precluded by the lady's presence in Shannon's version.

CHAPTER 5

THE SENSE OF PLACE IN ARTHURIAN FICTION FOR YOUNGER READERS

Raymond H. Thompson

During the Middle Ages, stories of King Arthur and his knights of the Round Table circulated most widely in the form of romance. Medieval romance, however, pays scant attention to the historical and geographical context of the events recounted. Thus, George R. Stewart, Jr., although he argues that Sir Thomas Malory is more specific than are his sources, nevertheless admits, "the geography [of medieval romance] is certainly hazy."[1] Moreover, while the setting is medievalized, few actual features of that setting are described, even though they are often heightened by exaggeration, as Dorothy Everett points out: "The dresses and armour, the feasts and hunts, were cut to the pattern of things known, but on those patterns the romancer embroidered every splendour his imagination could conjure up."[2] As a result, adventures take place in a world that is, by and large, removed from common experience by a combination of vagueness and exaggeration.

The novel genre, by contrast, with its concern for verisimilitude, does endeavor to create a plausible setting for the events that unfold, and so we should expect to find there a clearer sense of place. Certainly this is the case in William Mayne's *Earthfasts* (1966), which describes the Yorkshire Dales in closely observed detail:

> Below them, the way they had come, the town was laid out, castle and houses, on the arteries of the valley. The brow of Haw Bank hung above to one side, and far off was the Wold country and the North York Moors, the Cleveland and Howardian Hills with their white cliffs and plantations; and all tufted with the same cloud and drizzle.[3]

Earthfasts is placed in a modern setting into which the sleeping King Arthur and his knights are aroused by the removal of a candle from their cavern.[4] Arthurian novels are, however, placed in a wide variety of settings, ranging from the Dark Ages of the fifth and sixth centuries,[5] through the High Middle Ages portrayed in medieval romance and the contemporary setting familiar to all of us, to the future that may one day await humanity. They extend even to a supernatural otherworld filled with magical creatures and to a world with an alternate history as envisioned in *The Stolen Lake* (1981) by Joan Aiken. Indeed some novels include more than one such setting: in *The Third Magic* (1988), by Welwyn Wilton Katz, the protagonist is drawn from the contemporary world into the other world of Nwm, then moved back to our world during the Dark Ages, before returning to Nwm.

The Third Magic provides a map of Nwm, a practice common in fantasy fiction, and this attention to geographical and topographical accuracy is one means by which authors establish a sense of place in modern Arthurian fiction. Thus maps are supplied of the legendary Isle of Fincayra, visited by the young Merlin in T. A. Barron's five-novel fantasy series, "The Lost Years of Merlin" (1996–2000), and of post-Roman Britain in *The Lantern Bearers* (1959) by Rosemary Sutcliff. They help the reader to envisage the journeys of the protagonists within their world.

Maps are much rarer in novels set in the present and in the High Middle Ages. In the former, not only are the place names more familiar, but the important journeys are likely to take place in time, whether by modern young people traveling into the past or by figures from the past traveling, or sometimes surviving, into the present.[6] Nancy Bond does supply a map of the Cardigan Bay area of Wales in her novel *A String in the Harp* (1976), but that helps to locate not only place names that are difficult for most English speakers but also the sites where events occur in the sixth century as well as the present. In his Arthur trilogy, of which *Arthur: The Seeing-Stone* (2000) and *Arthur: At the Crossing-Places* (2001) have been published to date, Kevin Crossley-Holland also supplies maps of part of the Welsh Marches about the year 1200, but they relate to the narrator's life rather than to his visions of King Arthur. Even without maps, however, many authors still strive for topographical accuracy, as, for example, do both Susan Cooper in her series "The Dark Is Rising" (1965–77), which takes place primarily in a modern setting (albeit with journeys through time),[7] and E. M. R. Ditmas in *Gareth of Orkney* (1956), which is set in the High Middle Ages.

The latter tells the story of Gareth, the nephew of King Arthur, and it follows Malory's account closely. As a novel, however, it endeavors to provide more credible characterization and setting than is called for in the romance genre. Unlike Malory's "Tale of Sir Gareth," which starts with the arrival of Gareth at Arthur's court, Ditmas's novel opens on the main island of Orkney, from the cliffs of which Gareth and his two companions watch a ship approach. The geographical details of this opening scene are accurate, as a scrutiny of modern maps reveals: the ship rounds the point of Hunda,[8] a small island to the south. Since it is noon and the sun is shining on their northern island, the boys must shade their eyes with their hands to observe the vessel as it approaches from the south. Then one of them moves "further westwards so that he could overlook the little valley that cut the island at this, its narrowest, point." From this vantage point he spots a welcoming party approaching from "the castle and townlet of Kirkevaag in the north."[9] This is modern Kirkwall: "Placed on a gentle eminence overlooking the natural harbour, it also commanded the road to the southern bay and thus controlled the two safest landing-places in the island."[10] Even the "conical hill on the north-west of the valley in which was that subterranean chamber known locally as the Dwarf's House"[11] is an accurate description of Grain or Grainbank, an Iron Age souterrain (underground passage) near Kirkwall. The long passage through which one must enter is less than three feet high, and so Gareth is forced to crawl in order to enter and leave the chamber.

The attention to topography found in this completely original episode is preserved throughout the novel, as Gareth travels to Arthur's court at Caerleon-upon-Usk in South Wales, then to Lyonnesse on the south coast of Cornwall to rescue its Lady. Few novels set in the High Middle Ages are as attentive to topography as this, however. Like their romance models, they focus instead upon the process of learning lessons through experience, as is the case in *The Sword in the Tree* (1956) by Clyde Robert Bulla and in "Merlin's Knight School" (1993), first in a series of humorous tales by Michael Markiewicz about the childhood of Arthur and Cai. Yet some do exploit the geographical vagueness of their modes for humorous effect, as do two other novels based on Malory's story of Gareth: *The Dragon's Quest* (1961) by Rosemary Manning and *The Savage Damsel and the Dwarf* (2000) by Gerald Morris. In the former, Sir Gryfflet assures his friend the dragon that they cannot be lost:

> "I think we are still going in a westerly direction, aren't we? The sun always seems to be behind us."
> "Gryfflet," said the dragon, "does it occur to you that the sun is not always in the same place?"
> "Isn't it?" asked Gryfflet, looking alarmed.[12]

In the latter, Lynet is impressed by the dwarf's keen sense of direction:

> "I suppose women are different that way." Lynet sighed.

"Don't make yourself so special," the dwarf said with a snort. "As if getting lost was some trick that only women knew. I've known men who could get lost in their own bedrooms. The only difference is that men with no sense of direction don't brag about it, the way women do."[13]

Yet accurate topography, while of concern to knowledgeable readers, is but a start of the process of establishing a sense of place in modern novels. More importantly, the author must create a credible physical and cultural setting of a world that is often very different from that of modern readers. Thus while the geography of Bulla's novel is vague, the brief description of the foggy woods through which young Shan and his mother flee is as credible as the bed of nettles into which Arthur slips in Markiewicz's story. The location of the castle in which young Artos is reared in *The Dragon's Boy* (1985) by Jane Yolen is not well identified, but the setting is otherwise clearly visualized. Artos gets his feet soaked in pursuit of a hound in the watery fen near the castle: "The fen was a low, hummocky place full of brown pools and quaking mosses; and in the slow, floating waters there was an abundance of duckweed and frog-bit, mile after mile of it looking the same."[14]

A favorite device to facilitate the process of creating a sense of place is to send the protagonists on a journey, as in fact happens in all the novels just discussed. This allows authors not only to map out the geography of the route but also to give their characters a reason to observe more closely details of the new and unfamiliar surroundings that they encounter. In Diana L. Paxson's "Wild Man" (1995), Lunet journeys north in search of Mirdyn (Merlin) who is running mad among the wild men of the Great Caledonian Forest. She notices first how the "oak forest was giving way to stands of pine,"[15] and then she enters the Caledonian Forest itself:

> But where mature pines grew more sparsely the earth might be covered by a brilliant green carpet of moss, or on the higher slopes, with heather and bilberries. Sometimes the pines shared the ground with silver birch or shapely rowan, and where the bald crowns of the hills broke through the trees, sturdy junipers clung to the scree.[16]

In Monica Furlong's *Juniper* (1990), Juniper, the daughter of King Mark of Cornwall, is struck by the sparse furnishings in the hut of the wise woman from whom she hopes to learn the healing arts. She examines them closely, reflecting that the luxuries she "had been accustomed to at home seemed unimaginable here."[17] After struggling in vain to light a fire with moss and "big pieces of wood. . .it occurred to me that the twigs might light more easily."[18] Her efforts still prove unsuccessful, until she remembers seeing servants at home cleaning out the ashes before lighting the fire: "I took down my pyramid of wood, cleared away the ashes with a shovel that lay before the hearth, relaid the fire, and repeated the procedure with the tinderbox. This time, to my delight, the twigs flared up."[19] The situation is unfamiliar to the narrator because she is a princess, and it enables the author not only to describe the setting in detail but also to involve her young readers imaginatively in the task of lighting a fire, something they have less experience with these days than they might once have had. Later she travels to the house of another wise woman where she learns to spin and weave.

Whereas girls like Juniper learn domestic and healing skills, boys undergo different training. In *The Hidden Treasure of Glaston* (1946) by Eleanore M. Jewett, young Hugh is taken by his father to Glastonbury Abbey, where he learns the skills of a scribe: cutting new quills, mixing ink, cleaning and preparing parchments in the scriptorium. In Anne McCaffrey's *Black Horses for the King* (1996, expanded from her short story, "Black Horses for a King," 1995), Galwyn leaves his berth on his uncle's ship to follow Artos, Count of Britain, and in his service he learns all about the care of horses, particularly the craft of farriery—shoeing horses. On many an unfamiliar road and on his lord's distant farm, in stables listening to whickering horses and in forges "inhaling the odd odours of hot metal and coal,"[20] Galwyn observes closely, and the powers of observation that make him so apt a pupil allow the author to recreate his world in careful detail.

In Arthurian fiction, however, most boys train to be warriors (in the Dark Ages) or knights (in the High Middle Ages), and in the latter case they often learn the duties of page and squire in a distant household. Thus it is that Arthur leaves his home to become Lord Stephen's squire at Holt Castle in Crossley-Holland's *Arthur: At the Crossing Places*, and Terence leaves the hermitage to become Gawain's squire at Camelot in *The Squire's Tale* (1998) by Gerald Morris. The need to discharge their new duties efficiently gives them good reason to take careful note of their new surroundings.

In some of these novels, such as *Page Boy for King Arthur* (1949) and *Squire for King Arthur* (1955), both by Eugenia Stone, and Catherine Owen Peare's *Melor, King Arthur's Page* (1963), the primary concern is to supply information about life in the Middle Ages as well as to warn against the dangers of thoughtless behavior. Indeed, the thoughtlessness of Tor, the hero of Stone's first novel, allows the author to introduce readers to a number of activities in a typical medieval castle. Because he is a dreamer, Tor keeps forgetting his responsibilities—at one point, the castle nearly burns down because he becomes so engrossed in watching the squires joust that he forgets his duty to tend the fire. As a result, Tor is moved from task to task, helping in turn the cook, the falconer, and the armorer, before being promoted to the rank of page boy. For despite his mistakes, Tor is kind and brave.

The setting in these three novels, however, while it does endeavor to recreate the medieval world, is not localized. Indeed, the authors are more interested in providing insight into a typical medieval castle than in any one place in particular. The setting certainly presents challenges to the young protagonists, and in dealing with these, they learn the importance of responsible behavior. But it provides no clear sense of place. Indeed, the description of the Saxons in Stone's *Squire for King Arthur* blends elements of the Dark Ages and High Middle Ages in an anachronistic fashion.

Another variation upon this strategy of placing characters in an unfamiliar setting takes place in *The Third Magic* by Katz and *The Minstrel Boy* (1997) by Sharon Stewart. Here the protagonists, both Canadian teenagers, travel back in time from the twentieth century, observing earlier customs with inexperienced eyes.[21] In the latter novel, David proves inept at weapon drill and the various practical tasks, such as cleaning pots in cold river water, that are expected of young people, and his fumbling discomfort heightens our awareness of the harsh realities of life in Dark Age Wales.[22] Since everybody is expected to contribute to the survival of the clan, he is saved from expulsion because his musical talent (on guitar in his own time) enables him to learn to play the harp, and because of the help he receives from Emrys and Bear. Only later does he discover that they are the Merlin and Arthur of legend.

Among the many novels for younger readers, however, two stand out for their mastery of the sense of place. They are *The Sword in the Stone* (1938) by T. H. White and *The Lantern Bearers* by Rosemary Sutcliff. Like the novels of Stone and Peare, *The Sword in the Stone*, which describes the childhood of Arthur, is also concerned to provide insight into life in a typical medieval castle. We are given extensive detail about hawking and hunting, two of the major activities of the aristocracy. Both the kennels for the dogs and the mews for the hawks are carefully described:

> At one end of the Mews there was a little fireplace and a kind of snuggery. . . here there were a couple of stools, a cauldron, a bench with all sorts of small knives and surgical instruments, and some shelves with pots on them. The pots were labeled Cardamum, Ginger, Barley Sugar, Wrangle, For a Snurt, For the Craye, Vertigo, etc. There were leather skins hanging up, which had been snipped about as pieces were cut out of them for jesses, hoods or leashes. . .A special shelf, and the most beautiful of all, held the hoods: very old cracked rufter hoods. . .tiny hoods for the merlins, small hoods for the tiercels, splendid new hoods which had been knocked up to pass away the long winter evenings.[23]

Such careful, even loving, detail goes beyond mere instruction. White not only teaches the reader about the mews where hawks are kept but also helps us to recreate it by providing so full a picture.[24] His lists, moreover, suggest the untidiness of human life, of a place where work is ongoing:

> On the bench there was a jumble of oddments such as are to be found in every workshop, bits of cord, wire, metal, tools, some bread and cheese which the mice had been at, a leather bottle, some frayed gauntlets for the left hand, nails, bits of sacking, a couple of lures and some rough tallies scratched on the wood.[25]

Part of White's technique here is to invite comparison with a setting that is familiar to most people, even today. The workshop is still to be found in many homes and businesses, and most of us recognize the pattern of clutter, even if some of the details may vary. These are details, moreover, that a child would notice more readily than an adult, who is more likely to be concerned with the tasks to be completed in the workshop than with its contents. To the child, gazing with the eye of a visitor rather than a worker, such objects are both curious and fascinating.

When he describes places that are no longer familiar, White gives helpful advice about how to proceed.[26] The Castle of the Forest Sauvage, where young Arthur (or the Wart, as he is called) grows up, is still standing, he tells us, "and you can see its lovely ruined walls with ivy on them, standing broached to the sun and wind."[27] After describing its present appearance, he continues:

> If you are a sensible person, you will spend days there, possibly weeks, working out for yourself by detection which were the stables, which the mews, where were the cow byres, the armory, the lofts, the well, the smithy, the kennel, the soldiers' quarters, the priest's room, and my lord's and lady's chambers. Then it will all grow about you again. The little people—they were much smaller than we are, and it would be a job for most of us to get inside the few bits of their armor and old gloves that remain—will hurry about in the sunshine, the sheep will baa as they always did, and perhaps from Wales there will come the ffff-put of the triple-feathered arrow which looks as if it had never moved.[28]

Such imaginative creation comes more easily to children than to adults, and it is a vital element in most of the games they play. Thus the Wart's reaction to this world, so carefully recreated by the imagination, seems natural:

> This place was, of course, a complete paradise for a boy to be in. The Wart ran about it like a rabbit in its own complicated labyrinth. He knew everything, everywhere, all the special smells, good climbs, soft lairs, secret hiding-places, jumps, slides, nooks, larders and blisses. For every season he had the best place, like a cat, and he yelled and ran and fought and upset people and

snoozed and daydreamed and pretended he was a Knight, without ever stopping.[29]

Even when he describes a supernatural event, like Merlyn's transformation of the Wart into a fish, White helps us to visualize the setting by explaining how the world would look to a fish:

> In order to imagine yourself in the Wart's position, you will have to picture a round horizon, a few inches above your head, instead of the flat horizon which you have usually seen. Under this horizon of air you have to imagine another horizon of water, spherical and practically upside down—for the surface of the water acted partly as a mirror to what was below it.[30]

"It is," White confides, "difficult to imagine,"[31] but those of us who have swum underwater and looked up to the surface, or perhaps looked at the surface of a fish tank from below, will have some idea of what he describes. Such discoveries, moreover, are probably first made in childhood.

White does, to some extent, localize his story. The Castle of the Forest Sauvage is set in the Welsh Marches from which the Wart, Kay, and Ector travel to London for the tournament. As they pass through the countryside, however, it is the general terrain that White describes, instead of naming specific places. "The road, or track, ran most of the time along the high ridges of the hills or downs,"[32] he tells us. "On the whole it was an England without civilization. The better roads were cleared of cover for a bowshot on either side of them, lest the traveler should be slain by hidden thieves."[33] Such a description provides useful historical information about conditions throughout medieval England rather than in any one area. More importantly, however, it helps to visualize the landscape through which the travelers pass.

What enables White to go beyond mere geographical and historical authenticity, thus, whether for verisimilitude or instruction, and to provide a sense of place in *The Sword in the Stone*, is the care that he takes to help us recreate his world in our imagination. He succeeds because he provides such rich detail and helpful instructions on how to visualize that world. There is, however, another important element in that success: his affection for the world that he describes. This is noticeable from the start, in the description of the haymaking:

> It was July, and real July weather, such as they only had in old England. Everybody went bright brown like Red Indians, with startling teeth and flashing eyes. The dogs moved about with their tongues hanging out, or lay panting in bits of shade, while the farm horses sweated through their coats and flicked their tails and tried to kick horseflies off their bellies with their great hind hoofs.[34]

The affection recurs in the description of Christmas night in the Castle of the Forest Sauvage, with snow on the battlements "like extremely thick icing." And on the roofs of the village where "it occasionally slid off. . .when it saw a chance of falling upon some amusing character and giving pleasure to all"; "there was skating on the moat, which roared all day with the gliding steel, while hot chestnuts and spiced mead were served on the bank to all and sundry"; "cooks put out all the crumbs they could for the small birds"; and "reddest of all shone the cottage fires all down the main street of an evening, while the winds howled outside and the old English wolves wandered about slavering in an appropriate manner, or sometimes peeping in at the keyholes with their blood-red eyes."[35]

There is more than a note of humor in this picture-perfect depiction, but the affection is undeniable. White is, after all, drawing upon his own childhood memories and investing them with a happiness heightened not only by the safe distance of adulthood, but also by his concern over the approach of war.[36] As a pacifist, he considered mankind's suicidal march toward destruction to be as mindless as that of the ants whose behavior he castigates in the revised version of the story for *The Once and Future King* (1958). The hopes and idealism of youth were all the more precious for being so cruelly betrayed.

It is this sense of something precious that has been lost that gives such power to *The Once and Future King*. In this, White is true to the spirit of his source, Sir Thomas Malory, who laments at the conclusion of *Le Morte Darthur*, "Lo ye all Englysshemen, se ye nat what a myschyff here was? For he that was the moste kynge and nobelyst knyght of the worlde, and moste loved the felyshyp of noble knyghtes, and by hym they all were upholdyn, and yet myght nat thes Englyshemen holde them contente with hym."[37] Fuller development of the sense of loss lies in the future, when White continues with the books that were eventually assembled as *The Once and Future King*,[38] but the groundwork is laid in the affection and nostalgia with which the author depicts his settings in *The Sword in the Stone*. Ironically, the affectionate nostalgia and the sense of loss were to prove both the great strengths and weaknesses of White's work, but since the later books are for adult rather than younger readers, that is a subject that lies outside the scope of this essay. Here it must suffice to say that *The Sword in the Stone* develops such a powerful sense of place by the three means discerned: encouraging readers to use their imagination; providing it with a rich supply of detail in order to recreate the Arthurian world; and describing that world with an affectionate nostalgia. This is one of the reasons why White's book is recognized as one of the most important Arthurian novels for younger readers.

The other novel, I would argue, is *The Lantern Bearers* by Rosemary Sutcliff, which won the Carnegie Medal as the outstanding book for children in the United Kingdom in 1959. Whereas White's Arthurian world is set in the High Middle Ages, Sutcliff depicts Britain after the withdrawal of the last Roman garrisons in the fifth century. Aquila, a decurion commanding a troop of Auxiliary Cavalry, chooses to stay and fight for Britain rather than leave with his men. A Saxon raiding party attacks the family farm, however, and burns it to the ground after killing his father and their workers. His sister is abducted and he himself tied to a tree for wolves to devour. Another band of raiders finds him, however, and carries him off as a thrall. This harsh experience is compounded when he meets his sister again, for although she helps him escape, she refuses to leave her Saxon husband and their child. An angry and embittered Aquila makes his way to the camp of Ambrosius, the British leader, to resume his struggle against the invaders.

The dominant pattern in *The Lantern Bearers* is one of loss, suffering, and eventual redemption through love,[39] and it is both reflected and enriched by the careful use of setting, particularly the symbolism of the lantern and the damson tree. We first encounter "the old spreading damson tree" in front of the farmstead where Aquila and his family live. On leave from garrison duty, Aquila is "piercingly aware" that he is "living in a world that might fall to pieces at any moment," and it heightens his appreciation of his home and its occupants, particularly his beloved sister Flavia: "She drew up her knees and clasped her arms round them, tipping up her head to the sunshine that rimmed the damson leaves with gold and made the little dark damsons seem almost transparent."[40]

Shortly after, a wandering bird-catcher approaches, bearing a basket and a lantern on a pole; he, it emerges, is a messenger for those, like Aquila's father, who seek help from Rome. But just as "the sunlight faded. . .and the twilight came lapping up the valley like a quiet tide" with onset of night, so Aquila's "world had begun falling to pieces."[41] Recalled from leave, he learns that all remaining troops are being withdrawn from Britain and that the navigation light where his garrison is stationed will be left untended. As he walks by the tower, he notes, "The light was beginning to fade; soon the beacon would be lit, and the night after it would be lit, and the night after that, and then there would be no more Rutupiae Light."[42] Aquila, however, recognizing he "belonged to Britain," deserts the Eagles and, in a final gesture of both farewell to his old world and "defiance against the dark,"[43] he lights the beacon after the ships have sailed.

He returns to the farm, but when the Saxons come to slay and burn, they leave but "the scorched and shrivelled skeleton of the damson tree."[44] In captivity, Aquila learns that his family was betrayed by the bird-catcher, and that "more than one hearth was warm enough then, that's cold and blackened now."[45] Images of light and warmth, of "sitting on the sunwarmed steps where they had sat as children," are replaced by those of darkness and cold, of long winter nights "on the tide-swept, gale-torn shores of Western Juteland," and they reflect the bitterness and despair of Aquila's life as a thrall.[46] Even when he returns to Britain more than two years later, landing close to the Rutupiae Light, his prospects of escape remain bleak: "There was no beacon-light now in the windy spring darkness. . .coming back to his own world at last, [he] had found it dead and cold, and himself alone in it."[47]

Nevertheless, with his sister's help he does escape, and he takes service with Ambrosius to fight against the Saxons. He keeps people at a distance, however, "always in a kind of armour, and a man who does that cannot have friends."[48] The name he earns, "the Lone Wolf," links him with the Sea Wolves who destroyed his home. At Ambrosius's insistence, he reluctantly takes a wife, Ness, but his coldness blights their relationship, and this is reflected in the description of the apple orchard of her home. When he first sees her, it is sunny, filled with color and laughter, but this changes after he is promised her hand in marriage: "The gold was gone from the orchard, even the apples had lost their warmth of colour, and the branches swayed in the small, chill wind."[49]

To escape the darkness in his heart, Aquila must learn to care for others again. The scene in which he recognizes just how much his wife and infant son have come to mean to him is mirrored by the spring promise of another damson tree: "The damson tree that grew beside the door was thickening into bud, the shadows of its branches stirring and dappling on the old sunlit wall and over Ness herself."[50] Because he offers to let her leave with her father and the rest of her own departing clan should herself choose to do so, Aquila demonstrates the sacrifice that marks true love. But to gain full redemption, he must learn not only to care for his new family but also to forgive, and let go, his old one. His resentment at his sister for refusing to escape with him arises, after all, from a selfish possessiveness. He does take this final step when he saves his sister's son from among the enemy wounded after a battle, and helps him escape home to rejoin his mother. The enigmatic message that he sends, "I'm your long-lost brother,"[51] even acknowledges that he was at fault.

Later, a friend tells him,

> "It was once told me that the great beacon light of Rutupiae was seen blazing *after* the last of the Eagles flew from Britain. I have always felt that was. . .a symbol. . .I sometimes think that we stand at sunset. . . .It may be that the night will close over us in the end, but I believe that morning will come again. Morning always grows out of the darkness, though maybe not for the people who saw the sun go down. We are the Lantern Bearers, my friend; for us to keep something burning, to carry what light we can forward into the darkness and the wind."[52]

As he returns home that night, he has all at once "a feeling of great riches," flowing from the love of wife, son, sister, friends like Eugenus, Artos, and Ambrosius—and his own heart:

> He looked up at the old damson tree, and saw the three stars of Orion's belt tangled in the snowy branches. Someone, maybe Ness, had hung out a lantern in the colonnade, and in the starlight and the faint and far-most fringe of the lantern glow it was as though the damson tree had burst into blossom; fragile, triumphant blossom all along the boughs.[53]

Sutcliff is much more selective in the details with which she describes surroundings than is White. She did, after all, train as a miniaturist painter.[54] The details are, however, precisely observed and invested with a significance that enriches both characters and theme. The damson tree is an image of Aquila's heart: warm, sunlit, laden with fruit, leaves rimmed with gold in his happy younger days surrounded by those he loves; scorched by the red violence that destroys his home and family; dark and shriveled during his thralldom and early vengeful years, alone and angry; thickening into spring bud and dappling the wall with sun and shadow when he discovers how much he cares for his wife and son; finally bursting into fragile, triumphant blossom to celebrate the victory of love over hate. The lantern, which at the end of the novel casts its glow upon the damson tree, is a symbol of defiance against the dark, of preserving something of value amidst the ruin of one's hopes. The bird-catcher's lantern and the beacon at Rutupiae, representing the old links with Roman civilization, are both extinguished, enshrouding the world of the Romano-Britons in cold and wintry darkness. Yet hope endures, buried deep in the heart where it is nurtured by the care that we feel for others and receive in our turn—for friends and family, and even valiant foes like old Bruni—until finally it bursts into the flame of full-fledged love: "I feel as though I could warm my hands at you, in that gown," Aquila says, as he gazes at Ness in her "gown of thick, soft wool the colour of the apple flames."[55] The achievement has been hard won and it remains precarious, the darkness still threatens and may eventually overwhelm them all, but there is time, for a while at least, to feel grateful for present mercies, to appreciate what has been gained rather than lament what has been lost. The light that the Lantern Bearers carry forward into the darkness and the wind is, when all is said and done, the light of love, and it burns the more brightly in the night, and down through the ages, because of their unselfish sacrifices.

In medieval romance, scenes that provide a sense of place are rare enough that their appearance is noticeable, for example, the Grail Castle visited by Perceval in *Le Conte del Graal* by Chrétien de Troyes, and the frozen wilderness through which Gawain rides in *Sir Gawain and the Green*

Knight. As one would expect, such scenes are more plentiful in modern fiction where they serve to provide a credible context for the events that unfold, and this is particularly true of stories set in the modern period and Dark Ages. In the more thoughtful works, however, they may also help to develop character and theme: characters respond with courage and resourcefulness to the hardships of the journey and the unfamiliar conditions that they encounter in new places; theme is enriched by creation of mood like the nostalgic affection in White's *Sword in the Stone* and by the symbolism of features like the damson tree and the lantern in Sutcliff's *Lantern Bearers.* When authors choose to do so and possess the talent, they can create a sense of place that not only engages the imagination but also enriches their vision in the novel.

Finally, it is interesting to observe how these two fine novels complement each other. Both the Wart and Aquila feel deep affection for their home and the people who live there, and they leave them very reluctantly. Much of the bitterness that marks the later books of *The Once and Future King* and *The Book of Merlyn* (1977), as well as the attitude of Aquila, results from a deep sense of loss and an anger at the betrayal of that important childhood trust in the security offered by home. As a result, they both turn against their fellows. Aquila, however, finds redemption because he learns to open his heart again, to cherish his new home and family and not just resent past injuries, to carry the light "forward into the darkness and the wind." White, sadly, was less fortunate. At the end of *The Once and Future King*, he uses a very similar image, that of a candle in the wind, to describe Arthur's vision of using force to serve justice,[56] but the hope that it offers is undercut by the misanthropy of *The Book of Merlyn*. It is a warning against clinging too tightly to the things of this world, even to the places that we love.

Notes

1. "English Geography in Malory's 'Morte D'Arthur,'" *Modern Language Review* 30 (1935): 205 [204–09]. Anne Wilson, in *Traditional Romance and Tale: How Stories Mean* (Ipswich, UK: D. S. Brewer, 1976), maintains, "The purpose of these references to time and place is not only to give credibility to the pretence that the events of the story actually occurred historically, but also to distance the events of the story" (p. 57).

2. "A Characterization of the English Medieval Romance," in *Essays on Middle English Literature* (Oxford: Oxford University Press, 1955), p. 8 [1–22].

3. William Mayne, *Earthfasts* (Harmondsworth, Middlesex, UK: Puffin, 1969), pp. 71–72.

4. For a discussion of the cave legend attached to King Arthur and his knights, see *The New Arthurian Encyclopedia*, ed. Norris J. Lacy et al. (New York: Garland, 1991), pp. 76–77. For its appearance in modern fiction, see

Raymond H. Thompson, *The Return from Avalon: A Study of the Arthurian Legend in Modern Fiction* (Westport, CT: Greenwood, 1985), especially pp. 91, 98–99, and 103–04.

5. For a discussion of some attempts to establish an authentic Dark Age setting, see Dan Nastali, "Arthur Without Fantasy: Dark Age Britain in Recent Historical Fiction," *Arthuriana* 9.1 (Spring 1999): 5–22.

6. American novels that use this motif are discussed by Alan Lupack and Barbara Tepa Lupack, in *King Arthur in America* (Cambridge, UK: D. S. Brewer, 1999), pp. 303–05.

7. The author describes her care over topography in an interview that I conducted with her in 1989: see "An Interview," in Susan Cooper, *Dreams and Wishes: Essays on Writing for Children* (New York: McElderry/Simon & Schuster, 1996), pp. 193–94 [186–97]. This is reproduced electronically in Raymond H. Thompson, *Taliesin's Successors: Interviews with Authors of Modern Arthurian Literature* (1999) <http://www.lib.rochester.edu/ camelot/ intrvws/ cooper.htm> and also reprinted in full in this volume as "Interview with Susan Cooper."

8. E. M. R. Ditmas, *Gareth of Orkney* (London: Faber and Faber, 1956), p. 13.

9. Ditmas, *Gareth of Orkney*, p. 16.

10. Ditmas, *Gareth of Orkeny*, p. 25.

11. Ditmas, *Gareth of Orkney*, p. 19.

12. Rosemary Manning, *The Dragon's Quest* (Harmondsworth, Middlesex, UK: Penguin, 1974), p. 18. Like Ditmas, Manning takes care over geography, particularly when the dragon and Gareth pursue their respective quests, through the Mendip Hills, across the River Severn, and up the Usk Valley; see pp. 83–150, especially pp. 127–28.

13. Gerald Morris, *The Savage Damsel and the Dwarf* (Boston: Houghton Mifflin, 2000), pp. 22–23. The novels of both Manning and Morris are part of the ironic tradition in Arthurian literature: see Thompson, *Return from Avalon,* pp. 139–62, especially pp. 149–50.

14. Jane Yolen, *The Dragon's Boy* (New York: HarperCollins, 1990). This version, here published separately as a children's book, is a substantially expanded revision of a short story that first appeared in 1985 in *The Magazine of Fantasy and Science Fiction*; it was subsequently included in Yolen's collection of short stories and poems entitled *Merlin's Booke* (New York: Ace, 1986), pp. 73–92. The revision pays more attention to the setting.

15. Diana L. Paxson, "Wild Man," in *Camelot*, ed. Jane Yolen (New York: Philomel, 1995), p. 29 [17–38].

16. Paxson, "Wild Man," p. 29.

17. Monica Furlong, *Juniper* (New York: Knopf, 1997), p. 47.

18. Furlong, *Juniper*, p. 47.

19. Furlong, *Juniper*, p. 48.

20. Anne McCaffrey, *Black Horses for the King* (London: Corgi, 1997), p. 118.

21. For a discussion of the growth of Morgan's character in response to the new conditions that she encounters in Katz's novel, see Raymond H. Thompson's "From Inspiration to Warning: The Changing Role of Arthurian Legend in

Fiction for Younger Readers," *Bulletin of the John Rylands University Library of Manchester* 76.3 (Autumn 1994): 245–46 [239–47].

22. Interestingly, girls are also trained to fight (with knives). This is part of a growing trend toward female warriors in Arthurian fiction, albeit they are found mainly in adult fantasy such as Patricia Kennealy-Morrison's Keltiad series (1984–96) and *The King's Peace* (2000) by Jo Walton. King Arthur's daughter does fight, very successfully, disguised as the Black Knight in *A Kid in King Arthur's Court* (1995), a novel by Ann Mazer based on a Walt Disney film for younger audiences.

23. T. H. White, *The Sword in the Stone* (New York: Dell, 1963), pp. 13–14. I have chosen this edition since it is more readily available than the rare first edition.

24. For White's sources for such information, see Elisabeth Brewer, *T. H. White's "The Once and Future King"* (Woodbridge, Suffolk, UK: D. S. Brewer, 1993), pp. 188–206.

25. White, *The Sword in the Stone*, p. 14.

26. As Brewer observes, "His chosen setting allowed him to give way to his school-masterly tendency to instruct. . . .His real interest in the Middle Ages was above all in how things were done" (*White*, p. 19).

27. White, *The Sword in the Stone*, p. 46.

28. White, *The Sword in the Stone*, p. 48.

29. White, *The Sword in the Stone*, p. 48

30. White, *The Sword in the Stone*, p. 54.

31. White, *The Sword in the Stone*, p. 54.

32. White, *The Sword in the Stone*, p. 277.

33. White, *The Sword in the Stone*, pp. 277–78.

34. White, *The Sword in the Stone*, p. 10.

35. White, *The Sword in the Stone*, pp. 191–92.

36. Brewer identifies the form of the novel as pastoral: "the subject is the myth of the idyllic childhood. The form is pastoral, usually characterised by a pervasive nostalgia for the vanished 'dream days'. . . .The carefree life of the Wart and Kay in Sir Ector's castle. . .removes us temporarily from 'the real world' and brings back memories of childhood adventure and the intensity of childhood experience. . . .In creating his images of happy childhood, White drew on his own experience of life with his grandparents" (*White*, p. 23). Apart from this interlude, his childhood was unhappy.

37. Sir Thomas Malory, *The Works of Sir Thomas Malory*, ed. Eugène Vinaver, rev. P. J. C. Field, 3rd edn., 3 vols. (Oxford: Oxford University Press, 1990), 3: 861–62.

38. On the relationship between the books published as *The Once and Future King*, see Brewer; see also Alan Lupack, "*The Once and Future King:* The Book That Grows Up," *Arthuriana* 11.3 (Fall 2001): 103–14.

39. For a discussion of this pattern, see Thompson, "From Inspiration to Warning," pp. 244–45.

40. Rosemary Sutcliff, *The Lantern Bearers* (London: Oxford University Press, 1972), pp. 3, 2, 4.

41. Sutcliff, *The Lantern Bearers*, pp. 10, 12.

42. Sutcliff, *The Lantern Bearers*, p. 15.

43. Sutcliff, *The Lantern Bearers*, pp. 24, 21.

44. Sutcliff, *The Lantern Bearers*, p. 31.

45. Sutcliff, *The Lantern Bearers*, p. 48.

46. Sutcliff, *The Lantern Bearers*, pp. 5, 41.

47. Sutcliff, *The Lantern Bearers*, pp. 69–70.

48. Sutcliff, *The Lantern Bearers*, p. 132.

49. Sutcliff, *The Lantern Bearers*, p. 140.

50. Sutcliff, *The Lantern Bearers*, p. 171.

51. Sutcliff, *The Lantern Bearers*, p. 236.

52. Sutcliff, *The Lantern Bearers*, p. 246.

53. Sutcliff, *The Lantern Bearers*, pp. 247–48.

54. See her autobiography, *Blue Remembered Hills: A Recollection* (Oxford: Oxford University Press, 1984), p. 111.

55. Sutcliff, *The Lantern Bearers*, pp. 239, 238.

56. "The Candle in the Wind" is the title of the fourth book of *The Once and Future King*, and Sutcliff may well have borrowed the image from White. In an interview that I conducted with her in 1986, she says, "I loved T. H. White's *The Once and Future King*. It goes so deep and it's on so many levels" ("An Interview with Rosemary Sutcliff," *Avalon to Camelot* 2.3 (1987): 12 [11–14]. This is reproduced electronically in Thompson, *Taliesin's Successors* <http://www.lib.rochester.edu/camelot/intrvws/sutcliff.htm>.

CHAPTER 6

SUSAN COOPER'S "THE DARK IS RISING"

Charlotte Spivack

In recent years, Arthurian fantasy—particularly fantasy fiction by women—has proliferated so as to become a veritable subgenre of Arthurian literature. Mary Stewart, for example, in her landmark trilogy devoted to the life of Merlin, permitted the archetypal male wizard, through his intuitiveness, his sensitivity to nature, and his minimizing of power, to function in effect as the feminine side of King Arthur. Vera Chapman created a new character—King Arthur's daughter—to narrate part of the old story and endowed minor characters with strong personalities (like Bertilak's wife and Lynette) to narrate the rest. And both Marion Zimmer Bradley and Gillian Bradshaw, by retelling events from the point of view of major female characters, placed emphasis on human relationships and reactions rather than on battles and politics.[1] Such female points of view on conventionally masculine subjects have afforded readers new perspectives on the Arthurian legends as a whole.[2]

New perspectives and points of view are evident as well in the works of other female fantasy writers, especially those who gear their series toward younger readers and who incorporate younger characters in their fiction. Pamela F. Service, for instance, set her two-volume fantasy series, *Winter of Magic's Return* (1985) and *Tomorrow's Magic* (1987), in a new Dark Age Britain and revives Merlin as a teenager who must assist two of his schoolmates on a quest for Arthur and in a battle against Morgan le Fay and the mutants she commands. In her juvenile Arthurian novels, *The Night of the Solstice* (1987) and *Heart of Valor* (1990), L. J. Smith created an elaborate new—and often convoluted—Arthurian mythology that plays out in two worlds, Findahl (Wildworld) and Stillworld (Earth), as sorceress Morgana Shee falls in love with a Native American dreamsinger and later seeks to avenge the Wildworld magistrate, Thia Pendriel, who has had the dreamsinger put to death. Whereas Smith and Service emphasized the character of Morgan, popular and prolific author Jane Yolen, in her collection of tales *Merlin's Booke* (1986) and in *The Dragon's Boy* (1990), focuses largely on the character of Merlin as boy, man, and legend. In her "Young Merlin Trilogy," Yolen traces Merlin's unusual and generally unhappy childhood: in *Passager* (1996), an eight-year-old Merlin is abandoned in the woods and captured by a falconer, who tames him as he would a passager bird and helps him to relearn the things he has forgotten and to reclaim his identity; in *Hobby* (1996), after being orphaned again, Merlin assumes new identities as "Hawk" and "Hobby" (the name of a small falcon) and explores his new powers; and in *Merlin* (1997), the now twelve-year-old boy, living among the *wodewose*, or wild folk, comes into his magic.[3]

Perhaps the most interesting and most distinctive of the writers of children's Arthurian fantasy series, however, is Susan Cooper. Born in 1935 in Burnham, Buckinghamshire, in western England, Cooper moved to the United States in 1963. And she infused her remarkable five-book fantasy sequence "The Dark Is Rising," written between 1965 and 1977, with the myths and legends of her youth. "The Matter of Britain," she observed in an interview with Raymond H. Thompson (published in full in this volume), "was part of a great mass of stuff in my subconscious, which consisted of fairytale, folktale, myth—that whole range of material that had always appealed to me enormously since childhood."[4]

Cooper's importance in the Arthurian canon can be confirmed in part by the scholarly attention she has received. Critics who have treated her works usually focus on the elements of high fantasy, symbols, and voice in "The Dark Is Rising" series. Lois R. Kuznets, in " 'High Fantasy' in America: A Study of Lloyd Alexander, Ursula LeGuin, and Susan Cooper," suggested that Cooper's use of her original sources allies her to "the Arthurian myth of male development"—that is, to "the adolescent rite of passage in terms of the quest of an unacknowledged son for the phallic sword and/or uterine cauldron or grail"—and to all of that myth's "elitist trappings."[5] Raymond L. Plante, in "Object and Character in *The Dark Is Rising*," compared Cooper's series with Tolkien's *Lord of the Rings*; discussed the nature of the struggle between good and evil in the series; demonstrated how that struggle emphasizes both fate and ritual; and explored the various symbolic objects that Cooper incorporates in her text.[6] The chapter on Cooper in *Merlin's Daughters* (1987) offered a close reading of Cooper's novels, analyzed her use of theme and character, and discussed her work in the context of feminine fantasy fiction.[7] Emrys Evans, in "Children's Novels and Welsh Mythology: Multiple Voices in Susan Cooper and Alan Garner," noted that, in Cooper's series, her voice "develops [over] the period of writing." Evans analyzed some of the many narrative voices in the novels, which range from "the voice of the implied author, propelling the narrative and addressing itself clearly and directly to the implied (child probably, adult possibly) reader," to "the slightly different voice of a close observer of this particular scenery, this particular part of Wales at this time of year," to "the voices of the characters," and finally to the "'high' language, drawn from the area of what Cooper calls the High Magic, which informs the whole series."[8] Peter Goodrich, in "Magical Medievalism and the Fairy Tale in Susan Cooper's The Dark Is Rising Sequence," examined some of the functions and implications of medievalism in the series.[9] Michael D. C. Drout, in his essay on "Reading the Signs of Light: Anglo Saxonism, Education, and Obedience in Susan Cooper's *The Dark Is Rising*," noted that while critics have focused on Cooper's reworking of Celtic and Arthurian legends, her use of Anglo-Saxon source materials, which carry "coded meanings at a level that is not immediately apparent but that nevertheless operates to exercise ideological control of the text," "fundamentally shape[s] the text beyond the control of the author and beyond the conscious apprehension of the child reader."[10] And Raymond H. Thompson, in his various studies, particularly his pioneering *The Return from Avalon* and his *Taliesin's Successors: Interviews with Authors of Modern Arthurian Literature*, explored the ways that the young protagonists of Cooper's novels learn "heroic self-reliance" and that Cooper's work as a whole addresses the "timeless challenge" of the Arthurian dream.[11]

Even more enthusiastic than the critical response to Cooper's novels has been the reader response. Young readers, in particular, have embraced the five-volume "The Dark Is Rising" series as a superb children's Arthurian adventure. Appropriately set in Cornwall and Wales, the series' action takes place mostly in the contemporary world, but shifts often to the haunting past of the Arthurian fifth century. The principal characters are the vacationing Drew children: Simon, Jane, and Barney. With them is their great-uncle, Oxford Professor Merriman (Merry) Lyon, a figure based on Merlin. Eventually, the Drews meet two other children, Will Stanton, one of the Old Ones, an immortal race possessed of supernatural powers, and Bran Davies, who is ultimately revealed as the son of Arthur and Guinevere (who has brought the child forward in time in order to protect him); together, they embark on a search for the Grail and on other related quests.

The pervasive theme of the series is the struggle between the Light and the Dark, that is, good and evil, the dualities that underlie the Arthurian tradition. As wise Uncle Merry puts it, in the old days

> "the struggle between good and evil was more bitter and open than it is now. That struggle goes on all around us all the time, like two armies fighting. And sometimes one of them seems to be winning and sometimes the other,

but neither has ever triumphed altogether. Nor ever will," he added softly to himself, "for there is something of each in every man. Sometimes, over the centuries, this ancient battle comes to a peak. The evil grows very strong and nearly wins. But always at the same time there is some leader in the world, a great man who sometimes seems to be more than a man, who leads the forces of good to win back the ground and the men they seemed to have lost."[12]

That leader, of course, is King Arthur.

The Drew children's adventures begin in the Cornish town of Trewissick, where they are spending their vacation. Young Barney Drew, who is enchanted by the Arthurian legends, is quick to note that Cornwall is the Logres of King Arthur. In an obscure attic of the "Grey House" in which they are staying, the children find an ancient manuscript that contains a mysterious map. At first they think that the map must lead to a buried treasure, but what is hidden "over sea, under stone" (the title of the first volume in the series, published in 1965) is an object infinitely more precious: it is nothing less than the Holy Grail, a cup, heavy and strangely bell-shaped like the goblets that Barney had seen pictured in his Arthurian books. Despite efforts by certain members of the Dark to steal the Grail, the children succeed in keeping it safe and donating it to a museum, where it is identified as a gold chalice of "unknown Celtic workmanship, believed sixth century."[13] In preserving the actual chalice from the Dark forces, however, the Drew children lose a lead case that contains a second manuscript, which holds the key to deciphering the Grail's inscriptions, a key that is not restored until more than midway through the series. But Barney is confident that they will learn the Grail's secret—"one day."[14]

Throughout these lively events in the volume, the three children are very effectively characterized. They speak as children, not as little adults, and they are convincingly individualized. Jane, the middle child, is the most sensitive; Barney, the youngest, is playful and mischievous; and Simon, the oldest, is daring and determined. And like ordinary children, they have their petty differences. Of the adult characterizations, Uncle Merriman is the most effective. Brave and totally dependable, he helps the children and on occasion even saves their lives, but he is also always fun.

The representatives of the Dark are also individualized, each depicted in a subtly terrifying way. One example is Mr. Hastings, whose soft but ominous voice announces: "the dark will always come, and always win."[15] Jane first meets him when she is seeking the village vicar, who has moved and whose vicarage the dark, sinister Hastings is renting. His appearance is forbidding, and Jane immediately detects something evil about him. Her suspicions are later confirmed when it is revealed that Merriman has known Hastings by other names in other times. Although he is momentarily subdued by the power of the Grail at the end of the novel, Cooper hints that Hastings will appear again to tempt the children.

The Dark can also be totally deceptive. The housekeeper for the vacationing family is a village woman, Mrs. Palk, red-cheeked, beaming, a buxom image of homely virtues. She bustles about benevolently, offering cups of tea or cocoa, cheerfully singing while washing the dishes. Only intuitive Jane mistrusts her; everyone else accepts her for the domestic paragon she appears to be. But she betrays the children. She falsifies a message they asked her to give their uncle about their plans for the day, deliberately misleading him as to their whereabouts, as a result of which Barney is kidnapped (one of a pattern of child kidnappings and betrayals in the series). This duality—of appearance versus reality, of good versus evil (which is only hinted at here)—creates the conflict that underlies both the novel in particular and the series in general.

The second volume of the series, *The Dark Is Rising* (1973), which shares its title with the series as a whole, was the recipient of the Boston Globe Horn Book Award for Fiction and was a runner-up for both the Newbery and Carnegie Medals.[16] Cooper makes much more use of symbols in this book than in the first, and the text is somewhat denser in style. She also introduces several significant new characters who advance the series' Arthurian motifs. The child at the center of the plot is Will Stanton, the youngest of nine children in his family, who is celebrating his eleventh birthday on Midwinter Day. Will's birthday, the day upon which he comes into his magic, proves to be a very important date in the volume, since the powers of the Dark are strongest between Midwinter Eve and the twelfth day of Christmas (although they are briefly restrained by the Wild Magic on Christmas Eve). After meeting the mysterious Merriman, Will learns that they were both born with the same gift, and for the same high purpose. Naturally Will is surprised and baffled, but Merry soon explains: "You are one of the Old Ones, the first to have been born for five hundred years, and the last. And like all such, you are bound by nature to devote yourself to the long conflict between the Light and the Dark. Your birth, Will, completed a circle that has been growing for four thousand years. . .the circle of the Old Ones." Merriman then proceeds to tell Will about the nature of the quest he must undertake, namely to find and guard the six Signs of Light, magical objects that are hidden in various locations (and over various centuries) in the village of Buckinghamshire, where the boy lives. (The Signs, it is later revealed, are one of the Things of Power, which also include the Grail, the Golden Harp, and the Crystal Sword.) Will's destiny is to be the "Sign-Seeker," for only the Signs can vanquish the powers of the Dark, which is once again on the rise. And Merriman chants, "For the Dark, the Dark is rising."[17]

Cooper's concept of the Old Ones is central to the meaning of time, in both the book and the series. The title "The Dark Is Rising," for example, is a statement not only of events occurring in the present moment, which indeed it is, but also of events that occurred in Arthurian times. Similarly, while the Old Ones are contemporary beings who exist in the modern world, most have already lived for hundreds of years. One such fascinating character is the man who is first introduced as the Walker, a "shambling, tattered figure, more like a bundle of old clothes than a man."[18] When he first appears in the volume, he is attacked for no apparent reason by two rooks, which are rarely aggressive toward people.[19] The Walker, however, is no ordinary mortal; he is actually Hawkin, former liege man to Merriman, who has been sent forward in time by Merriman to deliver one of the Signs. "Hawkin is a child of the thirteenth century, Will," Merriman explains. "Seven hundred years before you were born. He belongs there. By my art, he has been brought forward out of it for this one day, and then he will go back again."[20] But Hawkin, it turns out, is tempted by forces of the Dark into betraying Merriman, his old master, and condemned to fearful centuries of walking, until he is of no more use to the Dark. The character, transformed from a bright-eyed young man into the ancient, ragged, and despised Walker, is at once horrifying and pathetically touching.

In addition to being able to travel through time, the Old Ones have further supernatural gifts and abilities. As Merriman points out, now that Will is eleven, he possesses certain magic. For instance, when he wants the fire in a room to go out, all he has to do is tell it to do so, and it does. Similarly, when he wants it to start burning again, he tells it to, and it does.

The six Signs of Light that Will is destined to find, save, and use against the Dark are water, fire, stone, bronze, iron, and wood. These Signs all have the same form—a circle quartered by a cross—and all are from nature and deeply imbedded in mythic symbolism through the centuries. Basically, water is associated with fertility and birth, fire with divine energy and purification, stone with durability, bronze with force and power, iron with strength and hardiness, and wood with protection and the maternal. Will acquires the first Sign, the Sign of Iron, as a gift from his neighbor, Farmer Dawson (after which Will has his first encounter with the Black Rider of the Dark); from the Walker, he demands and receives the Sign of Bronze, which he then places beside the first Sign on his belt. The third Sign, Wood, appears to him on Christmas Day, on the wooden panels of the home of Mrs. Greythorne, another neighbor (and, like Dawson, another of the Old Ones). That sign, she tells him, is "sometimes [called] the Sign of Learning";[21] and indeed along with that Sign, he discovers another valuable item that aids him in his quest: the magical Book of Gramarye, which Merriman pulls out of an old pendulum clock. The book, which is the oldest book in the world and which will be destroyed as soon as Will reads it, is written in the Old Speech. Now that Will is eleven and possessed of his new magic, he can read and speak the Old. Interestingly, however, at first he does not even know that he is reading it. It seems to him that the book is actually written in English and that he is speaking English, his everyday speech. The Old Speech comes so naturally to him that it does not seem any different from English. Like Will himself, the Book of Gramarye has special power: it totally absorbs the boy's mind. Merriman explains that Will needs to read it only once, for it will remain in him for all Time to come. Accordingly, Will seems to experience all that he reads, and when he finishes the book, he feels as if he has lived a hundred years. On that same day, Will also discovers the fourth Sign, Stone, as a light blazing from the wall. As he reaches for it, Will realizes that it is "a natural flint, grown in the Chiltern chalk fifteen million years ago."[22] But that night, as Will goes to bed, he watches the unnaturally heavy snow falling and recalls Merriman's warning of the "danger" ahead.

That danger soon arrives: nature seems to go wild as snows devastate all of England. And Will's family suffers various ills: his mother is injured and his younger sister kidnapped. But, in a dramatic scene that enacts the winter solstice and that moves the boy in time between the manor house of the present and of a century ago, Will is able to light the six candles known as the "candles of the winter" and to dispel the influence of the Dark, after which he finds the fifth Sign, Fire. That Sign is gold and set with tiny colorful precious gems. Jubilant, Will holds it high for others to see; as he does so, every light in the hall flickers with its brilliance. Yet immediately "there came a great crashing roar with a long wail of anger through it. The sound rumbled and came crashing out again"[23] as the Dark expresses its displeasure at Will's success.

The sixth and final Sign is perhaps the most unusual. In an instant Will finds himself back in the year 1875, on board a funeral ship; under its canopy he discovers the body of a dead king, who has been buried there for fifteen hundred years. In the king's hand Will spots a circular ornament, quartered by a cross, and engraved with eels and fishes, waves, and serpents, objects of the sea. He realizes excitedly that this is clearly the Sign of Water. After removing this sixth and final Sign, he rides out of the river alongside Merriman on the magical "white horse of the Light" and, back in real time, prepares to complete the "joining" of the Signs. More angry than ever, the Dark set fire to the ship by striking it with a lightning bolt. As Merriman tells Will: "They vent their spite, because they know they are too late."[24]

Will's sudden realization of himself in a different time is but a single example of time travel in this book (a popular motif in other children's fantasy stories as well, but one which Cooper uses especially well—to manifest a philosophical vision of time as continuous and organic). Throughout the series, Cooper handles this theme of time in various ways. Like Arthur and Guinevere, who travel between their own time and the present day, the Old Ones travel from one time to another; they also move from one location to another. While their means is not always specified, one device is through the Doors of Time, which become a literalized metaphor. Will uses them for his Christmas journey back in time, and Merriman uses them at the end of the volume. "The tall carved doors led out of Time."[25] In each case, just before the doors appear (always out of nowhere), enchanted music can be heard. Will first sees the doors at the beginning of the volume, soon after he has acquired the first two Signs, before he fully apprehends the doors' meaning: "before him, standing alone and tall on the white slope, leading to nowhere, were two great carved wooden doors."[26] And at the end of the book, as Will watches Merriman leave, "with the music singing in his ears" and the trees, the road, and the mist all "shaking, shivering," he sees the doors, "standing alone and upright in the Old Way," take shape. The music in Will's head is the same haunting, bell-like sound that always comes with the opening of the doors, and as Merriman passes through them, the music fades and sounds far away. The doors then close, and "the towering slabs of heavy, carved oak swung slowly together, together, until silently they shut" and the last echo of the enchanted music died.[27] Merriman's leavetaking, however, is not the end of Will's story; it is just the beginning.

Greenwitch (1974), the middle book in the series,[28] is more straightforward and somewhat less complex in its symbolism. A bit shorter than the other volumes, it is significant primarily as a transition. Here, thanks to the subtle orchestration of Merriman, the children from the first two books come together for their adventures: the three Drew children and Will Stanton join each other in South Cornwall, renewing the specific Arthurian theme of the Grail. The "Trewissick Grail," the chalice that was donated to a museum in London at the end of the first volume, has been stolen by an agent of the Dark, and it is up to the children to recover it.

The events occur during an annual spring ritual, and Cooper draws extensively on folklore for this part of the tale. The ritual involves the making of the Greenwitch, a huge image composed of leaves and branches, fashioned by the women of the village, and thrown into the sea in order to bring good luck in both fishing and harvesting; no men or boys may participate. Jane, who is invited to observe the ritual, responds very sensitively to the Greenwitch. She detects in the figure a profound sadness, and when Jane is given a chance to make the traditional wish, she does not wish for herself but rather for the happiness of the Witch. "Melancholy seemed to hover about [the Greenwitch] like a mist," writes Cooper; and Jane impulsively utters to her, "I wish you could be happy."[29] In the subsequent events, the wish becomes integral to the recovery of the stolen Grail chalice and to the deciphering of its inscription.

Later, in what Jane believes to be only a dream, the leafy creature reveals that she has a secret, a bright, shining thing in a cleft in a rock, which she makes Jane promise never to disclose. "It is mine. Mine, mine," repeats the Greenwitch. "But I will show you. If you promise not to tell, not to tell."[30] When Jane awakens, she has a "sudden flash of remembering" and thinks she recognizes the bright object of which the Greenwitch spoke. But Jane falls asleep again before she fully recaptures the memory. Meanwhile, Simon and Barney encounter one of the agents of the Dark, a wild-eyed man who is posing as a painter. In fact, the painter—whose bizarre canvases turn out to be magical spells—is a thief who has stolen and hidden the Grail and who now wants to steal the Greenwitch's secret as well. Summoning the Witch by means of a totem that he has taken from Barney, he demands that she give him the Thing of Power, the "secret" that she had mentioned to Jane and by which he hopes to "make himself one of the great lords of the Dark."[31] The Witch, however, refuses to relinquish it and instead, in anger, loosens her "Wild Magic" on the village. (Neither Light nor Dark, Wild Magic is simply the way of living things in the natural non-human world.) In the nightmarish episode that follows, the villagers are forced to reexperience the past, as a phantom ship appears and savage smugglers rush ashore. Soon afterwards, the Greenwitch disappears back into the sea, "dissipating into nothing." As for the supposed painter, he is cast by the Wild Magic to "outer Time, from which he may never properly come back."[32]

On the very night that "the whole village was hilla-ridden,"[33] Jane has another dream in which she hears the voice of the Greenwitch. Out of gratitude for the girl's concern, the Witch offers her the secret that she has guarded so carefully. When Jane awakens, in her hand is the lead case that contains the manuscript able to unravel the mystery of the Grail, the same case that was lost in the sea at the end of the first novel, *Over Sea, Under Stone*. (As housekeeper Mrs. Penhallow recalls on the novel's final page, on that same night, Jane's room was "clean as a pin," but the next morning it was a mess of "twigs and leaves, hawthorn leaves, and rowan and every-where a great smell of the sea."[34])

Ultimately, in a gypsy caravan in the yard of a local farm, the children discover a battered, damp, smelly cardboard box in a low cupboard. When Barney takes hold of the top of the box, it crumbles, and there, shining beneath their eyes, is the Grail. From the manuscript given to Jane by the Greenwitch, Merriman translates the Grail's inscription, which speaks of many amazing things, including a "raven boy," "silver eyes that see the wind," "a harp of gold," a pleasant lake where "the Sleepers lie," a "Grey King," six burning Signs, and a tall "midsummer tree."[35] *Greenwitch* thus provides a mysterious transition to the final two volumes, which continue the Arthurian adventures of the children.

The Grey King (1975), the fourth volume in the series, was also a prize winner: it won the John Newbery Medal for the Most Distinguished Contribution to American Literature for Children, the Tir na N'og Award, and a Carnegie Medal citation. Set in Wales, it is the most specifically Arthurian of the five works. The Drew children do not appear; the story focuses instead on Will, who has been sent to the Welsh home of relatives to recuperate from an illness that has likely been brought on by the Dark. An important character in the novel is Will's new friend, Bran Davies, adopted son of local sheep farmer Owen Davies. An unusual looking boy with pale skin, white hair and eyebrows, and yellow eyes, Bran (sometimes called "the raven boy") describes himself as albino in appearance; even Bran's beloved dog Cafall (who bears the same name as Arthur's dog) is white, almost as white as he is. By the novel's end, Bran is revealed to be the Pendragon, son of King Arthur and Queen Guinevere, sent forward in time to help the Light against the forces of the Dark.

When Will first meets Bran, he is unaware of his identity as the son of the great King, but the two boys quickly become good friends. Will, because of his illness, has forgotten about his own identity as an Old One and about the ongoing battle between the Dark and the Light. The meeting with Bran, however, immediately restores his memory of both and of the tasks he must perform in order to prevent the rising of the Dark; and, of course, Bran and Cafall prove helpful in his ongoing adventure. As "one of the Old Ones of the Light put here to hold back the terrible power of the Dark," Bran tells Will, "you are the last of that circle to be born on earth. And I have been waiting for you."[36] Having already achieved the six Signs of Light, Will now has a new quest to fulfill, for the golden harp, another of the "Things of Power," which will awaken the Six Sleepers. And he must face a new enemy: the Grey King, a High Lord of the Dark, who usually appears as a grey mist.

The forces of the Dark need cruel people to fulfill their brutal aims, and one such person in this book is Caradog Prichard, a Welsh farmer who becomes "an unwitting servant" of the Grey King.[37] (The "fool" Prichard is "not of the Dark," the Grey King later admits to Will. "But he is very useful. A man so wrapped in his own ill-will is a gift to the Dark from the earth."[38]) The local sheepmen have recently lost a number of their animals. When Prichard hears a sheep scream and sees what appears to be a large white dog with silver eyes taking up the chase, he assumes that Cafall is the villain, pulls his gun, and shoots the dog in the chest. (In fact, Cafall is chasing the actual sheep killer, one of the grey foxes—*milgwn*—that serve the Grey King by assuming various forms and colors and by wreaking havoc within the community.) The loss of his devoted dog leaves Bran griefstricken, and he rejects further thought of the Light and Dark conflict. In a very moving speech, Bran tells Will:

> "I wish you had never come here. I wish I had never heard of the Light and the Dark, and your damned old Merriman and his rhymes. . . . I am not a part of your stupid quest any more, I don't care what happens to it. And Cafall was never a part of it either, or a part of your pretty pattern. He was my dog, and I loved him more than anything in the world, and now he is dead. *Go away*."[39]

Cafall is not the only victim of the evil Prichard's brutal shot; the friendship between the boys, it seems, is also destroyed.

The episode involving the shooting of Cafall and the one directly preceding it exemplify Cooper's talent for creating intersecting worlds. In reading about Cafall, we see the daily life of the Welsh shepherds, the voices of the sheep on the slopes, the broken fence mended with barbed wire, the mountainside covered with bracken and gorse. But in the immediately preceding episode, we are transported to an otherworldly setting. Walking alone in the hills, the boys find a cleft rock, locally called Bird Rock, where they enter, not knowing what to expect. For a moment it seems as if they are "somewhere in another time, on the roof of the world."[40] They see stars, which disappear, then find themselves on a stairway that leads to an enormous cavernous room. At the end of the chamber are three thrones occupied by Lords in blue robes, one dark, one light, and one greenish-blue, like the sea. After Will states that he has come to claim the golden harp, the figure in the lightest robe tells the boys that they must first answer three riddles, "as the law demands." Bran is asked to identify the three elders of the world. The touch of Cafall's fur reminds Bran of feathers and provides him with the appropriate clue, allowing him to respond correctly— the three elders are the Owl, the Eagle, and the Blackbird, each associated with a specific Welsh location. Then Will is asked his riddle—to name the three most generous men of the Isle of Britain. Recalling what he had read in the Book of Gramarye, he names Nudd, Mordaf, and Rhydderch, but adds that Arthur was "*more generous than the three*." The answer is right, but the Lord in the darkest robe promptly asks another riddle—what is the shore that fears the sea? Will's mind fills with images of the sea, the shore (the beach), and the forest (the beech). He responds that it is the wood of the beech tree, for its "wood loses its virtue if soaked by water."[41] At this point, the Lord in the dark blue robe throws back his hood and reveals his face. It is Merriman, "a Lord of the Light," who, as one of the "Three Lords

of High Magic[, has] for many years had guardianship of the golden harp."
(Because in this place "there are no names" or allegiances, the other two
Lords are never identified. But Merriman alludes to the fact that one "is a
Lord of the Dark," while the third Lord is clearly King Arthur himself, the
"master in that hall.")[42]

The mysterious figure in the sea-blue robe, whom Merriman addresses
as "Sire," then speaks for the first time. He tells Will that there are two chests
between the thrones and that he must open the one on the right and take
out what he finds there. The chest is too difficult for Will to open alone,
but with Bran's help he succeeds. A sound of music is heard in the air, as
Will lifts in his arms "a small, gleaming, golden harp."[43] But the music in the
room abruptly gives way to thunder, and the Lord explains to Will that
the harp has High Magic in it, a power that may not be broken by either the
Dark or the Light. With Bran playing the golden harp as if it were an
instrument familiar to him, the boys leave through the cleft rock. Will's
quest is thus fulfilled, for now he has another "Thing of Power" with which
to stop the Dark from rising.

Will and Bran are eventually reconciled after Cafall's death, when Bran
travels to an old cottage near a lake (the place where "Gwen" [Guinevere]
and her baby first appeared to Bran's foster father Owen Davies and the
same "pleasant lake" mentioned in the Grail inscription) to warn Will
that Prichard is pursuing him and planning to shoot his new companion,
the black sheepdog Pen. Invoking the magic of the Old Ones and using the
golden harp he has recently acquired, Will is able to defend against
Prichard, diminish the powers of the Dark, and summon the Six Sleepers,
who ride magically out of the mountain near Bird Rock "glinting silver-
grey on their silver-grey mounts," with swords drawn in homage to their
leader, whom both Will and Bran now realize is King Arthur. The novel
ends with Caradog Prichard going mad, his mind permanently gone ("col-
lapsed into the wreck it must become" as "all control from the Dark left
him"[44]), and the heavy mist, called the Breath of the Grey King, closing
over the water, as the powers of the Dark vanish from the Lake.

Silver on the Tree (1977), the final volume in the series,[45] is the most profound as well as the most complex, a fitting finale to the marvelous adventure. Cooper here achieves a double level of time just as she had of place in
the earlier works. Merriman explains to Will that the two great risings of
the Dark, although more than a thousand years apart, actually coexist. One
rising "is in the time into which you were human-born. One is here and
now, fifteen centuries before that, when my lord Arthur must win a victory
that will last. . . . You and I have a part to play in the defence against each of
these two risings. In fact, the same part."[46] Will is baffled, but Merriman tells
him: "the times are linked, by our presence and by the place."[47]

A good illustration of this time linking occurs at the beginning of the volume, as Will stands in the front hall of his home admiring a Victorian print entitled "The Romans at Caerleon." In an instant, Merriman appears; together, he and Will return to the Roman amphitheatre depicted in the print, where they had earlier hidden the six Signs for safekeeping. Then, just as suddenly, the two Old Ones are back in the present, at an archaeological dig at the site of the same Roman amphitheatre. By reversing the earlier spell, Will releases the Signs. As he holds in his hands "the linked belt of crossed circles that was the symbol of the Circle of Light, ...time and space merged as the twentieth and the fourth centuries became for a Midsummer's instant two halves of a single breath."[48] Merriman then tells the boy that King Arthur has need of the Signs in his own time, and he also informs him that his final quest will be to find the crystal sword of the Pendragon, by which the Dark will at last be put to flight. Just before Merriman disappears with the Signs, he reminds Will: "we will strive at our separate tasks across the centuries, through the waves of time, touching and parting, parting and touching in the pool that whirls forever. And I shall be with you before long."[49] And, with the stars spinning around him, Will finds himself again "in the hall of his home, his hand on the frame of a sepia print that showed Romans building an amphitheatre at Caerleon." The episode gains further meaning from the parallel portrayals of two men whom Will meets at the site. The first is a homesick, fourth-century Roman centurion, working on the structure and complaining about the frigid English weather; the second is a twentieth-century American archaeologist, also homesick, also lamenting the weather, dreaming about his family back home. Cooper thus suggests that in any given landscape, history repeats itself while human nature remains a constant.

In this final volume of the series, the story is again set in Wales, although the plot at times continues to move to places and times outside of this world. The three Drew children are reunited with Will and introduced to Bran, whose whiteness and knowledge of Welsh (particularly his recitation of an old verse about a Lady, whom he identifies as one of the greatest figures of the Light) they find duly astonishing. The mysterious Lady soon appears to Jane, with whom she seems to have an affinity (as the Greenwitch earlier had); she tells the girl that Will and Bran must head for the Lost Land when it becomes visible between the land and the sea. Cryptically, she warns that a white bone will at first prevent them; a flying may-tree will save them; and only the horn can stop the wheel. But in a glass tower set among seven trees, they will find the crystal sword of the Light that will enable Will to complete his quest. After the Lady's visit, Jane is terrified by a gruesome monster that arises from a lake and demands that she reveal the Lady's words. Jane, however, refuses to betray the message, which she delivers only to the boys for whom it was intended.

On their fantastic journey to the Lost Land, which exists in the far past, Will and Bran meet Gwion, also known as Taliesin, who serves as their guide. After overcoming various obstacles, including a maze of mirrors, a giant skeletal horse (the "white bone"), and a gigantic deadly wheel of enchantment (which Will halts with his hunting horn and with the tree branches they have ritually collected), they eventually encounter the Land's sad king, Gwyddno, and assume possession of Eirias, the crystal sword that Gwyddno had fashioned and that shines like a "bright icicle." Yet, as Bran and Will sail away, with sword in hand, they witness not only the destruction of the Lost Land by the forces of the Dark but also the bravery of Gwyddno and his loyal retainer Gwion, who remain behind to face the flood. "The world tossed and roared in a dark endless turmoil, with no count of time passing."[50] Although Will loses consciousness in the tumult, soon he and Bran find themselves on a stretch of sand along the River Dyfi, where they are met by the Drew children.

Meanwhile, the Drews experience incredible adventures of their own, as Barney is kidnapped by the mysterious White Rider, who transports him to a past era as a hostage to be used in exchange for Bran and the crystal sword. Initally assumed to be a spy for the English against the Welsh, Barney is rescued by Will and Bran and returned safely to "a different place and a different time."[51] All five children are then reunited on Merriman's extraordinary "time-train."

The dramatic train scene involves another act of betrayal by a familiar character, Blodwen Rowlands, the wife of the children's friend John Rowlands. As Blodwen sits knitting in Merriman's compartment, the sound of her needles mingles with the sound of the train wheels, both of which seem to chatter "*into the dark, into the dark, into the dark.*" Immediately Jane's mouth goes dry, and she notices a mysterious group of horsemen galloping alongside the train. Uncle Merry confirms her suspicions: "This is the Rising, yes, the last pursuit. And the danger will grow now." As the engine shrieks and the train lurches forward, Merriman exposes Blodwen by revealing that she "belongs to the Dark." Defiantly—in a voice "all at once oddly different, soft and sibilant but with a new force behind it"—Blodwen announces that the Dark is "massed and waiting," that the sword Eirias is powerless to destroy the Lords of the Dark, and that even the Things of Power will be insufficient to help Merriman and the children find the tree they are seeking. Suddenly Merriman steps forward and shouts, "The Light throws you from this stream of Time,"[52] and with a cry of rage, she whirls away from them, into the "dark space" and onto the white horse ridden by the White Rider of the Dark who had earlier kidnapped Barney.

With Blodwen dispatched, the children abruptly find themselves on a boat, on their way to the midsummer tree, which blooms for a single day once every seven hundred years; they know that whoever cuts the silver blossom just as it opens will have the right to command Magic and to drive rival powers out of the world and out of Time. "Where the midsummer tree grows tall," chants Merriman, "by Pendragon's sword the Dark shall fall." Out of the mist appears another boat: at its prow is King Arthur, fresh from the Battle of Badon and still wearing around his neck the six Signs of Light acquired by Will. Arthur addresses Bran, who raises the sword Eirias in salute, as "my son"; and he returns to Will the Circle of Signs that "served its purpose and must now serve yours."[53]

In a rousing climax, the appearance of things changes wildly: black seems white, green seems red, the roar of thunder and the whirling black tornado of the Dark fills the air. As various characters from this and earlier volumes—Blodwen, the Lady, the White and Black Riders, Mr. Hastings, Herne the Hunter, the Sleepers (now changed into Riders)—reappear, the mistletoe breaks into bloom, and the Dark comes rising.

As Merriman and the children encircle the magical midsummer tree, each takes one of the six Signs: Simon, the smooth Sign of Iron; Jane, the gleaming Sign of Bronze; Barney, the rowan Sign of Wood; Merriman, the gold Sign of Fire; Bran, the crystal sign of Light; and Will, the black flint of Stone. With the aid of John Rowlands, who appears at the boy's side and places the Sign of Light into his own hand, Bran uses Eirias to cut the spray, which transforms into a white bird and flies away into the sky. Suddenly all six Signs burn with a cold light, too bright for eyes to watch. Two voices are heard crying out in fear, and both the Black Rider and the White Rider of the Dark fall backwards out of Time and disappear. Then all six hands are suddenly empty, as each Sign burns with its cold fire into nothing and is gone.

All are silent for a time, then Arthur bids farewell to his son Bran (who has decided to stay in the present) and tells Merriman, his "lion," that he will see him soon. Merriman, too, prepares to depart, since his work is done. And, except for Will, the children are left with no memory of their experience. "So," Merriman tells them, "the last magic will be this—that when you see me for the last time in this place, all that you know of the Old Ones, and of this great task that has been accomplished, will retreat into the hidden places of your minds, and you will never again know any hint of it except in dreams."[54] On the last page of *Silver on the Tree*, the Drew children, oblivious to all that has transpired, find themselves on a hill in Wales listening to music—or perhaps only to the sound of the wind in the trees—as they embark on a new but less fantastic adventure.

Unlike the other children, who are introduced early in the narrative, the character of Bran is not developed in detail until the final two volumes of the series. Earlier in the narrative, reference is made largely to his appearance. When Jane sees him for the first time, for example, the emphasis is on his albino skin and hair and on his eyes, which are "yellow, tawny, flecked with gold like the eyes of an owl; they blazed at her, bright as new coins."[55] It is only in the late volumes that we learn about the disappearance of Queen Guinevere, his mother, who ran away from her husband, King Arthur, and who left the baby Bran with Owen Davies, who has played the paternal role all the years since.[56] The time discrepancy is significant. Son of Arthur, this child from the past has grown up in the present with a contemporary father, the only real parent he has ever known. Thus, in the touching final episode, when Arthur tries to reclaim the boy and return with him to his own time, Bran declines. "I cannot come, my Lord," Bran says simply; "I belong here." He explains that he has "*loving bonds*" here, and these bonds, which he established in this life in his growing years on a farm in Wales, are ultimately more important to him than his role as Pendragon. He chooses to forget his participation in the transcendental work of the Light and instead to continue life as other mortals do. After giving the crystal sword and its scabbard to a "proud and loving" Arthur, Bran receives Arthur's blessing and embrace in return.

"The Dark Is Rising" series is not a traditional retelling of the Arthurian tales; it is a contemporary remythologizing. The five children encounter King Arthur both directly and indirectly in their travels back to his century and in their contemporary adventures with the forces of Dark and Light. But apart from Arthur himself, whose presence is strong yet who appears in person only briefly, just a few of the characters are specifically Arthurian: Bran, who is the son of the king; Merriman, who is a man of the king's century and who turns out to be his wizard, Merlin; Guinevere, who as "Gwen" moves briefly forward in time (but who never appears in the story); Gwion, who is also known as Taliesin, the king's legendary bard. (And, of course, there is the dog Cafall.) Yet the fact that the main characters and their adventures are actually contemporary stresses the timelessness and universality of the original Arthurian material.

The author's subtle handling of the theme of time intensifies this element of the original myth. As Arthur, Guinevere, and Merriman do, the children make several journeys through Time: Will moves through the Doors of Time and visits the manor house of a century ago, finds himself aboard an ancient funeral ship, and envisions Arthur and Guinevere in their own time; Jane watches from her window as incidents from history occur in the village below; Bran observes the past to learn about his royal parentage and his destiny. But such journeys are only one facet of the theme. When characters are destroyed or disappear, they are described as being thrown out of Time (as happens to the painter in *Greenwitch* and to the Black and White Riders near the end of *Silver on the Tree*); even death, after all, is just a dismissal of Time. And within the framework of Time, certain dates have special significance. It is Will's eleventh birthday when he comes to recognize, in *The Dark Is Rising*, that he is one of the Old Ones. His birthday is also Midwinter Day, which is the day of the winter solstice and the shortest day in the year. The middle of the winter thus coincides with the middle of Will's youth, with the decade of childhood behind him and the decade of adolescence ahead of him. It is at this time that he learns of his special quest for the six Signs. And it is on this Christmas Day that Will walks with Merriman into a different time—1875, a century earlier. And it is on the twelfth night of Christmas that the forces of the Dark produce a raging flood. Dates in the other novels have a similar and cyclic importance. In *Greenwitch*, it is the spring ritual designed to insure good harvests on land and from the sea; in *The Grey King*, it is Halloween, the traditional day of the dead and the first day of winter, according to the ancient reckoning of the calendar; in *Silver on the Tree*, it is Midsummer's Eve, which precedes the longest day of the year, an important festival for the Celts. And the series as a whole begins and ends in summer, thus coming full circle.[57] Both travel through time and significant dates in Time therefore contribute to the meaning of the adventure.

Apart from the time travel episodes, there are numerous examples of fantasy in the narrative. In *Silver on the Tree*, in the Lost Land, where Will and Bran go in search of the crystal sword, they encounter many magical obstacles, including a spectral horse, a skeleton with a hollow-eyed skull, dead yet alive, who collapses into a heap of white bones gleaming in the sun. In *The Dark Is Rising*, an antlered mask that has been given to Will by his brother comes alive during the Wild Hunt. In an episode in *The Grey King*, Will, who is walking on a mountain side, falls because the mountain shrugs. A piece of the path beneath his feet jumps to one side and back again, causing Will to lose his balance and tumble down. In the same book, the titular role is a fantastical figure of mist; when Will finds the golden harp, he sees the mist take shape as a figure so huge that it is wider than the field and reaches high into the sky. The outline of that figure is visible, but when Will looks directly at it, there is nothing there. At the very end of the book, the mist that pervades the valley—the mist that men call the breath of the Grey King—leaves, taking with it the ghosts of the grey foxes. The disappearing mist indicates that the Grey King has given up the battle against the Light.

There are also other minor episodes of fantasy interpolated in the children's adventure. In the final volume, for example, they encounter a terrifying sea monster, called the "afanc," which screams and thrashes furiously in the water. Terrified Jane loses consciousness and falls on the grass alongside the lake, and only Bran is able to dismiss the threatening creature and keep it from coming back. And at several crucial points in the narrative, mysterious music sounds, sometimes associated with the threat of the Dark and sometimes with the saving grace of the Light. But it is always magic, and is never explained. All of these examples of fantasy enhance the narrative by suggesting new dimensions of ritual and mystery.

One of Cooper's most successful techniques in the series is her creation
of a double level of conflict: she makes the Dark and the Light convincing
as opposing forces that represent ideas at the same time that she makes clear
that the forces and ideas are meaningless without their representation in
people, both mythic and contemporary. At the center of the Light is a "cold
white flame," and at the center of the dark is a "great black pit bottomless
as the Universe";[58] but both concepts are expressed through human beings.
The image of the Dark, presented as an independent force throughout history, is also an embodiment of the cruelty, prejudice, and hatred of humanity: the Dark could not rise without cruel and bitter people like Caradog
Prichard in *The Grey King* or the hateful English boys who bully a
Pakastani youth because of the color of his skin in *Silver on the Tree*. And
the Light could never withstand its onslaught without kind and gentle people like John Rowlands or without the bonds that unite people in mutual
trust. Bran's expressed preference for the *"loving bonds"* of humans thus
reflects a major theme of the series: that real though they are, the Dark and
the Light must derive their ultimate meaning from real human beings.

Young readers respond enthusiastically to the Cooper series. They can
identify with the five children protagonists, whom they find very convincingly
portrayed, and with the plot, which is complex yet appealing in its liveliness
and variety of episodes and in its integration of Arthurian lore. Also excellent
is Cooper's style, which ranges in expression to suit the complex narrative and
is almost symphonic in its rhythms and language. Above all, the series brings
the Arthurian material close to home, with episodes from the original tales
carefully integrated with contemporary experience. The children not only
learn about the original Arthur but also participate in Arthurian adventures
going on in the present—and often in traditionally Arthurian settings.
(Cornwall, as Barney observes, is the site of Arthur's Logres; the summit of the
mountain Cader Idris in *The Grey King* is known as Arthur's seat; one scene
even offers a reenactment of the battle of Mount Badon.) Time is not fixed;
the past is not remote. Magic and mystery flourish throughout.

"The Dark Is Rising" series is a brilliant and thoroughly enjoyable work
of literary adventure. And it confirms Susan Cooper's important place in
the Arthurian literary tradition, particularly the tradition of Arthurian
literature for children.

Notes

1. For a fuller discussion of these and other women writers of fantasy, see
   Charlotte Spivack, *Merlin's Daughters: Contemporary Women Writers of Fantasy*
   (Westport, CT: Greenwood Press, 1987).
2. As discussed at greater length in *Merlin's Daughters* (especially pp. 49–50),
   Cooper is not writing consciously as a feminist, but "her vision of life is

spiritually allied to the feminine as defined in contemporary psychological and anthropological theory. Her Celtic background, with its emphasis on the seasonal cycle and its sacramental view of nature, is the product of a matriarchal society." This feminine perspective is evident also in the development of the characters. In his interview with Cooper (reprinted in this volume), Raymond H. Thompson notes that "As the series progresses, Jane in particular grows more interesting." Cooper, in the same interview, concurs that "Jane is someone I wanted to write about again."

 3. Alan Lupack and Barbara Tepa Lupack, *King Arthur in America* (Cambridge, UK: D. S. Brewer, 1999).

 4. See Raymond H. Thompson, "Interview with Susan Cooper," on p. 162 [161–169] in this volume.

 5. Lois R. Kuznets, "'High Fantasy' in America: A Study of Lloyd Alexander, Ursula LeGuin, and Susan Cooper," *The Lion and the Unicorn* 9 (1985): 27, 29 [19–35].

 6. Raymond L. Plante, "Object and Character in *The Dark Is Rising*," *Children's Literature Association Quarterly* 11.1 (1986): 37–41.

 7. Spivack, *Merlin's Daughters*, pp. 35–52.

 8. Emrys Evans, "Children's Novels and Welsh Mythology: Multiple Voices in Susan Cooper and Alan Garner," in *The Voice of the Narrator in Children's Literature: Insights from Writers and Critics*, ed. Charlotte F. Otten and Gary D. Schmidt (Westport, CT: Greenwood Press, 1989), pp. 93, 94 [92–100].

 9. Peter Goodrich, "Magical Medievalism and the Fairy Tale in Susan Cooper's The Dark Is Rising Sequence," *The Lion and the Unicorn* 12.2 (1988): 165–77.

10. Michael D. C. Drout, "Reading the Signs of Light: Anglo Saxonism, Education, and Obedience in Susan Cooper's *The Dark Is Rising*," *The Lion and the Unicorn* 21.2 (1997): 231 [230–50].

11. Raymond H. Thompson, *The Return from Avalon: A Study of the Arthurian Legend in Modern Fiction* (Westport, CT: Greenwood, 1985), p. 178.

12. Susan Cooper, *Over Sea, Under Stone* (New York: Harcourt, Brace and World, 1965), ill. Margery Gill, pp. 71–72.

13. Cooper, *Over Sea, Under Stone*, p. 250.

14. Cooper, *Over Sea, Under Stone*, p. 252.

15. Cooper, *Over Sea, Under Stone*, p. 192.

16. It was also named an American Library Association Notable Book.

17. Susan Cooper, *The Dark Is Rising* (London: Chatto and Windus, 1973), ill. Alan E. Cober, p. 36.

18. Cooper, *The Dark Is Rising*, p. 7.

19. The rook is later revealed to be "an agent of the Dark" (*The Dark Is Rising*, p. 136). Early in the volume, the rooks also throw themselves against the skylight in Will's attic bedroom, a foreshadowing of other conflicts between Light and Dark in the novel.

20. Cooper, *The Dark Is Rising*, p. 86. Later, toward the end of the volume, when Will sees Hawkin again, he discerns a change in him. "He was more recognisably Hawkin now, though still the Walker in age. Will felt that he was

looking at two men in one. Hawkin was still dressed in his velvet green coat; it seemed still fresh, with the touch of white lace at the neck. But the figure within the coat was no longer neat and lithe; it was smaller, bent and shrunk by age. And the face was lined and battered beneath long, grey wisping hair; the centuries that had beaten at Hawkin had left only his sharp bright eyes unchanged" (p. 183).

21. Cooper, *The Dark Is Rising*, p. 80.

22. Cooper, *The Dark Is Rising*, p. 129.

23. Cooper, *The Dark Is Rising*, p. 171.

24. Cooper, *The Dark Is Rising*, p. 192.

25. Cooper, *The Dark Is Rising*, p. 216.

26. Cooper, *The Dark Is Rising*, p. 26.

27. Cooper, *The Dark Is Rising*, p. 216.

28. *Greenwitch* was also an award winner; it was awarded a Notable Book Citation from the American Library Association.

29. Susan Cooper, *Greenwitch* (New York: Atheneum, 1978), Frontispiece by Michael Heslop, p. 35. Later, Jane again expresses her concern about the Greenwitch: "The poor Greenwitch, all alone there in the sea. I hope the waves don't smash it all to bits" (p. 49). Later still, Jane worries that the Greenwitch "was unhappy. *Poor thing*, Jane thought, *it's always unhappy*" (p. 122).

30. Cooper, *Greenwitch*, p. 51.

31. Cooper, *Greenwitch*, p. 132.

32. Cooper, *Greenwitch*, p. 108.

33. Cooper, *Greenwitch*, p. 146

34. Cooper, *Greenwitch*, p. 131.

35. Cooper, *Greenwitch*, pp. 140–41.

36. Susan Cooper, *The Grey King* (New York: Atheneum, 1975), ill. by Michael Heslop, p. 33.

37. Cooper, *The Grey King*, p. 186.

38. Cooper, *The Grey King*, p. 137.

39. Cooper, *The Grey King*, p. 118.

40. Cooper, *The Grey King*, p. 84.

41. Cooper, *The Grey King*, pp. 91–95.

42. Cooper, *The Grey King*, pp. 96–97.

43. Cooper, *The Grey King*, p. 98.

44. Cooper, *The Grey King*, pp. 207–208.

45. Like *The Grey King*, Cooper's *Silver on the Tree* also won the Tir na N'og Award, for the best book written in English that takes place in Wales.

46. Susan Cooper, *Silver on the Tree* (New York: Atheneum, 1977), p. 28.

47. Cooper, *Silver on the Tree*, p. 41.

48. Cooper, *Silver on the Tree*, p. 41.

49. Cooper, *Silver on the Tree*, p. 46.

50. Cooper, *Silver on the Tree*, p. 204.

51. Cooper, *Silver on the Tree*, p. 222.

52. Cooper, *Silver on the Tree*, pp. 229, 233–34.

53. Cooper, *Silver on the Tree*, p. 239.

54. Cooper, *Silver on the Tree*, p. 268. A few pages earlier, John Rowlands faces a similar choice. The Lady tell him: "You may indeed remember the hard truth about the Light and the Dark, and the true nature of your wife, if you wish." John asks the Lady to choose on his behalf. "The lady sighed. 'He shall forget,' she said. 'It is better so'" (pp. 261–62).

55. Cooper, *Silver on the Tree*, p. 64.

56. Guinevere's appearance in twentieth-century Wales relates the theme of betrayal to an Arthurian motif. Her reason for leaving her own time is her fear that Arthur will not trust her because of her previous betrayal. She is convinced that having once betrayed a great trust, she cannot permit herself to be trusted again. Betrayal is an important underlying motif in the whole sequence, as demonstrated in the chapter on Cooper in Spivack, *Merlin's Daughters*, pp. 35–50.

57. For a more detailed discussion of the cyclic view of time, see Spivack, *Merlin's Daughters*, particularly pp. 48–49.

58. Cooper, *The Grey King*, p. 146.

CHAPTER 7

INTERVIEW WITH SUSAN COOPER

Raymond H. Thompson

Because she had to fly to California, I missed Susan Cooper on my first trip to the Boston area to interview authors in 1988. I had better luck the following year, fortunately, although the weather was predictably hot and humid since it was early July. After the drive up from New York City, her house in Cambridge was a cool and restful oasis. Even so, it seemed a world away from the rocky Cornish coast, the wintry Buckinghamshire village, and the wild Welsh mountains in which is set her series "The Dark Is Rising."

Composed of *Over Sea, Under Stone* (London: Cape, 1965), *The Dark Is Rising* (New York: Atheneum, 1973), *Greenwitch* (New York: Atheneum, 1974), *The Grey King* (New York: Atheneum, 1975), and *Silver on the Tree* (New York: Atheneum, 1977), it introduces the Grail and several Arthurian characters, the most important of which is Merlin. Though but one element in the broader context of the series, Arthurian tradition provides a dimension that resonates throughout, and it was fascinating to learn how that arose out of the homesickness she felt for the land of her birth. She told me that her second novel was set in her childhood home of Dorney in Buckinghamshire. I later had a chance to visit the village and to go through Dorney Court and the church in which so many of the events take place. That too was a hot and humid day, but one could still recapture in the mind's eye the wintry scene of Will's struggle against the Dark, so powerfully evoked in her book.

RT: What attracted you to the Arthurian legend as an ingredient in your series "The Dark Is Rising"?
SC: I haven't the least idea. It never occurred to me that I was writing about the Arthurian legend as such. I was just writing a series of fantasies which draw on everything I'd ever read, lived through, and absorbed

through general cultural osmosis. The Matter of Britain was part of a great mass of stuff in my subconscious, which consisted of fairytale, folktale, myth—that whole range of material that had always appealed to me enormously since childhood. I suppose I had read almost as much as was then in print, apart from very scholarly studies, about Arthurian legend, partly because I went to Oxford University and the English School at Oxford is very strong on earlier literature.

RT: So for you Arthurian legend was just one part of a wider tradition?

SC: Yes. One result of coming to live in America in 1963 was that I became extremely homesick and turned to reading about not just England, but Britain. Perhaps if I had stayed in England I would have been less focused on things British. I have a strong sense of the mythic history of the land. I grew up in Buckinghamshire, in what was then a countryish area twenty-two miles outside London. I had an awareness of the past that I never had to think about. There was an Iron Age fort a couple of fields away. There was a Roman pavement that somebody had found in his field. Windsor Castle I could see from my bedroom window. Things like that give a sense of layers and layers of time, and of the stories that stick to those layers and develop through them, even though you may not realize that you've got it. It's a great legacy for a writer. I was lucky.

RT: Did your appreciation of this legacy grow keener when you came to America?

SC: I think so. The English author J. B. Priestley was a friend of mine, and he used to write to me when I was going through this dreadful homesick period. In one of his letters he said, do not worry about being away from your roots; you will find you write better about a place when you are away from it. That certainly turned out to be true with "The Dark Is Rising" books. They were immensely British, yet all except the first were written either here in Massachusetts, or on a very small island in the Caribbean where we have a house.

RT: As a child, did you read Arthurian stories for younger readers?

SC: I suppose I must have done because I knew the legends, but I couldn't tell you which ones specifically.

RT: The experience at Oxford must have greatly increased your familiarity with Arthurian legend, then?

SC: Yes. We had to do a lot of background reading in the French sources, such as Chrétien de Troyes. I also read *The Mabinogion*, the chronicles, and many other works that I don't recall now. I didn't, however, refer back to the studies I did at Oxford when I wrote the books. No way. Whatever went into that room at the back of my head while I was at university, there it is in that room. I never consciously looked at it afterwards.

RT: You didn't reread Arthurian sources as a preparation for writing the book?

SC: No. The only thing I ever reread on purpose is *The Mabinogion*, and that not very often. Malory I dip into just because I love the prose.

RT: Did you read studies of the Arthurian era by archaeologists and historians?

SC: Yes. I read E. K. Chambers, R. S. Loomis, Leslie Alcock; and I think John Morris's *Age of Arthur* is fascinating because of the different threads. They were part of my general reading, however, rather than preparation for the series. I'm the kind of person who would go into a second-hand bookshop and look around for anything in that area that I hadn't read.

RT: Had you read any of the more modern versions of the Arthurian legend, such as Tennyson's *Idylls of the King* and *The Once and Future King* by T. H. White?

SC: Oh sure. At university I probably read everything Tennyson ever wrote. White I loved, but I hadn't read many modern novels about Arthur before I wrote the series. It was only when I started *The Dark Is Rising*, the second book in the series, that I realized I had four more books to write. Once I found I was writing fantasy which was being published for young adults, I thought, it's very dangerous to read anybody who is writing in this area. So I didn't. As a result, when I finished the last book I had this lovely orgy reading Alan Garner, C. S. Lewis, and a whole bunch of other writers. I enjoyed them enormously, especially Alan Garner. He's wonderful. We met each other, he and I, at a conference years later. It was like meeting your brother!

RT: Were you conscious of the fact that you were writing in the fantasy form in "The Dark Is Rising" series, particularly the later books, since the fantasy element is less obvious in *Over Sea, Under Stone*?

SC: Evolution, that was really. I wrote *Over Sea, Under Stone* when I was a very young journalist, before I left England. A publishing company called Jonathan Cape, which had published E. Nesbit, had a competition for a family adventure story, and I thought I would go in for this. So the book started off as an adventure story. It doesn't really draw much on Arthurian legend. It makes use of a grail, but not in the same way as the Grail legend. Very early on, however, this character called Merriman turned up, and the book turned itself into a fantasy. Once I was writing fantasy, I don't think I really thought about it. I just felt I'd come home. You don't say to yourself, I am writing fantasy. You don't even say to yourself, I am writing for kids. You just tell the story. Or you're really living in it and reporting on what you find. Of course what you find comes out of your own subconscious.

RT: Did you have in mind a particular age group when you were writing the series?

SC: No, I've never aimed at an age group. You write something and the publishers decide that. To some extent you're aware of your audience because you don't use enormously long Latinate words, for instance. Even then if somebody were to say, you can't use that word because it's too complicated, you can reply, let the kid look it up. This is the way children learn languages, by coming across words they haven't met before. I don't know whom I'm writing for. I write for me, I suppose.

RT: The conflict between good and evil, that is central to the series, is to some extent inherent in the Arthurian legend itself. Were you influenced by that when you were writing?

SC: No. I take more from the chronicles and *The Mabinogion* than from the medieval romances where that conflict is more marked, though that is something I only recognize in retrospect. I'm more interested in Arthur as *dux bellorum*, as the Dark Age war leader, than in the romantic image of the Round Table.

The struggle between the Light and the Dark in my books has more to do with the fact that when I was four World War II broke out. England was very nearly invaded by Germany, and that threat, reinforced by the experience of having people drop bombs on your head, led to a very strong sense of Us and Them. Of course Us is always the good, and Them is always the bad.

This sense must have stayed with me, and it put me into contact with all the other times that England has been threatened with invasion. We are such mongrels: we have been invaded over and over and over again from Scandinavia, from Ireland, from the Continent. This same fear and resistance—usually unsuccessful—has been repeated throughout British history. All that goes into the collective subconscious, and, especially if you come from a generation which went through this experience in childhood, it becomes very much a part of your own imagination. So there is this sympathetic link between my growing up and what it must have been like when the real Arthur—what we know about him—was alive. You find this reflected in the books, especially the last.

RT: What is the relationship between Arthur and Herne the Hunter in your series?

SC: One of the things I tend to believe, largely as a result of reading Robert Graves whom, I'm sure, many scholars find outrageous, is that there is a blurring of identity between an awful lot of figures. The mythic territory of the totally mythical Herne and the possibly-once-real Arthur can cross and overlap, and this happens with the figures in my story. So it is never possible to say, this character is precisely this, and that one is precisely that, because nothing is precise in myth. When you're using myth you can be precise for the purposes of your book, but you do it at your own peril. The mythic elements are all intended to be slightly out of focus, like an impressionist painting, and if you try to sharpen the focus you will lose something. You will lose the magic. The writer must tread gently.

RT: During the last battle in the final book, Arthur seems to disappear. Why was that?

SC: I don't know. That's just the way it happened. This is the story of the Dark and the Light, not a story about Arthur. It draws on myth only to the extent that the myth serves the story. The major Arthurian figure in my series is one that doesn't exist in Arthurian legend: Bran, the son of Arthur. He is my invention. It's with great temerity that an author departs from tradition like this, but you just do it. I think perhaps that he originates in the very strong image of betrayal that you find in the story of Arthur, Guinevere, and Lancelot.

RT: Why did you decide to make Bran the son of Arthur, rather than just an ordinary figure?

SC: I don't know. It was not a rational decision. I start a book knowing it's a road. You know the beginning, you know who's going with you on the road, you know roughly where they're going, but you don't know anything at all (at least I don't) about what's going to happen on the way. You find out as you go along. When I write a novel, I have two things. I have the manuscript as it comes out very slowly, from the typewriter or on the page or wherever; and at the same time I keep a notebook. It's full of random scraps from all over the place, and they often turn up in the books: quotations, images, historical allusions, etc. But in it I also talk to myself. I'm sure if I looked back at the notebook for *The Grey King*, I would find at some point a realization that Bran is going to be the son of Arthur, just as there was a point at which Merriman turned out to be Merlin. Your head does things before it tells you it's doing them.

RT: At what point did you recognize that Merriman was Merlin?

SC: At the end of *Over Sea, Under Stone* one of the characters, a small boy named Barney, says, "Merry Lyon. . .Merlion. . .Merlin." It was only when I reached that point in the writing that I realized who he was. I recognized it at the same time as Barney did. There must be some Jungian reason why the Merlin figure has a particular attraction for me, but I've never delved into it.

RT: Once you discovered Merriman Lyon was Merlin, did that place restraints upon how you were able to use him as a character because of the way he appears in tradition?

SC: No, he's my character, not the Merlin of tradition. Merriman is an Old One in my books, a figure of the Light that opposes the Dark, which is my rather obvious classification of good and evil. He doesn't have the ambiguous dark qualities of Merlin in Arthurian legend. The sinister side of Merriman Lyon, and indeed all the Old Ones, is that absolute good, like absolute evil, is fanatical. As one of my characters points out, there is no room for human ambiguity. Absolute good is like a blinding light, which can be very cruel, and to that extent Merriman is not a sympathetic character. He represents something, but what he represents is to do with those books and not to do with Arthurian legend.

RT: Were you aware that Taliesin had Arthurian associations when you included him in *Silver on the Tree*, the concluding novel in the series?

SC: No, I probably wasn't. I think he may have come from Robert Graves's *White Goddess*, which I read while writing the series.

RT: Do you have specific locations in mind for your settings, or are they an amalgamation?

SC: Oh, very specific. *Over Sea, Under Stone* and *Greenwitch* are both set in Trewissick, which is based on a village in southern Cornwall called Mevagissey. We used to go there when I was a child. *The Dark Is Rising* is set in the part of Buckinghamshire where I grew up. Every stick is real. It doesn't look that way now, a lot of it, but some of it does. The little church is still exactly the same. Huntercombe is based upon the village of Dorney and the Great Hall is Dorney Court, which I see is being used as Miss Haversham's house in a new television version of Dickens's *Great Expectations*. The Welsh setting in *The Grey King* and *Silver on the Tree* is around Aberdyfi, the village where my grandmother was born and where my parents lived. I took some liberties with the description at one point, combining two valleys into one, but otherwise it's exact. My aunt, who still lives there, occasionally has people knocking on the door and saying, is this the certain point from that book?

RT: Did you need to check details of the topography after you had started writing, or was your recollection clear enough?

SC: I had two ordnance survey maps pinned up in my study inside a cupboard door, so that if I wanted to check them I went to the cupboard. Also I used to go home every year. I can remember going out of the door from my parents' house when I was visiting Aberdyfi from America, to remind myself what it was like to go across the dunes and down to the sea in the very early morning. The images that I encountered on the way went into *Silver on the Tree*, where a character called Jane does just that. So I did things like that.

An awful lot of detail comes out of your memory, however. You don't know it's there until you start writing about it. In that same book Will and Bran are on a mountaintop on one side of the River Dyfi, and there appears a magical arching bridge which takes them down into a timeless place called the Lost Land. When I was writing that passage I had them on the mountaintop, and I didn't know what happened next. Then I remembered the last time I was home—being up on that particular mountain, looking out across the estuary of the River Dyfi. Ever since I was a child, I had known the legend about the drowned country, and I could almost see it. As I recalled that moment I thought, that's what they do! That's what happens! They go down there, over a bridge! It's lovely when that happens. That's what I meant by saying it's not a rational decision. You can't control it. You say, oh, I see! You even find yourself using images from dreams sometimes.

RT: Were you aware of legends about Arthur attached to any of these places?

SC: Yes. In the valley behind Aberdyfi, for example, is a stone where King Arthur's horse is supposed to have left a hoofprint. I'm interested in the creation of layers of myth. You can really see how the Arthurian legend has developed, and why it is so impossible to go backwards and say, this bit is true and this isn't. It's all true. How much of it is real is another matter and really irrelevant. This is like Camelot. Where was Camelot? Who cares really? It doesn't matter.

RT: The books comprise a series. Did you find that what you had written in the earlier books committed you to directions that you subsequently regretted, or wished you had more freedom to change?

SC: No. It was wonderful. It was like writing a symphony, in which each movement is different and yet they all link together. I wish my imagination would give me another shape like that because there are all kinds of satisfactions inside it. Things link together, an early book leads to something in a later book. When I wrote the first book, of course, I didn't envision a series, but later, when I first had the idea of writing, not just the second book, but the whole sequence, I drew up a plan on a piece of paper. I had little notes written down: I had the four times of the year—focused upon the solstices, Beltane, and such festivals—I had places, and, very roughly, the characters who were in each book. I remember that under *The Grey King* there was a boy called Bran, but I didn't know who he was. So that was the only thing that limited me.

There were things I had to remember from early books that had to be either resolved or referred to in later books. Once in a great while some particularly bright child will write me a letter saying, you never said what happened to. . . .But I didn't find it restricting. No.

RT: Are there any particular details you would like to change, looking back in retrospect?

SC: I would like to have developed the three Drew children more fully in the first book. They develop as the series progresses, but they're very corny kids' book characters in *Over Sea, Under Stone*, it seems to me. I hadn't gotten to know them.

RT: As the series progresses, Jane in particular grows more interesting, doesn't she?

SC: Yes. Jane is someone I always wanted to write about again. *Silver on the Tree* suffered from being the last book where I was tying up all the ends. It has too much in it. My head was going off in all directions. Its structure is not terrific. There was even more in it, but I took some out. Of course when you're dealing with the substance of myth, which is the fight between good and evil, I suppose, you have to provide the ultimate, terrific, enormous climax. It's almost impossible.

RT: Did the elements you had drawn from Arthurian legend contribute significantly to that feeling of congestion?

SC: I had to move away from it because it seems to me that the Arthurian legend is parallel to the Christian story of the leader who dies for our salvation. Whereas what my books were trying to say is that nobody else can save us. We have to save ourselves. *Silver on the Tree* contains a reference to a poem that I remember my mother reciting to me. It's about Drake being in his hammock, which recalls the local legend in Devon that Sir Francis Drake will come back to rescue England if we're ever invaded again. Similarly, Arthur will come back, and Christ—they are saviors. I didn't want to use that idea. The Arthur that I was using goes to Avalon, and saving the world is up to the people in it.

RT: So in a sense you had to keep Arthur from taking too strong a role within the story, didn't you?

SC: Yes. It wasn't a case of Arthur coming into the story, however, rather a case of the story moving into the time of Arthurian legend, because that is what happens. These books go in and out of time, traveling like a train or a boat, linking one part to another to form a continuity.

RT: I recognize that Arthurian legend is but one among many elements in your story, but what part of that legend did you feel was most important for you to include for your purposes?

SC: I didn't go to the legend. The legend is there at the back of my imagination, in that room where the imagination goes sometimes to draw on something. The part of you that's writing the story at a certain point reaches out and says, I want that bit. You don't sit down at the desk saying, today I'm going to use that bit. It's as if you're going into a garden to pick something that you're going to cook for dinner. You don't say, today

I want carrots and onions and green peppers. You go in and say to yourself, the broccoli looks good; I'll have some of that; there is one pepper on that bush; I'll take that. It's not organized. It's also as if something comes to help. Elements seem to say, I am here and I belong in this part of the story.

Of course picking, itself, is not the best image either, because the act of picking something is deliberate. It is very much a case of your consciousness being invaded at a certain point by something which belongs there.

RT: What you get then is Merriman, who's a guide for young people?

SC: Or Jung's wise old man.

RT: And Arthur who sides with the Light in the struggle against the Dark?

SC: Yes. He represents the Light, I suppose.

RT: They appear in the series because they emerge from your creative subconscious?

SC: We are all writing about the same things in the end. Nobody ever invents a totally original character or story. You're lucky if you can be part of the fabric.

RT: Have you any final comments?

SC: I should just repeat that I've never sat down and thought about the way I've "used" the Arthurian legend, or the Matter of Britain as I like to call it, why certain parts of it come into the story and not other parts. The imagination makes its own choices.

RT: Thank you.

This interview took place in Cambridge, Massachusetts, on July 2, 1989. Originally published as "An Interview" in Susan Cooper, *Dreams and Wishes: Essays on Writing for Children* (New York: McElderry/Simon & Schuster, 1996), it has been reproduced electronically in Raymond H. Thompson, *Taliesin's Successors: Interviews with Authors of Modern Arthurian Literature* (1999) <http://www.lib.rochester.edu/camelot/intrvws/cooper.htm> and appears here by permission of the author.

CHAPTER 8

SWORDS, GRAILS, AND BAG-PUDDINGS:
A SURVEY OF CHILDREN'S POETRY AND PLAYS

Dan Nastali

Youngsters of today can scarcely avoid contact with the Arthurian legend as they proceed through childhood, encountering it in comic books, films, computer games, and occasionally—one would hope—even in books. The characters and motifs embodied in the tradition have become as familiar as superheroes, and most children, although their knowledge might be shallow, can associate Excalibur with King Arthur as readily as the Batmobile with Batman. Acquaintance with the legend is one of the pop-cultural legacies of the twentieth century for English speakers everywhere as well as for many others who have been exposed to the products of Anglo-American culture.

Two minor contributors to this legacy have been the poetry and plays that have presented Arthurian subjects to children down through the years. Each has its own history, and while one has diminished to the vanishing point in our time, the other, to judge by the number of works put before the public, is flourishing. While the importance of the poems and plays produced for juvenile audiences may be slight in terms of shaping the Arthurian literary tradition, a review of their histories sheds light into some curious and lesser known corners of the tradition.

What did the children of the past know of King Arthur, and where did they meet him? There was a time before films and computers, before beautifully illustrated storybooks, before books for children (other than a scattering of religious texts and other didactic works) were produced at all. Although histories of children's literature generally assign its beginnings to the mid-eighteenth century when publications first began to be seriously marketed for juvenile audiences in England, young readers certainly had access to printed material from the late fifteenth century on, and especially to the popular literature that began to appear in abundance in the sixteenth century. It is here, in an era of communal literature, when anyone who could read could read anything, that one must start searching for the earliest Arthurian poetry and plays that children were likely to have encountered.

King Arthur's name was a familiar one to young and old by the late sixteenth century, but the image typically conjured by the name for most people was neither the warlord who defended post-Roman Britain against the Saxons nor the glorious ruler of medieval romance. The Arthur of the public mind was Spenser's Prince of Fairyland, and his stature was comparable to that of Guy of Warwick or Amadis of Gaul, two other characters popular in the fiction of the day. If one looks for the earliest printed Arthurian works in verse that would have been read by young people, one finds the *Faerie Queene*, but also, and perhaps more commonly, less literary works such as "Sir Lamwell," "The Jeaste of Sir Gawayne," and the lost ballad "A Pleasaunte History of an Adventurus Knyghte of Kynges Arthurs Couurte." Only a few such works eventually would find their way into the canon of children's literature, and those that did—"The Marriage of Sir Gawayne," "King Ryence's Challenge"—had to wait for rediscovery in the nineteenth century when a growing popular interest in medieval subjects coincided with a rapidly expanding market for juvenile literature.

Two works in verse, however, that remained in print and retained an audience among young readers from those early years of the popular press were Thomas Deloney's poem "The Noble Acts of King Arthur and His Knights" and the ballad version of the Tom Thumb story. Although the earliest extant copy of Deloney's ballad, which tells of Sir Lancelot's rescue of the knights held captive by Sir Tarquin, is a broadside printed in 1615, it was certainly in circulation before 1600 because it was familiar enough to be quoted by Falstaff in Shakespeare's *Henry IV, Part 2*. Often reprinted under the more common title "Sir Lancelot du Lake" (and not always attributed to Deloney), the ballad opens with the familiar stanza:

> When Arthur first in court began,
> And was approved king,
> By force of armes great victorys wanne,
> And conquest home did bring.[1]

In addition to appearing in many collections, the ballad was popular enough in the seventeenth and eighteenth centuries to inspire a number of burlesque songs, and as late as 1820, John Badcock included a version as a glee in his collection of popular songs, *New Lyre*:

> When Arthur first in Court began
> To wear long hanging sleeves,

He entertained three serving men
And all of them were thieves.[2]

In this version, the comic fates of the three knaves—an Irishman, a Scot, and a Welshman—are described in terms that most charitably can be called ethnically insensitive.[3] Although such politically incorrect humor was commonplace well into the twentieth century, this version had a limited life in collections for children, while Deloney's ballad continued to be included in children's verse anthologies as late as 1930.

"Sir Lancelot du Lake" clearly derives from the medieval narrative tradition and most likely directly from Malory. The origins of the Tom Thumb story are more obscure, and although literary historians and folklorists have found references in English to the little hero as early as the 1580s (as well as analogues in other languages), the earliest extant version of his story is Richard Johnson's prose tale, *The History of Tom Thumbe, the Little*, printed in 1621. The ballad version, upon which Johnson probably drew, exists in its earliest form in an edition printed by John Wright in 1630: *Tom Thumbe, His Life and Death*. There, in eight-line stanzas, is the story of the miniature boy whose birth results from the granting of a wish by Merlin and whose clever deeds eventually win him a place at King Arthur's court. Both the prose and ballad versions had long lives in the chapbooks of England and America, and in time the story was modernized, adapted in virtually every popular medium, and now holds a prominent place among the standard stories of children's literature.

In 1855, the British author Charlotte Yonge published her own *History of the Good Knight Sir Thomas Thumb*, describing his adventures in her preface as "without variety, and, in general, disagreeable; and even the name of King Arthur cannot raise him, appearing only as the vulgarized Arthur of nursery rhymes."[4] Indeed, the King Arthur who descended through the chapbooks and broadsides that fed the public's appetite for inexpensive diversions from the sixteenth into the nineteenth centuries was much diminished from the hero of the earlier chronicles and romances. Children who first encountered him in such verse met a two-dimensional figure distinguishable only by his most familiar artifacts—Excalibur, the Round Table—from any generic medieval king.

In 1784, the antiquarian Joseph Ritson included the oldest known version of another nursery rhyme, "When Good King Arthur Ruled This Land," in his collection *Gammer Gurton's Garland*:

When good King Arthur rul'd the land,
He was a goodly king,
He stole three pecks of barley meal
To make a bag pudding.[5]

The poem goes on to tell how he fed his noblemen and how his wife fried the leftovers the next morning. Sometimes entitled simply "King Arthur" or "Bag-pudding," this bit of nonsense, which may have originated as a song in a play, may be the most often reprinted Arthurian poem for children, and if it is difficult to recognize Arthur from the context, it is because there is no one there to recognize—in other versions, the king is Henry or Stephen.[6] (For a discussion of some of the musical versions of this poem, see the essay by Jerome V. Reel, Jr., chapter 10 in this volume.)

Similar children's poems with just as little substance but just as much gusto have appeared in various collections over the years. Another poem entitled "King Arthur" appeared in a collection by "L. H." in 1864, and is here given in full:

> When Arthur reigned in Camelot,
> A hundred knights at table sat;
> They never knew from day to day,
> Or what they drank, or what they ate.
>
> Except on Sunday—then the king
> His knights with beef and pudding fed;
> A flagon of beer was each man's cheer,
> And butter had they on their bread.[7]

And one more early lyric that may or may not refer to King Arthur but that has often been reprinted is "Arthur O'Bower":

> Arthur O'Bower has broken his band
> And he comes roaring up the land;
> The King of Scots with all his power
> Cannot stop Arthur of the Bower.[8]

This folk poem has found its way into many collections of nursery rhymes and reportedly was first recorded in a lost letter from Dorothy Wordsworth to Charles Lamb in 1804. It has been suggested that the poem is a riddle and that "Arthur" here personifies the wind, a conjecture supported by a comment by William Wordsworth to the effect that the rhyme was recited in his childhood at times of high winds.

Although the earliest of these poems were not written with a juvenile audience in mind, all undoubtedly became familiar to young readers early in their literary lives. While collections of old ballads and other poems appeared with increasing frequency after the success of Thomas Percy's *Reliques of Ancient English Poetry* in 1765, there was, in fact, very little poetry of any kind published specifically for children through the eighteenth century. Robert Bator notes that "original poetry for children had to await Jane Taylor, Ann Taylor, and others in *Original Poems, for Infant Minds*" (in 1804), which was soon followed by others. Virtually all of it was moralistic in content and cautionary in tone, and "amusement and imagination, if allowed at all, had to be matched with some more worthy purpose."[9]

By the early nineteenth century, the possibilities of adapting Arthurian stories began to become apparent to those writing for the growing market in children's literature. In what may be the earliest Arthurian works written expressly for a juvenile audience, Andrew St. John, in 1808, retold two long stories, "The History of Merlin, the Enchanter" and "Lancelot of the Lake," in his collection of prose adaptations of old chivalric *Tales of Former Times*. "An attentive perusal of the old English Metrical Romances first suggested to the Editor of these Tales," he wrote in his preface, "the idea that a series of stories founded upon acts of heroism, honour and generosity, and pursued according to the manners of former ages, might not be unacceptable to the youth of the rising generation."[10] The notion that Arthurian stories could furnish behavioral models for the young would be repeated throughout the century.

Thomas Love Peacock is best remembered by Arthurians for his Taliesin novel, *The Misfortunes of Elphin* (1829), but he also published, in 1817, what is probably the earliest original Arthurian poem written expressly for children in *The Round Table: or, King Arthur's Feast*. The poem is actually a lighthearted history of the British kings and queens, who are assembled by Merlin for a feast to alleviate the tedium Arthur complains of while awaiting the time for his return on his solitary island. The verse is unremarkable, but Peacock cleverly works in a memorable fact about each monarch:

> Now Stephen, for whom some bold barons had carved,
> Said, while some could get surfeited, he was half-starved:
> For his arms were so pinioned, unfortunate elf!
> He could hit on no method of helping himself.
> But a tumult more furious called Arthur to check it,
> 'Twixt Henry the Second and Thomas-a-Becket.
> "Turn out," exclaimed Arthur, "that prelate so free,
> And from the first rock see him thrown in the sea."[11]

The publication, in 1816 and 1817, of the first editions of Malory in almost two hundred years fed an already burgeoning taste for the gothic in literature and stimulated a revival of the Arthurian tradition that would expand throughout the century. The rediscovered world of the *Morte d'Arthur*, so familiar to modern readers (and discussed at length by Andrew Lynch in chapter 1 in this volume), would gradually supplant the fairy tale milieu in which Arthur had resided since the English Renaissance.

By the time Tennyson's first *Idylls of the King* reached print in 1859 (his "Lady of Shalott" had already been published in 1833, and "Sir Galahad" and "Morte d'Arthur" in 1842), knights were everywhere in the popular culture of the day. Tennyson's poetry codified the ideals. Mark Girouard writes, "It was Tennyson's version of chivalry, 'Live pure, speak true, right wrong, follow the King,' which provided what might be called the establishment ethic of chivalry."[12]

The impact of Tennyson's *Idylls* on children's literature was almost immediate, and it would continue to grow into the twentieth century even after the poet's works had fallen from fashion with the general public. Evidence of the early response to the *Idylls* may be found in the anonymous author's preface to the second printing of *Arthur's Knights: An Adventure from the Legend of the Sangrale* in late 1859: "The publication of Tennyson's last noble poem since the first edition of this trifle, may have given it an air of presumption, which induces me to add, that it was printed for the amusement of those young people who have some curiosity about the early English romances, and few means of gratifying it."[13]

First published in 1858, the ninety-page poem, in blank verse and a variety of stanza forms, introduced its young readers to the Grail quest with a narrative drawn primarily from Malory. Beginning with the vision of the "Holy Grale" at Arthur's court, the story follows the adventures of the major Grail knights and ends with the return of Bors to Camelot, where he recounts the glorious fates of Galahad and Percivale. Lancelot figures prominently in the poem, and his fathering of Galahad occurs during a brief marriage to Elene that ends with her death, but the reason for his failure in the quest is never made explicit. Anticipating the bowdlerization that characterizes the many prose retellings of Malory that would follow, the relationship between Lancelot and the queen is only hinted at in such passages as Percivale's account of a tournament:

> Queen Guinevere on high the while,
> Saw the tourney raging under,
> I marked the summer of her smile,
> Warming thee [Lancelot] to battle thunder;
> Pleased, the king to her 'gan say,
> "Lancelot makes marvelous play,"
> But she heard him not
> For the shouting of the crowd,
> And all around the echo loud,
> Of Lancelot, Sir Lancelot.[14]

Following several non-Arthurian poems, the volume ends with another poem, "Sir Hector de Marais," which serves as a coda to the book's title.

It tells of the long search by Lancelot's brother that ends in the chapel where the knight's body lies and also with a sobering moral:

> We too, we seek Sir Lancelot,
> Till youth and hope are fled;
> We find him, yet we find him not,
> For Lancelot is dead.[15]

In the United States, in that same year (1858), Thomas Bulfinch capitalized on the success of his retelling of the classical myths in *The Age of Fable* (1855) by publishing a companion book in his *Age of Chivalry; or, Legends of King Arthur*, and thereby offered the American public a large coherent body of Arthurian story before the *Idylls* were published. Alluding to his earlier book, he remarked in his preface, "if every well-educated young person is expected to know the story of the Golden Fleece, why is the quest of the Sangreal less worthy of his acquaintance?" And like his British counterpart Andrew St. John some fifty years earlier, Bulfinch saw in the Arthurian stories their value as models of behavior for the young. "The tales," he wrote, "though not to be trusted for their facts, are worthy of all credit as pictures of manners."[16]

Readers familiar only with modern editions of *Bulfinch's Mythology*—the omnibus which includes *Legends of Charlemagne* (1862) as well as the two earlier books—may think of the work as a collection of scraps of poetry strung together with a slight narrative and not, for that matter, a work written for a juvenile audience. In fact, the modern *Bulfinch* is largely the product of later editors—notably Edward Everett Hale in 1884 and J. Loughran Scott in 1898—who left little of the original author's text intact. Bulfinch's *Age of Chivalry*, which went through four editions by 1872, did indeed introduce its young readers to Arthurian poetry, but the poetry consists of scattered quotations from Chaucer, Spenser, Milton, the ballads in Percy's *Reliques*, and the verse of Thomas Warton, all gracing a straightforward, if bowdlerized, narrative drawn from Geoffrey of Monmouth and later chronicles, Malory, and the *Mabinogion*.

By the time Hale issued his revision, the Arthurian Revival was well underway, and the editor explained his approach in his own preface: "The popularity which Mr. Bulfinch's versions of the 'Stories of the Round Table' at once attained has demanded several repeated editions of his book. In this edition the book has been materially enlarged. . . .Since Mr. Bulfinch wrote, Mr. Tennyson. . .has published several additional 'Idylls of the King,' from which I have added some illustrations. I have also taken advantage of the greater space to retain the original language of Sir Thomas Mallory in many of the stories where Mr. Bulfinch thought it necessary to abridge, and I have inserted one or two new stories from the 'Mabinogeon.' "[17] Hale also added the non-Arthurian concluding section, "Knights of English History." The book was further overhauled some fourteen years later by Scott who, smitten as so many were by Tennyson, "our modern Homer," added even more of the *Idylls* as well as passages from the works of Arnold, Swinburne, Lowell, Schiller, and others. And mentioning his new adaptations of Malory, he states that he has "created a new work"— one which retains little of the 1858 original beyond Bulfinch's "splendid framework."[18]

In England, another anonymous poet published *Six Ballads About King Arthur* in 1881, retelling in jaunty ballad stanzas the same central episodes of Malory's *Morte* that would appear in countless prose works for children thereafter. Purged of any morally questionable detail, the poems present a bland version of Arthur's story, and perhaps the only insight into the author's personal views is discernible in the concluding poem, "The Death of King Arthur," which explains Mordred's success in turning the barons against Arthur:

> Now, all ye Englishmen, behold
> What mischief happened here:
> This King, who was the noblest king,
> And knight withouten peer,
>
> Who loved the fellowship of none
> But good and brave, who spent
> His life redressing crime and wrong,
> Was held in discontent.
>
> This old, *old* custom of the land
> Is not forgot, they say,
> That Englishmen are ne'er content,
> Not even at this day.
>
> This is their great default—no thing
> Pleaseth this people long.
> Thus happed it that false Mordred's force
> Waxed numerous and strong.[19]

Howard Pyle, the American author and illustrator best known to Arthurians for his series of four books retelling the old stories for young readers (1903–10), first turned his hand to the material by illustrating Tennyson's "Lady of Shalott" in 1881.[20] Two years later he published one of his classic children's books, *The Merry Adventures of Robin Hood*, of interest here for the two Arthurian ballads it contains. At one point in the narrative, following a bountiful meal, Little John sings "The Good Knight and His Love," in which a knight of Arthur's court, rejected by the lady he longs for, finds his anguish relieved by food and drink. The poem begins on a familiar note—"When Arthur, King, did rule this land, / A goodly king was he"—and ends with the lesson:

> "Then gat he back where was good sack
> And merry companye,
> And soon did cease to cry 'Alack!'
> When blithe and gay was he.
>
> From which I hold, and feel full bold
> To say, and eke believe,
> That gin the belly go not cold
> The heart will cease to grieve."[21]

At another point in the story, Arthur a Bland, one of Robin's companions, sings the ballad "The Wooing of Sir Keith," in which a loathly lady appears at Arthur's court and requests three kisses. After Lancelot, Tristram, Kay, and others refuse, the young knight of the title kisses her and breaks the spell she is under, revealing her, of course, to be a young beauty. Arthur's knights are much chagrined:

> In great amaze the knights did stare,
> Quoth Kay, "I make my vow
> If it will please thee, lady fair,
> I'll gladly kiss thee now."[22]

In Pyle's version of the old story, there is no need to relinquish sovereignty to the lady, for when the gallant Sir Keith drops to his knees and offers to become her slave, she bends to bestow her own kisses on him, proclaims that he is now her master, and gives herself, her wealth, and her lands to him.

Another ballad embedded in a prose narrative—although as a series of fragments that preface the chapters of a story purportedly based on the ballad—is "The Lay of Sir Marrok" by Allen French. Appearing first in the popular children's periodical *St. Nicholas Magazine* in May, 1902, "Sir Marrok" is French's original tale of a knight of Arthur's court who is turned into a wolf by a sorceress, undergoes terrible trials (including being hunted by Sir Tristram), but ultimately defeats the evil woman and regains his human form, his son, and his property. The story was expanded to novel length when it was published in book form in the fall of 1902. Although the "Lay" itself consists of a total of twenty-eight stanzas if magazine and book verses are combined, the "fragments" exist only to lend the tale a more archaic flavor and merely hint at the contents of the prose narrative as in the following set piece:

> Sir Tristram was a well-versed knight
> In harping and in minstrelsy;
> In hunting took he great delight,
> And best of all the hounds had he.[23]

St. Nicholas Magazine was one of the most popular of the children's periodicals with a life that extended from 1873 to 1943. Children's magazines, which began to flourish in both Britain and the United States in the 1820s and which were, in their early years, often church-sponsored and always moralistic in content, began to shift in their editorial aim toward entertainment by the middle of the nineteenth century.[24] Today, when teenage culture holds such sway in the marketplace, it is fascinating to look at the most popular children's periodicals of a century ago and note that their intended audiences inclusively ranged in age from the youngest readers to those entering adulthood; presumably, the children of each age would find the material that suited them in each issue, from nursery rhymes to surprisingly detailed expository pieces on, say, steamship technology.

Poetry in the juvenile periodicals included well known works by the great authors, often nicely illustrated, and a vast amount of original material. Typical of the treatments of Arthurian subjects is "The Last Knight" by William Hayne, published in *The Youth's Companion* in 1887, in which the poet provides a portrait of a forlorn Sir Bedivere, still obsessed with the events of Arthur's passing as he awaits the end of his own life:

> Companionless I roam the world
> From dreary shore to shore,—
> But soon my yearning eyes shall see
> Brave comrades gone before![25]

Another prolific author of magazine verse for both children and adults was Arthur Guiterman, whose verse appeared in *Colliers Weekly* and *Life* as well as *St. Nicholas* and *The Youth's Companion*. From the *Companion* in 1904 is a cautionary "King Arthur and the Half-Man," in which Arthur's repeated refusals to fight turn a feeble creature ("habit") into a raging giant. Finally shamed into fighting and defeating the menace, Arthur acknowledges the lesson he has learned:

> So panted Arthur: "Aye! Forsooth,
> He called me 'Fool'—and spake the truth.
> Yea, 'fool!' to scorn a feeble foe

While false indulgence made him grow!"
Boast not thy strength. Make no delay.
That foeman waxes day by day.
Strike swift! Let cravens flinch or flee
If Half-Man Habit challenge thee![26]

In December, 1918, *St. Nicholas* began a series of narratives in verse entitled "The Wondering Boy" in which the title character, a young dreamer
who loves romantic tales, shares adventures with Arthur's knights. Written
by Clara Platt Meadowcroft and handsomely illustrated by M. L. Bower, the
stories are not what one might expect from the prefatory lyric poem,
which suggests that some familiar tales will follow:

Wherever the battle is two to one,
Where faint hope gallantly fights,
Still over the Cambrian hills they come,
The King and his valiant knights.[27]

The mention of "Cambrian hills" provides the clue to what follows, for the
first of the knights to visit the boy is not Lancelot or Tristram but Iscawndred,
whose tread is so light that he does not bend a blade of grass when he passes,
and together the boy and the knight face down a tyrannical giant.

Although she presents her heroes as knights rather than as Celtic war-
riors, Meadowcroft's sources are the old Welsh tale of "Culhwch and
Olwen" and Lady Charlotte Guest's notes to her translation of the
Mabinogion. In subsequent ballads, the boy is visited by other companions
of the Welsh Arthur, all with marvelous powers—Taliesin the Knight of the
Radiant Brow, Sandde Byrd Angel and his singing sword, Coll the Juggler,
Peredur the Knight of the Magic Chess Board, and Kay, whose ability to
stay under water for days enables them to defeat a seagoing dragon. In the
seventh episode, Arthur himself is called from his rest beneath a hill to lead
a phantom fight against an unnamed army invading England:

High overhead rang joyous cries as his knightly legions came.
The English echoed the shouts below when they heard that magic name:
"Arthur is with us, the great High King! Arthur himself comes back!"
The air was filled with a cloudy fire, and they spurred to a fresh attack.

Nothing the strangers saw or heard; they were dulled of sense and soul;
Only they knew that the scattered band once more was a glowing whole;
Only they felt that this new-found strength was a force that could not yield;
And seized with a sudden nameless fear, they fled from the battle-field.[28]

In the final poem of the series, when the Wondering Boy wishes to know
where lost ships go, Merthyn arrives in his own ship of glass to transport

the boy to Avalon, where in a rather maudlin moment, he not only sees the happy folk who sailed on those lost vessels but also is greeted by "a faery dog. . .his little lost playmate, Sprite." If her verse is pedestrian, Meadowcroft must be credited for some originality in her choice of Arthurian material.

Most of the poems mentioned thus far have been narrative poems, which is to be expected in works that derive from the Arthurian tradition—a literary tradition that embodies its themes and symbols in stories. The nursery rhymes are somewhat disassociated, of course, because they typically depend for their ongoing lives on the pure pleasure of the verbal experience in reading and reciting them—they no more stimulate curiosity about the Arthurian tradition than "Old King Cole" would lead one back to his prototype in Geoffrey of Monmouth. But by the early decades of the twentieth century, narrative verse—written for both children and adults—was going out of fashion, and when Arthurian material appeared at all, it was likely to be in such novelties as "Arthur's Knights Tackle Caesar's Senators." This comic piece by Dervin Locksley, which appeared in the scouting magazine *Boys' Life*, recounts the tale of a football game between the knights and some ancient Romans that takes some silly turns and ends when Sir Bors steals the ball and is chased from the stadium by his coach, the Connecticut Yankee.[29] (See figure 8.1.)

Although narrative poetry has given way to prose fiction in the realm of storytelling, hundreds of modern-era poets have found material in the Arthurian tradition for lyric poems written for adult audiences. Typically such poetry has focused on characters and relationships, drawn on evocative settings with Arthurian associations, or offered observations on incidents in the stories. In recent years, poets have become so confident of the familiarity of educated readers with the material that they may simply color their works with oblique allusions to aspects of the tradition. Lyric poetry written for children is shallower and narrower, and there is much less of it. There are the old nursery rhymes that still appear in collections, and while the unexplored archives of the children's magazines of Britain and the United States undoubtedly hold more Arthurian verse, every discovery reinforces the notion that what remains hidden is more of the same.

Children's lyrics tend to be slight things, inspired by the most familiar characters and motifs. Eleanor Farjeon incorporates a few brief poems with the hero stories in her 1925 collection, *Mighty Men*, including "Is Arthur Gone to Avalon?":

Is Arthur gone
To Avalon
In a black boat, as I hear?
Yes, three tall Queens were there alone
To row and watch and steer.

He sidestepped as a tackler
dove

8.1   King Arthur's Knights engage ancient Romans in a football game in Dervin Locksley's "Arthur's Knights Tackle Caesar's Senators" in the scouting magazine *Boys' Life* (1930).

Who saw him go
And told you so?
His Knight, Sir Bedivere.
Now Arthur's crown is fallen low,
His sword lies in the mere,
And Arthur's gone
To Avalon
With a black boat for his bier.[30]

Stella Mead, in another collection of hero tales, similarly includes some poetry, including the lullaby "Arthur in the Arms of Merlin," the first stanza of which follows:

In his mantle richly 'broidered
Slept the little trustful child.

Merlin, old and fierce and wrinkled,
Gently on the baby smiled.
"Rest, my sweet one, slumber softly,
Merlin claims thee but to save,
Thou shalt grow to splendid manhood,
Kind and valiant, mild and brave.
Slumber here,
Have no fear,
Merlin takes thee but to save."[31]

Somewhat more inventive is James Reeves's "Avalon" in his book of alphabet verse, *Ragged Robin* (1961), in which a grave robber visits the sleeping Arthur and his queen and takes their jewels and rings, though in time, we are told, "they will rise again / And all false knaves be slain." In the same book, "Good Sir Kay," who is commanded to lock the gate while the lords and ladies are abed, may refer to the Arthurian figure.[32]

Any survey of Arthurian children's verse would be incomplete without reference to the works that virtually every British and American school child was exposed to in the late nineteenth and early twentieth century— the poetry of Alfred, Lord Tennyson. The earliest school reader based on the *Idylls of the King* may be an edition of *Elaine* published in "The Students' Series of English Classics" in Boston in 1894.[33] Typically such readers included background information on Tennyson and the Arthurian legend, notes, and other editorial matter and were printed in the small, inexpensive editions that today ubiquitously appear at used book sales. Selections from the *Idylls* continued to be issued by different publishers at the rate of one a year through the 1920s, and many of these school texts were often reprinted.[34] In the United States, the *Idylls* most frequently included were those "selected by the National Conference on Uniform Entrance Requirements in English as a basis for the examinations in 1915–1919": "The Coming of Arthur," "Gareth and Lynette," "Lancelot and Elaine," "The Quest of the Holy Grail," and "The Passing of Arthur."[35] It would have been difficult for anyone attending school in the years before 1930 to avoid exposure to Tennyson, and it is small wonder that youth organizations based on Arthurian and Holy Grail themes flourished during the period and often incorporated Tennyson's works as inspirational reading.[36] In addition to the *Idylls*, two of Tennyson's shorter poems were regularly placed before students (and have had greater staying power in the literature anthologies than the *Idylls*): "The Lady of Shalott" and "Sir Galahad," the first admired a century ago for its sweet morbidity as much as its rhythm and rhymes, the second for its muscular Christianity.

Spiritually akin to "Sir Galahad"—at least for American students—was James Russell Lowell's *The Vision of Sir Launfal*. First published in 1848, the poem tells of a knight who seeks the Holy Grail for many years without success only to learn that its true meaning is charity after he provides food and drink for a leper who reveals himself to be Christ. Considered a standard work of American literature by the end of the nineteenth century, Lowell's poem also began to appear in school editions in the 1890s and continued through the 1920s. By 1929, Lowell's "Vision" had faded, its pious message apparently offering little comfort or inspiration to Depression-era readers. By that same point in time, a decline in interest in Tennyson's verse was also discernible. Although selections of his poetry have continued to be included in anthologies, new editions of the *Idylls* intended for use in schools began to appear with less frequency—at five-year intervals on average through the twentieth century. When he is read by students today, Tennyson is typically treated as a period author and the *Idylls of the King* as an example of Victorian morality embodied in a fashion of the day.

By comparison to earlier periods, little poetry of any sort is written for children today, and although the modern Arthurian Revival has once again made the legend familiar to children in a host of forms and formats, the time is past when young readers will pick up a new book or magazine and find an Arthurian tale in verse. Children's plays, however, are quite another story. Each year of the recent past has seen more Arthurian plays produced for young audiences and, for that matter, published for performance by children.[37] If chances are high that a modern child will never read an Arthurian poem, they are much better that he will sooner or later experience a play that in some way draws on the legend. For purposes here, such peripheral works as toy theaters, puppet shows, radio dramatizations, television shows, and films will all be excluded, and the concentration will be on theatrical and published plays intended for children.

One must look to England for the earliest Arthurian works presented on stage and to the eighteenth century for any sort of juvenile audience, although those who did attend, we are told, did so in spite of warnings about the jeopardy in which the theater placed their morals: "But many ignored [such warnings], including, predictably, certain aristocrats and gentry, but also many pious middle-class persons, who if they did not condone participation in dramas, did not forbid seeing or reading them."[38] And what type of Arthurian works would an audience of that period have seen? A performance, perhaps, of one of the later versions of the scarcely traditional Dryden/Purcell semi-opera *King Arthur*, first staged in 1691 but modernized for audiences in the 1730s and most notably by David Garrick in 1770, whose "chief production task was to improve the spectacle, to oil the machinery of pageantry, to intensify the wonder of stagecraft."[39]

Henry Fielding's mock heroic Tom Thumb play *Tragedy of Tragedies* (1731), even less connected to its Arthurian roots than Dryden's work, received similar treatment in the eighteenth century at the hands of revisers, notably Kane O'Hara, who in 1780 turned the work into a "burletta," or burlesque opera. Another full-length play (which survives in the author's published works but may never have reached the stage) was Aaron Hill's *Merlin in Love* (1760), an operetta in five acts in which Merlin appears as a buffoon who tries to win the beautiful Columbine with his magic but becomes the butt of the humor. The presence of Harlequin and Columbine in Hill's play identifies the stage tradition it descends from—the pantomimes and burlesques that in the eighteenth century became popular "added attractions" as afterpieces to the tragedies and comedies that were the "feature presentations." Borrowing such stock characters as Harlequin from the Italian *commedia dell'arte*, these ancestors of the Christmas pantos that are still performed in Britain today were Anglicized with the addition of such popular figures as Tom Thumb, Jack the Giant-Killer, and Merlin, whose role was usually reduced to that of a comical stage wizard.

Examples of such entertainments, which sometimes traded on the titles of earlier works, are *Merlin; or, The British Enchanter*, a pantomime of 1731; a *Merlin's Cave* pantomime of 1750; *Merlin; or, The Enchanter of Stonehenge*, a 1767 entertainment; *Merlin's Cave; or, A Cure for a Scold*, an entertainment of 1788; Charles Dibdin's *Wizard's Wake; or, Harlequin and Merlin*, in 1802; *Merlin's Cave; or, Harlequin's Masquerade*, a pantomime of 1814; and Thomas Dibdin's *Merlin's Mount; or, Harlequin Cymraeg and the Living Leek* of 1825.[40] By the early nineteenth century, the British theater scene had become the rowdy and scandal-ridden province of aristocrats and lowlifes and it remained so until legislation in 1843 permitted new and smaller theaters to compete with Drury Lane and Covent Garden. Until that time, it is doubtful that many young people of the middle class were exposed to even the superficial and farcical depictions of Arthurian characters that occasionally appeared on stage.

The exceptions would have been the holiday entertainments that grew in sophistication and visual splendor through the early 1800s. At a time when melodrama ruled the legitimate theater, the popular taste for stage humor and spectacle was satisfied by what one historian has characterized as "vapid comic opera and stupid farce," which began to be redeemed, beginning in the 1830s, by more creative and imaginatively presented extravaganzas.[41] The first notable example to exploit an Arthurian theme was Isaac Pocock's *King Arthur and the Knights of the Round Table* (1834), which, like other Arthurian works of the time, took liberties both with traditional characters and with its source, Sir Walter Scott's *Bridal of Triermain*. The "grand chivalric entertainment," however, required a story only to excuse the elaborate stage effects, the action (which included jousting on horseback and the storming of a castle), and other visual delights.[42]

By the late 1830s, the tradition of Christmas pantomimes was solidly established, and if not as directly aimed at juvenile audiences as the pantos of
today, the plays still leavened the rude buffoonery of the burlesques with
more fanciful themes and treatments. An example is Richard Nelson Lee's
Harlequin and Mother Red Cap; or, Merlin and Fairy Snowdrop, a romantic
farce produced at the Adelphi Theatre in which Merlin, the "Astrologer of
the Olden Time," is cast in a malevolent role.[43]

Throughout the remainder of the century, other works with Arthurian
associations that would have drawn young people to the theater included
Thomas Longdon Greenwood's *Harlequin and Good King Arthur; or, the
Enchanter Merlin and the Queen of Fairyland* (1842); *Jack the Giant Killer,
or, The Knights of the Round Table* (1846); H. J. Byron's *Jack the Giant
Killer; or, Harlequin King Arthur and Ye Knights of Ye Round Table* (1859);
E. L. Blanchard's *Tom Thumb; or, Merlin the Magician and the Good Fairies of
the Court of King Arthur* (1861); H. S. Faucit's *Tom Thumb; or, Merlin the
Magician and the Fairy in the Grotto of Silver Shells* (1862); William Brough's
King Arthur, or, The Days and Knights of the Round Table (1863); F. W. Green's
*Jack the Giant Killer and Tom Thumb, or Harlequin, King Arthur and the Knights
of the Round Table* (1875); F. L. Moreton's *Jack the Giant Killer, or
Harlequin King Arthur, and the Seven Champions of Christendom* (1885); and
E. H. Patterson and H. Grattan's *Merry Mr. Merlin; or, Good King Arthur* (1895).
Such frivolities were not restricted to the British stage: W. M. Akhurst's *King
Arthur, or, Lancelot the Loose, Gin-ever the Square, and the Knights of the Round
Table* was produced in Australia in 1868, and an American musical by
F. B. Neilson, *King Arthur and Ye Knights of Ye Table Rounde*, was performed at
the University of Pennsylvania in 1894.

Although the appeal of this type of entertainment to young audiences
is obvious, the first work explicitly aimed at children may be *King Arthur:
A Juvenile Operetta*, with music by Herbert Longhurst and George G. Lewis
and a libretto by H. E. Turner, which premiered in London in 1896.
Although by this time the "orthodox" Arthurian story was already quite
familiar through the many editions and adaptations of Malory and the
verse of Tennyson, the creators of this musical felt perfectly free to present their own version. Thus we have Arthur knighting a Lancelot who is
in love with the king's daughter Elaine. Through the magical spells of King
Gore and his wife, the witch Endor, Lancelot breaks his knightly vows, is
condemned in court, and ultimately must be rescued by the sweet Elaine.

In the United States, the first theater program for young people was
established in New York City in 1903, and the early productions were for
the most part adaptations of such familiar literary works as L. Frank Baum's
The Wizard of Oz.[44] Without a review of theater records or newspaper
accounts, it is impossible to say whether Arthurian works were included in

the repertoires of the early companies, but it is altogether likely since such plays were being published and also being performed by church and school groups at the time. One of the earliest published Arthurian plays was Lena Dalkieth's "Sir Gareth of Orkney," which together with such other short works as "King Alfred and the Cakes" and "Scene from Uncle Tom's Cabin" was included in *Little Plays* (1905) along with suggestions on staging and "pictures of little actors from photographs."[45] The story is that of the kitchen knight's rescue of Lady Lyonors in spite of the scorn the young hero must endure from her sister Lynette.

Another dramatization of the Gareth story, drawn from Tennyson and dating from the same period, was the Reverend James Yeames's *The Young Knight*, one of the plays written for the Knights of King Arthur youth organization (discussed by Alan Lupack in chapter 9 in this volume). Plays were popular with such groups, offering opportunities to involve young people in activities that embodied ethical and spiritual ideals while at the same time trading on popular subject matter. The Grail quest was deemed especially uplifting, and there are records of an anonymous two-act play on that theme that was performed annually for decades at a Christian summer camp in Alabama. At the end of the play, after the questing knights reported on their adventures, the assembled campers would join in a ritual Grail procession.[46]

Not all such summer plays were so edifying. At about the same time, a camp in Maine performed "Good King Arthur," an elaborated musical version of the old nursery rhyme in which Arthur steals the barley meal and the queen makes bag-pudding. The lyrics were set to familiar tunes, with Guinevere, for example, singing to the tune of "The Campbells are Coming":

> The soup is all ready, and so's the roast;
> Potatoes and onions are done—almost!
> And now I must think of some delicate thing
> That's worthy to make a dessert for my King![47]

Another original play, edifying in its own way, perhaps, was the anonymous "King Arthur," a "posture play for seven boys" published in *Hygeia* in 1929 as a useful pedagogic exercise. Arthur here presents Lancelot, Tristram, Belvidere [*sic*], Galahad, and others each with a lesson on proper posture. The play ends as the knight determined to have the best posture is awarded a bride.[48] Of the more traditional plays, Tennyson was, not surprisingly, a popular source in the early decades of the century. C. W. Bailey, in his "King Arthur and the Knights of the Round Table" (1929), adapted his text from Tennyson's verse for a series of scenes ending with Arthur's passing.

His published text is illustrated with photographs of young actors in performance. Frank Jones did much the same in his *Life and Death of King Arthur* (1930), a play written for the boys of Wellesley School, Croydon.

By the 1930s, an active market was established for the publication of plays,[49] and while more original works began to appear, Arthurian plays for young audiences unadventurously drew again and again on familiar stories. An exception is Boyce Loving's *Galahad Jones* (1937), a modern comedy in which the hero, Tommy Jones, is inspired by books about King Arthur to introduce the concept of chivalry to the lives of those around him. Ridiculed for his efforts and called Galahad in jest, he attempts to rescue a damsel in distress and unwittingly uncovers a hijacking ring. If the story is not terribly original, Loving's play at least broadened the scope of Arthurian subject matter in juvenile drama.

A review of the subjects of Arthurian children's plays by decades does reveal some patterns, but one hesitates to assign too much meaning to them. While it is tempting to attribute the patterns to the shifting social ideals that authors, educators, and parents believed should be placed before young audiences, from a broader perspective—one that would encompass all of the media twentieth-century children have been exposed to—the subjects may simply reflect changing tastes in popular entertainment. In reality, both views have some validity.

Plays with the Holy Grail as a focal point appeared in each decade through the 1950s, but not in the 1960–70s. In the 1980s they returned, but as a relatively small percentage of the total number of Arthurian plays and probably not as a signal that the legend was a source of a resurgent spiritualism. Stories about Gareth, the kitchen knight, were popular until the 1950s but then disappeared, suggesting that behavior once considered inspirational is no longer, or, perhaps, that the abusive treatment of the boy by Sir Kay and the damsel he assists has become too alien or distasteful to modern children. The story of the charitable Sir Cleges and the Christmas cherries, traditionally set at Uther Pendragon's court, was once a seasonal favorite but now no longer seems to be.

Merlin and Morgan le Fay became the central figures in several plays of the 1980s and 1990s, a reflection of their popularity in an era when fantasy had made a strong comeback in popular fiction, films, and other entertainments. Merlin, it might be noted, is virtually always portrayed as a benevolent figure now, having almost entirely shed the darker role assigned him by Mark Twain, and Morgan is almost always a villainous sorceress. Adaptations and spin-offs of the *Connecticut Yankee story* have become more popular since the 1970s in children's plays as well as other media, possibly because the time travel plot device offers easy opportunities for humor based on anachronisms and historical contrasts. Gawain also has become a popular figure since the 1970s, with the Green Knight adventure adapted at least six times and his marriage to the Loathly Lady at least four—pleasant fantasies, perhaps, with accessible moral lessons for modern youngsters. (For a discussion of literary versions of *Connecticut Yankee* for children, see the essay by Elizabeth S. Sklar, chapter 3 in this volume; for a discussion of children's adaptations of *Sir Gawain and the Green Knight*, see the essay by Cindy L. Vitto, chapter 4 in this volume.)

The most consistently popular Arthurian plays throughout the twentieth century have been those with Arthur at their center, usually presenting in simplified form some central events of his life, from childhood to his marriage to his passing. Since the 1950s, the perennial favorite has been the story of the sword in the stone, which has the virtues of being self-contained, visually appealing, and easy to stage. (For a discussion of the sword motif in modern picture books, see the essay by Judith L. Kellogg, chapter 2 in this volume.) The popularity of the story in the second half of the century clearly has been stimulated by T. H. White's books—*The Sword in the Stone* in 1938, *The Once and Future King* in 1958—and the Disney animated film *The Sword in the Stone* in 1963. Several plays reveal their source in White's version in their depiction of Merlin and his relationship with the young Arthur—the conceit of the wizard living backward through time, for example, and the teaching of Arthur by transforming him into various animals.

By the 1970s, a bit more variety was beginning to appear in the plays. In Great Britain, Tim Porter was writing and producing his Arthurian "folk operas" for audiences young and old. These were lighthearted works with music and dance ringing changes on some well-worn themes. His *Sir Gawain and the Green Knight* was first produced by the Bude Grammar School in Cornwall and subsequently by touring companies.[50] The same story was the subject of two more notable dramatizations, one of which was commissioned for the first National Children's Arts Festival and performed at the Kennedy Center in 1977. The play by Dennis Scott (under the sponsorship of the National Theatre of the Deaf) features dialogue written for sign language interpretation and subsequently was produced in various regional venues. Another treatment of interest is the masque *Sir Gawayne and the Green Knight* written by Susan Cooper for the Christmas Revels in Cambridge, Massachusetts, in 1979. Cooper, better known for her Arthurian "Dark Is Rising" series of juvenile novels (discussed in chapters 6 and 7 in this volume by Charlotte Spivack and Raymond H. Thompson), has had her play produced in subsequent Revels in Cambridge and elsewhere.

There have been a number of comic treatments of Arthurian stories, as might be expected, though none is outstanding. V. S. Petheram's "The Troubles of King Arthur" (1960) features simplistic verbal and physical comedy as modern characters rehearse a play that is set in Arthur's court.

"The Knights of the Square Table" (1965) by Earl J. Dias simply plays on Arthurian names—for example, Queen Giddyvere—in a spoof for younger children. A similar approach is taken by Elinor R. Alderman in her "Hamelot" (1970). Little more sophisticated is *King Arthur's Calamity* (1972) by William Brohaugh and Dennis Chaptman, in which the villains are not Mordred and Morgan le Fay but Earl and Lady Nasty. Rich Kilcup's "Camel Lot" (1982) is yet another farce, involving a dragon who threatens the realm of King Arthuritis.

Far more original is another Tim Porter work first performed in Bristol in 1981, *The Marvels of Merlin*, with dialogue in sassy and anachronistic light verse. Scenes with traditional Merlin episodes frame the old Welsh tale of the winning of Olwen, and Arthur is presented as a "guileless naïve youth whom Merlin works like a glove-puppet."[51] And an improbable comedy—another production of the National Theatre of the Deaf presented in spoken dialogue and sign language—was *The Romance of Parzival and His Quest for the Grail: From the Horse's Mouth* (1982), by Shanny Mow and David Hays. The play was advertised as the "boisterous and bawdy misadventures of an innocent fool. . . . Parzival, the Charlie Chaplin of King Arthur's roundtable."

With a multitude of regional youth theaters operating across the United States and Great Britain by the late twentieth century, Arthurian productions began to appear everywhere, some using original scripts, others texts furnished by publishers specializing in children's plays. A representative sampling of local productions includes Charles Knoll's *King Arthur and the Magic Sword*, performed by the Theatre for Young America in Kansas City in 1983; Richard Gill's *The Magic of Merlin*, performed at the Polka Children's Theatre at Wimbledon in 1985; Gail Erwin's *Arthur, the Future King*, presented at the Emmy Gifford Children's Theater in Omaha in 1987; Nigel Bryant's *Merlin and the Sleeping King*, produced at the New Victoria Theatre in Newcastle in 1990; Lane Riosley's *Swords Beneath Camelot*, performed at the Stage Repertory Theatre in Houston in 1990; Ian Assersohn's *Lancelot Wins Again!*, first performed at the Cottesmore School in Sussex in 1994; Andrew Beattie's *Ordinary Jack*, performed at Eltham College in 1995; Chip Coffey's *Young King Arthur*, presented at the Kaleidoscope Children's Theatre in Atlanta in 1999; Kate Sheey's *Life Among the Ants*, presented at the Viaduct Theater in Chicago in 1999; and John Spurlong's *King Arthur in Avalon*, produced for the Youth Drama Festival in Cheltenham in 1999.

The variety of Arthurian material that reached the stage in the late twentieth century can be illustrated by the citation of a few more works. The 1983 Broadway musical *Merlin* was essentially a showcase for the magician Doug Henning and was quite successful, running for one hundred and ninety-nine performances. The plot had only the loosest connection with traditional stories—a young boastful Merlin must overcome an evil queen who intends to put her son, Prince Fergus, on Arthur's throne—but audiences were lured by the spectacle, the music, and, of course, the magic. A less ambitious *Merlin the Magnificent* by Stuart Paterson premiered during the Christmas season at the Royal Lyceum Theatre in Edinburgh in 1985. In this musical, Morgana le Fay steals away the boy Arthur, who must be rescued by Merlin before he can draw the sword from the stone. New productions of the play were staged at Dundee in 1987 and Manchester in 1989.

A much larger and more elaborate production featuring performances by young actors was *Pendragon* (1994), advertised as "a thrilling new exploration into the deeper and darker regions of Arthurian legend." Presented by the British National Youth Musical Theatre, the play set "poetry, puppetry, magic and mime" and a plot with several original twists to Peter Allwood's music. After Arthur becomes king in this version, Morgan transforms Guinevere into a Loathly Lady who trades the location of Excalibur in Lake Avalon for Arthur's promise to marry. His agreement breaks Morgan's spell and restores Guinevere's beauty. Accompanied by extensive publicity, including a television documentary on the creation of the production and a soundtrack album, the show has been staged at several sites in Great Britain, and tours have taken it to New York, Hong Kong, and Taiwan.

Far less ambitious works have toured, however, if not as far or as extensively. In 1996, a children's theater camp on Martha's Vineyard performed *Questionable Quest* by Cinda Fox, a play about a boy who becomes a knight after enduring a series of trials and eventually is transported to New York City by the wizard Merlin. The play's music was composed by the author's twelve-year-old son William. An expanded version was presented in Puerto Rico later in 1996, and the Island Children's Musical Theatre performed the play at the Beacon Theater in New York in 2000. Finally, to illustrate the global reach of the Arthurian legend today, *The Magical Mystery Tour* was written and performed in English by the students of the Scuola Media Dante Alighieri of Varese, Italy, in 2000. The story of the play reveals some knowledge of the traditional material, though it is colored, perhaps, by films and comic books: three students are transported into the past where they learn of a plot by Morgana to poison King Arthur. Obtaining the help of Robin Hood and William Wallace, they are able to keep Arthur alive until Merlin produces the Holy Grail, which cures the king and kills Morgana.

If *The Magical Mystery Tour* is an extreme example of the trend away from traditional Arthurian stories, it still exemplifies the modern tendency in all of the popular arts to reduce the best known characters to stereotypes, to reinterpret relationships and incidents with dispatch, and to refuse to be inhibited by tradition. Most current plays written expressly for children to perform range from the competent at best to the utterly inconsequential, and most are not very good drama. Today's publishers of Arthurian children's plays usually have catalogs that include similar dramatizations of the adventures of Robin Hood, Aladdin, Cinderella, and many other classic works of childhood. The Arthurian legend, one infers, holds no special place in such company; its presence simply reveals the familiarity it has developed within a fairly deep cultural stratum over the past century and a half.

Today's young people are much more likely to have their sense of Arthurian story shaped by film and television dramatizations (as Barbara Tepa Lupack suggests in chapter 12 in this volume) than by amateur or professional plays, and poetry's influence is all but nonexistent. In some respects, the plays and verse can be considered fallout from the twentieth-century Arthurian Revival rather than contributors of substance. Yet every new work has the potential to spark an interest, and as long as there are school plays to be performed, and as long as entrepreneurs are willing to mount expensive professional productions, the Arthurian tradition will supply subject matter. And among the writers, the young actors, and the children in the audiences, someone, perhaps, will be inspired to further explorations of the legend.

Notes

1. [Thomas Deloney], "Sir Lancelot du Lake," in *Reliques of Ancient English Poetry*, 3 vols., by Thomas Percy, ed. Henry B. Wheatley (1886; rpt. New York: Dover Publications, 1966), 1: 204–209.

2. John Badcock, "When Arthur First in Court Began," in *New Lyre* (London, [ca. 1820]); reprinted but misdated in Lina Eckenstein's *Comparative Studies in Nursery Rhymes* (1906; rpt. Detroit: Singing Tree Press, 1968), pp. 17–18.

3. A curious parallel to this song is the nineteenth-century folksong "King Arthur Had Three Sons," in which three rogues of different professions—a miller, a weaver, and a tailor—similarly come to unhappy, job-related ends.

4. [Charlotte Yonge], *The History of the Good Knight Sir Thomas Thumb* (Edinburgh: Thomas Constable, 1855), p. iii. The author weaves several Arthurian episodes from earlier sources into this literary version of Tom's adventures: Merlin's imprisonment in a hawthorn by Viviana, the Lady of the Lake; Arthur's battle with the giant Ryence; Gawayne and the Loathly Lady; Mordred's treachery (here the theft of Arthur's signet ring); the last battle at Camelford and Bedivere's return of Excalibur to the lake; and Arthur's passing to Avallon with Morgain. The story ends with the prophecy that Tom will one day return with Arthur. An extensive appendix provides background notes on Arthurian topics (as well as traditional and literary fairy lore) including passages from Malory, Spenser, Percy's *Reliques*, Arnold, and others. A poem, "Merlin the Prophet," is an English translation of Villemarqué's Breton verse about Merlin and the snake's egg.

5. [Joseph Ritson], *Gammer Gurton's Garland: or the Nursery Parnassus; a choice collection of pretty songs and verses, for the amusement of all little good children who can neither read nor run* (Stockton-upon-Tees: Durham, 1784).

6. William S. Baring-Gould and Ceil Baring-Gould, *The Annotated Mother Goose* (New York: Clarkson N. Potter, 1962), notes 3–5, pp. 142–43.

7. L. H., *Children's Songs for Town and Country Life* (London: Routledge, Warne, and Routledge, [1864]), p. 10.

8. Baring-Gould and Baring-Gould, *The Annotated Mother Goose*, p. 270.

9. Robert Bator, ed., *Masterworks of Children's Literature, Vol. 3: c. 1740–c. 1836, Middle Period* (New York: The Stonehill Publishing Company in association with Chelsea House Publishers, 1983), pp. xxiv–xxv.

10. Andrew St. John, *Tales of Former Times* (London: Printed for B. Crosby, 1808), p. v.

11. Thomas Love Peacock, *The Works*, ed. Henry Cole (London: Richard Bentley, 1875), p. 216. In 1814, Peacock published another didactic work with a medieval motif although there is nothing Arthurian beyond the name of the young knight in it: *Sir Hornbook; or, Childe Launcelot's Expedition. A Grammatico-Allegorical Ballad* (London: Printed for Sharpe and Hailes).

12. Mark Girouard, *The Return to Camelot: Chivalry and the English Gentleman* (New Haven: Yale University Press, 1981), p. 196.

13. "Preface" to the second edition (Edinburgh: R. and R. Clarke, 1859), pp. iii–iv. As an indication of the immediate popularity of the *Idylls*, John Pfordresher points out that of the first printing of forty thousand copies, ten thousand were sold in the first week. *A Variorum Edition of Tennyson's Idylls of the King* (New York: Columbia University Press, 1973), p. 34.

14. *Arthur's Knights*, p. 39.

15. *Arthur's Knights*, p. 127.

16. Thomas Bulfinch, *Age of Chivalry; or, Legends of King Arthur* (Boston: J. E. Tilton, 1858), pp. v–vi.

17. E. E. Hale, "Preface," to *The Age of Chivalry, or Legends of King Arthur* (Boston: S. W. Tilton, 1884), p. 7.

18. J. Loughran Scott, "Editor's Preface" to *Age of Chivalry or King Arthur and His Knights* (Philadelphia: John D. Morris, 1898), p. vi.

19. *Six Ballads About King Arthur* (London: Kegan Paul, Trench, and Company, 1881).

20. Alfred Tennyson, *The Lady of Shalott* (New York: Dodd, Mead and Co., 1881). A companion volume to *Yankee Doodle*, the book's illustrations— over thirty chromolithographic plates—were among the earliest American experiments in color-printed books for children, but the book was considered by Pyle to be a "total failure" according to an uncredited note in *Ladies of Shalott: A Victorian Masterpiece and Its Contexts*, the catalogue of an exhibition by the Brown University Department of Art in 1985, p. 137.

21. Howard Pyle, *The Merry Adventures of Robin Hood of Great Renown, in Nottinghamshire* (New York: Charles Scribner's Sons, 1883).

22. Pyle, *Robin Hood*.

23. Allen French, "Sir Marrok," in *St. Nicholas Magazine* 29 (May 1902): 592–620. The expanded version is *Sir Marrok: A Tale of the Days of King Arthur* (New York: The Century Company, 1902).

24. Although the past few decades have seen growing scholarly interest in juvenile periodicals, the field is so vast that the full range of Arthurian content

within it will never be uncovered. Kirsten Drotner, in her study *English Children and Their Magazines, 1751–1945* (New Haven: Yale University Press, 1988), indicates that there were "more than 450 titles, many of which appeared as sixteen-page weeklies and one of which ran for 108 years" (p. 7). R. Gordon Kelly's guide to *Children's Periodicals of the United States* (Westport, CT: Greenwood Press, 1984) lists four hundred and twenty-three titles, which he states "is a beginning—but a very limited one" (p. ix). Bibliographical records and subject guides, while extensive for some publications, are nonexistent for others.

25. William H. Hayne, "The Last Knight," in *The Youth's Companion* 60 (May 5, 1887).

26. Arthur Guiterman, "King Arthur and the Half-Man," in *The Youth's Companion* 78 (May 26, 1904): 260.

27. Clara Platt Meadowcroft, "The Wondering Boy," in *St. Nicholas Magazine* 46.2 (December 1918): 110. Subsequent poems in the series appeared in the following issues: April 1919; August 1919; September 1919; October 1919; November 1919; December 1919; and January 1920. It does not appear that the sequence was ever published in book form.

28. Meadowcroft, "The Adventure of the High King," in *St. Nicholas* 47:2 (December 1919), p. 111.

29. Dervin Locksley, "Arthur's Knights Tackle Caesar's Senators," in *The Boy Scouts Year Book*, ed. Franklin K. Mathiews (New York: D. Appleton and Co., 1930), pp. 157–59; published earlier in *Boys' Life*. The court of King Arthur merely provides the setting for a later comic narrative about a fat knight and a dragon in Jo Carr's "Sir Cumference: Knight of the Round Table" in *Boys' Life* (February 1966), pp. 46–47.

30. Eleanor Farjeon, "Is Arthur Gone to Avalon?" in *Mighty Men* (New York: D. Appleton, 1925), p. 159.

31. Stella Mead, "Arthur in the Arms of Merlin," in *The Land of Legends and Heroes* (London: James Nisbet and Co., 1929), p. 165.

32. James Reeves, "Avalon" and "Kay," in *Ragged Robin* (London: William Heinemann, 1961).

33. Alfred, Lord Tennyson, *Elaine*, ed. Fannie More McCauley (Boston: Leach, Shewell, and Sanborn, 1894).

34. For those who preferred the stories in prose form, about twenty retellings of various *Idylls* also were published for children between 1899 and 1930, in some cases merged with Malory adaptations in story collections.

35. William Boughton, "Preface" to Tennyson's *Idylls of the King* (Boston: Ginn and Company, 1903; new edn., 1925), p. v.

36. Such youth groups have been described by Alan and Barbara Tepa Lupack in their *King Arthur in America* (Cambridge, UK: D. S. Brewer, 1999), pp. 59–70. Further evidence of the potency of Tennyson's Arthurian poetry may be found in the juvenile fiction of the era in which children are depicted as inventing games, performing in plays, and setting behavioral standards with Tennyson's characters as models. Some examples: Marjorie Richardson's story, "Launcelot's Tower," in *St. Nicholas Magazine* (1891), Annie Fellows Johnston's *Two Little Knights of Kentucky* (1899), Amy Le

Feuvre's *Legend-Led* (ca. 1900), Lucy Maud Montgomery's *Anne of Green Gables* (1908), and Booth Tarkington's *Penrod* (1914).

37. The increase may be illusory to some degree because there is no comprehensive single source of information on such works, and current available sources—bibliographies of children's literature, reviews, publishers' catalogues, internet websites—necessarily focus on recent works.

38. Mary V. Jackson, *Engines of Instruction, Mischief, and Magic: Children's Literature in England from Its Beginnings to 1839* (Lincoln: University of Nebraska Press, 1989), p. 242.

39. Harry William Pedicord and Fredrick Louis Bergmann, notes to *King Arthur* in *The Plays of David Garrick, Vol. 7: Garrick's Alterations of Others, 1757–1773* (Carbondale: Southern Illinois University Press, 1982), p. 419.

40. The texts of only a few such works were published, and while some survive in manuscript, others are known only through contemporary reviews and advertisements. Information about individual works may be found in several studies, including Sybil Rosenfeld's *The Theatre of the London Fairs in the 18th Century* (Cambridge UK: Cambridge University Press, 1960); Lillian Gottesman's "The Arthurian Romance in English Opera and Pantomime, 1660–1800," in *Restoration and 18th Century Theatre Research* 8.2 (November 1969): 47–53; and Roger Simpson's *Camelot Regained* (Cambridge, UK: D. S. Brewer, 1990).

41. Allardyce Nicoll, *British Drama: An Historical Survey from the Beginnings to the Present Time*, 4th edn. (London: George G. Harrap, 1947; rpt. 1958), pp. 332–33.

42. Simpson, *Camelot Regained*, p. 125.

43. Simpson, *Camelot Regained*, p. 126.

44. Lowell S. Swortzell, "Children's Drama," in *The Reader's Encyclopedia of World Drama*, ed. John Gassner and Edward Quinn (New York: Thomas Y. Crowell Company, 1969), pp. 125–26.

45. Lena Dalkieth, *Little Plays* (London: T. C. and E. C. Jack [1905], "Told to the Children" series no. 14).

46. The scholar Mildred Leake Day, who attended the Alabama camp in 1938, reproduced the text of the play from a typescript in the journal *Quondam et Futurus* 10.1–2 (Fall 1989–Winter 1990): 12–22. She reported that her mother had participated in the same play at the camp in 1916. A subsequent letter to the journal indicated that the correspondent had participated in a similar play at a camp in the Ozarks in the 1940s.

47. Laura E. Richards, "Good King Arthur," in *Fairy Operettas* (Boston: Little, Brown, and Company, 1916), p. 74.

48. "King Arthur, Posture Play," in *Hygeia* 7 (August 1929): 826.

49. Swortzell, "Children's Drama," p. 126.

50. Porter described the development of his work from his college assignment to write a children's opera to its repeated performances in the 1970s in "The Early History of an Arthurian Folk-Opera" in *Pendragon* 12.2 (December 1978): 7–9.

51. Tim Porter, "On the Road with King Arthur," in *Pendragon* 20.4 (Autumn 1990): 22.

CHAPTER 9

ARTHURIAN YOUTH GROUPS IN AMERICA:
THE AMERICANIZATION OF KNIGHTHOOD

Alan Lupack

One contemporary American reaction to Alfred, Lord Tennyson's lofty views of knighthood was to satirize them. Another, however, was to translate idyllic notions of knighthood into an American setting, as some American authors did by redefining knighthood in terms of moral achievement rather than nobility of birth, inherited wealth, or physical prowess. James Russell Lowell, for example, in *The Vision of Sir Launfal*, opened the most exclusive of knightly clubs, achievers of the Grail, to any person willing to be charitable.

In a book entitled *Twentieth Century Knighthood: A Series of Addresses to Young Men* (1900), Louis Albert Banks succinctly defined the notion of symbolic, moral knighthood. Banks observed: "We do not all have splendid physiques, and some deeds of hardihood in which the old knights rejoice are beyond our power, but the higher deeds of the loftier chivalry, of upright thinking, of pure conduct, of self-denying devotion, are within the reach of every one of us."[1] The highly idealized notion of knighthood that lies behind such a statement is, of course, based on literary rather than historical examples. Banks obviously could not have been thinking of actual feuding barons or struggles for the throne when he wrote that "Chivalry during its golden days made the world a much pleasanter place in which to live. It did away with low suspicions and jealousies and filled the land with an atmosphere of noble hospitality and courtesy" or that "no spirit of discord or peevishness was ever allowed in these knights toward one another."[2]

Much of Banks's book is a catalogue of chivalric virtues coupled with exempla illustrating how those virtues have been demonstrated in the modern world. Knightly simplicity of character, for instance, is illustrated by an anecdote about Abraham Lincoln carrying a trunk for a little girl so that she would not miss her train. But it is not only the famous or powerful like Lincoln, a congressman at the time of the story, who can act like the heroes of medieval romance. Banks also finds chivalric qualities in the common man. He tells of a sailor who is asked what he was doing when Commodore Winfield Scott Schley was "pulverizing Cervera" (i.e., Admiral Pascual Cervera y Topete) near Santiago, Cuba, in the Spanish-American War. The sailor's response that he was "shoveling coal down yonder" in the "lower regions of the ship" prompts Banks to comment: "everybody knows that it was the knightly loyalty of the coal shovelers and engineers down in the smothering and sweltering furnace rooms that made the victory possible."[3] Other knightly virtues are exemplified by stories about Americans as famous as Ulysses S. Grant, who showed compassion by allowing Robert E. Lee to keep his sword after his surrender, and as ordinary as a train inspector who refused to be provoked by a rude passenger. The point is that "the real gentleman, of the old knighthood or the new, is not to be judged by his employment, but by the personal honor evinced in his character and conduct."[4]

Since "chivalry emphasized the theory that it is natural for youth to be courageous, and that it is the greatest shame for a young man to lack courage," it provided, in Banks's view, a fine model for modern youth. "I am profoundly convinced," he wrote, "that our own age would be greatly improved, and the outlook of civilization distinctly brightened, if there might be a wide stimulation of manly courage in the hearts of American youth. I do not mean physical courage only, but the courage to face the great moral and social and political problems of our time, and ride them down with the dauntless valor of youth. It is as natural now as it was in the days of chivalry for young men to dream dreams and see visions of courageous achievement."[5]

A contemporary of Banks whose ideas had much greater influence also believed chivalry to be valuable in the development of American youth. In 1901, a minister named William Byron Forbush (1868–1927) wrote a book whose title, The Boy Problem, reflects a serious concern of its age. Forbush divided the stages of a boy's life into infancy (until the age of six), childhood (from six to twelve), and adolescence (from twelve to manhood),[6] a scheme altogether consistent with the psychological theory of his day. (G. Stanley Hall, sometimes referred to as the "father of American psychology," for example, not only wrote a brief introduction to Forbush's book, but also outlined similar stages in the development of boys in his own two-volume study of Adolescence, published in 1904.[7]) According to Forbush, it is in adolescence, the last of these stages, that the boy problem arises because the boy "has become endowed with the passions and independence of manhood while still a child in foresight and judgment. He rushes now into so many crazy plans and harmful deeds." In addition, "the very sensitiveness, longing and overpowering sense of the new life. . .is often so concealed by inconsistent and even barbarous behavior that one quite loses both comprehension and patience."[8]

According to Forbush, the moral dangers of this stage in a boy's growth are balanced by great potential, for this period is "the time for shaping ideals."[9] The notion of shaping ideals aligned Forbush once again with contemporary theory, especially with Banks, who saw the manly courage of knighthood as a model to be imitated by boys who need to deal with societal problems, and with Hall, whose assessment of the condition of youth in America is that "our young people leap rather than grow into maturity." This "leap" occurs largely because, as America is "conquering nature" and "achieving a magnificent material civilization. . .our vast and complex business organization. . .absorbs ever more and earlier the best talent and muscle of youth. . .[and] we are progressively forgetting that for the complete apprenticeship to life, youth needs repose, leisure, art, legends, romance, idealization, and in a word humanism."[10] Referring again to the significance of such legends later in his study, Hall says: "some would measure the progress of culture by the work of reinterpreting on ever higher planes the mythic tradition of a race, and how this is done for youth is a good criterion of pedagogic progress."[11]

Interestingly, it was in the stories of King Arthur and the Knights of the Round Table that Hall saw "perhaps the very best ideals for youth to be found in history."[12] Hall's singling out of the Arthurian legends was no doubt based in part on his knowledge of and admiration for an organization founded by Forbush to put into practice some of Forbush's own theories about the development of adolescent males. In 1893, Forbush established the first of what was to become a network of clubs for boys called the Knights of King Arthur. These clubs, felt Hall, captured "the spirit of fealty and piety" that made the medieval legends in general and "the literature of the Arthuriad and the Sangrail" in particular so wholesomely appealing to young boys; and he spoke of the clubs as "an unique order of Christian knighthood for boys."[13]

Of course, there were many societies for young boys in addition to Forbush's Knights of King Arthur, some of them based on chivalric virtues and some not. Hall refers to groups such as "the Captains of Ten," which promoted "a spirit of loyalty to Christ"; "the Agassiz Association," which encouraged "personal work in natural science"; and "the Princely Knights of the Character Castle," which tried to inculcate "the principles of heroism" in boys.[14] The most successful and long-lasting was the Boy Scouts, whose founder, Sir Robert Baden-Powell, modeled his club largely on Forbush's Knights of King Arthur and on another American group, the Woodcraft Indians. Scouts, in fact, were encouraged to read stories of chivalry; and many of the virtues espoused by the Scouting movement derived from Baden-Powell's notions of chivalry.[15]

After the Scouts had been founded, Forbush himself advised the adults who guided each of his Castles, as the local clubs were called, to "buy the manual of the Boy Scouts." But he made a clear distinction between the two: "While the Knights may use and should use scouting and camp methods, its appeal is a higher one than that of the Scouts. It deals with the fraternal, the emotional and the intellectual, with a constant emphasis on the spiritual. The very ideals of the two movements show the difference; the ideal product of the Scouts is the scout, the agile frontiersman; the ideal product of the Knights is the knight, the Christian gentleman. The Scout movement may do this latter, the Knights can do nothing less or else."[16]

Forbush originally founded his organization for boys between the ages of thirteen and sixteen, a time when they "are said by psychologists to be in the knightly period, and it is just then that they respond to the ritual, regalia and the glamor of exclusiveness."[17] The general plan, outlined by Forbush in a pamphlet called *Knights of King Arthur: How to Begin and What to Do*, was fairly simple and flexible. Each Castle, he wrote, is "a fraternity, private but not secret, self-governing and under the control of the local church. It is based upon the oldest English Christian legend, that of the Round Table. It is a revival of the nobler side of medieval chivalry. The thought is to fulfill the prophecy of King Arthur that he would return to re-establish a kingdom of righteousness, honor and service." Such clubs became ways of channeling what was believed to be the instinctive tendency in adolescent males to form gangs into a means of doing good deeds and developing character. Hall discussed "the propensity of boys from thirteen on to consort in gangs" and concluded that "Every adolescent boy ought to belong to some club or society marked by as much secrecy as is compatible with safety."[18]

In the course of his membership in Forbush's clubs, a boy progressed through the stages of Page, Esquire, and finally Knight. In order to help him focus on particular virtues, "Each boy takes the name of some ancient knight or some hero, ancient or modern, and tries to represent his knightly traits."[19] The fact that the heroes the boys emulate need not be knights of Arthur's court—or even knights at all—implies that for Forbush, as for Banks, the force of the example was more important than consistency with the Arthurian stories. In a book called *The Boys' Round Table*, which Forbush coauthored, he suggested that boys adopt the name of such Arthurian heroes as Launcelot, Gawain, Bedivere, Percivale, Bors, and

Gareth; but the boys might also choose names of saints such as Luke, George, and Francis, or of other heroes such as Alfred, Roland, Ivanhoe, Ulysses, Luther, Christopher Columbus, or even Thor.[20] Forbush was determined that the boys "actually live out the knightly life together, and their 'gang' spirit, instead of tending, as is usual, towards the ideals of the noisiest or most dominant boy, which are probably lower than the average, are lifted toward the ideal of the best manhood."[21] If consistency suffered because of the eclectic models allowed, Forbush and the others who organized Castles were unconcerned, so long as the proper models were followed and the proper ideals were fostered.[22]

Since Forbush's conception of the Arthurian stories was based largely on Tennyson, he conceived of Merlin as "the venerable counsellor of Arthur." Therefore, in each of his clubs, the adult responsible for guiding the boys was known as the Merlin. By assuming the role of Merlin rather than of the king himself, the adult leader would be seen as an advisor rather than a ruler so that the Castle would "feel that it is self-governing." The Merlin was to take a seat "before and below the throne" to emphasize that "what he gives the Castle is his wisdom and not his authority."[23]

The Merlin could help the boys organize "tournaments," which were "usually athletic," and "quests," which were "co-operative deeds of kindness."[24] Among the good deeds performed by some of the Castles, Forbush cites such things as cleaning up and beautifying parts of town, providing lunch and hot coffee for policemen on Halloween, earning money to place a King Arthur memorial window in a church (in Rutland, Vermont), sending magazines to a church mission in Alaska, and giving King Arthur Flour to the poor.[25]

A particular honor was reserved for a member who performed exceptional service. That boy would be allowed for one evening to adopt the name of Sir Galahad and to sit in the Siege Perilous. Each Castle was to have such a seat, and the privilege of occupying it could be conferred only by the unanimous consent of the other members.[26] It is some indication of the kind of ritual the clubs promoted that the Siege Perilous, usually covered with a red cloth, was "to be treated reverentially" and that "in some Castles it is almost a superstition that it shall not be uncovered even by accident."[27] This sense of ritual was enhanced by the fact that the boys generally wore some sort of costume, ranging from simple sashes to tunics or more elaborate dress, including shields decorated with heraldic emblems and swords or spears. (See figure 9.1.) Boys could purchase and wear pins and badges identifying them as members when out of uniform. In addition to the ceremony for granting the right to sit in the Siege Perilous, there were other formulaic ceremonies—for example, for the installation of the officers of the Castle, such as the Chamberlain, the Heralds, and the Seneschal.

9.1 A Castle of Knights, one of the many Knights of King Arthur boys' groups founded by William Byron Forbush to remediate "the boy problem." (From Forbush's *The Knights of King Arthur* [1916].)

Although boys were seen as more problematic than girls, a female parallel to the Knights of King Arthur known as the Queens of Avalon (originally Queens of Avilion) was established in 1902, nine years after the Knights. Whereas the boys' clubs were directed by a Merlin, the girls were guided by a Lady of the Lake. As did the Knights, the Queens of Avalon strove to revive medieval values. The society "represents itself as the revival of the group of royal ladies, who, in the Arthurian legends, lived on the magic island of Avalon, the land of flowers and fruit, of peace and purity, of wholesomeness and healing, and ministered to humanity with graciousness and beauty. It is the Kingdom of Ideal Womanhood."[28] Forbush chose Avalon as the group's controlling symbol because he believed that the isle, "bright though misty, may correspond in the idealism of girls to what the Holy Grail does in the idealism of boys; that, a vision to be won by the chivalrous; this, a social condition to be earned by the pure in heart. And the ideal is truly feminine—woman the nurse and healer of mankind, in youth and age, rules by her virtue the kingdom where all men live in peace and purity."[29]

Forbush's clubs continue to be of significance not only in the study of the history of pedagogy and adolescent psychology; they also bear on American cultural and literary history in two important ways. First, they were a means of democratizing the Arthurian legends by making them accessible to anyone willing to live a morally noble life. And second, they were a way of spreading knowledge of and interest in the Arthurian legends.

In his various handbooks and manuals, Forbush suggested Arthurian books for reading and Arthurian illustrations for viewing, though, like the names of persons to be imitated and the names of Castles, readings went far beyond the strictly Arthurian. In *The Boys' Round Table*, Forbush and coauthor Frank Masseck provided a reading list[30] that included various retellings of the legends, such as *The Boy's King Arthur* by Lanier; the *Idylls of the King* and other Arthurian poems (like "Sir Galahad," which presented an idealized model of virtue) by Tennyson; Bulfinch's *Age of Chivalry*; and the Arthurian ballads from Percy's *Reliques of Ancient English Poetry*. In the manual on *How to Begin and What to Do* to start a Castle, the novice Merlin was instructed to have available for the boys a "library of books of King Arthur and other heroic stories" as well as reproductions of Edwin Austin Abbey's Holy Grail paintings for the Boston Public Library.[31] And in his *Queens of Avalon* guide, Forbush recommended, among other books, Mary MacLeod's *The Story of King Arthur and His Noble Knights*. He noted that one Court of girls read regularly from Tennyson's *Idylls*; and he made it a requirement that any girl chosen as a Queen of a Court must have completed all of the *Idylls*, just as to advance to the degree of Knight a boy had to memorize the lines from Tennyson's "Guinevere," which begin "In that fair Order of my Table Round," the lines that contain the impossible vows to which Arthur makes his knights swear.[32]

The emphasis placed on Tennyson is due, of course, to the conception of the *Idylls* as a morally appropriate example. The spiritual ideal, after all, was foremost in Forbush's clubs, which is why sitting in the Siege Perilous was deemed the highest honor and why Abbey's Grail images were recommended for viewing. Forbush also suggested that each Castle "be adorned with beautiful pictures" and that "the most familiar and easily obtained is Watts' Sir Galahad." He even advised that a copy of Watts's painting be given to every member of the Castle.[33]

The very extent of the clubs is noteworthy as an indicator of increasing interest in the Arthurian legends. Writing in *The Knights of King Arthur: The Merlin's Book of Advanced Work* in 1916, Forbush observed: "there have been over 3,000 Castles. There have been over 350 Courts of Queens and over 200 Camps of the Brotherhood of David. It is believed that over 125,000 young people have been identified with the King Arthur movement."[34] And the entry on Forbush in *The National Cyclopædia of American Biography*[35] estimates that the Knights of King Arthur had one hundred and thirty thousand members by 1922. Though the movement extended to Canada, Mexico, England, Jamaica, and New Zealand,[36] its spread throughout the United States, where it was not limited to any one region of the country, was by far the most impressive. In his various publications, Forbush referred to Castles of the Knights of King Arthur and Courts of the

Queens of Avalon in such places as Bangor, Maine; Milford, New Hampshire; Boston, Massachusetts; Hartford, Connecticut; Columbia, Pennsylvania; Otterbein, Indiana; Versailles, Ohio; Estherville, Iowa; Lincoln, Nebraska; Fargo, North Dakota; Telluride, Colorado; Cheyenne, Wyoming; Marshall, Texas; Seaside, Oregon; and San Francisco, California. Equally impressive is the longevity of the clubs. As late as 1940, the Knights of King Arthur and Queens of Avalon were still being recognized as organizations that could help young people; and, in isolated cases, Castles lasted much longer.[37] And so in cities and towns all over America for a period of more than fifty years, boys and girls were playing at being Arthurian heroes and heroines and participating in basketball game "tournaments" and "quests" to beautify towns or feed the poor.

When dealing with any sort of American Arthurianism, we must always ask why a legend based on a hierarchical system headed by a monarch is attractive in a land where such things are alien to our national values. Forbush seems to answer this question by translating the hierarchy from a social to a moral realm. A youngster advanced in the peerage of the Knights of King Arthur or the Queens of Avalon not by being from a wealthier or nobler family than the average person but by being better and by doing more of the kind of good deeds that anyone can do. The clubs' compatibility to American values was enhanced by the fact that some of those boys and girls, as members of an Arthurian Castle or Court, could take names such as Roosevelt or Edison,[38] or Clara Barton, Dorothea Dix, or Louisa Alcott.[39]

This notion of the legends as suitable to American youth was embedded in Forbush's understanding of the Arthurian material and of the clubs he founded. In *The Boys' Round Table*, the manual for the Knights of King Arthur, Forbush and his coauthor Masseck noted that "Although the framework of the order is a monarchy, there is nothing dictatorial about its management" and also that "the most cogent reason yet given for the roundness of the [i.e., Arthur's] table is that at a round table there is no head, and so there can be no jealousy. Thus we have, in a democracy under leadership, the ideal form of organization for boys."[40] The democratic and patriotic nature of the clubs was evident also in the two banners that each Castle was to have, "the Castle flag and the American flag."[41] And in his book on the *Queens of Avalon*, Forbush observed that those who are attracted by the poetry of legends such as those surrounding Avalon and dreams of places like Utopia and the New Atlantas (Forbush's spelling) "may even think it fair to place the real Avalon on the shores of the New World, toward which all such dreams have tended."[42]

Forbush's notion of Arthur's returning through his organization and of Avalon's being located on the shores of the New World may have been romantic enthusiasms, but in a very real sense Arthur, or at least the stories surrounding him, did indeed have a rebirth through the Knights of King Arthur and related groups. After all, some one hundred and thirty thousand youngsters—not to mention the Merlins and Ladies of the Lake guiding them—were taught to read and to dream about and to imitate in their daily lives the legends of Camelot.

Forbush's was not the only group to increase interest in the Arthurian tales and knowledge of the texts in which they were treated as a way of dealing with "the boy problem" in America. In *The Boys' Round Table*, Forbush and Masseck mentioned "several imitations" of their order and "a number of independent societies having the main features of our order. . .without acknowledgment to their parent organization."[43] One man, a minister named Perry Edwards Powell, founded a strikingly similar organization that he described in a book called *Knights of the Holy Grail: A Solution to the Boy Problem.* Though he claimed that his "new order is original" and that it "evolved independently," borrowing from Forbush is evident both in the title of his book and in the structure of the organization itself.[44]

Powell's Knights went through two of the three degrees that Forbush's did, Esquire and Knight, and were led by a Merlin. Like Forbush's Knights, Powell's clubs were designed to deal with the boy problem by channeling the "gang spirit" and appealing to the "mystic, private, clannish, chivalrous, and. . .religious" instincts of boys.[45] One of the few differences between the groups is that Powell's was a little more openly religious and so the Merlin was usually a pastor who was to be "in supreme charge and his will obeyed." Such authoritarianism might make the Knights of the Holy Grail appear less democratic and less well-suited to an American setting, yet Powell looked to James Russell Lowell's very American poem *The Vision of Sir Launfal* as a model. Of the two poems that Powell believed set forth the story of the Grail "in epic measure," Tennyson's idyll "The Holy Grail" and Lowell's poem, he considered the latter to embody particularly American values: "The Britisher is aristocratic and can not free himself from his pedigree and environment. But the American voices all the traditions of his favored Republic, and we find Lowell's Sir Launfal a social Knight."[46] The co-importance of Galahad's chastity and Launfal's charity was emphasized in Powell's ritual of initiation into the order of knighthood, in which there were four lectures. The first was on confessing Christ before the world; the second was on chastity, for which Galahad was the model; and the third discussed charity, as exemplified by Launfal. In the fourth, on the Holy Grail, the candidate was told: "The Holy Grail is in the world to-day, and is in the Church as of old. Galahad saw it within the shrine at the holy altar, and there can you, in the Holy Supper of our Lord. Sir Launfal saw it in the sweet works of love and there you may ever behold it."[47] This final lecture was followed by a reading from Lowell's poem of the lines which state that the Holy Grail is the cup that Launfal filled at a stream for the leper who is actually Christ.

Another youth group centered on the Grail was the Order of Sir Galahad, which was affiliated with the Episcopal Church. Like Forbush and Powell, this group strove to inculcate into boys and young men a sense of modern chivalry. The manual for leaders of the organization observes that "Long ago chivalry centered about life on horseback. It is only in our day that the common man, the pedestrian, is coming into his own."[48] The modern chivalry is represented by numerous small deeds: "Helping lame dogs over stiles, leading blind men across the crowded street, kicking a board with a nail in it out of the path, tearing up an indecent picture, killing by forgetfulness a bad story, writing a letter to say you're sorry when a friend is in trouble, visiting some one who is ill, giving up your seat in the street car,—all these and a hundred other things are cases where we can exercise in small, unrecorded ways the little daily deeds that make up the chivalrous boy and man."[49]

Members of the Order progressed through stages, as did those in other chivalric groups. They began as Lads, then became Pages, Esquires, Knights, and Counsellors. The Order of Sir Galahad was designed so that boys growing into manhood would not leave the club but would progress to the highest rank of counsellor and thus guide the younger members. The Manual for Leaders outlines the story of the Grail as represented by the Edwin Austin Abbey murals. And the group had a symbolic coat of arms, a white shield with a red cross, which contained five stars, and a blue lion rampant. The colors "make up the national tri-color of our flag and that of England, whence we get the story of Sir Galahad." Thus, as with Forbush's group, there is a patriotic element (and a democratic element, since the King is a knight whom the other knights have chosen). The colors have another symbolic value; red represents courage; white, purity; and blue, truth. The five stars suggest the five degrees of the order; the cross represents the Church; and the lion stands for strength.[50]

Powell's Knights of the Holy Grail and the Order of Sir Galahad seem to have remained relatively small and not to have achieved the national membership that Forbush's Knights or another similar organization called the Knighthood of Youth did. "Directed by the National Child Welfare Association and intended primarily for school children from 7 to 12 years old,"[51] the Knighthood of Youth program had enrolled "more than a hundred thousand boys and girls in various parts of the United States"[52] by 1930. And in 1934 the *New York Times* reported that there were "now 370,000 children enrolled in the 'Knighthood of Youth' clubs."[53]

The Knighthood of Youth was designed to provide moral training in a manner analogous to the training in health habits offered in the schools, that is by "a definite, concrete program which the child can pursue and by which he can measure his improvement"; but character training was also meant to "fire the imagination, and arouse the will power of the child at the habit-forming age."[54] One of the principal ways of doing this was through stories of King Arthur and his knights. One book written "to captivate the imagination and hold the attention of every boy and girl reader in the upper elementary grades" at the same time that it aids and encourages "character building by giving the child an example. . .of the highest development of individuals" was a series of stories "based on Malory's *Morte d'Arthur* and the *Mabinogion*"[55] called *Knights Old and New* by Alice M. Hoben. In an introduction to this book, John H. Finley observed that the author "has given careful consideration to the Knighthood [of Youth] program and has included text material and activities that make the volume especially useful for the pupils in schools that have adopted the program."[56]

Classes enrolled in the program devised codes of conduct and charts with questions about their behavior, such as "Did I knowingly break any law of the class code? Did I brush my teeth today, both night and morning? Did I meet difficulties or defeat in a sportsmanlike manner?" and so on. A chart was labeled "A List of Daily Adventures"; each question was called either a "dragon" or an "adventure"; and the list was said to contain "reminders of the adventures which young knights may undertake."[57] In these and other ways, the moral and democratic concept of knighthood underlying the Knighthood of Youth was apparent. Though the children were told stories about King Arthur and his knights and about the crusaders, they also discussed men and women who might be considered "modern knights," people like Thomas Edison, who could be called "the *knight of electricity*," or Charles Lindbergh, "a *knight of the air*."[58]

To understand the impact of clubs such as the Knighthood of Youth, the Knights of King Arthur, and the Knights of the Holy Grail, one must imagine the members of these groups, nearly half a million in all, thinking of themselves and of those they admired—not only heroes like Edison or Lindbergh but also policemen, firemen, politicians, inventors, nurses, and the other common men and women who do their jobs well out of a sense of duty—as knights of the modern world. The concept of knighthood was thus absorbed into the popular culture and transformed from something attainable only by the nobility to a state expected of the moral youth or adult.

The scope and cultural significance of this transformation are evident in the literature that was influenced either specifically by the youth groups or generally by the notion of moral knighthood and that, in turn, was another way of spreading knowledge of the Arthurian legends in America. There were, for example, the rituals designed to initiate members into the various ranks of the respective organizations. Such rituals made use of Arthurian stories while being themselves a new form of Arthurian drama. In addition, plays and pageants were written specifically for the groups. In *The Boys' Round Table*, there is an advertisement for "'The Young Knight, or How Gareth Won His Spurs', a dramatization of Tennyson's 'Gareth and Lynette', for castle use, by the Rev. James Yeames."[59] There must have been numerous other local productions. Forbush himself compiled a collection called *Songs of the Knights of King Arthur* that contained original verses intended to be sung to traditional tunes. And the Knighthood of Youth groups "wrote and encouraged others to write stories and poems relating to knighthood of all times."[60] (See, in this volume, the essays on Arthurian songs and music for young people, chapter 10, by Jerome V. Reel, Jr., and on various Arthurian dramatic youth performances, chapter 8, by Dan Nastali.)

Many Arthurian works written about or for children also used notions of symbolic knighthood similar to those fostered by the youth groups. One novel called *The Gang of Six: A Story of the Boy Life of Today* (1906) is clearly an outgrowth of such clubs. In an introductory note the author, Horace M. Du Bose, refers to the three stages of childhood outlined by Forbush and others and even quotes Forbush on the "possibilities of danger or help" that the gang spirit presents.[61] Du Bose's didactic novel is the story of Harry Wilmot, a young man who sets about to reform six street urchins by organizing them into a club modeled on the Round Table that meets in a cave they call a "castle."

An obvious influence on *The Gang of Six*, as on the groups formed by Forbush and Powell, is Tennyson. At one point, Wilmot warns his boys that "The tempter will come every day" and describes the statues in Arthur's palace "that showed beasts overcoming men; there were also statues showing men overcoming beasts; then there were statues showing men in armor with their swords in their hands; and above all, there were statues showing men with wings starting from their shoulders and with flames of fire on their brows. These were to show how men must fight to overcome evil, and after overcoming how they must continue to use the sword of truth to win the highest glory."[62] The descriptions of these statues are obvious paraphrases of the four zones of statuary in Camelot as described by Tennyson in the "Holy Grail" idyll:

> And four great zones of sculpture, set betwixt
> With many a mystic symbol, gird the hall;
> And in the lowest beasts are slaying men,
> And in the second men are slaying beasts,
> And on the third are warriors, perfect men,
> And on the fourth are men with growing wings. . .[63]

What Du Bose omits, of course, is the statue of the nearly godlike king that Tennyson places "over all." Perhaps this omission indicates a deliberate avoidance of the monarchical setting of the British Arthurian stories. A similar democratizing of the legends seems to be at work elsewhere in the novel.

Almost as if he were following Forbush's injunction to his Merlins to inspire boys "with the poetry of the King Arthur Plan,"[64] Wilmot relates the story of Yarkin, "a shepherd boy who desired to become a knight."[65] After Yarkin tells Arthur that he was instructed in knighthood by the voice of one who claimed to be the sister of Purity and Faith, a voice he heard under a hawthorn tree, Arthur makes him a squire to Sir Christopher and changes his name to Hermas. Young Hermas then follows his lord for a year and a day, all the time learning obedience. He also serves the king by capturing two caitiff knights; and, for his faithful and obedient service, he is made a knight. But when Sir Hermas goes to the castle of Purity and Faith seeking the sister whose beautiful voice inspired him, he finds that there are just two daughters. The third, Obedience, only seemed to be a sister, for "how should Purity and Faith be without *Obedience*?" Hermas "had heard the voice of obedience calling him, and it was this obedience whom the squire had worthily loved and whom the knight had sought to woo. He could not be sad, therefore, because he had lost an unseen bride, but rejoiced because he had gained forever the favor of one whom he knew."[66]

The story is noteworthy because of the use of an Arthurian context to promote a virtue appropriate to young boys. But it is also significant that the hero of the story is a shepherd boy who becomes a knight. The shepherd boy is not, as it might turn out in a medieval romance, someone who is sired by a knight or nobleman and whose nobility is ultimately discovered. He is actually a commoner whose nobility is moral rather than hereditary. Thus Yarkin, who becomes Hermas, is a perfect model for the American urchins that Harry Wilmot is trying to rehabilitate and for other boys who will be inspired with the poetry of the Arthurian plan.

The symbolic interpretation of knighthood seen in *The Gang of Six* and indeed in all the clubs based on the Arthurian legends contributes to the creation of thoroughly original uses of Arthurian material in works designed to exemplify how the concept of knighthood can be utilized to instruct children. This is not to say that tradition is wholly ignored, for the concept of knighthood and often of a particular character or characters frequently comes from earlier sources. Such is the case with Du Bose's view of the stages of knighthood, which provide the moral framework for instruction even though the novel is otherwise totally nontraditional.

Two didactic novels, each with the same title *Little Sir Galahad*, take a similar approach. The earlier of the two (1904), by Lillian Holmes, is the story of a crippled boy named David. Arthur Bryan, David's friend, plays at being King Arthur[67] and laments to his mother that David cannot play knight because of his disability. But Mrs. Bryan offers the example of Galahad and quotes from Tennyson's poem "Sir Galahad": "My strength is as the strength of ten, / Because my heart is pure." As in the vision of Sir Launfal, the Grail that Holmes's little Sir Galahad can achieve is not a material object but a spiritual quality. Mrs. Bryan says that the knights other than Galahad "thought they were looking for the cup out of which Christ drank at the Last Supper. What is really meant and what they wanted, was the presence of Christ, their King."[68]

David proves his worthiness by doing good deeds such as not becoming angry with a three-year-old who breaks his slate and, after regaining his ability to walk, by carrying books for a girl whose brothers unchivalrously make her carry their books as well as her own.[69] When he cheats in school and so fails to live up to the knightly code, David confesses; and then "instead of feeling like a coward, he again had the strength of ten, because his heart was pure from dishonor."[70] Ultimately David recovers his health and finds wealthy relatives who provide for his education and the employment of his poor aunt, the woman who cared for him in his illness. But "whenever he seems inclined to be exultant about his returning strength, she reminds him of the better strength which the years of lameness taught him."[71]

The second of the *Little Sir Galahad* novels was written by Phoebe Gray in 1914. As in Holmes's story, there is a strong didactic bent, one of the chief messages being the dangers of alcohol. Also as in Holmes's story, the little Sir Galahad of the title is crippled, a condition that occurred when his "jovially stimulated" father dropped him. Charlie, the title character, is enrolled by a young friend, Mary Alice Brown, in a group called the Galahad Knights. Mary Alice is herself the victim of a father who beats her and her mother when he drinks. And the young boy who founded the Galahad Knights, Francis Willett, falls in with the wrong crowd at college and is expelled because he gets drunk and steals a car. Having forgotten the ideals of the group he founded, Francis loses his reputation and almost his life because of alcohol.

It is Charlie who remains true to his quest and is dubbed "little Sir Galahad" by the renowned doctor who saves Francis's life. The doctor finds Charlie's "fidelity to his quest for the Grail. . .infinitely fine and touching" and observes, in a sentiment reminiscent of the inspiration for the Arthurian clubs of Forbush and Powell, that "the development of these rare little souls is the vital problem of our country."[72] The doctor himself ultimately joins the Galahad Knights as reformed by Charlie and goes to help "the wounded, the suffering, the poverty-stricken people of prostrate Belgium," where he enlists soldiers for the organization.[73]

The crippled son of a poor farmer can be the exemplar of Grail Knighthood because, as in the clubs and in much of the American Arthurian literature, knighthood is symbolic. Charlie himself defines that noble concept as it occurs in the novel: "Well, us fellers are pledged, just like Sir Galahad, to do everythin' to help and purtect folks that's weaker'n us. Our sword is Brotherly Love, and our shield is made of Faith, Courage, Symp'thy, and Willin'ness," and the Grail "stands for Perfect Manhood" and is "full of a dullicious drink, called Unselfishness."[74]

Symbolic notions of the Grail and of knighthood also play a part in a novel in the "Little Colonel" series by one of the most popular turn-of-the-century American authors of juvenile literature. In her epigraph (a passage from the novel) to the tale of *Two Little Knights of Kentucky* (1899), Annie Fellows Johnston sets the tone for her Americanization of chivalry: "Knighthood has not passed away. The flower of Chivalry has blossomed anew in this New World, and America, too, has her 'Hall of the Shields.' "[75]

The New World chivalry is exemplified by Keith and Malcolm MacIntyre when they befriend a boy named Jonesy, who is abandoned by the tramp with whom he has been traveling. To raise money so Jonesy can stay in the care of a kindly but poor old professor, the two boys decide to organize a benefit. Their Aunt Allison pleads with her mother, the boys' grandmother, to allow them to hold the benefit by pointing out that it is a way for them to learn the lesson of *The Vision of Sir Launfal* that what is important is "Not what we give, but what we share, / For the gift without the giver is bare." The grandmother agrees because she feels that "If this little beggar at the gate can teach them where to find the Holy Grail, through unselfish service to him, I do not want to stand in the way."[76] The benefit itself is to take the form of a pageant in which "the old days of chivalry" will live again through readings from *The Vision of Sir Launfal* and Tennyson's *Idylls*, accompanied by tableaux in which the children don the garb of knights and ladies.

The boys exhibit the New World chivalry not by dressing up as knights but by performing an act of charity. The professor tells Keith that because of his good intentions, "thy shield will never be blank and bare. Already thou hast blazoned it with the beauty of a noble purpose, and like Galahad, thou too shalt find the Grail."[77] And when Keith says that if he and Malcolm could keep Jonesy from growing up to be a tramp, that would be "as good a deed as some the real knights did," their aunt calls them "my dear little Sir Galahads."[78] Later she tells them of Tennyson's Sir Galahad, "whose strength was as the strength of ten because his heart was pure."[79] The symbolic nature of their knighthood is underscored when Aunt Allison gives the boys a badge of knighthood, a white enamel flower with a small diamond in the center. Though they "can't wear armour in these days," wearing "the white flower of a blameless life," like the badges Forbush's Knights of King Arthur wore, is meant to remind them that they "are pledged to right the wrong wherever you find it, in little things as well as great."[80]

In addition to the fact that two little boys with good hearts can be knights of the New World, the Americanization of knighthood is apparent in another way in *Two Little Knights of Kentucky*. When the boys, forgetting the chivalry they are supposed to represent, taunt their cousin Ginger because she cannot be a knight, she asserts that she can be a patriot, which is "lots better." Aunt Allison responds that "they ought to mean the same thing exactly in this day of the world"[81] and then gives Ginger a badge appropriate for the patriot knight, "a little flag whose red, white, and blue was made of tiny settings of garnets, sapphires, and diamonds." The flag is to be a reminder to her of the values espoused by the boys in the code they have adopted from Tennyson: "Live pure, speak truth, right the wrong, follow the king; else wherefore born?" Aunt Allison explains the connection between the American flag and modern knighthood: "there is the white for the first part, the 'live pure,' and the 'true blue' for the 'speak truth,' and then the red,—surely no soldier's little daughter needs to be told what that stands for, when her own brave father has spilled part of his good red life-blood to 'right the wrong' on the field of battle."[82]

The link between the American flag and knighthood strengthens the reading of another tale by Johnston as an Americanization of the concept of knighthood. In a short prose work called *Keeping Tryst: A Tale of King Arthur's Time* (1906), she tells the story of a page boy named Ederyn who asks a minstrel if it is possible for him to become a knight. Told that some win knighthood by slaying dragons or giants or by going on crusades, Ederyn is advised to "forget thy dreams of glory, and be content to serve thy squire. For what hast such as thou to do with great ambitions? They'd prove but flames to burn away thy daily peace."[83] A year later the minstrel returns to say: "there *is* a way for even such as thou to win the honours thou dost covet." The opportunity arises because Arthur wishes to establish "round him at his court a chosen circle whose fidelity hath stood the utmost test. Not deeds of prowess are required of these true followers,. . . but they must prove themselves trustworthy, until on hand and heart it may be graven large, '*In all things faithful*.' "[84] Ederyn must undergo and pass a series of tests of his faithfulness by keeping tryst despite obstacles and temptations. Since he answers each call to keep tryst without neglecting his duty, first as a page and then as a squire, he is finally knighted by the king.

The notion that a young person becomes a knight of the Round Table because of moral integrity rather than prowess or nobility of birth is the very basis for the Arthurian clubs and for the symbolic knighthood in the literature under discussion. Ederyn is much more like American knights from Sir Launfal to the Black Knight of the 1954 movie of that name than he is like the heroes of medieval romance. He is no dragonslayer or giant killer or crusader. Like the twentieth-century knight of whom Banks wrote, he does not have a splendid physique, and some "deeds of hardihood in which the old knights rejoice" are beyond his power; "but the higher deeds of the loftier chivalry, of upright thinking, of pure conduct, of self-denying devotion, are within his reach."[85] Johnston's message is that any person of character can possess this moral strength. And because it is not a condition of birth or wealth, it becomes an appropriate model for American youth and a means by which the hierarchical realms described by Malory and Tennyson can be made compatible with American ideals.

Notes

This essay is a revised and expanded version of an essay that first appeared in *Studies in Medievalism*, Vol. 6 (1994).

1. Louis Albert Banks, *Twentieth Century Knighthood: A Series of Addresses to Young Men* (New York: Funk and Wagnalls, 1900), p. 129.
2. Banks, *Twentieth Century Knighthood*, p. 9.
3. Banks, *Twentieth Century Knighthood*, pp. 50–51.
4. Banks, *Twentieth Century Knighthood*, p. 95.
5. Banks, *Twentieth Century Knighthood*, p. 14.
6. William Byron Forbush, *The Boy Problem: A Study in Social Pedagogy* (Boston: Pilgrim Press, 1901), p. 9.
7. G. Stanley Hall, *Adolescence: Its Psychology and Its Relations to Physiology, Sociology, Sex, Crime, Religion and Education*, 2 vols. (New York: Appleton, 1904). The stages are outlined in the preface to the first volume. Others concerned about the development of boys recommended the chivalric clubs. John L. Alexander, in a book called *Boy Training* (New York: Association Press, 1911), lists both Forbush's Knights of King Arthur and the Knights of the Holy Grail among "organizations supplementary to the home, school and church in a boy's development" (pp. 169–70).
8. Forbush, *The Boy Problem*, pp. 23 and 24.
9. Forbush, *The Boy Problem*, p. 11.
10. Hall, *Adolescence*, I, pp. xvi–xvii.
11. Hall, *Adolescence*, II, p. 444.
12. Hall, *Adolescence*, II, p. 532.
13. Hall, *Adolescence*, I, pp. 442–44.
14. Hall, *Adolescence*, I, pp. 418–19.
15. Cf. Mark Girouard, *The Return to Camelot: Chivalry and the English Gentleman* (New Haven: Yale University Press, 1981), pp. 254–55.
16. Forbush and Forbush, *The Knights of King Arthur: How to Begin and What to Do*, pp. 20, 21.
17. Forbush, *The Coming Generation*, p. 352.
18. Hall, *Adolescence*, II, pp. 396, 429.
19. Forbush and Forbush, *The Knights of King Arthur: How to Begin and What to Do*, p. 4.

20. Forbush, *The Boys' Round Table*, pp. 55–56.
21. Forbush, *The Coming Generation*, pp. 352–53.
22. The same impetus is behind books such as *Heroes Every Child Should Know* (New York: Grosset & Dunlap, 1907), ed. Hamilton Wright Mabie, which provided models for youth, including such diverse personages as King Arthur and Sir Galahad, Daniel and David, Saint George and King Alfred, George Washington and Abraham Lincoln. Another book of tales with a more specifically religious purpose, Basil Mathews's *The Splendid Quest: Stories of Knights on the Pilgrims' Way* (Cleveland: The World Syndicate Publishing Co., 1929), also combines, as two of its thirteen stories of quest, the tales of Abraham Lincoln's abolition of slavery and Galahad's achieving of the Grail.
23. William Byron Forbush and Dascomb Forbush, *The Knights of King Arthur: How to Begin and What to Do*, p. 7.
24. William Byron Forbush, *The Coming Generation* (New York: Appleton, 1912), p. 352.
25. Forbush and Forbush, *The Knights of King Arthur: How to Begin and What to Do*, p. 23.
26. William Byron Forbush and Frank Lincoln Masseck, *The Boys' Round Table: A Manual of the International Order of the Knights of the Round Table*, 6th edn., revised (Potsdam, NY: Frank Lincoln Masseck, 1908), p. 35.
27. William Byron Forbush and Dascomb Forbush, *The Knights of King Arthur: The Merlin's Book of Advanced Work* (Oberlin, OH: The Knights of King Arthur, 1916), p. 30.
28. William Byron Forbush, *The Queens of Avalon*, 4th edn. (Boston: The Knights of King Arthur, 1925), p. 7. Forbush's view of Avalon is no doubt based on the description in Thomas Wentworth Higginson's *Tales of the Enchanted Islands of the Atlantic* (New York: Macmillan, 1898), a book Forbush recommends to the girls who join the Queens of Avalon. Higginson describes Arthur's resting place as a "green and fertile island which each year is blessed with two autumns, two springs, two summers, two gatherings of fruit,—the land where pearls are found, where the flowers spring as you gather them—that isle of orchards called the 'Isle of the Blessed.' No tillage there, no coulter to tear the bosom of the earth. Without labor it affords wheat and the grape. There the lives extend beyond a century. There nine sisters, whose will is the only law, rule over those who go from us to them. The eldest excels in the art of healing, and exceeds her sisters in beauty. She is called Morgana, and knows the virtues of all the herbs of the meadow" (p. 92).
29. Forbush, *The Queens of Avalon*, p. 11.
30. Forbush and Masseck, *The Boys' Round Table*, pp. 128–32.
31. Forbush and Forbush, *The Knights of King Arthur: How to Begin and What to Do*, p. 22.
32. Forbush, *The Queens of Avalon*, pp. 26, 24, and 33; Forbush and Forbush, *The Knights of King Arthur: The Merlin's Book of Advanced Work*, p. 27.
33. Forbush and Masseck, *The Boys' Round Table*, p. 139.

34. Forbush and Forbush, *The Knights of King Arthur: The Merlin's Book of Advanced Work*, p. 55. The Brotherhood of David was an organization for boys younger than those admitted to the Knights of King Arthur. The ideal was to make use of "entirely different legendary material from that of the Round Table" so as not to "take the edge off the King Arthur idea when the time comes for it"; but since there was "some demand for a preparatory stage for boys from ten to thirteen in which the King Arthur stories are used in very simple fashion," Forbush established a group called the Yeomen of King Arthur (Forbush, *The Knights of King Arthur: The Merlin's Book of Advanced Work*, p. 43).

35. Published in New York by James T. White in 1933.

36. Cf. Forbush and Masseck, *The Boys' Round Table*, p. 18.

37. Cf. Merle Colby, *Handbook for Youth* (New York: Duell, Sloan, & Pearce, 1940), p. 272.

38. Forbush and Masseck, *The Boys' Round Table*, p. 56.

39. Forbush, *The Queens of Avalon*, p. 12.

40. Forbush and Masseck, *The Boys' Round Table*, pp. 18, 29.

41. Forbush and Forbush, *The Knights of King Arthur: How to Begin and What to Do*, p. 7.

42. Forbush, *The Queens of Avalon*, p. 11.

43. Forbush and Masseck, *The Boys' Round Table*, p. 18.

44. Perry Edwards Powell, *The Knights of the Holy Grail: A Solution of the Boy Problem* (Cincinnati: Press of Jennings and Graham, 1906), p. 20. Powell even includes Forbush's *The Boy Problem* in a list of recommended readings for his Merlins (p. 83). And Powell, even more than Forbush, saw similarities and ways of cooperating with the Boy Scouts. In his book, *The Knights of the Holy Grail and Boy Scouts* (Cincinnati: Press of Jennings and Graham, 1911), Powell noted: "The Grail and Scouts, though two separate societies, work together as pleasantly as husband and wife or twins" (p. 146).

45. Powell, *The Knights of the Holy Grail*, pp. 20, 9.

46. Powell, *The Knights of the Holy Grail*, pp. 15–17.

47. Powell, *The Knights of the Holy Grail*, p. 74.

48. *The Manual for Leaders of the Order of Sir Galahad Incorporated, A Club for Boys and Men of the Episcopal Church* (Boston: The Order of Sir Galahad, 1921), p. 55.

49. *The Manual for Leaders of the Order of Sir Galahad*, p. 55.

50. *The Manual for Leaders of the Order of Sir Galahad*, p. xv.

51. Mary S. Haviland, "'Knighthood of Youth'—A New Solution of an Old Problem," *School Life* 2.2 (October 1926): 36.

52. Julia Williams, "A Year with The Knighthood of Youth," *The Journal of the National Education Association* 19 (1930): 9.

53. "370,000 in Child Clubs," *The New York Times*, February 14, 1934: 24: 2.

54. Haviland, "'Knighthood of Youth,'" p. 36.

55. Alice M. Hoben, *Knights Old and New*, intro. John H. Finley (New York: D. Appleton, 1929), p. iii.

56. Hoben, *Knights Old and New*, p. v.

57. Williams, "A Year with the Knighthood of Youth," p. 9.

58. Williams, "A Year with the Knighthood of Youth," p. 9.

59. Forbush and Masseck, *The Boys' Round Table*, p. 179.

60. Williams, "A Year with the Knighthood of Youth," p. 10.

61. Horace M. Du Bose, *The Gang of Six: A Story of the Boy Life of Today* (Nashville, TN: Publishing House of the M. E. Church, South; Smith & Lamar, Agents, 1906), p. 8.

62. Du Bose, *The Gang of Six*, p. 84.

63. Alfred, Lord Tennyson, *The Idylls of the King* (New York: Bantam, 1965), p. 187.

64. Forbush and Forbush, *The Knights of King Arthur: How to Begin and What to Do*, p. 4.

65. Du Bose, *The Gang of Six*, p. 42.

66. Du Bose, *The Gang of Six*, p. 48.

67. Lillian Holmes, *Little Sir Galahad* (Chicago: David C. Cook, 1904), p. 18.

68. Holmes, *Little Sir Galahad*, pp. 22–23.

69. Holmes, *Little Sir Galahad*, pp. 27–28, 35–36.

70. Holmes, *Little Sir Galahad*, p. 34.

71. Holmes, *Little Sir Galahad*, p. 64.

72. Phoebe Gray, *Little Sir Galahad* (Boston: Small, Maynard and Co., 1914), p. 222.

73. Gray, *Little Sir Galahad*, pp. 372–74.

74. Gray, *Little Sir Galahad*, p. 193.

75. Annie Fellows Johnston, *Two Little Knights of Kentucky: Who Were the "Little Colonel's" Neighbours* (Boston: L. C. Page and Co., 1899), p. 116.

76. Johnston, *Two Little Knights of Kentucky*, pp. 96–97.

77. Johnston, *Two Little Knights of Kentucky*, p. 109.

78. Johnston, *Two Little Knights of Kentucky*, pp. 120–21.

79. Johnston, *Two Little Knights of Kentucky*, p. 121.

80. Johnston, *Two Little Knights of Kentucky*, pp. 121–22.

81. Johnston, *Two Little Knights of Kentucky*, p. 122. An earlier book, *Annals of the Round Table and Other Stories* by Jennie M. Bingham (New York: Phillips & Hunt, 1886), presents young girls in a club called The Round Table. Though the club is largely literary, the girls decide that the club's aim should be "mutual help" (p. 9) and its members go on to lead lives of service to society.

82. Johnston, *Two Little Knights of Kentucky*, p. 123.

83. Annie Fellows Johnston, *Keeping Tryst: A Tale of King Arthur's Time* (Boston: L. C. Page and Co., 1906), pp. 8–9.

84. Johnston, *Keeping Tryst*, pp. 12–14.

85. Banks, *Twentieth Century Knighthood*, p. 129.

CHAPTER 10

GOOD KING ARTHUR: ARTHURIAN MUSIC
FOR CHILDREN

Jerome V. Reel, Jr.

Of the many forms of Arthurian popular culture for young people, among the most interesting and diverse is Arthurian music. That music takes many forms, from nursery rhymes to individual songs for infants and children, from pantomimes to theater pieces, from rock operas to concept albums geared especially to teenagers and young adults.

Perhaps the most immediately recognizable individual Arthurian song for children is "Good King Arthur." A nursery song, it was typically sung by mothers to their children as they engaged in "mother play," lively interactions that were critical to child development: mother and child would play hand games, holding up their thumbs at the right moments to coincide with the rhymes. Like most nursery songs, "Good King Arthur" was brief:

> When good King Arthur ruled this land
> He was a goodly King;
> He stole three pecks of barley-meal,
> To make a bag-pudding.
> A bag-pudding the Queen did make,
> And stuffed it well with plums,
> And in it put great lumps of fat
> As big as my two thumbs.
> The King and Queen did eat thereof,
> And noblemen beside;
> And what they could not eat that night,
> The Queen next morning fried.

Like those of most nursery rhymes, the words to "Good King Arthur" are traditional. (In fact, as Dan Nastali demonstrates in his essay, chapter 8 in this volume, that nursery rhyme dates back at least as far as 1784, the year in which Joseph Ritson published it in his collection *Gammer Gurton's Garland*.) Interestingly, the first twentieth-century publication of "Good King Arthur"—in a 1901 edition designed by Edward B. Edwards, a Munich art house, and published by G. Schirmer in New York[1]—included both English and German words, which suggests just how extensive was the reach of the rhyme.

Although the words are traditional, there appears to be no traditional tune surviving; so each new issue of the song had its own tune. The music for the 1901 version, for example, was created by German composer, teacher, and pianist Carl Reinecke (1824–1910), whose music owed debts to Felix Mendelssohn and Robert Schumann and who is perhaps best remembered for his most performed work, a sonata entitled *Undine*.[2] Similarly, distinguished African-American composer Ulysses Kay (1917–95) set to music "King Arthur" (1948), a later version of the same nursery rhyme.[3] Kay, who had received his education upon the advice of his uncle King Oliver, a well known jazz cornetist, was noted for his distinctly American musical style; and his "King Arthur," which has been reissued many times since 1948, is typical of that style.[4] Among the most recent settings of the nursery rhyme is one by Elizabeth Poston (1905–87), a noted English pianist, composer, and collector of folk music. Poston wrote in the preface to her collection:

> Nursery rhymes are themselves: they are basic. They have here returned to base. In our modern world they appear in many forms. Those that are meant for the home but that add elaborate displays in the accompaniment serve only to show up how resistant are these tough, enduring little entities of his own folklore that are every child's heritage, to attempts upon their real nature. These offered here belong where they begin, on mother's knee, and find unadorned their simplest essential.[5]

Nevertheless, over the years, changes have occurred not only in the music but also in the words of the familiar "Good King Arthur." In 1966, in a version by American Paul Kapp, "stole" became "took" and "peck" became "bag." Thus Kapp's first verse began:

> When good King Arthur ruled this land
> He was a goodly King;
> He took three bags of barley-meal
> To make a bag pudding.[6]

The change from "peck" to "bag" reflected the fact that the new audience to whom Kapp's work was directed was most likely American, for whom the word "peck," meaning "a measure," was passing from common usage. But the substitution of "took" for "stole" spoke to a desire to cleanse the lyrics for the child less likely to understand "rascally royals." A 1969 version set by another American composer, Earl Bichel, substituted "bought" for "stole" or "took" as the implications became softer yet and the idiom increasingly familiar.[7]

In all, during the twentieth century, thirteen composers from at least three different countries—Germany, Great Britain, and the United States—set to music "Good King Arthur," and a number of the nursery rhyme collections in which these versions have been published were issued multiple times.[8] (Only in one period, the recent past, is there no record of publications.) Thus, throughout most of the last century, infants and small children in America, Germany, Britain, and the Commonwealth (and, no doubt, in other countries as well) have received their first exposure to a part of the Arthurian legend through the familiar rhyme.

Arthurian songs for older children, those between the ages of six and ten, are generally found in graded school collections. And the song most frequently included in those collections is "Fairest Isle," from *King Arthur* by Henry Purcell (1659–95) and John Dryden (1631–1700). (*King Arthur* is a semi-opera, an English theatrical form in which the principal actors do not sing.) "Fairest Isle" is set for Emmeline, Arthur's beloved, and is, though not easy, within the range of preadolescents. Usually the first stanza is the only one so set:

> Fairest isle, all isles excelling;
> Seat of pleasures and of loves,
> Venus here will quit her dwelling
> And forsake her Cyprian groves.
> Cupid from his fav'rite nation
> Care and envy will remove;
> Jealousy that poisons passion
> And despair that dies for love.[9]

Ninety-three different printings of the song survive in the British Library; of those, at least half appear to be for the elementary age group. At least one printing carries both English and German words, and several are in Welsh.[10]

Existing in greater abundance are Arthurian songs for middle school youth, young people ten to fifteen years who were moving from puberty into adolescence. One of the earliest songs for this group is the "Song of King Arthur's Knights" by William George Cusins (1833–93), based on

Alfred, Lord Tennyson's *Idylls of the King*, which became the basis for many poems and the inspiration for much art of the period. Another example of an Arthurian song is Rutland Boughton's "King Arthur Had Three Sons," composed in 1905 and printed in 1909 as *Choral Variations* (1st Set). Once again, the words (dating back to a nineteenth-century folk song) are traditional:

> King Arthur had three sons
> He had three sons of yore
> And he kicked them out of door
> Because they could not sing.
> Because they could not sing,
> Because they could not sing,
> He had three sons of yore
> And he kicked them out of door
> Because they could not sing.
> That he did!

The same verse was set again twelve years later by Thomas Keighley. In his composition, Keighley described each of the sons, as Boughton had:

> The first was a miller, that he was.
> The second, he was a weaver, a weaver, that he was.
> Third he was a little tailor boy
> And he was mighty clever, that he was.
> He was mighty clever, that he was;
> He was mighty clever.[11]

Keighley's text then took a turn similar to that in the nursery song "Good King Arthur":

> Now the miller stole some grist for his mill, that he did,
> And the weaver stole some wool for his loom,
> And the little tailor boy he stole some corduroy,
> To keep those three rogues warm, that he did. . .

But in another turn, which was intended to remind the preadolescent of the "wages of sin," the words continued:

> Oh the miller he was drown'd in his dam,
> And the weaver he was killed at his loom,
> And old Nick he cut his stick with the little tailor boy
> With the broadcloth under his arm, that he did!

That final allusion to the cutting of the stick derived from the royal exchequer, who recounted each shrieval transaction as a notch on a tally stick. At the conclusion of the sheriff's accounting, the tally sticks were cast into

the fire and burned. The lesson for the preadolescent about the consequences of his actions, however, was a bit arcane; the reference to the tally
stick was lost beyond Great Britain—and, in the twentieth century, lost
even there.

Just prior to the entry of the United States into World War I, the song was
published again in the United States by Robert Foresman in his *Sixth Book
of Songs*, which was intended for thirteen- to sixteen-year-old male singers.
Foresman used a tune that he identified as an "English Folk Song" and noted:
"In selecting folk music, usual care has been taken to be both comprehensive
and significant. Only those folk songs have been included which bear
significant markings of their own racial quality, the quality which makes them
distinctly Celtic or Slavic or Latin or Teutonic in feeling."[12] In his version,
Foresman set down only the first verse, and he ignored the catalog of bad
behavior found in the British settings by Boughton and Keighley.

A variant in 1953 by J. P. B. Dobbs recast the song in a musical setting
for adolescent female voices.[13] No longer were the rogues royals; now they
had become servants. This sanitizing of the text, which occurred at about
the same time as similar changes in "Good King Arthur," suggested a new
admiration for the British royal family in the years that followed World
War II. (Dobbs's version, coincidentally, was published around the time of
the coronation of Elizabeth II.) Only five years later, American musicians
Warner Imig and Bill Simon set the entire traditional song for mixed
voices. While Imig and Simon went back to the miller, weaver, and tailor,
they changed the Devil Nick's task to "took the stick" from "cut the stick,"
an allusion incomprehensible to an American audience.[14]

A less humorous, more serious approach in music for adolescents in this
age group occurs in "Song of King Arthur's Knights" (1927) by Ralph
Baldwin, with words written by Abbie Farwell Brown. The song's musical
setting is reasonably sophisticated and includes special texts and bass lines
for the young male voices. In theme, the author envisions Arthur's knights
riding across the whole world "treading holy ground. / For love has toiled
before us, / Where heroes trod."[15]

These sentiments of Baldwin's were similar to Sallie Hume Douglas's in
"Follow the Gleam," the verse song she wrote seven years earlier with the
aid of Helen Hill Miller. "Gleam" songs were quite popular at the time:
early in the twentieth century, Josef Holbrooke, who was more famous for
his large pieces, composed "Follow the Gleam," using Tennyson's text, for
his *Six Characteristic Songs*; and in 1920, Sir Charles Villiers Stanford composed a piece for the same words.[16] Douglas's intended singers were female
collegians, and her Grail narrative celebrated familiar chivalric virtues:

To the Knights in the Days of old
Keeping watch on the mountain heights

> Came a vision of Holy Grail
> And a voice through the waiting night.
> Follow, follow, follow the gleam
> Banners unfurled, o'er all the world.
> Follow, follow, follow the gleam
> Of the chalice that is the Grail.

The occasion for the writing of Douglas's song was a contest held at the Young Women's Christian Association student conference at Silver Lake, New York, in 1920. After composing the music, Douglas recalled that the "poem, 'Follow the Gleam,' had as its background the legend of the Holy Grail so artistically portrayed by the immortal Tennyson and by Sir Thomas Malory in his works and by Richard Wagner in his opera *Parsifal*. The legend of the Holy Grail has been consistently a challenge for piety, purity, compassion, fellow-suffering and the renunciation of low desires." The music that was initially used—and that remains the most popular—was adapted from Douglas's *Garden of Paradise*. Helen Hill Miller, who became a distinguished biographer best known for her life of George Mason, was also present at the Silver Lake conference. Never fond of the sentiments it expressed, Miller even offered to pay to modify the use of the song at the closing ceremony of YWCA conferences. A second tune for the words was written in 1927 by Gena Branscombe. The second verse (common to both versions) ran:

> And we who would serve the King
> And loyally Him obey
> In the consecrate silence know
> That the challenge still holds today.

For her part, Douglas remembered that "Obedience was exacted from the Knights of Old and it is the condition of Knighthood still. It is the price of knighthood—allegiance to the 'Light that shall bring the dawn.' To 'Follow the Gleam,' then, is to live his or her life supremely and victoriously for such alone is the vision of the Grail and the life abundant."[17]

The religious, almost liturgical, use of Arthurian legend is not unique to Douglas's "Follow the Gleam" or the other popular variants of it. The early years of the twentieth century saw several efforts to create ritual societies around the legend. Perhaps the earliest use was by William Byron Forbush, an American minister who was concerned that modern (that is, late nineteenth- and early twentieth-century) youth had little or no moral reinforcements to their character at the most crucial stage of their development. In their study of *King Arthur in America*, Alan Lupack and Barbara Tepa Lupack discuss Forbush's creation in 1893 of the Knights of

King Arthur and the importance of that society in the history of youth. They note that Forbush's Knights lasted at least through 1940 and established about three hundred "castles," as the local units were called.[18] (Alan Lupack also writes about Forbush's and other clubs in his essay on youth groups, chapter 9 in this volume.) Forbush, in 1911, published a compilation of songs for use in the "castles." In most cases, the music for these songs was adapted from existing tunes usually not in copyright. The first song in the collection, for instance, was set to "Tannenbaum," therein described as "Maryland, My Maryland":

> Upon King Arthur's throne tonight
> The royal sword is flashing bright;
> The dew of youth is on us laid,
> The dew of heaven upon our blade.
>
> *Chorus*
>
> Then lift the heart and raise the song
> Of manly voices fresh and strong;
> To knightly manhood pledged are we,
> In life and love and loyalty.

A few of the songs in Forbush's collection had music composed especially for them. "Upon King Arthur's Throne," for example, had a second tune composed by Wallace A. Sabin, a fellow of the Royal College of Organists. In all, sixteen songs made up Forbush's collection.[19]

While songs, both secular and Christian, for elementary and middle school–aged children were fairly plentiful, songs written for an older juvenile audience (young people fifteen and older) were rather unusual until the 1960s. An exception was an early piece, the 1926 graduation song from the students of the University of London, with words by John Drinkwater and music by John Ireland (1879–1962). Ireland was a highly regarded English composer who had attended the Royal College of Music, studied with Sir Charles Villiers Stanford (author of *Six Characteristic Songs*, based on Tennyson's Arthurian work), received a Bachelor of Music degree from the University of Durham (in 1905), and later taught at the Royal College. Much of his music has not survived, but *A Graduation Song for the University of London*, which was a chorus for equal voices and included the line "We are Not Knights of Lyonnesse," was published by Curwen in 1926.[20]

By the 1960s, however, a number of songs appeared that were aimed specifically at middle and late teens. For example, *Sunshine Superman*, an album recorded in 1966 by Donovan Leitch, one of the British rock stars who was part of the "British invasion," included the Arthurian track "Guinevere."[21] While the musical style could be described as "folk rock," the song avoids the obvious Guinevere, Arthur, and Lancelot triangle.

The opening lines—"Guinevere of the royal courts of Arthur, draped in a gown of white velvet, silk and lace"—have a winsome quality, while the refrain—"The jester he sleeps but the raven he peeps, through the dark foreboding sky over Camelot"—begs for the tragic triangle to be revealed. Three years later, Crosby, Stills and Nash recorded their own song, also titled "Guinnevere," with words and music by David Crosby (b. 1941). The song managed to combine the group's classic rock style with Donovan's poignancy and to underscore the queen's Celtic origin by descriptions of her as "green eyed" and of "golden hair."[22] Guinevere was not, however, the only subject of such popular Arthurian songs. On his album *Reflets* (1970), Alan Stivell (b. 1944), an accomplished musician who came from a Breton family and began piano and harp lessons at age of five, wrote and composed the song "Broceliande."[23]

A change from folk and soft rock songs was ahead, as the classic heavy rock group Led Zeppelin recorded "The Battle of Evermore" (1971), which introduced the apocalyptic theme of the "day of destiny" into much popular music. Merlin, as Dan Nastali observed, soon became the Arthurian character most appealing to rock musicians of the 1970s and into the early 1980s—"a protean figure equally at home" in such soft rock songs as "Merlin" (1973) by Climax; progressive rock tunes such as "Merlin, the Magic Man" (1974) by If; so-called "Kraut rock" such as "Merlin" by the German band Amon Düül; and the five-song suite ("Merlin," "Tintagel," "The Sword in the Stone," "King's Enchanter," and "Niniane") on the album *Merlin* (1981) by the Dutch progressive rock band Kayak.[24] Even Al Stewart, on his album *24 Carrots* (1980), recorded and released a Merlin song, "Merlin's Time." "Merlin isn't the one you're probably thinking of," Stewart wrote; "he's the Scottish warrior poet." Yet the first stanza

> And I think of you now
> As a dream that I had long ago
> In a kingdom lost to time

certainly evokes an Arthurian image. It continues:

> In the forest of evening
> The archer is bending a bow
> And I see you bring him bread and wine.[25]

The sacred image of the high priest Melchizedek greeting the arriving Abraham with bread and wine and of Jesus serving his disciples bread and wine connotes the creation of a royal priesthood reminiscent of the fellowship of the Round Table.

By the 1980s, Arthurian songs were remarkably diverse in subject and theme. Jana Runnalls's "Spirit of Avalon" (1985), on her new-age album *Ancestral Dreams*, was both ritualized and feminist. Kenny Loggins took a more light-rock approach in his song "Back to Avalon" (1988), which depicted Avalon as a place for lovers. Laura Zaerr's *The Harper in the Hall* (1988) echoed—and in some parts even quoted—medieval music and, perhaps more importantly, anticipated the trend of using distinct musical styles such as the medieval and, later, the Celtic forms for Arthurian texts. Among the best and most popular of those Celtic styles was the album *The Visit* (1992), by Loreena McKennitt, which contained the rather extended repetitive, almost hypnotic setting of Alfred, Lord Tennyson's "Lady of Shalott." And Jag Panzer, a heavy metal rock group from Colorado, on their album *The Age of Mastery* (1988), recorded "The Moors," which described the Lancelot, Guinevere, and Arthur triangle from Lancelot's perspective. What tied together many of the works of this period was their reference to the end of the Arthurian age, and, by extension, to the changes in contemporary Western society.

Other rock groups also recorded Arthurian pieces—although sometimes the Arthurian element appeared only in the title, as in Deep Purple's *The Book of Taliesyn* (produced in 1968 in Sheffield, Great Britain). Similarly, two other examples of compact discs with suggestive titles—*The Wayward Sons of Mother Earth* by Skyclad (1991) and *Siege Perilous* by Kamelot (1998)—contained no Arthurian matter in their lyrics. Indeed, as Michael Rewa has noted, these musical works reflected a long tendency of British popular artists to use Arthurian characters and Arthurian images without significant Arthurian material in the works themselves.

By contrast, *Imaginations from the Other Side* (1995) by the German group Blind Guardian made specific Arthurian references, particularly to Merlin, the Holy Grail, and Avalon. The last, which occurs in "A Past and Future Secret," references "the future king's crown" and alludes to "end time." The disc also contains "Mordred's Song," which suggests that Mordred knew from early on that he personally was doomed to failure. Also in 1995, Amorphis, a heavy metal group, recorded *The Karelian Isthmus*, a doom-themed album that contained the song "Grail's Mysteries," written and composed by Esa Holopainen, and "The Sign from the North Side," which declared "True Celtic Power from the Cape of Cornwall." Yet another dark heavy metal group, Cradle of Filth, issued *Dusk and Her Embrace* (1996), whose last band, "Haunted Shores," references Caliburn, Pendragon, Arctorius, Camelot, and Avalon. The movement by all of these groups toward "end time" continued the apocalyptic vision begun by Led Zeppelin; and the darkening vision that permeated so much of the heavy and dense rock music certainly mirrored and reflected on the mood of much of alternative society.[26] The numerous Arthurian-themed rock albums appealed especially to younger audiences and were almost as important for their narrative lines as for their scores.

In addition to those works written as individual songs were a number of Arthurian theater pieces that were written and composed with youth in mind. The English pantomime, which by the early nineteenth century had developed into "family" entertainment, owed its origin in part to the *commedia dell'arte* and in lesser part to the English medieval plays best exemplified by the Saint George plays. These two elements merged, although by no means exclusively, with the legend of King Arthur.

Among the nineteenth-century family-style productions (several of which are also discussed by Dan Nastali in chapter 8 in this volume) was *Merlin's Mount; or, Harlequin Cymraeg and the Living Leek*, one of the popular pantomimes that featured Arthur's wizard.[27] Noted in the *Times of London* (December 2, 1825), it was teamed with *All in One Night; or, the House on the Heath* and *The Three Crumpiers; or, the Baron and His Brothers*. Written by Thomas John Dibdin (1771–1841), it mixed the comic and the romantic.[28] Its wonderful scenic display, moreover, allowed transformations of "a chest of glass, a bull's head, a barber's cue and powder-puff with a chair and umbrella, into an elephant with Pantaloon seated on his back under a canopy in the Eastern fashion. . ." The reviewer noted that "a pugilistic encounter between two kangaroos was the source of great merriment, whilst it conveyed a fair satire upon a practice fit for the brute creation alone to engage in."[29]

Another Merlin pantomime was *Harlequin and Mother Red Cap; or, Merlin and Fairy Snowdrop*, by London-born Jonathan Blewitt (1782–1853),[30] with a libretto by Richard Nelson Lee (1806–72). Originally produced for the Christmas season, it premiered on December 26, 1839. Its plot was simple: Mother Red Cap, owner of a public house, tries to marry her daughter off to Squire Resolute. But Merlin intervenes and, with the help of Fairy Snowdrop and other fairies, reunites the daughter with her beloved Ploughboy.[31] Besides the traditional two-part show with the grand transformations, the pantomime had immediate royal allusions. A hamper brought from Germany was opened to reveal a "diminutive figure clothed in the tinsel of a petty German prince, who, after strutting around for a minute or two, is joined by a young lady (spontaneously produced, and of the gentleman's own size) who he very ceremoniously takes by the hand, and so leads off. This, we need hardly say, was an allusion to Queen Victoria and Prince Albert."[32] *Mother Red Cap* was paired with *Jack Sheppard and the Knight of the Dragon*, which concluded with a grand procession of nobles wearing "armour, arms, dresses, and paraphernalia worn at the Eglinton Castle tournament."[33]

In April of 1846, *Jack the Giant Killer, or, The Knights of the Round Table* was performed at the Royal Surrey Theatre.[34] The burlesque work, according to Roger Simpson, derived from early eighteenth-century chapbooks. (A version of that burlesque may have been performed as early as August 18, 1810, at the Lyceum.[35]) Set in Arthur's time and at Arthur's court, *Jack the Giant Killer* found Jack doing battle with the giant Galligantus, defeating him, and rescuing the daughter of a duke. Arthur rewarded him with the hand of the duke's daughter. A choral glee opened the entertainment:

> When Arthur first our king became
> He wore a coat of sleeves
> He entertained all Knights of fame,
> And none of them were thieves.[36]

The similarity, both in meter and in slighting references to the upper orders, of that glee to "Good King Arthur" is striking.

Another piece similar in theme, *Jack the Giant Killer; or, Harlequin King Arthur*, was written and composed by Henry James Byron (1835–84).[37] Byron wrote burlesques that satirized grand opera's many excesses, and his *Harlequin King Arthur* was produced at the Princess's Theatre in 1859. A Christmas burlesque, it preceded a pantomime and as such attracted family audiences. A revised version in 1878 was produced at the Gaiety.[38]

Whether the consequence of the "sacral nature" that Tennyson's *Idylls* laid on the legend or of an even more radical change in taste, the Arthurian pantomimes and burlesques aimed at children in the earlier Victorian era began to diminish, to be replaced by songs, traditional (as in "Good King Arthur") or other. However, one work in the late nineteenth century by W. Carlile Vernon set to a text by E. H. Patterson and H. Grattan premiered in Newcastle on December 16, 1893. Not strictly a pantomime, *Merry Mr. Merlin; or, Good King Arthur* was described as an extravaganza.[39]

The last years of the nineteenth century also saw the emergence of a dramatic musical form known as "school opera." Because little of the form was published, it is hard to ferret out the extent of school opera written on any topic. Nonetheless, this focus on youth had early advocates. The noted German childhood education expert, Friedrich Froebel, in 1837, established kindergartens that emphasized education through play.[40] School opera was an outgrowth of that movement.

One early school opera was by the English composer Herbert Longhurst (1819–1904) with the libretto by George Lewis. Entitled *King Arthur: A Juvenile Operetta* (1896), the work was populated by Arthurian characters, but the deviations from the standard character motivations were probably deemed necessary, given the tender ages of the performers, who appear to have been early adolescents. In this work, Lancelot loves Elaine, King Arthur's daughter, rather than Guinevere, Arthur's wife. (Of course, the name "Elaine" was that of two different women who loved Lancelot, Elaine of Astolat and Elaine of Carbonek.) The focus of the plot, however, is not on Lancelot's loves but on a bandit crew led by King Gore. The band, urged on by Gore's wife, Endor, a witch (a Biblical allusion), plans to destroy Lancelot through the use of witchly enchantment and drugs. Succumbing to the devilish plan, Lancelot is put on trial for the offenses and for living beyond his means, something no late Victorian should have wanted to do. In the meantime, Arthur's court jester, Pompo, has fallen in love with Gore's chambermaid, Dame Slut. Through her, the plot against Lancelot is revealed and the witch is punished, as the school opera finishes on the chorus "Sorrow Ended."[41] Thus, in plot, *King Arthur* seems closer to the pantomime than to the more serious works that followed.

After the turn of the century, British composer Dorothea Hollins wrote the libretto and the music for another school opera, probably designed to be presented under the auspices of the church. *The Quest: A Drama of Deliverance* (1910) was loosely based on the story of the Holy Grail.[42] Set in the Wood of the World, the cast included King Arthur and Galahad along with Saint Augustine, Dante, Sir Thomas More, and Sir Philip Sidney. The music, though called significant by the author, was not specified. She noted, however:

> Being designed for music, which supplies more than half of the significance needed, the lyrics in this drama are purposely less closely wrought than the blank verse.

After the horrifying years of World War I, the Grail theme faded in British usage but returned in an American work, *The Consecration of Sir Galahad*. Written and composed in Boston in 1923 by Eugene and Elizabeth Shippen, it was definitely a church opera. The music was adapted from a number of sources and remained popular until the outbreak of World War II.[43] The work was described as "a cross between a procession and a play. Reduced to its simplest terms, it was symbolic group action," created to enrich the plainness of non-Anglican Protestant churches and designed to take place in the chancel. Some of the words were taken from Alfred, Lord Tennyson. Like Hollins's *The Quest*, Shippens's *The Consecration* used Gregorian chant. Other music suggested included the Adagio from Charles Marie Widor's Fifth Symphony, the Andante from Louis Vierne's First Symphony, and the Communion in G by Alexandre Guilmant.

A third Grail opera, *Galahad: A Pageant of the Holy Grail* (1924), was written and composed by Linwood Taft, but it does not seem to have had the popularity of the Shippens's work. Part of a series called "Pageants with Purpose," *Galahad* was based on Malory and had ten parts, which began with the young child Galahad and followed through the "Loathly Damsel" episode and the overcoming of the "Seven Deadly Sins." Its music was drawn primarily from Richard Wagner's *Parsifal* and from the works of other composers, such as Antonin Dvorak and Frederic Chopin.[44] Also published in the "Pageant with a Purpose" series was another Grail quest opera, Dorothy Clark's and Georgia Lyon Unverzagt's *The Vision of Sir Launfal*. Although this is the only *Launfal* opus specifically for youth, *Launfal* spawned several dramatic vocal pieces. Its words inspired by James Russell Lowell's poem, the work was first produced at the Saint Johnsbury Academy, on May 31, 1927. The music was drawn from a variety of composers, including Sallie Hume Douglas, George Friedrich Handel, and Sir John Stainer.[45] A few years later, Reverend Mr. E. Harvey Herring similarly set his *Youth's Quest for the Holy Grail*[46] (published in 1933 by Morehouse, a Milwaukee press) to music from a variety of sources. Herring's setting was probably the last Arthurian youth opera before the Depression, the rise of Nazi youth movements, and the horrors of World War II; and the popular Grail as Christian symbol would not be taken up again so strongly again, even after the war's end.

Normalcy did not return quickly, either to society or to art, after 1945. Among the first specifically youth-oriented performance Arthurian pieces was *Tommy Pitcher* (1952), a school opera aimed at younger children. It was written by Paul Tripp and composed by George Kleinsinger (1914–82), who had created a number of youth operas, although none as unusual as *Tommy Pitcher*, the tale of a Tennessee boy who imagines himself a Knight of the Round Table who needs to conquer a giant (the Tennessee River) and thus make the world a better place. The obvious allusion was to the Tennessee Valley Authority, a project whose governmental sponsorship was the occasion of many attacks by American conservatives. Kleinsinger used the Welsh folk tune "Ashgrove" as the leading musical theme of the work, which was premiered in Stockbridge, Massachusetts.[47]

Of greater musical interest was an effort by W. Gillies Whittaker and Jane Dawkins, one year earlier, to scale down the musical requirements of the Purcell *King Arthur* for youth performance. While Gillies's and Dawkins's notes suggest that *King Arthur* could be presented either as an operetta or a cantata, the publication by the Oxford University Press came with production notes, costume instructions, and illustrations, and was set for equal voices in two parts.[48] In the four scenes—"In the Saxon Camp," "In the Fens," "King Arthur's Victory," and "King Arthur's Happy England"—the Saxons who have invaded England rely not just on their military prowess but also on the magical evil spirits that they call up. But the "Good Spirits" who protect Britain ultimately lead "the bewildered soldiers [who follow Arthur] on the right path" to victory.

The most widely seen Arthurian music effort aimed at youth in this era was, no doubt, the Walt Disney full-length animated film, *The Sword in the Stone* (1963). Based on T. H. White's first book of his *Once and Future King*, the film told the story of the boyhood of Arthur ("Wart") and of Merlin's efforts to prepare him for the kingship that he will assume after he pulls the sword from the stone. The film's workmanlike musical score was composed by Richard Sherman, a "house" composer for the Disney enterprise. Sherman's brother, Robert, provided the lyrics for the six songs: "The Legend of the Sword in the Stone," "A Most Befuddling Thing," "That's What Makes the World Go Round," "Higitus Figitus," "Blue Oak Tree," and "Mad Madam Mim." Of them, "Higitus Figitus," with its pig Latin and its memory of the Sorcerer's Apprentice from *Fantasia*, was probably the most memorable.[49]

Arthurian musical youth performance works remained popular, and one of the finest was *Culhwch and Olwen*, set by William Mathias (b. 1934) for treble voices and composed in 1971 to the words of Gwyn Thomas. The tale of Culhwch's tasks and his eventful wooing of Olwen is retold with heavy use of a chorus of courtiers, knights, ladies, and assorted folk.[50] Appropriately, this Celtic tale was set by one of Wales's most renowned composers.

Another notable composer was Timothy Porter, who in 1973 wrote and produced *The Entertaining of the Noble Head*, a musical entertainment in eight parts that were played without a break. Of the twelve singers, eleven also played instruments. While Porter quotes the tunes "Holly and the Ivy" and "Lead Kindly Light," his highly original score was meant to be played by nonprofessionals (but more advanced than "amateur"). The story parallels the Celtic god, Bran of the alder tree, with King Arthur. Bran was decapitated and his head, which had continued to talk, was eventually buried on what is now Tower Hill in London. So long as it remained undisturbed, Britain would be safe from invasions. Arthur, in a prideful moment, exhumed the head and announced that the British would now have to depend on him for protection.[51] A reviewer wrote that the music itself "possessed the power to strike fire from the performers and, fitfully, to create and sustain the atmosphere of portentous mystery. . . ."[52]

Timothy Porter added to his Arthurian output in 1981 with a new pantomime, *The Marvels of Merlin*. Among the many characters were Ygerna, Ector, Cei, Bedwyr, and Culhwch. The last part was taken by a female, while the stepmother was played by a male, in the tradition of the pantomime. When the musical opened, Vortigern declared:

I am the tyrant Vortigern,
And while I rule, this realm shall burn!

Woe to this land of low-born curs
That peace and plenitude prefers
To good old-fashioned tyranny
And really right-wing kings like me!

The first half of the plot centers on the tale of Vortigern and the tower at Dinas Emrys. Merlin sings:

But I can tell you what's below;
A pool of water black as sloe,
And deep within, two hollow stones,
And in the hollows, dragons' bones
The dragons waken every night
And till the grey of dawn, they fight.
Their fighting shakes the solid land,
And your great tower can never stand
While earth so trembles through and through.
Dig deep, and find if I speak true!

Of course, he did, and later, as the first act ended, the boy Arthur pulled the sword from the anvil. As was the custom in pantomimes, the second act told an entirely different story—the tale of Culhwch in the thrall of his stepmother, who was a witch. After a giant refused his dare, Culhwch (with a reference to Charles I) cut off the giant's head and married his beloved Olwen. The pantomime ended with Merlin enchanted by Nimue.[53]

In between those two Porter pieces, another British composer, Richard Blackford (b. 1954) composed *Sir Gawain and the Green Knight* (1978). The cast consisted of preadolescent boys and girls who sang all of the lead roles except for the Green Knight, his wife, and Morgana le Fay. (While the Green Knight and his wife sang, Morgana did not.) In the composer's note, Blackford revealed that he considered the story to be "an odyssey, an adventure into unknown territory."[54] The librettist was John Emlyn Edwards. Inasmuch as *Sir Gawain and the Green Knight* was suggestive of a journey, the music in Camelot began in a familiar modal form but became increasingly discordant with the appearance of the Green Knight. By the entrance to the Green Chapel, the music made use of all twelve tones. In the return to Camelot, the music returned to the modal; and the opera concluded with the Coventry Carol. Since its premiere in Blewbury, Oxford, in 1978, Blackford's opera has enjoyed a number of performances.

On December 11, 1980, Douglas Coombes premiered his school opera *Scatterflock and the Glastonbury Thorn* to a text also by John Emlyn Edward. It was intended for treble voices accompanied by keyboard, with strophic songs in a traditional musical form and pleasant music in two forms: folk

style tunes and seasonal carols. Scatterflock, a shepherd boy from the village
of Glastonbury, meets Joseph of Arimathea as Joseph comes to the "green
and pleasant land." The village is preparing to celebrate Apple-Howl, a traditional gathering of the greens guaranteed to chase all demons from the
homes and fields. Joseph responds, "I bring you a tree that is evergreen with
the richest flower in the world." Of course, the tree alludes to the cross, and
the flower is Jesus. In a naïve, even arrogant resolution, the folk rapidly convert to Christianity. The intention of the piece was to delay the youth's movement from a place of childhood faith to the materialistic, secular society. The
opera yearned, in fact, for a society that might never have existed.[55] *Scatterflock's*
story drew most directly on the legend of the transportation of the Thorn and
the Grail to Britain rather than on other aspects of the Arthurian matter.

In *The Magic Sword* (1982), another play presented during the Christmas
season, Ken Hill and Alan Klein created a pleasant entertainment based on
the Gawain story for children. Sung by adults, it featured Gawain as the
bearer of the sword who battles for good and for justice. *The Magic Sword*
opened on December 2, 1982, at the Newcastle Playhouse in Newcastle
upon Tyne. The cast of characters included Merlin, Morgan le Fay, a fiery
dragon, and a giant bear. A reviewer noted: "the music and lyrics, it is true,
may be somewhat sparse but visually it is a pleasing production. . ."[56]
(For a discussion of literary adaptations of the Gawain story for children,
see the essay by Cindy L. Vitto, chapter 4 in this volume.)

Richard Blackford returned to the Arthurian world—and specifically to
the story of Gawain—for his school opera, *Gawain and Ragnall*, which premiered on April 4, 1984, and which had been commissioned by the
Children's Opera Company of Cannon Hill Arts Center in Birmingham,
UK. This time Blackford's librettist was Ian Barnett, and the only adult
character was Gromer Somer Jour, sung by a bass baritone; the girls are
sopranos and the boys are trebles. Scored for an orchestra of twelve, *Gawain
and Ragnall* told the well known tale of Sir Gawain's saving the honor of
Arthur's court by willingly agreeing to marry a hag. When Gawain and
Ragnall are alone she tells him she is under a curse laid by Gromer Somer
Jour so that she appears as a hag for twelve hours of each day and as a fair
beauty for the other twelve. Her question to Gawain is whether he prefers
her to be hideous for court or hideous for the bedchamber. Gawain's reply
that she should choose—a recognition of a woman's sovereign authority over
her self and her body—breaks Gromer Somer Jour's spell, for it answers the
riddle of what a woman most wants. As such, the use of the legend and its
composition as a school opera in 1984 helped reinforce the growing women's
rights movement.[57] The year after Blackford's opera, Timothy Porter
composed and presented his third work, *Lancelot or the Tale of the Grail* (1985),
a very accessible youth piece that was aimed at the family market.[58]

Other aspects of the legends also became the subjects of musical entertainments for children. Another school opera *A Computer Whiz at King Arthur's Court* (1990), by Dick and Karen Zylstra, derived from Mark Twain's *Connecticut Yankee in King Arthur's Court*,[59] which, by this time, had inspired efforts in a variety of genres (as Elizabeth S. Sklar demonstrates in her essay, chapter 3 in this volume). In *A Computer Whiz*, the hero, a computer specialist, is knocked unconscious during a mugging and awakens in King Arthur's court; but apart from the introduction of the Black Knight Lord Ballymore, the story generally follows Twain's plot.[60] Yet another "Connecticut Yankee" school opera for a youthful audience was Larry Nestor's *A Connecticut Yankee*,[61] which adapted Twain's story to music.

Fittingly, Arthur's youth also became the subject of musical works for young people. Following the growing interest in the Boy King, Gail Erwin composed a cantata for schoolchildren, *Arthur, the Orphan King* (1992). The text was written by Kate Schrader.[62] *Adventures with Young King Arthur* (1995) continued the youth-interest trend. Composed by Kevin Stites to a text by David Lewman, *Young King Arthur* was, in part, a reverse version of the "Connecticut Yankee" story line, with the time travel moving both ways.[63] A few years later, in 1997, Paul Reakes devised a pantomime entitled *King Arthur: A Pantomime Adventure in Camelot*. The instructions, however, carried no notice of the music that should have been used.[64] Even more recently, Wilfred Maria Danner premiered *Merlin in Soho* (2001) in Berlin, a children's opera that used adult singers but focused on a youth audience.[65] Another example of time travel that moved in both directions, it was set alternately in London and in a Celtic forest, where Merlin meets a sorceress named Migrane. Eventually, she joins Gwenamara and Nimue as loving pursuers of Merlin.

Youth-oriented Arthurian performance pieces such as these were only one notable form of popular musical Arthuriana. Another was the Arthurian concept album, a musical form introduced in the late 1960s and early 1970s in which the words and music tell a single story on a record (or now a compact disc). Among the most interesting concept albums was British musician Rick Wakeman's *Myths and Legends of King Arthur and the Knights of the Round Table* (1975). Wakeman's *King Arthur* was actually his third concept album—the first two were *The Six Wives of Henry VIII* (1973) and *Journey to the Centre of the Earth* (1975), which included the tracks "Merlin" and "Guinevere"—but it was certainly his most influential insofar as it brought the Arthurian legend to a modern young audience using that audience's mode of musical communication. Wakeman (b. 1949), a serious footballer and a well trained classical pianist, had been accepted in 1968 by the Royal College of Music to study clarinet, piano, orchestration, and modern music. But, finding the classical education too limited, he left after only a year. Following a path that predated his short stay at the Royal College, he joined one rock group after another; in the early 1970s, he served as pianist for Cat Stevens's hit recording, "Morning Has Broken." Wakeman's *King Arthur*, a kind of rock opera, was divided into seven parts: "Arthur," "Lady of the Lake," "Guinevere," "Sir Lancelot and the Black Knight," "Merlin The Magician," "Sir Galahad," and "The Last Battle." The recording, done at the Morgan Studios in London, used the Nottingham Festival Vocal Group and the English Chamber Choir and Orchestra. A few years after the work was first recorded, Wakeman produced a stage production in London, but it was not a success.[66] The concept album, however, remains popular and is still available for purchase.

Over the years, other Arthurian-themed concept albums appeared and proved almost as popular with young audiences. Some of those albums, such as the eclectic *Land of Merlin* (1992) by Jon Mark, a New Zealand composer, followed the historical music path by using Celtic forms. Mark's *Land of Merlin* focused on the boyhood of Arthur and derived from the wellspring indicated by T. H. White, a theme that really lay at the base of much of the post–World War II school opera. The narrative began in Cornwall, which Mark identified as the "land of Merlin." From there, the locus sharpened to Tintagel, the "rocky and desolate" birthplace of Arthur, a young, carefree boy who is introduced to the Celtic world of mystery by Merlin. In a passage that reflects White, in fact, Merlin reveals to Arthur the "wonderful and magical mysteries of life." With that education completed, Merlin takes Arthur on a journey across Bodmin Moor to receive the blessing of the Christian church in the person of the Abbot of the Forest Sauvage. (It would follow that Arthur is taken to an abbot and not a bishop, given the privileged place that abbots held in the Celtic Christian church.) Merlin and Arthur then journey on to the court (perhaps Castle d'Or) to meet the king and queen of Cornwall, in essence to meet the historical world. Thus, Arthur—having been introduced to the Celtic, the Christian, and the historical worlds in which he must function—bids his childhood farewell and sets his face toward his coming kingship. For those whose interest is in the narrative, Mark's may be the most satisfying of the concept albums.[67]

Alan Stivell, who earlier wrote and recorded the single track "Broceliande," turned in 1991 to the fuller scope of the legend in *The Mist of Avalon*. Stivell's music style was much wider-ranging in form than was Mark's. As an accomplished Breton harpist, Stivell used Celtic forms effectively, particularly Breton folk tunes, but on occasion he based his score also on ecclesiastical forms and on rock. Stivell opened *The Mist of Avalon* by introducing three of the great women, namely the Lady of the Lake, Morgan, and Guinevere. (Interestingly, "Morgan" is instrumental and not vocal.) The story continued with references to the Grail, Arthur's journey to Avallac'h, and the promise of Arthur's return. Fittingly the strophic, almost ecclesiastical style was used in the sections entitled "Camelot" and "The Return," while "Strink Ac Graal" assumed a more secular form.[68]

Three other interesting concept albums were published in 1994. The first was Maire Breatnach's *Voyage of Bran*. The music, composed and performed by Breatnach, was also in the Celtic idiom. The narrative was edited from Breatnach's text and described the journey of the Celtic god Bran or Bran the Blessed, his decapitation, the taking of the head to London, and its burial there.[69] The second concept album, Patrick Cassiday's *Children of Lir*, might be considered even further outside the Arthurian circle. However, the tale of the children who are turned into swans in order to protect them from their evil stepmother was so close in matter to the Lohengrin legend as to warrant mention. (The score, while it has some Celtic styles, is really a late Romantic piece.)[70]

If Bran's voyage and Lir's children stretch the bounds of the Arthurian matter, Peter Allwood's *Pendragon* (1994) was directly in the center of it. Allwood's concept album, performed by the British National Youth Musical Theatre, presented the early years of Arthur, beginning with his conception by Uther Pendragon and the Lady Ygraine, continuing with his boyhood under the tutelage of Ector, his freeing of the sword from the stone, and his encounters with his half-sister Morgan, and concluding with his marriage to Lady Guinevere, which opens the young king's eyes to the notion of woman's sovereignty over herself. The listener is left to ponder the effect this notion of sovereignty would have had in the traditional legend. Unlike most of the other concept albums, *Pendragon* was staged at the Horsham Arts Centre in London on June 4, 1994, a performance that was captured on disc.[71] The music was in a soft rock form with occasional borrowings from English folk and church music.

A much darker work was *The Final Experiment* (1995) by the Dutch group Ayreon.[72] A prologue establishes the year as A.D. 2084, by which time humankind has almost destroyed itself; a few surviving scientists attempt a time-mind travel experiment that will take them back to sixth-century Britain and into the mind of a blind minstrel. Merlin serves as the controlling force in this effort to persuade Arthurian Britain to change its destiny by learning to live in peace. Once the prologue ends, the rock opera (as it was termed) is divided into four acts. The first depicts the minstrel's difficulty in comprehending the messages he has been given. He laments:

If I have died, then this must be hell,
If I am alive, I cannot break this gruesome spell
I am seeking relief and finding more
I have fallen into oblivion.

The minstrel is guided, in Act II, to Arthur's court, where he is welcomed as "worthy." Act III finds him, through his music, warning the court of the great dangers facing civilization. In his vision, he sees the fate of the world plummeting into the hands of technocrats and computer experts while the old order passes into ice. After that ice age, in which most of mankind disappears, the earth warms again and an age of fire appears. Merlin steps forward into this vision of "end time" to intervene and appeal directly to twentieth-century man to mend his ways. Thus, besides the eschatological message, the album suggests a theme of a lost, past golden age that humanity could, if it dared to, reattain.

A number of other concept albums were produced around this time. Medwyn Goodall, a Cornish musician, composed several such albums, including *Excalibur* (1990), *Merlin* (1990), *Tintagel, Castle of Arthur* (1995), *The Grail Quest* (1996), *The Gift of Excalibur* (1996), and *The Fair Queen Guinevere* (1996), all of which featured new age instrumental music with Celtic elements (as in Goodall's album *The Druid* [1996]).[73] A much different interpretation of the legends was evident in the concept albums of the rock group The Soil Bleeds Black, composed of brothers Mike and Mark Riddick. In thirty-four brief tracks, *May The Blood of Many a Valiant Knight Be Avenged* (1996) retold the entire tale of the Gawain and the Green Knight,[74] with emphasis on the hunts and also on the Green Chapel test that occurred on January the first, which in the old Christian liturgical calendar was the Feast of the Circumcision. *The Kingdom and Its Fey* (1997), also by The Soil Bleeds Black, presented even more of the "Matter of Britain," although in a more dreamlike and raw style. The score included "Behold Thou my Crest," "The Charm of Making" (which was the first of the group's references to John Boorman's movie *Excalibur*), "Dragon Arte," "He Shall be King," and "Neath Mountain Sleep." The last track provided an alternate end to the Arthurian legend by offering the idea of a mountain cave where Arthur and his knights sleep, awaiting the recall to Britain.[75] The Soil Bleeds Black continued their musical exploration of the Arthurian legend with *March of the Infidels* (1997), which included sound clips from the *Excalibur* score and concluded with the "Temptation of Mordred."[76] Their recent album *The Maiden, the Minstrel, and the Magician*, produced in 1998, focused on the Lancelot and Guinevere affair with "Next Morning, He Must Away," "A Song for Guinevere," and "Journey's End."[77]

In addition to these many forms of Arthurian music for children and young audiences, there remains at least one other category to mention: youthful compositions. At least two such works (apart from rock albums, often composed and performed by youthful musicians) have survived. Olivier Messiaen (1908–92), now noted both for his adult composition of three Tristan-related titles[78] and for religious music, in 1917, at the age of eight, composed *La Dame de Shalott*, a late Romantic piano study that has since been recorded. He wrote:

> The piece was composed after Tennyson's poem "The Lady of Shalott." The obvious lack of experience in this work will be forgiven when one learns that I was born in December 1908 and wrote it at the beginning of 1917. I was then only eight years old! I was at Grenoble and still ignored every thing about musical techniques though I played the piano (very badly). . . . In this "Lady of Shalott" a child's imagination runs unleashed. Nothing is missing: the castle, the inflections of the spoken word, the song of Lady Shalott (weaving!). Sir Lancelot on horseback, the broken mirror, the tapestry which flies out of the window, the fallen willow leaves, and the death of the lady who lies in a boat drifting down the river (bacarole!). Despite its extraordinary naïvety, this is my opus 1.[79]

Another youthful composer was Roger Sessions (1896–1985), who composed an opera *Lancelot and Elaine*, in 1909, when he was only thirteen. He remembered that at that time he was full of Wagnerisms. Two years later, he entered Harvard and received the Bachelor of Arts at the age of eighteen.[80]

As demonstrated, then, a wealth of Arthurian music survives for young people at almost every stage of childhood and adolescence. For the very young, the form is usually nursery rhymes, which have had an almost immeasurable impact on generations of infants and youngsters. For children, the form is often individual songs or graded school collections, including the song books and rituals of the various Arthurian-styled societies. For older children and young adults, the forms are more varied: school operas, pantomimes, youth performances, and folk and rock songs and albums. As with other types of Arthuriana in popular culture, these various musical forms have often corresponded to or reflected social trends and development. More importantly, perhaps, the "once and future" tales of King Arthur and his knights and ladies of Camelot—in their numerous musical reinterpretations—have flourished and will continue to fascinate young audiences for years to come.

Notes

1. Carl Reinecke, *Fifty Children's Songs: With German and English Words* (New York: G. Schirmer, 1901), No. 40.
2. Stanley Sadie, ed., *The New Grove Dictionary of Opera* (London: Macmillan, 1994), Vol. 3, pp. 1282–83.
3. Ulysses Kay, "King Arthur" (New York: Pembroke Music Company, 1978).

4. Nicholas Slonimsky, ed., *Baker's Biographical Dictionary of the Twentieth-Century Classical Musicians* (New York: G. Schirmer, 1997), p. 761, and Shaylor L. James, *Contributions of Four Selected Twentieth Century Afro-American Classical Composers: William Grant Still, Howard Swanson, Ulysses Kay, and Olly Watson*, Doctoral Dissertation, Florida State University, 1988, pp. 177–219.

5. Elizabeth Poston, *The Baby's Song Book* (New York: Thomas Y. Crowell Company, 1972), pp. ii, 142–43.

6. Paul Kapp, *Cock-a-doodle-doo! Cock-a-doodle-dandy!* (New York: Harper and Row, 1966), p. 7.

7. Earl Bichel, *How Many Strawberries Grow in the Sea?* (Chicago: Follett Publishing Company, 1969), pp. 28–29.

8. The other composers, in chronological order, include L. E. Orth, *Sixty Songs from Mother Goose* (Boston: Oliver Ditson, 1901), pp. 69–70; L. Bridgen, *Songs for Children* (London: J. Williams, 1906); J. Moorat, *Thirty Old Time Nursery Songs* (New York: Thames and Hudson, 1980, a reprint of the 1912 edition); R. Mayhew, *Good King Arthur* (New York: Harper-Columbia, 1919); I. Bertail, *The Complete Nursery Song Book* (New York: Lothrop, Lee, and Shepherd, 1947; third printing, 1962); L. Ager, *King Arthur* (London: B. Feldman, 1969); and two for whom no publication date has been found, namely E. Newton, *The Ernest Newton Community Song Book* (London: Keith Prowse Music Publishing, Co., n.d.); and A. Weir, *King Arthur* (New York: Mumil Publishing Co., n.d.).

9. Henry Purcell, *King Arthur* (London: Faber Music Limited, 1970.) This is a piano/vocal score.

10. British Library F: 659.g. (16).

11. Thomas Keighley, "King Arthur Had Three Sons" (London: Stainer and Bell, 1917).

12. Robert Foresman, *Sixth Book of Songs* (New York: American Book Company, 1917), p. 3. The song is on pp. 118–19.

13. J. P. B. Dobbs, "King Arthur's Servants" (London: Curwen, 1953). In this version, the words were "cleaned up" by W. G. Whittaker, who first published the lyrics in a collection of northern folk songs in 1921.

14. Warner Imig and Bill Simon, "King Arthur" (New York: Carl Fischer, Inc., 1958).

15. Thaddeus Giddings, Will Earhart, and Ralph Baldwin, *The Home Edition* (New York: Ginn and Company, 1927), pp. 314–17.

16. Jerome V. Reel, Jr., "Sing A Song of Arthur," in *King Arthur in Popular Culture*, ed. Elizabeth S. Sklar and Donald L. Hoffman (Jefferson, NC: McFarland, 2002), p. 126 [123–37].

17. Text: "Copyright 1923 by Sallie Hume Douglas, Honolulu." Her memory and that of Helen Hill Miller of the writing of the tune and of the words are in the archives of the Mariam Coffin Canaday Library of Bryn Mawr College and were conveyed to me by Caroline Rittenhouse, College Archivist. I thank Isabel Caszeau for the reference.

18. Alan Lupack and Barbara Tepa Lupack, *King Arthur in America* (Cambridge, UK: D. S. Brewer, 1999), pp. 59–68.

19. William Byron Forbush, *Songs of the Knights of King Arthur* (Detroit: The Knights of King Arthur, 1911).

20. *A Graduation Song for the University of London* (London: Curwen, 1926).

21. W. M. Donovan Leitch, "Guinevere," in *Sunshine Superman* (New York: Peer International, 1967). Also see Michael P. Rewa, whose important essay "The Matter of Britain in British and American Popular Music" appeared in *Popular Arthurian Traditions*, ed. Sally K. Slocum (Bowling Green, OH: Bowling Green State University Popular Press, 1992), pp. 104–10.

22. David Crosby, "Guinnevere," in *Crosby, Stills and Nash* (Atco Records, 1969).

23. Stivell, "Broceliande," in *Reflets* (Arthurian Home Page).

24. Dan Nastali, "Arthurian Pop: The Tradition in Twentieth-Century Popular Music," in *King Arthur in Popular Culture*, p. 149 [138–67].

25. Colin Larkin, *The Guiness Encyclopedia of Popular Dance* (London: Guiness Press), Vol. 6, pp. 4357–58.

26. Kayak's 1981 album was reissued as a compact disc in 1996 by Atlantic Records. Jana Runnall's *Spirit of Avalon* was recorded in London by Stroppy Cow Records in 1985. Kenny Loggins's "Back to Avalon" was issued by Columbia Records in 1988. Rosewood Music recorded Laura Zaerr's *Harper in the Hall*, also in 1988. The 1992 compact disc *The Visit* by Loreena McKennitt was produced by Warner Brothers. Jag Panzer included "The Moors" on the Century Media album *Age of Mastery*. Deep Purple's *Book of Taliesyn* was recorded in 1966 and reissued in 1996 by Spitfire Records, a division of HEC Enterprises. Skyclad's *The Wayward Sons of Mother Earth* was recorded and produced by Noise International, 1992, which also produced *Siege Perilous* with Kamelot. Century Media recorded and produced Blind Guardian's *Imaginations from the Other Side* in 1995. Amorphis's *The Karelian Isthmus* was produced by Relapse Records, also in 1995. Cradle of Filth's *Dusk and Her Embrace* was released by Fierce Recordings in 1996.

27. Roger Simpson, *Camelot Regained: The Arthurian Revival and Tennyson, 1800–1849* (Cambridge, UK: D. S. Brewer, 1990), p. 257.

28. Sidney Lee, ed., *Dictionary of the National Biography* (Oxford: Oxford University Press, 1901), Vol. 15, p. 9.

29. *Times of London*, December 27, 1825, p. 3.

30. James Brown and Stephen S. Stratton, *British Musical Biography: A Dictionary of Musical Artists, Authors, and Composers* (London: William Reeves Ltd., 1897), p. 52. The playbill is in the Theatre Museum Collection in London. Also see the *Examiner*, December 29, 1839.

31. Simpson, *Camelot Regained*, p. 126.

32. *Times of London*, December 27, 1839, p. 2.

33. Playbill, Theatre Museum Collection, London.

34. British Library Additional Manuscripts 42992 ff. 679–710.

35. British Library Additional Manuscripts 42992 ff. 679–710.

36. Simpson, *Camelot Regained*, pp. 127–28.

37. The *Dictionary of National Biography*, 8, pp. 607–09, lists his birth date as 1834. The text of the burlesque is in the Lamont Collection, The Loeb Music Library, Harvard University.

38. The text for this work is in the Lamont Library of Harvard University and was published by T. H. Lacy (London) in 1859.

39. A. Nicoll, *History of English Drama* (Cambridge, UK: Cambridge University Press, 1959), Vol. 5, p. 515.

40. D. C. Alpine, *The Influence of Froebel's Mother Play and Nursery Songs or Kindergarten Song Books, 1887–1918*, Doctoral Dissertation, University of Maryland, 1972.

41. Herbert Longhurst and George Lewis, *King Arthur* (London: Curwen, 1896).

42. Dorothea Hollins, *The Quest: A Drama of Deliverance* (London: Williams and Norgate, 1910), p. 11.

43. Eugene Rodman Shippen and Elizabeth Blount Shippen, *The Consecration of Sir Galahad* (Boston: Beacon Press, 1923), pp. 6, 37.

44. Linwood Taft, *Galahad: A Pageant of the Holy Grail* (New York: A. S. Barnes, 1924).

45. Dorothy Clark and Georgia Lyons Unverzagt, *The Vision of Sir Launfal* (New York: A. S. Barnes, 1928).

46. E. Harvey Herring, *Youth's Quest for the Holy Grail* (Milwaukee: Morehouse, 1933).

47. George Kleinsinger, *Tommy Pitcher* (New York: Chappell, 1954).

48. Henry Purcell, *King Arthur and the Saxons*, arranged by W. Gillies Whittaker and Jane Dawkins (Oxford: Oxford University Press, 1951).

49. Richard Sherman, *Sword in the Stone* (Anaheim, CA: Wonderland Music, 1962).

50. William Mathias, *Culhwch and Olwen* (Cardiff: University of Wales Press, 1971).

51. Timothy Porter, *The Entertaining of the Noble Head*. (Unpublished score furnished to me by the kindness of the composer. The work was written in 1973).

52. Hugo Cole, "Spring from Celtic Roots" ([London] *Country Life*, September 14, 1978), p. 704.

53. Timothy Porter, *The Marvels of Merlin*. (Unpublished score furnished to me by the kindness of the composer. The work was written in 1981.)

54. Richard Blackford, *Sir Gawain and the Green Knight* (Oxford: Oxford University Press, 1978), p. ii.

55. Douglas Coombs, *Scatterflock and the Glastonbury Thorn* (Potten: Lindsay Music, 1981).

56. *The Newcastle* (UK) *Journal*, December 10, 1982, p. 3.

57. Richard Blackford, *Gawain and Ragnall* (Oxford: Oxford University Press, 1984).

58. Timothy Porter, *Lancelot or the Tale of the Grail*. (Unpublished score furnished to me by the kindness of the composer. The work was written in 1985.)

59. Dick and Karen Zylstra, *A Computer Whiz in King Arthur's Court* (Louisville, KY: Aran Press, 1990).

60. Information provided by Dan Nastali from his and Phillip C. Boardman's forthcoming *Arthurian Annals*.

61. Larry Nestor, *A Connecticut Yankee* (Denver: Pioneer Drama Service, 1990). The reference was furnished by Elizabeth Sklar.

62. Gail Erwin, *Arthur, The Orphan King* (Melville, NY: Pro Art, 1992).

63. Kevin Stites, *Adventures with Young King Arthur* (Woodstock, IL: Dramatic Publishing, 1995).

64. Paul Reakes, *King Arthur: A Pantomime Adventure in Camelot* (New York: S. French, 1997).

65. Wilfred Maria Danner, *Merlin in Soho*. (Unpublished. Premiere in Berlin.) This reference was furnished by Alan Lupack and Barbara Tepa Lupack.

66. Rick Wakeman, *Myths and Legends of King Arthur and His Knights of the Round Table* (London: Rondor Music, 1975).

67. Jon Mark, *Land of Merlin* (Tucson, AZ: Celestial Harmonies, 1992).

68. Alan Stivell, *The Mist of Avalon* (Montreal: Dreyfus, 1991).

69. Maire Breatnach, *The Voyage of Bran* (Dubkin and Starc Records [distributed by Atlantic Records], 1994).

70. Patrick Cassiday, *The Children of Lir* (Dublin: Lir Records [distributed by Atlantic Records], 1994).

71. Peter Allwood, *Pendragon* (London: Josef Weinberger, Ltd., 1994). I am indebted to Kevin Harty for this reference.

72. Arjin Anthony Lucassen, Ayreon, *The Final Experiment* (Maashlus, Netherlands: Transmission Recordings, 1995).

73. Medwyn Goodall, *The Druid* (Netherlands: Oreade Music, 1996); *Excalibur* (UK: New World Cassettes, 1990); *Merlin* (UK: New World Cassettes, 1990); *Tintagel: Castle of Arthur* (Netherlands: Oreade Music, 1995); *The Grail Quest* (Netherlands: Oreade Music, 1996); *The Gift of Excalibur* (Netherlands: Oreade Music, 1996), and *The Fair Queen Guinevere* (Netherlands: Oreade Music, 1996).

74. The Soil Bleeds Black, *May the Blood of Many a Valiant Knight Be Avenged* (Herndon, VA: Riddick Brothers, 1996).

75. The Soil Bleeds Black, *The Kingdom and Its Fey* (Herndon, VA: Riddick Brothers, 1997).

76. The Soil Bleeds Black, *March of the Infidels* (Herndon, VA: Riddick Brothers, 1997).

77. The Soil Bleeds Black, *The Maiden, the Minstrel, and the Magician* (Herndon, VA: Riddick Brothers, 1998).

78. These three are *Harawi, Cinq Rechants*, and *Turangalia: A Symphony*.

79. Oliver Messiaen, Liner notes to the recording on Erato ERA 9113 and 9114.

80. David Ewen, *Composers Since 1900* (New York: H. H. Wilson, 1969), pp. 519–22 and David Slonimsky, *Baker's Biographical Dictionary of Musicians* (New York: Schirmer Books, 1992), pp. 1688–89. The opera in manuscript form is in the Princeton University Library.

CHAPTER 11

ONCE AND FUTURE KINGS: THE RETURN OF
KING ARTHUR IN THE COMICS

Michael A. Torregrossa

The idea of the return of King Arthur has been an important element of the legend since the Middle Ages, and creative artists have represented Arthur as a Once and Future King in an unprecedented number of works during the twentieth century, an era that Valerie M. Lagorio described as "witnessing an Arthurian renascence even greater than that of the Victorian Age."[1] Over the past one hundred years, Arthur has adopted various forms, guises, and even genders to effect his return in modern works, including fiction, poetry, drama, film, television, radio, and folklore. In particular, the comics medium—both the comic book and the comic strip—has employed the enduring motif of Arthur's return to create innovative approaches to the legend. This essay will focus on one particular aspect of Arthur's fictional restoration in the comics by exploring his return through reenactment.

Compared to the Arthurian legend itself, the comics are a very young art form. Comics historians believe that the medium originated in the nineteenth century, but the comics as we know them today, a hybrid form of text and image, did not become fixed until the early decades of the twentieth century.[2] Like other forms of twentieth-century popular culture, the four-color world of the comics readily embraced the legend, and the "Arthurian comic" has flourished since the comic strips and comic books of the 1930s, a decade during which Milton Caniff featured an Arthurian episode in *Dickie Dare* (Associated Press, 1933–34), the strip that preceded his *Terry and the Pirates*, and Ralph Fuller depicted the adventures of a medieval peasant in King Arthur's court in his *Oaky Doaks* (Associated Press, 1935–61). Not long afterwards, Harold "Hal" R. Foster (1892–1982), originally the illustrator of the *Tarzan* Sunday strip, abandoned the jungle for the halls of Camelot and began the long-running and critically acclaimed *Prince Valiant in the Days of King Arthur* (King Features Syndicate, 1937–present), which is now under the direction of John Cullen Murphy and his son Cullen Murphy. The strip premiered on Sunday, February 13, 1937, and chronicles the adventures of its eponymous hero, Prince Valiant of Thule (modern Norway). In the formative years of the strip, Foster concentrated on Valiant's attempts to become a Knight of the Round Table; later, as Arthur's knight and emissary, Valiant sought adventure all over the world, including pre-Columbian North America. Respected for its artistry and storytelling, Foster's *Prince Valiant* has been reprinted worldwide, and, like other Arthurian texts, the strip has spawned its own progeny and been adapted to comic books, two feature films, and an animated series designed for family viewing.

While at present the legend makes only infrequent appearances in comic strips (apart from *Prince Valiant*), Arthurian plots and characters continue to feature prominently in the comic book, a format best defined as a periodical composed of a series of comic strips.[3] The series *Camelot 3000* (DC Comics, 1982–85), by writer Mike W. Barr and artist Brian Bolland, and *Mage: The Hero Discovered* (Comico, 1984–86), by writer and artist Matt Wagner, represent the corpus of comic book study for most Arthurian enthusiasts, but there also exists an enormous amount of lesser known material produced since the 1930s and 1940s. The majority of these works, including such recent series as *Excalibur* (Marvel Comics, 1988–98 and 2001), *Knights of Pendragon* (Vol. 2 [Marvel Comics UK Ltd., 1992–93]), and the anthology series *Legends of Camelot* (Caliber Comics, 1999), are geared for readers of all ages. However, the Arthurian legend has also featured in recent years in a number of works more graphic in content and imagery that are designed for mature readers (but, as with most comics, are often read by younger ones as well), such as *Butcher Knight* (Top Cow-Image, 2000–01), *Knights of Pendragon* (Vol. 1 [Marvel Comics Ltd., 1990–91]), *Knewts of the Round Table* (PAN Entertainment, 1998), and *Lady Pendragon* (Maximum Press, 1996; Image Comics, 1998–99 and 1999–2000).[4] In addition to these series, other comic books have also looked to the legend by presenting stories in which familiar characters interact with Arthurian figures. For example, over the years, superheroes like Batman, Superman, Wonder Woman, Swamp Thing, and Iron Man have all paid visits to Camelot, while non-powered heroes such as Walt Disney's Goofy and Donald Duck, the Three Stooges, Italian comic writer Alfredo Castelli's Martin Mystère, and the perennially young teens of Archie Comics' Riverdale have also undertaken adventures with Arthurian themes. Despite its prevalence and endurance, however, the Arthurian comic, like comics in general, has received little scholarly attention.[5] Yet writers of the comics have made interesting use of the return of King Arthur, and their treatment of this aspect of the legend in the context of Arthurian literature and popular culture deserves further study.

In a recent essay, Carl Lindahl observed that the concept of a return of King Arthur is an example of what folklorists term a belief legend, and he proposed several categories to describe the use of this theme in popular belief. One of those categories was "return-through-reenactment," which Lindahl defined as occurring when "hero worshippers restore the vanished hero by playing his part."[6] While Lindahl's definition is excellent and offers a good starting point for discussion of mythic material, his classification requires some modification for consideration of fictional texts, especially comics. Thus, for the purposes of this discussion, I have expanded on Lindahl's definition and divided it into three subsections: works that present a return of Arthur through the reenactment of traditional narratives (in which other characters assume Arthurian roles and reenact events from the Arthurian legends, such as the Grail quest or the battle to save Camelot); works that depict reenactment in its more common form as invocation (in which the legend itself rather than the actual return of Arthur brings hope); and texts that employ the analogous theme of Arthur's return through substitution (in which non-Arthurian characters assume the role of Arthur himself but do not specifically reenact events from his legend).

Over the years, Arthur's return has been reenacted in various ways and in diverse media, and, as is consistent with literary and cinematic tradition, a number of comic books have included stories in which characters reenact the Arthurian legend for inspiration and hope in dark and troubling times. A good example is James Felder's "Last Light" (in issue No. 27 [May 1997]) of the Marvel Comics' series *What If. . .?* (Vol. 2), which chronicles episodes from alternate universes and which gets its name from the question asked by Marvel's writers. This particular story from the series appears to be influenced by events from David Michelinie's "Knightmare" in *Iron Man* (Vol. 1, No. 150 [September 1981]) and builds upon writer Roy Thomas's various accounts of the fall of Camelot in the Marvel universe (a term used to refer to the shared world of all of the comics published by Marvel Comics).[7] Felder introduces a new Black Knight, Eirik Garrettson, who assumes the identity after the death of his uncle, Sir Percy of Scandia (a Knight of the Round Table and the original Black Knight, who was introduced in 1955 by Stan Lee and Joe Maneely in *The Black Knight* [1955–56]), and who vows to maintain Arthur's dream by fighting off a threat to its preservation.[8] Felder's approach to Arthur's return is comparable to the story by Charles Vess and Elaine Lee in *Prince Valiant* (1994–95), the most recent comics adaptation of Foster's classic strip. In this four-issue series published under the Marvel Select imprint, Valiant and his extended family struggle to preserve Arthur's dreams while attempting to free the deceased king's heir, the infant daughter of Valiant's son and Modred's daughter, from the clutches of her great-grandmother Morgause.[9]

An even more interesting variation on the reenactment theme occurs in *Legionnaires Annual* (No. 1 [1994]), in which writers Mark Waid and Ty Templeton offer an "Elseworlds," an alternate version of the DC Universe (the shared world of DC Comics). In this story, the Legion of Super-Heroes, a team of teenaged heroes based in the thirtieth century and introduced by Otto Binder in *Adventure Comics* (No. 247 [April 1958]), is made to fit into the frame of the Arthurian legend.[10] Cosmic Boy, Saturn Girl, and Lightning Lad—founding members of the Legion—assume the roles (and the love triangle), respectively, of Arthur, Guinevere, and Lancelot, while their base on Station Avalon serves as a type of Camelot, with the remaining Legionnaires standing in for the Knights of the Round Table and also undertaking a version of the Grail quest. Cosmic Boy even reenacts a variant of the boy king's freeing the sword from the stone when he uses his magnetic powers to extract an antigravity mineral from a mass of molten rock.

At the most basic level of reenactment, a number of comic books merely invoke the Arthurian legend and the hope for the future that it inspires, as writer Chris Claremont does in the context of the comics' most popular group, Marvel's X-Men family of titles.[11] Created by Marvel legends Stan Lee and Jack Kirby, the X-Men first appeared in 1963, as a team of teenaged, mutant heroes led by their teacher, the telepathic Professor Charles Xavier, a visionary who dreams that one day mutant-kind and baseline humanity will be able to coexist peacefully. Until that time, Xavier, affectionately known as Professor X, teaches his pupils how to survive, as the now clichéd expression goes, "in a world that hates and fears them" because of the accident of genetics that bestowed their unnatural abilities upon them. Claremont, who began to work on *X-Men* in the mid-1970s, revitalized the series. By the 1980s the X-Men were a hot property, but the book had no connection to the Arthurian legend until the end of the decade, when Claremont began to prepare the way for his spin-off series, *Excalibur*.[12] First in *Uncanny X-Men* (No. 229 [May 1988]), Claremont has Roma, then guardian of the omniverse and daughter of the Marvel Comics' version of Merlin, offer the X-Men a new chance at life by using a mystic portal she calls the Siege Perilous.[13] But one X-Man, Colossus, counters her proposal with these words:

> What then of the **dream**—our teacher, Professor Xavier's dream—that brought us together. . ./. . .and now, more than ever, gives our lives meaning? You call us "heroes" and "legends." To me, Roma, those are labels,

with little meaning. Another person's description of me, not my own. I am **Piotr Nikolievitch Raspustin**—I am **Colossus**—I am an **X-Man**. That is important, **that** is what matters. And while I breathe, I will fight with all my heart for Xavier's dream, and the better world it represents![14]

Inspired by their teammate's eloquence, the X-Men decide that their mentor's dream of a peaceful coexistence is worth living for and decline Roma's proposition. The final pages of Claremont's *Excalibur Special Edition, 1987* (1988), in a story entitled "The Sword is Drawn," develop this exchange by discussing the need for someone new to champion Xavier's dream now that the X-Men are believed to be dead. (In *Uncanny X-Men*, the X-Men fought against an ancient evil and appeared to perish in the final, televised battle.)

In *Excalibur Special Edition, 1987*, a prestige format book that launched the ongoing series *Excalibur*, Phoenix II (Rachel Summers) draws an explicit parallel to Xavier's dream and King Arthur's dream of Right for Might when she explains to a group of wounded X-Men and two other heroes with connections to the team that the sword Excalibur became the symbol of Arthur's dream and "*the means of keeping the legend alive and vital through the ages.*"[15] The name Excalibur later serves as the title of the series as well as the appellation for the new team founded to pay homage to both Arthur and the fallen X-Men. Also entitled *Excalibur, Marvel Press Poster* (No. 46 [August 1988]), with artwork by series' artists Alan Davis and Paul Neary, commemorates this union with a spectral image of King Arthur extending the blade of his sword over the newly formed team of heroes in apparent approval of their evocation of his legend. In an interview with comics historian Peter Sanderson, Claremont explained that he christened the new team after Arthur's sword because *Excalibur* has a "figurative" connection to the Arthurian legend:

> If the X-Men are the legend of King Arthur, then this team is striving to be the sword that embodies that legend. As Excalibur the sword came to symbolize the dream that bound England, the ideal that inspired Arthur, so this team of people are striving to exemplify the legend the X-Men have become, so the legend will not be twisted, tainted, perverted, or destroyed.[16]

As Phoenix reminds her friends (and Claremont's readers), Arthur's dream did not die; rather, it transformed into a legend offering hope during increasingly troubled times. Phoenix continues, saying, "*The X-Men thought enough of Professor Xavier's dream to offer up their lives. Is it so much to ask that we fight to preserve it? The sword Excalibur represented* **hope**. *It was light in the darkness of fear and hate.*" She then asks her friends, "Do we want— / —have we the right— / —to snuff it out?" The nascent team decides that they "like this dream. It's worth fighting for," and Claremont concludes this work of Arthurian invocation by declaring that "the dream is reconsecrated. . . /. . .and **Excalibur**. . ./. . .that most ancient and noble blade. . . ./. . .once more redrawn."[17]

Even though he has continued to work with both comic books and the Arthurian legend, Claremont himself has not expanded on the aformentioned connections between Arthur's and Xavier's dreams.[18] However, later writers at Marvel have made some intriguing contributions to the Arthurian mythos in the Marvel universe. For example, as revealed in a two-part story by Fabian Nicieza in X-Force (Nos. 24–25 [July–August 1993]), Professor Xavier's rival, Magneto, takes the concept of the otherworldly Avalon, where Arthur is said to rest until his return, and again combines stories by creating a new Avalon, a physical refuge for mutants, in an orbiting space station. Appearing over the span of several years, the majority of the Avalon stories occurred in Uncanny X-Men and X-Men, but the concept was also explored by writers of other books. For instance, although moved to the Savage Land of the Antarctic, the name Avalon serves a similar purpose in Warren Ellis's X-Calibre (1995), one series that chronicles the alternate timeline of "The Age of Apocalypse" crossover, where Xavier has died but (like the team of Excalibur in the mainstream Marvel universe) Magneto and his X-Men take up Xavier's dreams.

More recently, writer Steve Seagle made light of Claremont's association of Xavier with Arthur, when, in Uncanny X-Men (No. 364 [late June 1999]), a reluctant X-Man refers to the X-Men's devotion to Professor X: "Ugh! It's enough to make me **puke** the way you upworlders fall all over yourselves like the Knights of the Round Table trying to prop up a stricken **King Arthur**!"[19] Such negative reaction aside, Xavier, like Arthur, nonetheless continues to inspire his X-Men (and his readers) to dream of a better world. Recent issues of Uncanny X-Men, X-Men, and X-Treme X-Men (Claremont's new book) demonstrate that the lessons Xavier teaches at his school for the "gifted" at 1407 Graymalkin Lane in Salem Center, Westchester County, New York, help to shape a better future where Xavier's (and by extension Arthur's) dream could come true.[20]

At about the same time he began working on X-Men but over a decade before Excalibur, Claremont invoked the legends of King Arthur and his Knights of the Round Table in another origin story, that of Marvel Comics International's Captain Britain, a British hero who combined the studious side of Spider-Man's alter-ego Peter Parker with the nationalistic overtones of Captain America and who later became one of the founding members of Excalibur.[21] In Captain Britain (Vol. 1, No. 2 [October 20, 1976]), young research assistant Brian Braddock reaches into the stone circle, which Claremont refers to as the Siege Perilous; chooses an amulet (an emblem of life) over a sword (a symbol of death); and is transformed by Merlin into his superheroic alter-ego Captain Britain, as Roma (here in the guise of the Goddess of the Northern Skies) tells him to "*Be **one** with thy brothers of the **Round Table**—with **Arthur** and Lancelot, Gawain and **Galahad**, with them all....*" Then evoking T.H. White (or his adapters Alan Jay Lerner and Frederick Loewe), Claremont has Roma advise the new hero: "Be *thou* what they were—a *hero*! Strive forever to maintain the rule of *Right*—of law and *justice*—against those who rule by *Might*."[22] While Claremont did not remain with *Captain Britain* long enough to develop the new hero's connection to King Arthur, more recent comics writers have allowed his creation to achieve Arthur-like status in two alternate versions of the Marvel universe.

The first of these subsequent reinterpretations of Captain Britain occurs in the coming attractions publication *Marvel Vision* (No. 25 [January 1998]), in which writer Matt Smith rewrites the hero's origin by having Brian Braddock perceive the true nature of Merlin and Roma's testing of him. Understanding that the talismans represent an equilibrium, he chooses *both* the "amulet of life" and the "sword of death" in order to be transformed into the "perfect man," a change that causes many to "believe he is Arthur come back to life—the once and future king."[23] Offering an alternate future of the Marvel universe, a flashback in Jim Krueger's *Universe X* (No. 2 [November 2000]) reveals how King Britain (the transformed Captain Britain) came to possess Excalibur. After years of struggling to reconcile his dual status as a man "dipped in magic" but "clothed in science," Captain Britain eventually realizes that the choice set before him by Merlin and Roma was, in essence, a clue to uniting the rational and the supernatural sides of his being. As in Smith's version, he then claims Excalibur, the Sword of Might that he refused in *Captain Britain* (Vol. 1, No. 2), and heals the rift within himself. Braddock's newfound sense of completeness allows him to assume command of England in the wake of events leading into Krueger's earlier *Earth X* series (1999–2000), when the inhabitants of the Earth suddenly find themselves transformed into mutants. The reinterpretation of Captain Britain has not been limited to alternate timelines. Braddock also takes up the Sword of Might as the result of events in Ben Raab's *Excalibur* (Vol. 2 [2001]), a series with even closer ties than Krueger's work to the mainstream continuity of the Marvel universe. However, as in *Universe X*, the sword is revealed to be Excalibur, and in claiming it Braddock becomes king of Otherworld and successor to Arthur in that realm.

Comic book writers at companies other than Marvel Comics have invoked the legend in similar ways. One of the more recent examples appears in a story arc written by Dan Jurgens for DC Comics' *Aquaman* (Vol. 5).[24] Created by Mort Weisinger and Paul Norris, Aquaman (the alias of Arthur Curry) made his first appearance in *More Fun Comics* (No. 73

[November 1941]) and was originally just a superhero who patrolled the oceans. Over the decades, Aquaman's origin was rewritten, and writers reintroduced him as the offspring of a woman from the undersea city of Atlantis. After aiding the city several times, he eventually ascends to the throne upon the death of its king. Later reworkings of his origin make Aquaman's claim to the throne hereditary, since his mother is now the daughter of the king of Atlantis.[25] Even though he was King *Arthur* Curry for several decades, the obvious association with the King Arthur of Camelot was not exploited until Jurgens's introduction to *Aquaman* (Vol. 5, No. 63 [January 2000]), in which Atlantis is described as "*an underwater Camelot, its **king** a monarch, a hero, and **more**.*"[26] The conclusion of the arc in Jurgens's *Aquaman* (Vol. 5, No. 68 [June 2000]) draws a further parallel between the two King Arthurs: Atlantis, like Camelot, will endure, "thanks to King Arthur's vision and leadership."[27] More recently, after almost sixty years of service to the DC universe, Aquaman apparently perished in Jeph Loeb's "A Day Which Will Live in Infamy" in *JLA: Our Worlds at War* (No. 1 [September 2001]), but, like his namesake, Arthur Curry is a Once and Future King who returns in a story arc in *JLA* (Nos. 68–75 [September 2002–January 2003]) by writer Joe Kelly. A new *Aquaman* series by Rick Veitch premiered in February, 2003, and offers the continuing adventures of the Sea-King, who has been granted new powers by the Lady of the Lake and charged to use those powers to heal the world.

In addition to reenactment and invocation, the motif of substitution is a popular approach to portraying the textual return of the king. While narratives of Arthur's restoration through substitution are certainly the most interesting, he is not the only figure from the legend to return in this way in the comics. For example, several of his knights are reincarnated in *Camelot 3000*, while his half-sister Morgan Le Fay frequently appears in various Marvel comics to take possession of her modern-day descendants.

As described here, both Captain Britain and Aquaman have recently appeared as a type of substitute for Arthur, but the original comic book example of a substitute Arthur occurs in the untitled sixth story of Periodical House's *Captain Courageous Comics* (No. 6 [March 1942]), in which young Arthur Lake draws the sword from the stone and is transformed into his superheroic alter-ego, the Sword. Before every adventure, Lake must free the sword to change himself and his friends, Lance Larter and Moe Lynn, into their secret identities as Lancer and Merlin.[28] Although it does not present a return of Arthur directly, a more recent example of substitution occurs in Mike Lackey's three-issue adaptation for Marvel Comics (1993–94) of the syndicated, animated series *King Arthur and the Knights of Justice* (Bohbot Entertainment, 1993–95), created by Jean Chalopin, both of which feature a college football team (led by quarterback

Arthur King) that is taken back in time by Merlin's magic to battle the evils of Morgana and her warlords of stone in place of King Arthur and his knights, whom she has imprisoned.[29]

A variation on this motif, in which Arthur's surrogate is manipulated into serving in his stead, occurs in Venetian comic book writer and artist Hugo Pratt's "Un Songe d'un matin d'hiver," originally published in the French comics anthology *Pif Gadget* in 1972. In this episode of Pratt's *Le Celtiche* arc, the Faerie guardians of Britain maneuver adventurer Corto Maltese into assuming the role of Arthur, who cannot return because he must sleep for another five centuries, to thwart a German invasion attempt during World War I.[30] Similarly, in Marvel Comics UK's *Knights of Pendragon* (Vols. 1–2), by Dan Abnett and John Tomlinson, the Green Knight, an elemental being with some ties to his namesake in the medieval poem *Sir Gawain and the Green Knight*, organizes a band of heroes to continue his eternal struggle against the evils of the Bane and their dark master, the Red Lord. Both series suggest that King Arthur has been reincarnated as Adam Crown, a young man who serves as one of the Green Knight's champions.[31] Marvel Comics' Black Knight III also becomes a substitute for the absent Arthur. First introduced by Roy Thomas in *The Avengers* (Vol. 1, No. 48 [January 1968]), this modern-day Black Knight, the alias of Dane Whitman, has always had aspects of a Once and Future King about him. Whitman, a descendant of Sir Percy of Scandia, the original Black Knight, travels (on occasion) through various time periods to thwart Mordred wherever and whenever he appears.[32] Whitman's Arthurian parallels are refined in John Ostrander's *Heroes for Hire* (No. 2 [August 1997]), where the Lady of the Lake informs him (despite other Marvel stories to the contrary) that Arthur is truly dead and that he is the current Pendragon, the champion of Avalon, and thus the successor to Arthur in this age. To fulfill his new role, Whitman must prepare to face a threat to Avalon, an impending doom that has yet to be explained or featured in print.

Despite their variety, none of the aforementioned substitute Arthurs has achieved the popularity of Matt Wagner's *Mage* trilogy, which, although still incomplete, remains the most widely known example of the motif of substitution in Arthurian comics. In *Mage: The Hero Discovered*, the first book of the trilogy, protagonist Kevin Matchstick encounters the first of three Mages, Mirth (short for Myrddin, the Welsh name for Merlin), and finds himself charged with superhuman strength and speed. Mirth later explains that Matchstick has been empowered to combat the forces of Darkness (the Umbra Sprite, in this series, and his son, the Pale Inchanter, in the second), and Wagner suggests that Matchstick will reenact the role of a Grail knight by seeking out the Fisher King, the ultimate champion of the forces of Light.

In spite of the fact that he employed the Malorian epitaph ("*Hic iacet Arthurus, Rex quondam Rexque futurus*") in advertisements for the series and offers clues throughout the series, Wagner does not reveal the identities of his main characters until *Mage: The Hero Discovered* (No. 13 [June 1986]), after the Umbra Sprite's agents have killed Matchstick's friend, Edsel, about midway through the issue. At this pivotal point, Mirth reveals that Edsel's "line has *always* carried the weapon for you— / —awaiting you and this moment." Gesturing to Edsel's baseball bat, embedded lengthwise in an upright dumpster by an angry Matchstick, the Mage then proclaims, "You are the *Pendragon*, who before was called Arthur. And you *cannot* turn back from what *now* has been awakened—your other half. . . /. . .your weapon: *Excalibur!*"[33] In the next issue (No. 14 [August 1986]), entitled, perhaps ominously, ". . .Or Not To Be," Mirth offers a longer explanation of each character's exact role in the narrative. Edsel is the current incarnation of the Lady of the Lake, since her "roots, too, are *ancient* and *fey*. She *used* to like lakes instead of cars"; Matchstick is King Arthur, though "not king exactly. And not Arthur exactly," although his "heart is the heart of the Pendragon returned—confused as it may be."[34] And, as expected, Mirth reveals himself to be Merlin when he announces, "you see Kevin, *we* have always been student and teacher. King and wizard. Hero and Mage."[35] To complete his return, Matchstick is granted possession of Excalibur, which he reclaims from the dumpster in a scene reminiscent of Arthur's drawing the sword from the stone. Later, some time after his defeat of the Umbra Sprite, Matchstick takes up his quest to seek out the Fisher King; he begins to wander North America and confronts various supernatural entities. Although Matchstick has yet to find the Fisher King, his greatest challenge to date occurs in the second part of Wagner's trilogy, *Mage: The Hero Defined* (1997–99), in which his very identity as the Pendragon is questioned. (The series will conclude in the projected third part of the trilogy, *Mage: The Hero Denied*.)

Continuing the theme of substitution, other comic books employ the idea of Arthur's physical descendants, who (like his other surrogates) find themselves called upon to take up his legacy and defend the world against the enemies of the powers of good. Such stories appear in several comic books designed for older readers, as in Paul Jenkins's *Hellblazer* (Nos. 111–12 [March–April 1997]), from DC Comics' Vertigo imprint, where occultist John Constantine discovers that his drunken friend, Rich the Punk, is Arthur's descendant, or in Barry Blair's *Pendragon* (1991) for Aircel Comics, a two-issue series in which Valerie Pender, Arthur's female descendant, clad in a bikini and wielding Excalibur, emerges to aid Merlin, her college professor at New York University, in his fight against a magic-wielding Mordred. Other variants of the motif of Arthur's descendants feature more traditional superheroes and are thus even more appealing to younger readers, as in Marvel Comics' *Doctor Strange, Sorcerer Supreme* (Nos. 3–4 [March and May 1989]), a two-part story by Peter B. Gillis introducing Dafyd ap Iowerth, a character Gillis describes as Arthur's spiritual descendant and who aids a number of superheroes as they confront the evils of the Dragon of the Moon. Sometimes Arthur's relatives assume his role. An early example occurs in Jamie Delano's "The Bloody Saint" from DC Comics' *Hellblazer Annual* (No. 1 [1989]) featuring his cousin and heir Kon-sten-tyn (Constantine). More recent works focus on the women of Camelot. It is Guinevere who claims Excalibur after Arthur's death and becomes champion of a Marion Zimmer Bradley-esque Avalon in the three volumes of Matt Hawkins's *Lady Pendragon* series, while Anna, Arthur's sister (introduced by Geoffrey of Monmouth in his *Historia Regum Britanniae*), awakens in Kevin Gunstone's *Warrior Nun Brigantia* (2000), a three-issue spin-off series of Antarctic Press's popular *Warrior Nun* series, to face their half-sister Fata-Morgana and to recover the head of Bran the Blessed from her Nazi allies during World War II.

Conclusion

Collectively, these examples of Arthur's return through reenactment, invocation, and substitution from the comics demonstrate that, as in contemporary popular fiction, film, and other media, the theme of Arthur's restoration remains one of the most vital components of the Arthurian legend. This fact appears all the more relevant as we move further into the twenty-first century and discover that, even in the new millennium, crises of unimaginable proportions create the need for familiar heroes.[36] Undoubtedly, one such hero will be Arthur, for, as the comics discussed illustrate, he is the Once and Future King.

Highly malleable, the Arthurian legend transmutes as willingly today under the guidance of each new creative artist as it transformed in the Middle Ages, when the core of the legend first evolved. The representations of Arthur in the comics—from *Prince Valiant* to the *Uncanny X-Men* and from *The Black Knight* to *Lady Pendragon*—are part of the corpus of Arthurian texts. Largely neglected or ignored by Arthurian scholars, these works chronicling the adventures of the four-color king and his legend deserve to be better known, as examples both of the evolution of the legend and of the assimilation of Arthur into popular culture, particularly youth culture. Moreover, because they represent a medium that can be accessed by young readers, comics allow the legends to be shared and passed on to a new generation, one that can create its own Arthurian narratives and provide future returns for its beloved Once and Future King.

Notes

This essay is based on a paper presented at *Camelot 2000*. I am grateful to Professors C. David Benson, Mary Alice Grellner, Kevin J. Harty, Eugene K. Kannenberg, Jr., Alan Lupack, Meradith T. McMunn, Thomas J. Roberts, Elizabeth S. Sklar, and Charlotte T. Wulf for their continued interest in my research; to Anthony and Ann Marie Torregrossa for their encouragement and support; and to the members of the Comics Scholars Discussion List and the Arthurian Comic Book Discussion List on Yahoo! (especially Dan Nastali, Rodney Parrish, Cory Rushton, Alan Stewart, and Jason Tondro) for their input and assistance.

1. Valerie M. Lagorio, "Foreword," *Interpretations* 15.2 (1984): v.

2. For the history of the comics and related topics, see the following: Robert L. Beerbohm and Richard D. Olson's "The American Comic Book: 1842–1932. In the Beginning: New Discoveries Beyond the Platinum Age," pp. 226–34, and "The American Comic Book: 1933-Present. The Golden Age and Beyond: Origins of the Modern Comic Book," pp. 242–49, both in *The Overstreet Comic Book Price Guide*, ed. Robert M. Overstreet, 30th edn. (New York: HarperCollins, 2000); M. Thomas Inge's "Comic Strips: A Bibliographic Essay," *International Journal of Comic Art* 3.1 (2001): 217–50 and "Comics Books: A Bibliographic Essay," *International Journal of Comic Art* 3.2 (2001): 295–328.

3. The comic book, moreover, usually represents a collaborative effort, which combines the talents of writer, penciler, inker, colorist, letterer, and editor; comic strips, by contrast, are often the work of a single individual. Given the limited space provided here, I will be referring to the comics by writer's name, series title, issue number, publisher, and date. A listing of all the Arthurian comics cited here appears (with more complete citation information) in the "Select Bibliography of Arthurian Comics."

4. As these titles illustrate, comics have evolved from a medium long thought to be merely material for children to texts that can also be appreciated by adult readers and critics. For details on the audience of the comics, see the following works: Amy Kiste Nyberg's *Seal of Approval: The History of the Comics Code* (Jackson: University of Mississippi Press, 1998); Salvatore Mondello's "Spider-Man: Superhero in the Liberal Tradition," *Journal of Popular Culture* 10.1 (1976): 232–38; Greg S. McCue and Clive Bloom's *Dark Knights: The New Comics in Context* (Boulder: Pluto Press, 1993); Patrick Parsons's "Batman and his Audience: The Dialectic of Culture" in Roberta E. Pearson and William Urrichio, eds., *The Many Lives of the Batman: Critical Approaches to a Superhero and His Media* (New York: Routledge, 1991), pp. 66–89; Matthew J. Pustz's "EC Fan-Addicts and Marvel Zombies: Historical Comic Book-Reading Communities," pp. 36–65, and "From Speculators to Snobs: The Spectrum of Contemporary Comic Book Readers," pp. 66–109, both in his *Comic Book Culture: Fanboys and True Believers* (Jackson: University of Mississippi Press, 1999); and Bradford W. Wright's *Comic Book Nation: The Transformation of Youth Culture in America* (Baltimore: Johns Hopkins University Press, 2001).

The consensus among comics historians now is that the majority of comics were never marketed exclusively to a preteen audience, but the public, at least in America, often perceived them as such.

5. In 1984, Alan Stewart became the first Arthurian enthusiast to devote his energies to the Arthurian comic, and he later observed (in "King Arthur in the Comics," *Avalon to Camelot* 2.1 (1986): 12 [12–14]): "Over the centuries, the legend of King Arthur has been recounted in virtually every medium of expression known to humankind. Most of these are represented in Arthurian studies, but the popular artform known as the comic strip has been largely neglected, despite the fact that comics remain one of the most widely disseminated and experienced media of our time." In comparison to the heightened interest in Arthurian film following Kevin J. Harty's pioneering work in the late 1980s, little has changed in the status of the Arthurian comic as a topic for research in the years following Stewart's initial lament, despite the fact that the comics (with the exception of works of popular fiction that are often equally ephemeral) exceed most other media of twentieth-century Arthurian popular culture in terms of the sheer number of items produced. At present, scholarship on the Arthurian comics is still in its infancy, but the following studies offer useful overviews of the subject: Sally K. Slocum and H. Alan Stewart, "Heroes in Four Colors," in *King Arthur Through the Ages*, ed. Valerie M. Lagorio and Mildred Leake Day, Vol. 2 (New York: Garland, 1990), pp. 291–308; Alan Stewart, "Camelot in Four Colors: The Arthurian Legend in Comic Books, *Amazing Heroes* 55 (September 15, 1984): 80–97; Alan Stewart, *Camelot in Four Colors: A Survey of the Arthurian Legend in Comics*, June 2002 <http://www.camelot4colors.com>; and Jason Tondro, "Camelot in Comics," in *King Arthur in Popular Culture*, ed. Elizabeth S. Sklar and Donald L. Hoffman (Jefferson, NC: McFarland, 2002), pp. 169–81. See also Michael Torregrossa, "*Camelot 3000* and Beyond: An Annotated Bibliography of Arthurian Comic Books Published in the United States ca. 1980–1998," *Arthuriana* 9.1 (1999): 67–109, a revised version of which appears online as part of the *Arthuriana/Camelot Project Bibliographies*, May 2000 <http://www.lib.rochester.edu/camelot/acpbibs/comicbib. htm>.

6. Carl Lindahl, "Three Ways of Coming Back: Folkloric Perspectives on Arthur's Return," in *King Arthur's Modern Return*, ed. Debra N. Mancoff (New York: Garland, 1998), pp. 19 [13–29].

7. Thomas's most recent account of the fall of Camelot occurs in Roy Thomas and Dann Thomas's *Black Knight* (Nos. 1–2 [June–July 1990]).

8. For details on the original Black Knight, see Peter Sanderson, "Black Knight," *Marvel Age* (No. 88 [New York: Marvel Comics, May 1990]): 26–27; Peter Sanderson, *Marvel Universe* (New York: Harry Abrams, 1996), p. 131.

9. In addition to the reenactment noted earlier, Vess and Lee also invoke the section titles of T. H. White's novel *The Once and Future King* in the individual titles of the four issues.

10. For further details on the Legion, see Les Daniels, *DC Comics: Sixty Years of the World's Favorite Comic Book Heroes* (New York: Bullfinch Press-Little, Brown, and Co., 1995), pp. 122–23.

11. In general, the comics are full of examples invoking the Arthurian legend, such as the presence of round tables and enchanted weapons embedded in stones (see Tondro, "Camelot in Comics," pp. 174–77), but actual references to Arthur and his predestined return are much rarer, as I attempt to show here.

12. For the X-Men, see Les Daniels, *Marvel: Five Fabulous Decades of the World's Greatest Comics* (1991; New York: Harry Abrams, 1993), pp. 111–13, 167–72, 185–87, 193–95; Sanderson, *Marvel Universe*, pp. 208–49; Peter Sanderson, *Ultimate X-Men* (New York: Dorling Kindersley Publishing, 2000).

13. The Siege Perilous first appeared in Claremont's untitled origin story for Captain Britain in *Captain Britain* (Vol. 1, No. 1 [October 13, 1976], where it appears to be a ring of stones, so presumably it has evolved since then. According to Marvel continuity, Roma is the daughter of Merlin III of Otherworld, the Merlin who most frequently appears in comics published by Marvel's British imprint. Both also make their first appearance in *Captain Britain* (Vol. 1, No. 1), but subsequent texts suggest that this Merlin is also the Arthurian Merlin (classified as Merlin I). See Torregrossa, "*Camelot 3000* and Beyond," for further details on the distinction between these versions of Merlin.

14. Chris Claremont, "Down Under," *Uncanny X-Men* (No. 229 [New York: Marvel Comics, May 1988]), p. 30. Since this is my first quote, some comments need to be made concerning format. Punctuation in the comics remains erratic, while most text is presented in all capital letters. I have endeavored to present punctuation as is (including bold and italic effects), but I have on occasion introduced a virgule to signify divisions made by panel breaks or speech balloons. However, I have amended and regularized capitalization in all instances to reflect more standard usage.

15. Chris Claremont, "The Sword is Drawn," *Excalibur Special Edition, 1987* (New York: Marvel Comics, 1988), p. 46.

16. Peter Sanderson, "High Caliber: The Story Behind *Excalibur*," *Amazing Heroes* 134 (February 1, 1988): 30 [22–30].

17. Claremont, "The Sword is Drawn," pp. 46, 47, 48. Phoenix herself has become the vehicle for both preserving and continuing Xavier's dream, when she travels into the distant future to become the Mother Askani and forms her own band of mutant freedom fighters, as revealed in Scott Lobdell's *Adventures of Cyclops and Phoenix* (Nos. 1–4 [1994]) and *Askani'son* (Nos. 1–4 [1996]) and also in the prequel to these series, John Francis Moore's *X-Men: Phoenix* (Nos. 1–3 [1999–2000]). See also Scott Lobdell, *X-Men Books of the Askani* (No. 1 [1995]).

18. Claremont's most notable combination of the two after *Excalibur* has been in his *Sovereign Seven* (1995–98) creator-owned series for DC Comics, which features a character named Toby Merlin, a military base called Camp

Camelot, and at least one appearance each of Excalibur and a character presumed to be Mordred. Given these elements, one might expect Claremont to have produced a number of Arthurian story arcs, but the series was canceled before Claremont could further develop this aspect of the book.

19. Steve Seagle, "The Hunt for Xavier! Part Five: Escape from Alcatraz," *Uncanny X-Men* (No. 364 [late June 1999]), p. 11. This negative feeling toward an Arthurian connection to the X-Men is also present in the fan base, as evidenced by the response given by Jim McLauchlin, a columnist for *Wizard: The Comics Magazine*, to another fan's suggestion of an alternate invocation of the legend than that proposed here. Clearly unaware of the cited examples, McLauchlin replied to Jeremy Adams of Spencer, Ohio, "C'mon. Comics are geeky enough without some Monty Python 'Holy Grail'-types wedging their way into some convoluted 'Mutants of the Round Table' angle" ("Magic Word," *Wizard: The Comics Magazine* 120 [September 2001]: 14 [8, 10, 12–14]).

20. Like the spread of Arthur's dream through the narratives of various media, Xavier's dream and the hope for the future it provides has also been represented in a number of recent reinterpretations of the X-Men, including Bryan Singer's film *X-Men* (20th Century Fox, 2000), Joe Casey's *X-Men: Children of the Atom* (Nos. 1–6 [Marvel Comics, 1999–2000]), Mark Millar's *Ultimate X-Men* (Marvel Comics, February 2001–present), and in both the animated series *X-Men: Evolution* on the WB Network (Film Roman, 2000–present) and its more recent comic book adaptation by Devon Grayson (Marvel Comics, February 2002–present).

21. Sanderson, "High Caliber," p. 27; Sanderson, *Marvel Universe*, p. 236.

22. Chris Claremont, "From the Holocaust—A Hero!," *Captain Britain* (Vol. 1, No. 2 [Manchester, UK: Marvel Comics International Ltd., October 20 1976]), pp. 3–4.

23. Matt Smith, "Time Slip: Captain Britain," in *Marvel Vision* (No. 25, ed. Timothy Touhy [New York: Marvel Comics, January 1998]), p. 28 [28–29].

24. Volume numbers are often difficult to figure out with DC Comics. The *Aquaman* series from 1994 to 2001 was the fifth series called *Aquaman*, but Steve Horton classifies this series as Vol. 3, since he treats the two *Aquaman* limited series of the 1980s separately ("Aquaman: Sixty years of water-logged adventures," *Comic Buyer's Guide* Vol. 31, No. 38 [whole No. 1453] (September 21, 2001): 23 [22–24]). *The Overstreet Comic Book Price Guide*, 30th edn., p. 275, also lists it simply as the "3rd Series."

25. Michael A. Chaney, "The Dismantling Evolution of Heroes: Aquaman's Amputation," *International Journal of Comic Art* 1.2 (Fall 1999): 56–60 [55–65]; Laura Gjovaag, "Aquaman Biography," *The Unofficial Aquaman Guide*, August 2002 <http://www.eskimo.com~tegan/aqua/bios/aquaman.html>; Steve Horton, "Aquaman," pp. 22–24; Len Wein and Marv Wolfman, "Aquaman," in *Who's Who: The Definitive Directory of the DC Universe* No. 1 (New York: DC Comics, March 1985), p. 19.

26. Dan Jurgens, "King Arthur," *Aquaman*, (Vol. 5, No. 63 [New York: DC Comics, January 2000]), p. 3. But see Tondro, "Camelot in Comics," pp. 176–77, for suggestions that an earlier writer on the series, Peter David, was also using Aquaman to reenact the Arthurian legend. In addition to David's run on the series, a story apparently outside of regular continuity appears in "Battle Royal" in *Adventures in the DC Universe*, No. 15 [June 1998], where writer Steve Vance presents the Lady of the Lake in need of a time-traveling Aquaman to free Excalibur from an underwater stone before she can bestow it upon his more famous namesake.

27. Dan Jurgens, "Blood Realm," *Aquaman* (Vol. 5, No. 68 [New York: DC Comics, June 2000]), p. 21.

28. For details on the Sword, see Bill Nolan's "The Sword!," *Pure Excitement Comics* (Vol. 1, No. 12 [August 1999]) <http://www.fortunecity.com/victorian/hartford/103/12intro1.html>

29. The treatment of Arthur's return here might be inspired in part by Babs H. Deal's *The Grail: A Novel* (1963), which features a reenactment of Arthurian characters in a college football coach, his wife, and his star quarterback (Raymond H. Thompson, "Deal, Babs H[odges]," in *The New Arthurian Encyclopedia*, ed. Norris Lacy [New York: Garland, 1996], p. 112). However, in the cartoon, Arthur King is the quarterback, his best friend Lance has no feelings toward Guinevere, and Merlin assumes the role of coach (as made explicit in an episode entitled "The High Ground").

30. With the exception of the radio drama *The Saviours: Seven Plays on One Theme* (1942) by Clemence Dane [Winifred Ashton] where Arthur returns as the Unknown Soldier, Arthur's reappearance during World War I is something of a rarity, yet Pratt makes interesting use of the Arthurian legend here. In addition to characters from Shakespeare's play *A Midsummer Night's Dream* invoked in the title, Merlin and Morgana are among the island's guardians, while, borrowing episodes from Geoffrey of Monmouth, Rowena, a German spy and the wife of an Englishman named Vortigern, and her two brothers, Hengist and Horsa, engineer the plot against England.

31. Originally, Abnet and Tomlinson claimed that the Pendragons were only empowered by the various spirits of the Pendragon that once possessed the Knights of the Round Table (e.g., Captain Britain is early on possessed by the spirit of Lancelot and struggles against a friend possessed by the Pendragon of Gawain, which forces him to reenact that knight's search for the Green Chapel), but, in the second volume, they suggest that all of the Pendragons, and not just Adam Crown, were reincarnations of Arthurian figures.

32. For example, due to Merlin's machinations, Whitman spends time in the twelfth century aiding Richard I at the Crusades because Mordred has allied with Prince John, as revealed in Steven Englehart's "A Dark and Stormy Knight" in *The Defenders* (Vol. 1, No. 11 [December 1973]). For further details on Whitman's adventures as the Black Knight, see Stewart, "Camelot in Four Colors," pp. 84–86.

33. Matt Wagner, "Mark Me," *Mage: The Hero Discovered* (No. 13 [Norristown, PA: Comico, June 1986]), pp. 20–21.

34. Matt Wagner, ". . .Or Not to Be," *Mage: The Hero Discovered* (No. 14 [Norristown, PA: Comico, August 1986]), p. 9.

35. Wagner, ". . .Or Not to Be," p. 11.

36. Although no comic book has yet brought Arthur back to face the new post–September 11, 2001 threats, the comics have exalted some of the 9/11 heroes. See, e.g. *Babylon 5* creator J. Michael Straczynski's 9/11 tribute in *The Amazing Spider-Man* (Vol. 2, No. 36 [Marvel Comics, December 2001]), where Spider-Man states, "with our costumes and our powers we are writ small by the true heroes. . .Ordinary men. Ordinary women. Made extraordinary by acts of compassion. And courage. And terrible sacrifice" (10–11).

Select Bibliography of Arthurian Comics

Although the comics are, in general, a collaborative medium, titles are listed here by writer only. Series with Arthurian content are listed in one entry for the entire run of the series, while single, Arthurian-themed issues are listed separately. Where relevant, reprint information is included.

References

Abnett, Dan and John Tomlinson. *Knights of Pendragon* Vol. 1, Nos. 1–18 (London: Marvel Comics Ltd., July 1990–December 1991).

——. *Knight of Pendragon* Vol. 2, Nos. 1–15 (London: Marvel Comics UK Ltd., July 1992–September 1993). [The first four issues were titled *Pendragon*.]

Barr, Mike W. *Camelot 3000* Nos. 1–12 (New York: DC Comics, December 1982–April 1985). Rpt. in a collected edition as *Camelot 3000*. New York: DC Comics, 1988.

Biondolillo, Tom. "The Story of Sir Geraint & Lady Enid." *Legends of Camelot: Quest for Honor* (Plymouth, MI: Caliber Comics, 1999).

Blair, Barry. *Pendragon* Nos. 1–2 (Westlake Village, CA: Aircel Comics-Malibu Graphics Publishing Group, November–December 1991).

Caniff, Milton. *Dickie Dare*. New York: Associated Press, 1933–34. Rpt. in a collected edition as *The Complete Dickie Dare*. Agoura, CA: Fantagraphics Books, April 1986.

Captain Courageous Comics No. 6/6 (New York: Periodical House/Ace Magazine, March 1942).

Claremont, Chris. Untitled. *Captain Britain* Vol. 1, No. 1/1 ([Manchester, UK]: Marvel Comics International Ltd., October 13, 1976): 1–7. Rpt. in *Captain Britain Annual* No. 1. Manchester, UK: World Distributors (Manchester) Ltd., 1978. Pp. 5–11.

Claremont, Chris. "From the Holocaust—A Hero!" *Captain Britain* Vol. 1, No. 2/1 ([Manchester, UK]: Marvel Comics International Ltd., October 20, 1976): 2–9. Rpt. in *Captain Britain Annual* No. 1. Manchester, UK: World Distributors (Manchester) Ltd., 1978. Pp. 13–20.

———. "The Sword is Drawn." *Excalibur Special Edition, 1987.* New York: Marvel Comics, 1988.

———. *Sovereign Seven* Nos. 1–36 (New York: DC Comics, July 1995–July 1998).

———. "Down Under." *Uncanny X-Men* No. 229 (New York: Marvel Comics, May 1988).

Claremont, Chris, Alan Davis, Scott Lobdell, Ben Raab, et al. *Excalibur* Vol. 1, Nos. 1–125 (New York: Marvel Comics, October 1988–October 1998).

Delano, Jamie. "The Bloody Saint." *Hellblazer Annual* No. 1/1 (New York: DC Comics, 1989): 1–48.

Ellis, Warren. *X-Calibre* Nos. 1–4 (New York: Marvel Comics, March–June 1995).

Englehart, Steve. "A Dark and Stormy Knight." *The Defenders* Vol. 1, No. 11 (New York: Marvel Comics Group, December 1973).

Felder, James. "Last Light." *What If. . .?* Vol. 2, No. 97 (New York: Marvel Comics, May 1997).

Fitzgerald, Brian. *Knewts of the Round Table* Nos. 1–5 (Corona, CA: PAN Entertainment, 1998).

Foster, Harold R., John Cullen Murphy, and Cullen Murphy. *Prince Valiant.* New York: King Features Syndicate, 1937–present. Rpt. in collected editions published by Fantagraphics Books (Agoura, CA; Westlake, CA; and Seattle, WA), from 1987–present, and by other publishers worldwide.

Fuller, Ralph. *Oaky Doaks.* New York: Associated Press, 1935–61. [Reprint information not available.]

Gillis, Peter B. "Dragon Circle." *Doctor Strange, Sorcerer Supreme* No. 3 (New York: Marvel Comics, March 1989).

———. "Dragon's Dream." *Doctor Strange, Sorcerer Supreme* No. 4 (New York: Marvel Comics, May 1989).

Gunstone, Kevin. "The Battle for Britain: Part I." *Warrior Nun Brigantia* No. 1/1 (San Antonio: Antarctic Press, June 2000): 1–16.

———. "The Battle for Britain: Part II." *Warrior Nun Brigantia* No. 2/1 (San Antonio: Antarctic Press, August 2000): 1–16.

———. "The Battle for Britain: Part III." *Warrior Nun Brigantia* No. 3/1 (San Antonio: Antarctic Press, October 2000): 1–16.

Hawkins, Matt. *Lady Pendragon* Vol. 1, No. 1 (Anaheim: Maximum Press, March 1996). Rpt. as *Lady Pendragon* Vol. 1 #1 Remastered (Fullerton, CA: Image Comics, February 1999).

———. *Lady Pendragon* Vol. 2, Nos. 1–3 (Fullerton, CA: Image Comics, November 1998–January 1999).

———. *Lady Pendragon* Vol. 3, Nos. 1–10 (Fullerton, CA: Image Comics, April 1999–August 2000).

Holland, Charles. *Butcher Knight* Nos. 1–4 (Orange, CA: Top Cow-Image Comics, December 2000–June 2001).

Jenkins, Paul. "Last Man Standing: Part Two, No More Heroes." *Hellblazer* No. 111 (New York: Vertigo-DC Comics, March 1997).

———. "Last Man Standing: Part Three, Human Punk." *Hellblazer* No. 112 (New York: Vertigo-DC Comics, April 1997).

Jurgens, Dan. "King Arthur." *Aquaman* Vol. 5, No. 63 (New York: DC Comics, January 2000).

———. "Blood Realm." *Aquaman* Vol. 5, No. 68 (New York: DC Comics, June 2000).

Krueger, Jim. Untitled. *Universe X* No. 2 (New York: Marvel Comics, November 2000). Rpt. in a collected edition as *Universe X, Volume 1*. New York: Marvel Comics, February 2002.

Lackey, Mike. *King Arthur and the Knights of Justice* Nos. 1–3 (New York: Marvel Comics, December 1993–February 1994).

Lee, Stan. *The Black Knight* Nos. 1–5 (New York: Margood Publishing [for Atlas Comics], May 1955–April 1956). [A number of these stories have been reprinted over the years, but to date there does not exist a complete edition.]

Limke, Jeff. Untitled. *Legends of Camelot: Merlin* (Plymouth, MI: Caliber Comics, 1999).

———. Untitled. *Legends of Camelot: Sir Balin and the Dolorous Blow* (Plymouth, MI: Caliber Comics, 1999).

Martin, Joe. "Excalibur: A Tale of Renewal." *Legends of Camelot: Excalibur* (Plymouth, MI: Caliber Comics, 1999).

Michelinie, David. "Knightmare." *Iron Man* Vol. 1, No. 150 (New York: Marvel Comics Group, September 1981).

Nicieza, Fabian. "Prisoners of Fate." *X-Force* Vol. 1, No. 24 (New York: Marvel Comics, July 1993).

———. "Back to Front." *X-Force* Vol. 1, No. 25 (New York: Marvel Comics, August 1993).

Ostrander, John. "Blowup!" *Heroes for Hire* No. 2 (New York: Marvel Comics, August 1997).

Pratt, Hugo. "Un Songe d'un matin d'hiver." First published in *Pif Gadget* (1972). Rpt. in a collected edition as *Les Celtiques* (Paris: Casterman, 1975) and other translations for the international market, including *The Celts* (Harvill Press, October 1996) for Americans and the British. An abbreviated version of the arc also exists as *Corto Maltese, Volume 4: A Mid-winter Morning's Dream* (New York: Nantier Beall Minoustchine, 1987).

Raab, Ben. *Excalibur* Vol. 2, Nos. 1–4 (New York: Marvel Comics, February–May 2001).

Seagle, Steve. "The Hunt for Xavier!, Part Five: Escape from Alcatraz." *Uncanny X-Men* No. 364 (New York: Marvel Comics, Late June, 1999).

Smith, Matt. "Time Slip: Captain Britain." In *Marvel Vision* No. 25 (New York: Marvel Comics, January 1998): 28–29. Ed. Timothy Touhy.

Souder, Daniel. "The Enchanted Lady." *Legends of Camelot: The Enchanted Lady* (Plymouth, MI: Caliber Comics, 1999).

Thomas, Roy and Dann Thomas. "The Rebirth of the Black Knight." *Black Knight* No. 1 (New York: Marvel Comics, June 1990).

Thomas, Roy and Dann Thomas. "In the Dread of Knight." *Black Knight* No. 2 (New York: Marvel Comics, July 1990).

Vance, Steve. "Battle Royal." *Adventures in the DC Universe* No. 15/2 (New York: DC Comics, June 1998): 13–22.

Veitch, Rick. *Aquaman* Vol. 6, Nos. 1+ (New York: DC Comics, February 2003–present).

Vess, Charles, and Elaine Lee. *Prince Valiant* Nos. 1–4 (New York: Marvel Comics, December 1994–March 1995).

Wagner, Matt. *Mage: The Hero Discovered* Nos. 1–15 (Norristown, PA: Comico, February 1984–December 1986). Twice rpt. in collected editions: 3 oversized volumes (Norfolk, VA: The Donning Company/Publishers, March 1987–October 1988) and 8 comic-sized volumes (Fullerton, CA: Image Comics, October 1998–September 1999).

———. *Mage: The Hero Defined* Nos. 1–15 (Fullerton, CA: Image Comics, July 1997–October 1999). Rpt. in four collected editions, as *Mage: The Hero Defined* (Fullerton, CA: Image Comics, 2000–01).

Waid, Mark and Ty Tempelton. "Castles in the Air." *Legionnaires Annual* No. 1 (New York: DC Comics, 1994).

CHAPTER 12

CAMELOT ON CAMERA: THE ARTHURIAN
LEGENDS AND CHILDREN'S FILM

Barbara Tepa Lupack

The Arthurian legends have had a deep and pervasive influence on popular culture, especially film. As Kevin J. Harty, who has written extensively and incisively about Arthurian cinema, observed, "since 1904 the major names in the film industry both before and behind the camera have been associated with Arthurian film."[1] *Parsifal* (1904), for example, an attempt to capitalize upon the successful New York production of Wagner's opera at the Metropolitan Opera House in New York in late December, 1903, was the earliest American Arthurian film and the most ambitious and costly film Edwin S. Porter made while working for the Thomas A. Edison Company. Unusual for its length as well as for its elaborate sets and trick photography (action shot from the audience's point of view and exaggerated acting to suggest that the actors are actually singing), *Parsifal* had to be withdrawn from circulation because of copyright problems.[2] Other Arthurian silent films followed, including *Launcelot and Elaine* (Vitagraph, 1909; dir. Charles Kent), based on Tennyson's poem from the *Idylls of the King* and hailed for its artistry in blending action with narration and for innovative cinematic techniques that included shots inside a dark cave and close-ups of the tournament in which Launcelot fights to win the queen's favor,[3] and *The Lady of Shalott* (Vitagraph, 1915; dir. C. Jay Williams), which also drew on Tennyson's poetry for inspiration, although for more comedic purposes.[4]

Among these early Arthurian films was one of particular significance. *Knights of the Square Table, or The Grail* (Edison, 1917; dir. Alan Crosland) reflected the attempts by Robert Baden-Powell, the founder of the scouting movement, to model the organization in part on the fellowship of the Round Table. With a screenplay written by the National Field Scout

Commissioner James A. Wilder, *Knights of the Square Table* tells parallel stories about two groups of boys, one a gang of delinquents, whose leader's prize possession is Howard Pyle's *The Story of King Arthur and His Knights*, and the other a group of Scouts. After the leader of the delinquents is wounded in a robbery in which he is forced to participate, the Grail Knight appears and cures him; afterward, he and his gang join up with the Scouts.[5] This film, which reflected contemporary social belief that "the boy problem" could be remediated by channeling adolescent male energies in constructive ways (such as the various popular youth clubs, discussed by Alan Lupack in chapter 9 in this volume), *Knights of the Square Table* was quite likely the earliest of Arthurian films produced primarily for children.

Over the years, in both short and feature films, numerous other filmmakers have drawn on the Arthurian legends to educate, edify, and entertain younger viewers. They have depicted familiar Arthurian characters in both traditional and nontraditional situations. They have brought contemporary young people to the Arthurian world and the Arthurian world to contemporary young people. And through a new medium, they have continued to spark interest in an old but enduring story.

One of the difficulties in discussing Arthurian cinema for children, however, is that it is not always easy or possible to distinguish between children's and adult Arthurian films. For instance, *Knights of the Round Table* (MGM, 1953; dir. Richard Thorpe), the first MGM production in CinemaScope, was not specifically intended for children, but many younger viewers watched and enjoyed the spectacle, which, according to the opening credits, was "based on Sir Thomas Malory's *Le Morte D'Arthur*" and which featured many of the legend's traditional characters, albeit in some unusual ways. (Morgan le Fay, for example, supports Modred, whom she wants to install as king and with whom she plots to destroy her half-brother; Arthur is an adult, not a boy, when he pulls the sword from the stone; and Elaine, here the sister of Sir Percival, becomes the wife of Sir Lancelot, with whom she lives happily for a time in the northern country.) And the fifteen-part serial *Adventures of Sir Galahad* (1949), which starred George Reeves (who later gained fame as Superman on television), recounted, in cliffhanger fashion, how Galahad won his knighthood after rescuing Excalibur; the exciting (if at times confused) story of adventure and combat appealed not only to adults but also to boys—and girls—of the period. (See figure 12.1.) More recent films such as *Monty Python and the Holy Grail* (1974), *Knightriders* (1981), *Indiana Jones and the Last Crusade* (1989), *The Fisher King* (1991), and *First Knight* (1995), all geared to a wide market, have had a great following among younger audiences as well. While it would certainly be fascinating to examine the impact of such Arthurian films on young people or to discuss the influence of *Star Wars*, *Harry Potter*, and other non-Arthurian

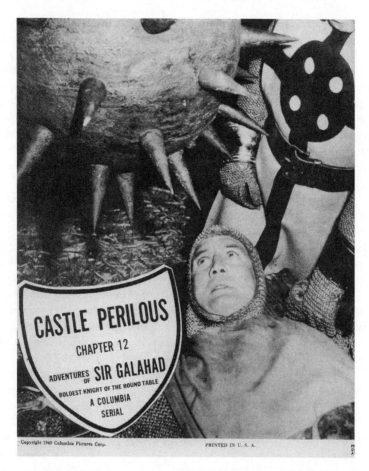

12.1 Galahad (George Reeves) ultimately wins knighthood by rescuing Excalibur in the cliffhanger serial *Adventures of Sir Galahad* (1949).

films that employ Arthurian motifs, the films to be considered here will, for the most part, be limited to those that are both explicitly Arthurian and clearly aimed at younger viewers.

Unsurprisingly, some of the most popular children's Arthurian films have been based on the most American retelling of Arthurian material: the Connecticut Yankee transported to King Arthur's court. Drawing, often very loosely, on Mark Twain's classic *A Connecticut Yankee in King Arthur's Court*, those films attempted to copy the novel's humor and convey the inventiveness of the Yankee. But like the adaptations of the Connecticut Yankee story for adult audiences—including the popular silent film,

A ConnecticutYankee at King Arthur's Court (Fox, 1920; dir. Emmett J. Flynn),
featuring Harry C. Myers; the first sound version, *A ConnecticutYankee* (Fox,
1931; dir. David Butler), starring American icon Will Rogers as Hank
Morgan; and the musical remake *A ConnecticutYankee in King Arthur's Court*
(Paramount, 1949; dir. Tay Garnett), starring crooner Bing Crosby as
Hank[6]—virtually all of the children's films failed to evoke the darkness of
the ending of the novel and the disturbing aspects of Hank's character.[7]
But, as the adult versions had done, most of the film adaptations for children (which Elizabeth S. Sklar has characterized as "cookie-cutter films" for
their homogeneity[8]) at least tried to update the familiar story by introducing elements of topical interest.

The animated *A Connecticut Yankee in King Arthur's Court* ([Australian]
Air Programs International, 1970; dir. Zoran Janjic), the earliest version
specifically for younger viewers, featured a blond-haired, lantern-jawed
Hank Morgan (voiced by Orson Bean) and a plot that was surprisingly
faithful to Twain's story. Hank, a manager of a steel mill, is struck on the
head and sent to Camelot, where he blots out the sun, frees the princess
pigs, organizes newspaper and telephone service throughout the kingdom,
and dispatches motorcycle-riding knights to rescue Arthur, who is arrested
while posing as a peasant. His biggest challenge, however, arises when he
returns from a six-month-long honeymoon in France with Sandy to find
Arthur dead and Merlin agitating to restore "the Old Order." With only
fifty-four knights—and some clever use of magnets and floodgates—he
defeats Merlin's army of thirty thousand before reawakening in a hospital
room in contemporary Connecticut. While the animation is somewhat static by contemporary standards, this television version of Twain's classic
American tale is laudable for its frank allusions to Hank's cynicism and
violence.

A sixty-minute live-action version of *A Connecticut Yankee in King
Arthur's Court* (WQED/Pittsburgh Public Television/*Once Upon a Classic*,
1978; dir. David Tapper), starring Richard Basehart as King Arthur, Roscoe
Lee Browne as Merlin, and Paul Rudd as Hank, proved even more ambitious. Knocked out during a "fire" in his factory (actually, a boiler machine
letting off steam), Hank comes to in Camelot, where he is nearly gored by
Sir Sagramore (Frederick Coffin). Brought to Arthur's court, Hank must
match wits with Merlin, here a regal, chess-playing figure who speaks in
rich, Shakespearean tones. After Hank makes the sun disappear and engages
in other inventive trickery that includes the development of forks, indoor
plumbing, newspapers, telegraphs, and even a mirror, he seems poised to
win the battle of "royal magician vs. royal technician." But when he uses a
gun ("the Great Equalizer") to dispatch Sagramore during a fight, he is
condemned by Merlin for introducing "a weapon that kills, an improvement

we can do without," and scorned by his beloved Sandy and all of the other citizens of Camelot. His "dream" soon over, Hank is stunned to find himself back in nineteenth-century Connecticut. "One of the most thoughtful adaptations of the original story,"[9] this version of *Connecticut Yankee*, with its interesting ragtime musical accompaniment, tried to recreate much of Twain's dialogue and plot, even down to scenes usually omitted in most adaptations, such as Arthur's visit to the smallpox hut. (There is, however, no mass slaughter of knights at the end, only the suggestion of the extent of the destruction that technology forbodes.) Notably, the use of a black Merlin anticipated other later confluences of Arthurian legend and black American culture, from the Merlin-like character Brother Blue in George Romero's *Knightriders* to the multicultural knights in animated series such as *King Arthur and the Knights of Justice* and in live-action features such as *Kids of the Round Table*.[10]

Another interesting spin on the familiar story appeared that same year in a Walt Disney film, *Unidentified Flying Oddball* (Walt Disney Productions, 1978; dir. Russ Mayberry), released in Britain as *The Spaceman and King Arthur*, in which robotics engineer Tom Trimble (Dennis Dugan), the victim of a NASA malfunction, is sent to King Arthur's court. Upon arriving in Camelot, Tom is captured, condemned to be burned at the stake (but saved by his flame-retardant space suit), and forced to fight Sir Mordred (Jim Dale). Just before the fight, however, Tom substitutes his look-alike robot Hermes, who is hacked apart but repaired after the contest. Although he wins a seat at the Round Table, Tom—whose "magic" includes a copy of *Playtime* men's magazine as well as such devices as a laser gun ("the magic candle"), a radio transmitter by which he communicates with Hermes, a Polaroid camera, a lunar rover, a jet pack, and a NASA spacecraft complete with rocket engines, thrusters, and magnetic fields—is anxious to return to the present, but not before he turns his spacecraft around for one last stop in Camelot to pick up his new girlfriend Alisande (Sheila White).

Another children's version, *A Connecticut Yankee in King Arthur's Court* (NBC-TV, 1989; dir. Mel Damski), a made-for-television Christmas special, went even further in reinterpreting Twain for a younger audience: it transformed the adult Connecticut Yankee into an actual child—in this case, a saccharine and precocious Connecticut kid, Karen Jones (played by Keshia Knight Pulliam from American television's landmark and long-running situation comedy, *The Cosby Show*). Knocked off a horse at an after-school equitation class, she is revived in Camelot as the prisoner of Sir Lancelot. Conveniently, Karen's backpack survives the fall as well as the time travel; its contents—a "lightning box" that traps people "in flatness" (i.e., a Polaroid camera); a Walkman; a tape recorder—make "Sir Boss" (a.k.a. "Lady Boss," "Grand Diva," and "Head Honcho") so powerful that

Arthur (Michael Gross) grants her both a blacksmith shop and the position of Prime Minister and accedes to her request for one percent of all revenues. Once established at court, Karen begins lecturing the women of Camelot on the dangers of carving ivory (and redirects their energies to needlepointing "Save the Elephant" pillows for each knight); teaches Guenivere (Emma Samms) and her ladies-in-waiting the twin arts of aerobics and of self-defense; devises a plan by which to improve personal hygiene while ridding the kingdom of poverty (peasants will manufacture and sell toothbrushes, which knights will advertise on their shields); and impresses upon Arthur the fundamentals of feminism and equality. Having saved Camelot from the machinations of Merlin (Rene Auberjonois) and the evil Mordred (Hugo E. Black), bowdlerized for a younger audience into Arthur's nephew, Karen floats away from Camelot in a hot air balloon that her young friend Clarence has copied from one of her textbooks.

Karen Jones was just the first of many young persons to make the backward journey in Arthurian films. In *A Kid in King Arthur's Court* (Walt Disney Pictures, 1995; dir. Michael Gottlieb), thirteen-year-old Calvin Fuller (Thomas Ian Nicholas), who plays for a Little League baseball team called the Reseda Knights, falls through a crack during an earthquake and ends up in King Arthur's time. Mistakenly fetched by Merlin (Ron Moody), who needs a "knight" to restore Camelot to its former glory, Calvin wins the trust of King Arthur, played by the veteran actor Josh Ackland; brings a certain kind of California cool to the court by teaching the princesses Sarah (Kate Winslet) and Katey (Paloma Baeza) to rollerblade and by introducing them to rock-and-roll music via a compact disc player and to the wonders of a Swiss Army knife; and provokes the evil Lord Belasco (Art Malik), who wants to marry Sarah and assume Arthur's throne. After helping the Black Knight (who turns out to be Princess Sarah in disguise) defeat Belasco, Calvin—now "Sir Calvin of Reseda"—returns to the twentieth century with a new sense of self-confidence, in time to hit a home run for his team.

In *A Young Connecticut Yankee in King Arthur's Court* (Filmline International Images, 1995; dir. Ralph L. Thomas), a Canadian film released the same year as Disney's *A Kid in King Arthur's Court*, the protagonist is Hank Morgan (Philippe Ross), a seventeen-year-old high school student and aspiring rock musician from Bridgeport, Connecticut. Nearly electrocuted while trying to fix a transamplifier on an electric guitar, Hank awakens in Camelot, where he becomes the prisoner of the young "knight" Alisande (Polly Shannon), fiancée of Sir Galahad. After being sentenced to burn at the stake for his evil wizardry in capturing another knight's soul "on parchment" (actually, Polaroid film), Hank escapes death by blotting out the sun (courtesy of the computer in his toolbox, which survives his time travel) and by calling on his own "royalty," the royalty of rock, including "Aretha, Queen of Soul" and "Elvis, the true King." Afterward, the newly knighted "Sir Dude" helps to bring a new order to Arthur's kingdom by rescuing Lancelot from an assault by Morgan Le Fay (Theresa Russell) and her evil accomplice Sir Ulrich (Jack Langedijk); restoring vitality to the relationship between Guinevere and Arthur (whom he advises to bathe and thereby to improve his personal hygiene); and scaring Galahad into embarking on a quest for the Holy Grail (an alternative to having to face Sir Dude in a joust). An allergic reaction to jasmine in the love potion that Merlin has prepared for Alisande makes Hank sneeze himself back to contemporary Connecticut—and to an audition for the part of Galahad in the school play opposite the new girl, Alexandra (also played by Polly Shannon). Apart from its generally bad acting, the film is notable for the campy performance of Merlin (Michael York), who spends much of the film looking for the powerful "King" Elvis; for the colloquialism of King Arthur (Nick Mancuso), who dispenses such royal wisdom as "hang on, sister," and "never kick a man when he's down"; and for the Valley-girl-inflected feminism of Alisande.

   Kids of the Round Table (Melenny Productions, 1995; dir. Robert Tinnell), another Canadian film produced in the same year as *A Young Connecticut Yankee in King Arthur's Court*, also drew on the Connecticut Yankee story, although a bit more obliquely. Young Alex (Johnny Morina), fascinated by the legends of Arthur, organizes his friends into a multicultural band of modern Round Table Knights and turns an old shed into their castle. After the band is assaulted—and scattered—by a group of older boys led by bully James "Scar" Scarsdale, Alex runs away but loses his footing and falls down a hill. There he finds a brilliant sword embedded in a large stone and encounters Merlin (Malcolm McDowell), who apparently resides in the "basement" of a nearby tree. The sword, Alex learns, is Excalibur; and Merlin instructs him in its proper use. Over the next few days, Alex repeatedly calls on Excalibur's power. But when he misuses that power to beat up his new classmate Luke (Jamieson Boulanger), a rival for the affection of Jenny (Maggie Castle), the sword disappears. Yet Merlin's lessons about loyalty and honor remain with Alex, who redeems himself by saving Jenny, Luke, and his other friends from the clutches of local criminals led by James's father, ex-con Butch Scarsdale. The film ends as another youngster in another city discovers the sword in the stone—and, it is implied, learns (as Alex did) that Excalibur is not an object but rather a symbol of what is best in people. *Kids of the Round Table*, based on an original story by Robert Tinnell, differs from other children's adaptations of *Connecticut Yankee* in its attempt to blend elements of Twain's story with a retelling of the Arthur–Lancelot–Guinevere (Alex–Luke–Jenny) love triangle in terms that adolescents could appreciate. Yet its message that anyone can become Arthur, or at least Arthur-like, on his own merit reinforces the democratic message that underlies much of the American Arthurian tradition, from James Russell Lowell's classic poem *The Vision of Sir Launfal* in the nineteenth century to the Arthurian youth groups of the early and mid-twentieth century and beyond.

Johnny Mysto, Boy Wizard (Kushner-Locke Productions, 1996; dir. Jeff Burr) also gives Twain's story a few new twists. Teenaged amateur magician Johnny Mysto (Toran Caudell) stages a magic show in his backyard, but his tricks are so poorly executed that only his audience disappears. That same night, Johnny and his friend Glenn pay a visit to Blackmoor, a professional magician they have seen on cable television, in order to acquire some of his trade secrets. At first Blackmoor (Russ Tamblyn), a self-described "has-been entertainer," dismisses the boys, but then he gives Johnny the magical "ring of Astarte," which he says will transform him into a true magician. Indeed, with the ring on his finger, Johnny begins to exhibit surprising powers, which he cannot always control: rabbits, for instance, keep coming out of his hat. And when he places his sister Andrea in a box, she disappears for real. With Blackmoor's assistance, Johnny travels back in time to locate Merlin (Ian Abercrombie) for help in restoring her. It turns out, however, that Merlin also needs Johnny's services: he has apparently sent the ring "through time" in order to summon a modern hero who can save the land from the evil Malfeasor (Michael Ansara) and rescue the imprisoned Arthur and Guinevere. Using both the ring and Arthur's sword Excalibur and relying on his companions Blackmoor and "Sprout" (a young girl about Andrea's age whom Merlin has befriended), Johnny defeats Malfeasor; earns knighthood for himself and Blackmoor; and ultimately is returned to the present, where he releases Andrea from her captivity. The child characters in *Johnny Mysto*—Johnny, Andrea, Glenn (whom Johnny magically transforms into the image of Andrea to fool the housekeeper while he tries to rescue the real Andrea), and the heroic "Sprout" (Amber Rose Tamblyn)—are all lively and appealing; and, along with Merlin, who also plays a prominent role, they manage to sustain interest in the adventure despite the numerous plot turns, which are often unresolved.

Excalibur Kid (Kushner-Locke Productions/Castel Films, 1998; dir. James Head), another film by the same production company, tells a similar story. Fifteen-year-old Zack (Jason McSkimming) is unhappy about his family's upcoming move to an unnamed city because it means he will have to quit his high school fencing team. After denouncing his parents as "fascists" and storming out of the house, he wishes aloud that he could live in "a different time, a time of chivalry, when skill with the sword mattered," a wish that Morgause (Francesca Scorsone) readily grants. Taking advantage of his youth and naïveté, she manipulates Zack into pulling Excalibur from the stone and claiming kingship before Arthur can. It is up to Merlin (François Klanfer)—who, reminiscent of Disney's Merlin in *The Sword and the Stone*, assumes animal form as a horse, rat, and dog—to restore Arthur (Mak Fyfe), defeat Morgause, and return Zack to his own time. Once home, Zack has no recollection of his Arthurian adventure; nonetheless, the experience gives him a new sense of self, similar to Calvin Fuller's burst of self-confidence following his visit to Camelot in *A Kid in King Arthur's Court*, and defines him as a new hero for a new time.

In the most recent *Connecticut Yankee* adaptation by Disney, *A Knight in Camelot* (Disney Television, 1998; dir. Roger Young), the Yankee is Dr. Vivien Morgan (Whoopi Goldberg), a dreadlocked, fast-talking physicist from West Cornwall, Connecticut. When an experiment with gravitational particles sends her back to Camelot, she is captured by Sir Sagramour (Robert Addie); brought before the king (Michael York); and thrust into adventures both familiar (a sentence to burn at the stake—averted, in this case, by reference to the "Scientific History/Natural Disasters" file on her laptop computer) and original (the tortures proposed by a jealous Guinevere [Amanda Donohoe], who cannot wait to dispatch the "ogre"). Using technologies such as a Swiss Army knife and a boom box that brings the rhythms of Chubby Checker and Motown to the citizens of Camelot, Morgan earns Arthur's trust, attains knighthood, and begins to reform the kingdom. Her reforms, particularly the implementation of a labor force of paid workers rather than slaves, lead Arthur to recognize the inequity of his "king's laws" and to rededicate himself to relieving the suffering of his people. "If we could do but this," he announces, "what a kingdom Camelot would be." Coming from a protagonist who is both black and female, Morgan's observations about the unfairness of slavery have a special relevance. Perhaps that is why, when her zeal to achieve "the greater good" temporarily blinds her to the importance of the individual (a blindness that successfully hints at the dark side of Twain's Yankee, a side usually ignored in *Connecticut Yankee* adaptations), Morgan's lapse seems inconsistent both with her character and with the easy comic resolutions of the plot. The film's underlying (and decidedly child-friendly) message of democracy and equality is also evident in the prominence of Clarence the page (Simon Fenton), who, though "common born," has—as Arthur tells the court— "a prince's bearing, a lion's heart, and a son's loyalty" and who achieves his knighthood, along with Sagramour's lands and properties, after exposing that knight's treachery. What most distinguishes this version of *Connecticut Yankee* from other reinterpretations, however, is the twist in the ending: back in her lab, Dr. Morgan encounters a dapper, modernly dressed Merlin and learns that it was he who had manipulated her entire adventure as a way of teaching Arthur the importance of the values of honor, loyalty, pride, and courage—values explicitly linked to American values. After Morgan asks Merlin if she can accompany him as his apprentice, the two move together through the doorway of the lab into the vast swirling universe beyond and into new adventures. Vivien Morgan thus becomes a new age Vivien to the age-old Merlin, just as the familiar Connecticut Yankee story keeps getting refined and reinterpreted for a new age.

Whereas the children's versions of *Connecticut Yankee* generally send contemporary characters into Arthur's court, other Arthurian children's films reverse the motif and bring Arthurian characters into modern times (more often than not, to contemporary California). The clash of modern and dark age or medieval cultures provides much of the comedy, both intentional and unintentional, in these situations. *Merlin's Shop of Mystical Wonders* (Berton Films, 1995; dir. Kenneth J. Berton), for instance, offers an Arthurian story— actually, two stories—within a story. When a storm knocks out the television reception in his home, a former scriptwriter (Ernest Borgnine) tries to entertain his young grandson with tales of Merlin, Arthur's magician. The tales, however, have nothing to do with Arthurian times; rather, they take place in northern California, where Merlin (George Milan) and his wife Zurella (Bunny Summers) have established a very unusual boutique, full of forests and gremlins, in order to "awaken the world. . .to bring magic back." In the first story, a wife stops by the shop and wishes on Zurella's talisman for a baby; her wish comes true in a bizarre way when her obnoxious, overbearing husband misuses spells from Merlin's book of magic and turns himself into an infant. In the second story, a toy monkey (a birthday gift to Merlin from his rival Morgana) that is stolen from the shop brings death and devastation to its new owners before being reclaimed by Merlin. Though neither an exciting nor even a well-edited film, its very grossness probably appealed to certain young viewers.

Merlin returns again in an even more contrived and convoluted film, *Merlin: The Return* (Peakviewing Production, 2000; dir. Paul Matthews). His challenge this time is to keep the evil Mordred (Craig Sheffer) from passing through a portal into the present day; to rescue Guinevere (Julie Hartley) and Lancelot (Adrian Paul), whom Mordred has kept imprisoned in another dimension for fifteen hundred years; and to help Arthur (Patrick Bergin) retrieve Excalibur, which he lost to Mordred during their last battle at Stonehenge. Through a medium, Mordred is in contact with an attractive scientist, Matthews (Tia Carrere), who is conducting her own unconventional experiments with electromagnetic energies (the same "magnetic flow of earth" from which Mordred's powers derive). Believing that Merlin's magic is waning, Mordred is determined to exploit his weakness. But two young people—Richie (Byron Taylor), who has recently moved with his widowed mother to her family home in England, and his new friend and neighbor Kate (Leigh Greyvenstein), daughter of the medium Matthews is using to channel Mordred—join forces with Merlin (Rik Mayall) and Arthur (who has been thrust forward in time) to defeat Mordred (who, after being impaled by Excalibur, explodes and disappears). For his courage, Richie is later knighted by Arthur. (In a sexist parallel, Guinevere gives her wedding ring to Kate as a reward for her bravery.) With low-budget Indiana Jones–like special effects (such as the demon–skeletons of women whom Mordred has sacrificed and dispatched through the portal to take over the bodies of Arthur's knights and of local citizens) and innumerable appearances and disappearances (as characters pop inexplicably or accidentally from one dimension into another), *Merlin: The Return* is surely one of the most poorly plotted and badly acted children's Arthurian films ever produced.

Another Merlin in a contemporary setting appears in *The Sorcerer's Apprentice* (Peakviewing Productions, 2001; dir. David Lister), a film by the same production company and starring the same young actor in a similar plot of sword and sorcery. In this film, the old magician (Robert Davi) is transformed into the gruff but likeable neighbor of a lonely fourteen-year-old boy, Ben Clark (Byron Taylor), whose family has recently relocated from South Africa. After Ben is threatened by bullies in the local "Burger Barn," Milner (an anagram of Merlin) comes to his rescue; later, Milner teaches Ben the secret to performing real magic. "To believe," he tells the boy, "is to do." And indeed, as Ben starts believing, both in Milner's magic and in himself, he discovers a new confidence and courage. That newfound courage, however, is tested when Ben comes to Milner's aid after Morgana (Kelly LeBrock) returns, as she has every century for fourteen hundred years, to claim the magic staff that will give her the power to rule the world. Ben, it turns out, is the incarnation of the original "staff-bearer" of "Fingall's staff," an Excalibur-like talisman that was hidden in stone centuries earlier by Merlin and that is now on display in an exhibit of ancient artifacts at the museum curated by Ben's father. Together, Milner/Merlin and Ben, his apprentice, defeat Morgana, preserve the staff, and restore the magic crystal (originally part of the staff) that Morgana had stolen. To be sure, the film takes great liberties with the Arthurian tradition (not least of which is the film's omission of Arthur himself),[11] and it is full of odd, incongruous images, including Merlin as a gentleman farmer tending his cottage garden and a very busty Morgana being chauffeured from place to place in a huge black Land Rover by her bumbling familiars. But the film's suggestion that the modern world needs ancient magic echoes, albeit clumsily, the notion that Arthur will return in the time of most need and reinforces the redemptive potential of the legend.

Merlin and Morgana meet again in *Arthur's Quest* (Crystal Sky Productions, 2000; dir. Neil Mandt).[12] When Morgana, one-time apprentice to the legendary magician, uses her evil magic to defeat Uther Pendragon, Merlin takes advantage of a portal in time to transport five-year old Arthur along with Uther's sword, Excalibur, which Morgana needs in order to rule. In Northern Valley, California, where the portal deposits them, Merlin (Arye Gross) embeds the sword in a marker at the local high school ("home of the Kings") and entrusts the boy to the care of a kind and attractive young woman, Caitlin Regal (Alexandra Paul). Ten years later, when the portal reopens, Merlin returns to reclaim the future king, who now goes by the name "Artie Regal" (Eric Christian Olsen). But Morgana (Catherine Oxenburg), skimpily clad in leather and accompanied by her dark knights, makes the same passage, and the battle for Arthur and Excalibur begins. Posing as the new high school principal "Miss Blackheart," Morgana wreaks havoc by implementing five-minute-long classes, teaching shop students to make swords and spears, and reinstating suspended gang members and appointing them to student government. Meanwhile, Artie pulls the sword from the stone marker and—together with his friend Gwen (whom Morgana's knights had earlier taken hostage), his teacher Mr. Winthrop (an enthusiast of myth who wrote his doctoral thesis on Arthur and other heroes of legend), Merlin, and Caitlin (of whom Merlin is now enamored and who also is briefly held captive)—prepares for a showdown with Morgana at the planetarium, the highest point in the city, just as the portal is about to open again. Although Morgana fights as fiercely as her leather bikini will allow, she is overcome and destroyed by the power of Excalibur, after which Artie is reunited with Uther Pendragon (since "brave men never die") and returned to his rightful place in history. Mr. Winthrop is left behind to offer the prologue to the new and ever-evolving Arthurian story: "And King Arthur was never without his sorcerer Merlin, Merlin's wife, Secretary of State Caitlin the Bold, or his Vice King, Lady Gwen the First." And, Winthrop adds, in addition to the Round Table, Arthur is "credited with inventing primitive forms of roller skates, hamburgers, and video games."

In *Lancelot: Guardian of Time* (Alpine Pictures/Anubis Productions, 1999; dir. Rubiano Cruz), it is not Merlin but Lancelot (Marc Singer) who travels forward in time. The evil sorcerer Wolvencroft (John Saxon), who intends to change history by preventing the young Arthur from becoming king, has removed the sword in the stone from the "protection" afforded by English soil and transported it to late twentieth-century America. Lancelot, who materializes suddenly—and still astride his white charger—on a beach in Venice, California, must rely on his newfound friend Michael Shelley (Jerry Levine) and Michael's sister Catherine (Claudia Christian) to help him track down the legendary stone, which "Mr. Wolf" is exhibiting at a local museum. Before defeating Wolvencroft and using the sorcerer's black crystal to return with Arthur to Camelot, Lancelot has numerous forgettable adventures, including a battle with a dinosaur skeleton, which comes to life and tries to devour him. (Meanwhile, the ridiculously coiffed Arthur engages in equally silly escapades: in a local park, he steals food and is confronted by angry picnicers, who address him as "weiner boy" and warn him to "put the hot dog down.") The film ends as Catherine, a feminist author who earlier expressed her skepticism about the existence of chivalric heroes, uses Lancelot's ring and glove to join him in Camelot as his lady. The film is a preposterous mix of Arthurian characters and Harlequin romance, replete with teen idioms (i.e., "Buzz off, butt munch"). Even the youngest and most undiscriminating viewer would find this haphazardly plotted tale of a long-haired, latter-day Lancelot in Los Angeles disappointing.

By contrast, the best of these youth-oriented films use the Arthurian motifs not simply to illustrate the clash of cultures but also to bring about healing, itself an important Arthurian motif, of the child protagonists.[13] *The Four Diamonds* (The Disney Channel, 1995; dir. Peter Werner), a made-for-television cable release, focused on Chris Millard, a fourteen-year-old boy who died in 1972. Based on an original short story that Millard wrote soon after he was diagnosed with cancer, the film concerns a young squire at King Arthur's court who must earn the four diamonds—courage, wisdom, honesty, and strength—in order to win knighthood. But the film actually tells two stories: Millard's own life story and the Arthurian fantasy that he writes to distract himself from his disease. Accordingly, the principal actors play dual roles. Tom Guiry, for example, is both Chris and Sir Millard, the squire; Jayne Brook is both Chris's mother and the wise hermit who guides him in his quest; and Christine Lahti, Chris's doctor, also appears as evil Queen Raptemahad, who holds the diamonds. As Kevin J. Harty noted in a review of the film, *Four Diamonds* uses "one of the key tropes of the Arthurian legend, the return to Camelot—a return, in this case, for healing. The real Chris Millard—already at age twelve familiar with the stories of King Arthur—taps into this trope by finding in the world of Arthur an almost allegorical universe parallel to his own." In the Arthurian universe, "Sir Millard is successful against all foes and meets all challenges. He also finds the virtues that Chris needs to live in his other, real world."[14] As a reinterpretation of the Arthurian story, *Four Diamonds* is thus as powerful as most other children's versions are predictable. And while Chris is not healed physically by his quest, he finds a different kind of cure: the spiritual strength to face his impending death, a strength upon which others (including the film's young viewers) can also draw.

The Mighty (Miramax Films, 1997; dir. Peter Chelsom), adapted from the novel *Freak the Mighty* by Rodman Philbrick, is another affecting film about healing and strength. The main characters are two unusual and surprisingly sensitive boys, Maxwell Kane (Elden Henson) and Kevin Dillon (Kieran Culkin), sometimes called "Freak." In appearance, the two are polar opposites: Max, huge and hulking, self-conscious about his size and withdrawn from social contact, is presumed to be stupid, even retarded; Kevin, small, misshapen by a degenerative disease, and handicapped even further by his crutches and leg braces, is bright and good-humored. But both share an uncommonly strong bond: traumatized—Max, by having witnessed the murder of his mother by his father; Kevin, by the realization of his impending death—and ostracized by their peers, they create their own world based on their reading of James Knowles's *King Arthur and His Knights* and then impose the Arthurian chivalric values of their ideal world on the real world around them. Daily "walks" (with Kevin riding high on Max's strong shoulders) through their rundown neighborhood become heroic quests: together, they protect a girl from an abuser; retrieve a stolen handbag; and scheme to rescue Max from his psychotic father, who has just been released from jail. They are often accompanied on their adventures by medieval knights, who materialize magically to assist them in defeating their opponents. After Kevin's death, Max retreats into his former isolation before recalling—and being emboldened by—his friend's legacy of optimism and courage. In the final scene, as Max releases into the sky one of Kevin's favorite toys, the knights reappear, to pay a final tribute to the noble young boy and to acknowledge the heroism of his companion, who perseveres in his absence.

Like *The Mighty* and the various versions of *Connecticut Yankee*, some of the most memorable and imaginative Arthurian films for children over the years have been adapted from literature. *The Sword in the Stone* (Walt Disney Productions, 1963; dir. Wolfgang Reitherman), for example, probably the best known Arthurian animated film—and one that is still popular with children today—was based on the first book in the tetralogy by T. H. White. The film focuses on Merlin's education of Wart (the young Arthur) and culminates in Wart's drawing the sword from the stone and accepting, reluctantly, the kingship for which the wizard has been preparing him. Like Wart himself, Wart's lessons about life (and especially about the ways in which knowledge and wisdom can be used to defeat stronger opponents) take many forms: Merlin transforms the boy into a fish, a squirrel, and a bird. But, as Raymond H. Thompson has observed, despite the ingenuity of the individual scenes, "the novelty palls." Because so much time is spent on chases and transformations, "particular devices recur predictably."[15] Nevertheless, according to Alice Grellner, the film remains "true to at least one aspect or dimension of White's vision, while eliminating or downplaying much of the novel's multifaceted, ambivalent, misogynistic, often contradictory, and darkly pessimistic view of human nature."[16] Even forty years after its original release, *The Sword in the Stone* continues to entertain viewers with its warm portrait of Wart; its outstanding animation, for which Disney is rightly famous; and its easy sing-along songs. (See the essay by Jerome V. Reel, Jr., chapter 10 in this volume, for discussion of this and other Arthurian music.)

Another shorter animated film, *Merlin and the Dragons* (Lightyear Entertainment, 1990; dir. Dennis J. Woodyard), already considered by some to be a classic, was adapted from a story by prolific Arthurian storyteller and children's writer Jane Yolen (who, in turn, adapted it from the works of Nennius and Geoffrey of Monmouth). Based on the illustrations of Alan Lee and narrated by actor Kevin Kline, *Merlin and the Dragons* tells the story of young Arthur, the newly crowned king, who is having bad dreams. To console him, Merlin shares with Arthur his own dream—of a feared and fatherless Welsh boy named Emrys, who has an odd way with animals and who makes up harmless predictions that start coming true. When Vortigern arrives in North Wales, he orders the locals to build him a tower; but the tower collapses. Each time the tower is rebuilt, it collapses again. Only Emrys is able to decipher the mystery: that the tower cannot stand because it is built on two giant stones, below which two dragons battle. The red dragon, who symbolizes Vortigern, is soon killed by the white dragon, who symbolizes Uther Pendragon. Arthur realizes that Emrys is actually Merlin and that the recounting of the dream is meant to be instructive, just as his own dreams are. "Thank your dreams for waking you up," Merlin tells Arthur. "Great men have great dreams." By paralleling the experiences of the youthful king and his closest advisor, *Merlin and the Dragons* recounts the Vortigern story in a nontraditional but effective way for children.

The Quest for Olwen[17] (METTA/Soyuzmultfilm, 1990; dir. Valeri Ugarov), produced the same year as *Merlin and the Dragons* and originally shown on Welsh television, drew on another literary work, the tale of "Culhwch and Olwen" from the *Mabinogion* by Lady Charlotte Guest. Cursed by his stepmother to love only Olwen, daughter of the evil giant Ysbaddaden, Arthur's cousin Culhwch embarks on a quest to win the hand of his beloved. Ysbaddaden, however, is also under a curse: he will die on his daughter's wedding day. Consequently, to prevent her marriage and his own death, he sets tasks for Olwen's suitors that he believes are impossible to meet. But, with the aid of the Knights of the Round Table and some sympathetic animals (a colony of industrious ants, a monumental eagle, a giant salmon), Culhwch undertakes—and achieves—each task: he finds seeds that never grew and replants them to raise flax for Olwen's veil; he retrieves a comb and scissors from a wild boar so that Ysbaddaden's hair can be cut for the wedding; and he draws blood from the Black Witch so that Ysbaddaden's beard can be softened and shaved. Once properly groomed, the giant glances at his reflection in a mirror and, as predicted, dies. And Culhwch, at last, marries Olwen. The film, which uses elegant images but minimal animation, simplifies the medieval tale; but the result is a charming adaptation for children.

Another quest tale, *The Legend of Percival: The Search for the Holy Grail* (Gateway Films, 1993; dir. Judith Bost), based on Wolfram Von Eschenbach's version of the Grail story, used original still illustrations (rather than standard animation) and voice-over narration to tell the story of Percival, whose mother Heart Sorrow tried to keep him ignorant of the world but who nonetheless became one of the most renowned of Arthur's knights. The thirty-minute-long cartoon includes many traditional episodes and situations—from Heart Sorrow's instructions to her son, some of which (like her admonition not to ask foolish questions) complicate and delay his quest; Percival's encounter with the Red Knight; his meeting of Blanche Fleur; his visit to the enchanted palace of Amfortas, where he glimpses the Grail but fails to ask the single question that can cure the wounded Fisher King—but it ends rather abruptly and inconclusively, with the young Percival setting off once again in search of the Grail. Bert Olton writes that the abrupt termination is deliberate: the videotape film, produced by Gateway, a Christian video supplier, was—Olton suggests—designed to serve a religious teaching purpose and, to that end, was accompanied by an instructional guide supposed to foster discussion by outlining "several endings to the legend, some with Percival finding the Grail, others with Percival's son, Lohengrin, finding the Grail."[18] Despite (or, arguably, because of) its religious orientation, however, *The Legend of Percival* provides a good introduction to the meaning of the quest for young viewers.

A more recent animated film, *Quest for Camelot* (Warner Bros., 1998; dir. Frederik Du Chau), was a full-length feature based very loosely on Vera Chapman's novel *The King's Damosel*. Kayley, the young heroine who dreams of becoming a knight, must rescue Excalibur and save Camelot from the evil Sir Ruber, who wants to be king and who, ten years earlier, had killed Kayley's father, the good knight Sir Lionel. Ruber is aided by the beastly Griffin and the awesome Ogre. But despite the menace that Ruber poses, Kayley persists in her quest. With the help of the blind hermit Garrett and several creatures from the Forbidden Forest, including Ayden the falcon and the two-headed dragon Devon and Cornwall, she wins back Arthur's sword and restores the kingdom. (See figure 12.2.) As a reward for her heroism, Kayley—along with Garrett—is made a knight of the Round Table. Though hardly a landmark film, *Quest for Camelot* (which did rather poorly at the box office) reflects a trend in certain recent works of Arthurian fiction and film toward more innovative and democratic approaches to the legends by focusing on female characters.

12.2 Kayley, assisted by the falcon Ayden and the two-headed dragon Devon and Cornwall, wins back Arthur's sword and restores the kingdom in the animated film *Quest for Camelot* (1998).

Arthurian filmmakers have also looked to media other than literature for the sources of their stories. While not, strictly speaking, a children's Arthurian film, *Prince Valiant* (Twentieth-Century Fox, 1954; dir. Henry Hathaway) was based on the long-running Harold R. (Hal) Foster comic strip that premiered in February, 1937, and that was widely read by young-sters, generations of whom first became acquainted with the Arthurian legends through its story lines. Like the MGM film *Knights of the Round Table* that had been released a year earlier, *Prince Valiant* used CinemaScope to offer viewers a variety of spectacular effects, including a climactic scene in which the castle held by enemy Vikings is destroyed by fire. Overthrown and driven into exile, the king of Scandia spends years in hiding with his wife and son, Prince Valiant (Robert Wagner). After reaching manhood, Valiant journeys to Arthur's court, where he is befriended by Sir Gawain (Sterling Hayden), who trains him to become a knight; falls in love with a beautiful princess, Alita of Ord (Janet Leigh); and faces the treachery of Round Table knight Sir Brack (James Mason), the illegitimate son of Uther, who has assumed the guise of the Black Knight in order to betray Valiant's family and usurp Arthur's throne. By his brave acts, Val restores his father's kingship and receives his own knighthood—and, of course, wins Alita's hand in marriage. His story illustrates the lesson about nobility and knighthood that underlies other Arthurian films of the period and that reit-erates the notion of courageous achievement promoted by the boys' clubs and the didactic literature derived from Tennyson earlier in the century (discussed by Alan Lupack and Andrew Lynch in chapters 9 and 1 in this volume). King Arthur alludes to that very fact when Valiant first arrives in Camelot: "Knighthood cannot be had for the asking. It is not enough to be highborn. Knighthood must be won," with deeds of moral courage. As a film, *Prince Valiant* recalled the popular Western, particularly in such plot devices as the trusty weapon (in this case, a singing sword), the faithful horse who warns its owner of impending danger, the rope tricks (Valiant uses his mattress roping as a lasso, hitching one end to a turret and then scaling the castle wall), and the barroom-style brawling.

Prince Valiant was remade in 1992, in a version even more accessible to children. *The Legend of Prince Valiant*, an animated cartoon production for the Family Channel, featured situations and characters loosely based on Hal Foster's strip and voiced by familiar actors (Robby Benson as Valiant, Tim Curry as Gawain, Samantha Eggar as Guinevere, and Efrem Zimbalist, Jr. as King Arthur). Developed for television by David J. Corbett (with Dianne Dixon as story editor) and produced in France and Korea by the Sei Young Animation Company, the series originally comprised twenty-six episodes, each approximately twenty-two minutes long, which dealt with modern issues such as the conflicting demands of conservation and commercial development.[19] The first three episodes, later issued on video, focused on Valiant and his family, who are forced by invading soldiers to flee their castle; on Valiant himself, who dreams of traveling to Camelot to become one of King Arthur's knights; and on the young woman Rowanne, daughter of Cedric the blacksmith, who assists Valiant and joins him on his quest for Camelot, where she too (in keeping with the trend of empowering female heroines) hopes to join the fabled Round Table.[20]

Another *Prince Valiant* film (Constantin Film Production, 1997; dir. Anthony Hickox) followed five years later but proved less successful than the earlier adaptations. Claiming Foster's comic strip as its source and utilizing portions (or at least suggestions) of the actual strip as introductions and segues to the live action, *Prince Valiant* told the story of how Valiant regained the throne of Thule and became a knight of the Round Table. As the film opens, Gawain (Anthony Hickox) is wounded in the joust by Prince Arn; Valiant (Stephen Moyer), Gawain's squire, dons his armor, defeats his opponent, and wins the admiration of Princess Ilene (Katherine Heigl), Arn's fiancée. Meanwhile Morgan (Joanne Lumley), having exhumed Merlin and stolen his book of enchantments from his grave, leads her men into Arthur's castle, where they make off with Excalibur. Knowing that war lies ahead, King Arthur commands Valiant to escort Ilene to safety in her home in Wales. Predictably, the couple falls in love en route. But various complications arise and numerous adventures follow—including an encounter with the fire-throwing Jabberwocky, a fall that sends Valiant and Ilene down the river, a meeting with a friendly dwarf in a tavern, and several close encounters with man-eating reptiles—before Valiant recovers Excalibur, which Morgan has taken back to Sligon (Udo Kier) in Thule.

Soon (though arguably not soon enough), most of the main characters are dead: Arn, Gawain, Morgan, Sligon, Sligon's evil warrior Thagnar, Morgan, even Ilene, who is brought back to life by the sword's magic. After restoring Excalibur to Arthur and securing peace between the two kingdoms, Valiant receives both knighthood and the king's blessing to marry Ilene. The film is truly a triple threat: bad acting, bad plotting, and bad dialogue. (For example, as they are about to fight, Valiant asks if there are any rules, to which Thagnar replies "He who dies first, loses.") Apart from some unintentionally bad special effects (paramount among them the unconvincing mammoth-sized reptile clad in armor), even young viewers fond of the comic strip would find this film adaptation unsatisfying.

As the Family Channel production of *Prince Valiant* had, two other animated television series recast Arthurian characters and motifs in topical ways. *King Arthur and the Knights of Justice* (Bohbot Entertainment, 1992) featured members of a New England football team, the Knights, headed by a player whom sportwriters call Arthur the King. After suffering a bus accident outside of New York, they are transported to "Castle Camelot" in Arthur's time. In order to return home, the Knights (who have names like Lance—and Lug, Trunk, Darren, Wally, and Brick) must find the Keys of Truth before rescuing King Arthur and his knights, who have been trapped by Morgana in the Cave of Glass, and free Guinevere, who has been kidnapped by Morgana's evil accomplice. The popular television series, which conflated Arthurian and sports motifs,[21] spawned a comic book series of the same name that chronicled some of the Knights' adventures as well as a host of toy merchandise, including action figures, and a Play Station video.

Whereas *King Arthur and the Knights of Justice* was oriented toward a younger male audience, *Princess Gwenevere and the Jewel Riders* (Bohbot Entertainment/New Frontier Entertainment, 1995), with its strong female heroines, was an adventure cartoon series designed primarily for girls. In the series, Avalon is a magical kingdom controlled by Merlin "for the good of all." When the outlaw Lady Kale (an anagram for the Lady of the Lake) imprisons him, he scatters the Seven Crown Jewels that she needs to rule. Only the Jewel Riders, a heroic band of youngsters and forest animals led by young Princess Gwenevere, can counter Lady Kale's "antimagic," recover the jewels, rescue Merlin, and ultimately save the kingdom. Like *King Arthur and the Knights of Justice*, *Princess Gwenevere and the Jewel Riders* translated the Arthurian story into an idiom easily accessible to preteen female viewers and generated numerous toy, book, and game products that appealed to its young audience.

Arthurian animation, however, was not limited to series developed for television or to feature-length films. In fact, even before Arthur himself became a familiar subject in those media, his kingdom of Camelot offered an appropriately heroic setting for numerous short cartoons. The first of those, as Michael N. Salda has demonstrated, dates back to "Wotta Knight" (1947), in which Sir Popeye engages in a joust with Sir Bluto, the Black Knight from Brooklyn, to decide who will win the chance to rouse the Sleeping Beauty (Olive Oyl) in a tournament that is open to all "Ye Knights of Ye Round Table / NO SQUARES ALLOWED."[22] Similarly, the Arthurian dimension was suggested but not developed much further in several subsequent cartoons. For instance, in *Crusader Rabbit* (1949–51), the first syndicated, made-for-television cartoon series, Crusader and his companion, Rags Tiger, hailed from Galahad Glen. And in "Knights Must Fall" (Warner Bros., 1949), Bugs Bunny utilized a variety of Twain-inspired technological maneuvers—including a pool cue, a drill, a spring, an empty suit of armor, a straight pin, a manhole cover, and a donkey-mounted bomber—to defeat Sir Pantsalot of Dropseat Manor, who has challenged him to a joust.[23]

Bugs Bunny returned to Arthur's world in other later cartoons, including "Knight-Mare Hare" (Warner Bros., 1955), directed by the legendary Chuck Jones, which again adapted the *Connecticut Yankee* motif to the cartoon medium. This time, as Bugs is sitting under a farmer's tree drying his ears with a metal hair dryer and reading aloud from Burton's *Tales of Knighthood and Gallantry*, he is struck on the head by a falling apple. The blow sends him back into medieval times, where he meets a dragon (whom he mistakes for a "big horny toad") and defeats his opponent, "Sir O of K, Earl of Watercress, Sir Osis of the Liver, Knight of the Garter, and Baron of Worcester-ooster-shooster-sister-shire." Later, Bugs encounters "Merlin of Monroe," a bug-eyed old sorcerer who uses magical powder to turn him into a pig. (The resourceful rabbit then uses the same powder to turn Merlin into a jackass.) Bugs eventually decides to hit himself in the head with an apple in order to reverse his time travel. Back in the farmer's field, he is left to wonder whether his experience was reality or just a bad dream ("knight-mare"). And in "Knighty Knight Bugs" (Warner Bros., 1958), the Academy-Award-winning Best Animated Short Film that year, Bugs the jester is dispatched from the court of the "noble knights of the Round Table," which includes such famed champions as Sir Osis of Liver and Sir Loin of Beef, to recover the Singing Sword that has been stolen by the Black Knight (Yosemite Sam). After encountering the slumbering dragon who guards the sword, Bugs engages in a medieval chase scene involving drawbridges, catapults, moats, lariats, dynamite, and the ever popular croquet mallet before he leaves the Black Knight's castle, sword—singing—in his hand.[24]

Bugs's most explicit and protracted Arthurian adventure occurs in the short feature film *Bugs Bunny in King Arthur's Court* (Chuck Jones

Enterprises, 1977), a classic of Arthurian animated filmmaking that incorporates elements of the earlier cartoons. The rascally rabbit, thinking that he is heading for the Georgia Peanut Festival, burrows his way into Camelot, where he immediately becomes the "pwisoner of [the] wance" (i.e., the prisoner of the lance) of the lisping Sir Elmer of Fudde. After performing some Twain-like magic by blotting out the sun, Bugs asks King Arthur (Daffy Duck) for a boon: a fire-breathing dragon that he can use as a source of power for his new enterprise, an armor works. Within two years, everyone in the kingdom is sporting Bugs's armor. Thoughtfully—and entrepreneurially—Bugs even manufactures special suits of armor for "endangered species," including foxes, squirrels, and deer. When Sir Elmer of Fudde (seconded by Merlin of Monroe, the Baron of Yosemite) challenges Bugs (seconded by Sir Porké of Pigge) to a joust, Bugs bests his opponent: with technology such as magnets, a boomerang-like device that repels arrows, a catapult, gunpowder, and a revolving wheel made of hatchets, he manages repeatedly to crash Elmer into the castle wall and dunk him into the adjacent moat. Finally, after drawing the sword (which he thinks will make a good carrot slicer) from the stone, Bugs gains the allegiance of Porké, Daffy, and even Elmer and Merlin, and becomes the new king, "Arth-Hare."

Arthurian characters also appeared in various other cartoons and cartoon series, including "Mr. Magoo's King Arthur" (UPA, 1964), in which Magoo, as Merlin, guides Arthur through some of the most momentous events in his life, including the pulling of the sword from the stone, the formation of the Round Table, the betrothal to Guinevere, the acquisition of Excaliber [sic] from the Lady of the Lake, and his coronation as king of all England; "Scared a Lot in Camelot" (Hanna-Barbera, 1976), on Scooby-Doo/Dynomutt Hour; "Excalibur Scooby" (Hanna-Barbera, 1984), on The New Scooby-Doo Mysteries;[25] "Sir Gyro de Gearloose," on Disney's Duck Tales (Disney, 1987), in which the three nephews of Scrooge McDuck and their friend, the "gadget-man" Gyro, encounter the evil wizard Moreloon and come up with inventive ways to battle fiery dragons and evil knights like Sir Lessdred; "Smurfs of the Round Table," on The Smurfs (Hanna-Barbera-Sepp, 1990); "The Pig Who Would Be Queen," on Muppet Babies (Marvel/Jim Henson Productions, 1988); and on two episodes of Animaniacs (Warner Bros., 1993): "Spell-Bound" (in which Pinky and the Brain, two mutant mice, try to use Merlin's book of spells in order to gain control of the world) and "Sir Yaksalot." Rocky and His Friends (Jay Ward Productions, 1959–61), one of the most consistently clever and sophisticated children's animated programs ever produced, incorporated Arthurian themes into several of the show's segments. On "Peabody's Improbable History," the scholarly, bespectacled canine Mr. Peabody and his boy companion Sherman journeyed through the Way-Back Machine to Arthur's time; and the clever parodies in "Fractured Fairy Tales" retold the stories of Tom Thumb (here, a juvenile delinquent whose situation is reversed by Merlin) and Sir Galahad (so named because a town clerk asks Mr. Galahad if he has chosen a name for his son and the elder Galahad replies, "Yes, Sir").[26]

Another notable example of Arthurian animation is *Arthur and the Square Knights of the Round Table*, also known as *Arthur! And the Square Knights of the Round Table* (API, 1968; dir. Zoran Janjic), a series of television shorts created by Australia's Air Programs International (the same team behind the first animated version of *Connecticut Yankee* [1970]) and later compiled on video, in which Arthur engages in "amazing" and anachronistic adventures. In the various episodes, Morganna and the Black Knight plot to steal Excalibur and gain power in Camelot; Lancelot escapes from his own wedding ceremony and later rescues Guinevere from a giant; Merlin gets a head cold and loses some of his magical powers, to Morganna's delight; Arthur and Lancelot use a mouse to win back Camelot from an Eastern emperor and his elephant; and Merlin and Lancelot join forces to retrieve Arthur's crown and sword from an octopus before Morganna does. Michael N. Salda has observed that, as the characters engage in mundane acts such as trying to get into the bathroom in the morning, shopping for hats, and planning parties, "the humor comes from the odd juxtaposition of old and new, ideal and actual. The series aims at deflating any elevated ideas we might cherish about chivalric life.... Overall these are clever cartoons that approach Arthuriana with a distinctly modern sensibility."[27]

Camelot featured prominently in several other animated films, all of which shared the same title. *Camelot* (Golden Films/Sony Films, 1997; dir. Greg Garcia) incorporated but sanitized elements of the traditional Arthurian stories in order to give young viewers a happy ending. In this animated musical version, Merlin finds the baby Arthur in a burning hut and brings him to Avalon, where Vivien resides with her sister Morgause and other priestesses. For a time, Arthur is blissfully happy: Merlin schools him by transforming him into various animals and objects (mouse, hawk, dolphin, tree); he and Morgause fall in love and form a union; and he pulls the sword from the stone. But then he must follow his destiny by making "the crossing" to England. Once there, he slays a dragon and saves Guinevere, whom he weds; creates a fellowship of knights at Camelot; meets "Mordred of Avalon," whose love of and loyalty to Arthur parallels that of Lancelot; and watches sadly as the jealousy between Mordred and Lancelot leads to the undoing of his dream. Although Arthur and Lancelot pledge to pursue peace by signing a treaty, Mordred challenges Lancelot's word, and a battle ensues. Arthur, Lancelot (who fights at the king's side), and Mordred are killed, but not before Guinevere reaffirms her love by rushing to Arthur's side. Nonetheless, as Merlin had predicted, Arthur leaves behind "a Camelot to remember" before he returns to Avalon, because "only Avalon is forever." And indeed, back in Avalon, where he "waits still," Arthur is greeted by Merlin and Vivien, hailed for never drawing his sword unjustly or giving up on his people, and reunited with Morgause. *Camelot* puts an unsual spin on the familiar story: there is little enmity, for instance, between Arthur and Mordred, with whom he has no bonds of kinship (apart from the fact that Mordred, too, is "of Avalon"). Rather, Mordred is jealous of Lancelot and Guinevere for having enjoyed more years than he in Arthur's company. And it idealizes Arthur's relationships, including those with his two wives, Morgause in Avalon and Guinevere in Camelot. Nevertheless, *Camelot* is a pleasant and age-appropriate reworking of the Arthurian story.

Camelot: The Legend (Tundra Productions/Good Times Home Video, 1998; dir. William R. Kowalchuk), another animated musical cartoon, is narrated by Merlin, who purports to know "the whole story" and who weaves into his retelling many typical Arthurian characters and events. The film opens as Arthur, Guinevere, Merlin, and Mordred are riding to Cornwall for a meeting of kings. Unknown even to Merlin, Mordred has arranged to have the king and queen attacked and killed. But before his hired thugs can complete their crime, the royal pair is rescued by Sir Lancelot, newly arrived from France.[28] Mordred's mother, it turns out, is the "evil witch" Morgan, whom Merlin has shut up in a cave; her only view of the world is through the magic sword, which projects television-like images of daily events onto the wall of the cave. Together, mother (blowzy, overweight, and dressed in low-cut, short-skirted outfits that accentuate her avoirdupois) and son (black-eyed, beak-nosed, and sporting a single Michael Jackson-like curl on his forehead) plot revenge by kidnapping Guinevere, undermining Arthur and Merlin, and making "French Fries" out of Lancelot. Ultimately, they are frustrated in their efforts by a combination of factors, including Morgan's unsuccessful spellcasting (she uses sneezing powder instead of a love potion on Lancelot's gloves), Guinevere's prowess with a sword (a skill she learned from Lancelot), and Arthur's willingness to accept blame for misjudging his queen after seeing Lancelot kissing her hand in chaste allegiance. Mordred, revealed at last to be a traitor, leaves Camelot; the entrance to Morgan's cave is sealed forever; and Arthur and Guinevere rule wisely and well, with Lancelot as their first knight. And so, concludes Merlin, "the legend of Camelot lives on in the hearts of all those true believers who want equality, justice, and opportunity for all people." *Camelot: The Legend* attempts to modernize the legend by mixing traditional episodes, such as Lancelot's crossing of the sword bridge in order to rescue Guinevere, with elements of topical, juvenile comedy, as in the scenes in which Guinevere and Merlin attempt to fool Morgan and Mordred by switching clothing or in which Morgan, after mistakenly using the love potion on herself, tries to seduce Merlin. But ultimately the film—unable to integrate the comic slapstick with the darker, more serious elements of the legend—lacks a consistent tone or perspective.[29]

A final Camelot-oriented Arthurian cartoon, also entitled *Camelot* (Burbank Animation/Anchor Bay Entertainment, 1997; dir. Richard Slapczynski), is reminiscent of Disney's *The Sword in the Stone*, especially in its attempt to show how a young Arthur, with Merlin's help, came to be king. The cartoon features some nontraditional characters, including a dying King Gerdlach (Arthur's father), who entrusts his son to the wizard, and a young foundling named Cynthia, who becomes Merlin's apprentice (to the chagrin of Arthur, who covets the role yet lacks the facility with magic that it requires). But when the evil usurper Sir Baldrick captures Arthur in order to prevent him from assuming the throne, Cynthia and her forest friends rescue him. And once Arthur is established as king—and after Merlin retires to write the story of Camelot—she becomes wizard of the kingdom. Bert Olton concludes that, despite its departures from Arthurian tradition, the cartoon is "a better-than-average reworking of the story of Arthur" and is "a charming version that should pique children's interest."[30] Similarly, Michael N. Salda suggests that while *Camelot* does not rise to the level of "a good Arthurian film," it nonetheless has "a good sense of its youth audience" and a "story-line [that] proceeds clearly from start to finish."[31]

Animation, while easily accessible and popular with youngsters, is not the only way the legends have had an impact on the small screen: a number of live-action television shows and series drew—and continue to draw—upon Arthurian themes and motifs. As early as 1948, in "Squareheads of the Round Table,"[32] a classic Three Stooges episode set in the "Days of Old," Moe, Larry, and Shemp played three troubadours on their way to King Arthur's court, where they help to reunite Cedric the blacksmith with his beloved Elaine, Arthur's daughter, and to defeat the evil Black Prince, who covets Arthur's throne. (The episode, originally produced by Columbia Pictures, has entertained generations of television viewers, young and old, and can still be seen in syndication as well as on video.)

Even more significant than the Stooges' escapade was *The Adventures of Sir Lancelot* (NBC-TV, 1951). The live-action series consisted of thirty episodes (ten of which are currently available on video).[33] Starring William Russell as Sir Lancelot, Ronald Leigh-Hunt as King Arthur, Jane Hylton as Queen Guinevere, and Cyril Smith as Merlin, the series focused on Lancelot's many noble and knightly acts, such as his prowess and generosity in battle against other knights, which wins him a seat at Arthur's Round

Table; his defense of the besieged castle of Sir Urgan; his rescue of the squires kidnapped by thieves seeking possession of Excalibur; his bringing together of his squire, Brian (Robert Scroggins), and the fair lady, Lilith (Shirley Cooklin), and, later, of Anguish's daughter, Kathleen, and her beloved; his recovery of an emerald given to Guinevere and, later, of the Ruby of Radnor, which possesses enough power to threaten even the king; and his help in reuniting the bewitched King Rolf with his loyal son, Damien. Interestingly, in an early example of television/product merchandizing, the Lisbeth Whiting Company produced a board game that allowed children to identify further with the brave knight. "Adventures of Sir Lancelot," was based—as the box announced boldly—"on the exciting NBC TV series" and marketed as "The Official Game" of that popular show. Depending on the color of their game pieces, players assumed the roles of Sir Lancelot, the Green Knight, Merlin the Magician, or King Mark; and as they attempted to capture either Camelot or Westbury Castle, they encountered hazards such as the "Spear Pit," the "Dragon Trap," the "Bow and Arrow Trap," and the rather anachronistic "Alligator Pit."

Over the next decades, numerous television series and shows for young viewers also took up Arthurian themes. Some focused specifically on youthful characters in the legends. *Arthur of the Britons*, for example, depicted Arthur's boyhood and portrayed some of the hardships of life in sixth-century Britain. Alternatively titled *Arthur, Warlord of the Britons*, the British television series originally aired in twenty-four episodes on the Harlech Television Channel in 1972–73.[34] A video film version, *King Arthur, The Young Warlord* (Heritage Enterprises, 1975; dir. Sidney Hayers, Patrick Jackson, and Peter Sasdy), abridged the series into a ninety-minute version that consisted of just a few of the show's original episodes. Despite some ragged transitions between scenes, the film offered an unidealized view of the young Arthur and depicted some of his adventures, beginning with his own death, which Arthur stages in order to bring together leaders of the divided Celtic tribes and to demonstrate how they, by working— literally—in unison, can remove the sword from the stone and resist Cedric, their mutual Saxon enemy. In other episodes, Arthur turns a young boy from enemy to ally; reveals Mark's rough nature to his prospective bride Rowena, whom Arthur loves; tricks Mark into helping him rescue Kai (his stepbrother) and Llud (his stepfather) from their Saxon captors; and even manages to achieve a brief truce with Cedric, with whom he exchanges symbolic gifts. (Arthur gives Cedric a handsome shield and receives in return a brilliant sword; the exchange suggests that the weapons of war can become instruments of peace as well.) Another British television production, *The Boy Merlin* (Thames Television, 1978; dir. Vic Hughes), dwelt on Merlin rather than Arthur and was part of a series for children about magic

and the supernatural.[35] Thames Television was also behind other important
Arthurian television programming of some interest to younger viewers
(although oriented primarily to adult audiences), including the most recent
version of *Gawain and the Green Knight* (1991; dir. John Michael Phillips),
which—as Robert J. Blanch and Julian L. Wasserman observed—cast the
tale as a psychological adventure and allowed the film "to remain true to
the poem's larger themes."[36] The same year, the British Broadcasting
Company produced *Merlin of the Crystal Cave* (1991), a strong adaptation
of Mary Stewart's novel.[37] And the long-running, cult-favorite BBC television series *Doctor Who* incorporated the Arthurian legend in at least one
episode, the four-part "Battlefield" (originally broadcast in 1989),[38] in
which Doctor (a Time Lord) and Ace (his female friend) receive a distress
signal from the future and land in the Earth village of Carbury, where they
discover armed and warring knights who have recently emerged from
spaceships. All the space knights are in search of Excalibur, which rests in
Lake Vortigern. One group is led by Mordred, who is determined to
destroy the Doctor (whom he believes to be Merlin). For help, Mordred
calls on his mother Morgaine, who is in possession of nuclear missiles. As is
typical of the *Doctor Who* episodes, the time-traveling Doctor (Sylvester
McCoy) resolves the situation—in this case, by containing Mordred and
Morgaine and by restoring Arthur's sword.

American television producers also turned to Arthurian material. While
the various television adaptations of *A Connecticut Yankee in King Arthur's
Court* in the 1950s and 1960[39]—by Westinghouse Studio One, Kraft
Theatre/ABC-TV, NBC-TV, and Ford Startime—were intended for adult
viewers, later programs offered more youth-accessible Arthurian fare. In
Mr. Merlin (1981–82), for instance, Barnard Hughes starred as Merlin, a
garage owner and mechanic with a teenaged apprentice, Zachary Rogers,
to whom he tries to teach a responsible brand of his magic. The popularity
of the short-lived series was evident in the amount of spin-off materials,
including "Mr. Merlin" lunchboxes, books, puzzlebooks, and other toy and
game items. *Merlin: The Magic Begins* (1997), another program with a similar youth orientation, was—according to Bert Olton—a two-hour pilot for
a television series with a projected twenty-two follow-up episodes
(although there is no record that the subsequent episodes were ever made
or shown). The pilot told the story of the young Merlin, who was just
learning of his powers, and of his struggles to save the king, Uther
Pendragon, from his advisor, King Vidus, who was trying to steal his
throne.[40]

Over the years, Arthurian themes and characters have also been incorporated in episodes of numerous television shows familiar to young viewers,
from *Highway to Heaven*, *The Twilight Zone*, *MacGyver*, *Quantum Leap*,

Northern Exposure, Thirty-Something, Star Trek, and *Babylon-5* to current shows such as *Touched by an Angel, Third Watch,* and *The Dead Zone.* The popular educational children's show *Between the Lions,* produced by PBS/Corporation for Public Broadcasting, even features a regular Arthurian-influenced vocabulary-building segment, "Gawain's Word," in which two jousting knights, each representing a particular syllable, literally bump into each other and form whole words.[41] And several original adult-oriented television movies and miniseries released within the last decade were full of special and magical effects that appealed to young audiences as well. *Guinevere* (Lifetime Productions, 1994; dir. Jud Taylor), a seriously flawed made-for-cable movie based on the feminist novels of Persia Woolley, depicted Guinevere (Sheryl Lee) as a woman educated in the cult of the goddess and equal in skill to any man and featured likeable actor Noah Wylie as her love interest, Lancelot. *Merlin,* a four-hour miniseries (NBC-TV, 1998; dir. Steve Barron), attempted to do for Arthur's wizard what *Guinevere* did for his queen: that is, to recount, in Merlin's own voice, the events of his life. But *Merlin* took liberties with the familiar stories, both by expanding the role of the wizard (played by Sam Neill) and by introducing intriguing new characters like the shape-shifting gnome, Frik (Martin Short). *The Mists of Avalon* (TNT [Turner Network Television], 2001; dir. Uli Edel), an unsatisfying adaptation of the cult-classic novel by Marion Zimmer Bradley, paid homage to the legend's female characters, including Morgaine (Julianna Margulies), Viviane (Angelica Huston), Morgause (Joan Allen), and Gwenhwyfar (Samantha Mathis), each of whom is empowered to the detriment of the male characters surrounding her. Of far more interest, especially to young audiences, is an original eight-hour miniseries about the life of King Arthur currently in production for Dream Works/HBO (Home Box Office) by two of Hollywood's biggest talents, producer Steven Spielberg and actor/producer Tom Hanks;[42] their fascination with the legend is one more suggestion of its enduring and universal appeal.

A final category of children's Arthurian film deserves brief mention: video productions geared to very young viewers. For example, in *Merlin's Magic Cave* (World TV Company/Embassy Home Entertainment, 1977), a young Morgan (presumably, but not definitively, Morgan Le Fay) takes viewers into the magician's cave. Morgan, who observes that Merlin (glimpsed only in still illustrations) used to love to tell stories to children in the kingdom, then introduces other familiar though non-Arthurian tales from various lands. And in the thirty-minute-long "A Visit with King Arthur" (Coombe-Grove Productions, Inc., 1983; dir. Denny Fisher), one installment in a series in which the puppet-students in the class of Miss Twiddle (Dian Hart) at the fictitious 5th Street School make "visits" to various historical times and places, Laura Hushpuppy dreams that she is in Camelot, where she meets a very unregal King Arthur (comedian Marty Allen). Also featured are Laura's schoolmates Toby Turtle, whose lack of courtesy gets Laura thinking about medieval chivalry in the first place, and Penelope Giraffe, who precipitates Laura's dream-journey by telling her about Guinevere.[43]

In the nineteenth and early twentieth century, youngsters learned about King Arthur largely through literature, from Tennyson's *Idylls* and "Sir Galahad" to James Russell Lowell's widely read, widely taught poem *The Vision of Sir Launfal* and the various adaptations and illustrated retellings of Malory (discussed by Andrew Lynch in chapter 1 in this volume). Today, many children receive their first exposure to the Arthurian stories from Camelot on camera. On the big screen and on the small screen, in live-action and in animated versions, in films and series based on traditional characters and in films and videos that introduce non-Arthurian characters into Arthurian settings—the legends of Arthur have become familiar and accessible to younger viewers. While many of the productions seek largely to entertain, the best of those works continue to provoke, to challenge, to instruct, to edify. And, like earlier forms of Arthurian juvenilia, they mirror timeless values, celebrate tradition as well as Yankee inventiveness, and evoke visions of courageous achievement that today's children and adolescents can emulate. In all of these ways, children's Arthurian films confirm the enduring appeal of the legends and demonstrate how widely—and often effectively—they have been adapted for young people.

Notes

1. Kevin J. Harty, "The Arthurian Legend in Film: An Overview," *Cinema Arthuriana* (New York: Garland, 1991), pp. 3–4 [3–28].
2. Kevin J. Harty, "Cinema Arthuriana: An Overview," *Cinema Arthuriana: Twenty Essays*, Revised Edn. (Jefferson, NC: McFarland, 2002), pp. 7–8 [7–33].
3. Harty, *Cinema Arthuriana*, p. 5.
4. According to Einar and Gunnar Lundquist in *American Film Index: 1908–1915*, p. 333, *The Lady of Shalott* was released on March 15, 1915. The scenario, written by Cecilie B. Peterson, was "inspired by the poem by Tennyson." The cast included Flora Finch, Kate Price, William Shea, Jay Dwiggins, and Constance Talmadge.
5. See the following: Harty, *Cinema Arthuriana*, p. 6; *Cinema Arthuriana: Twenty Essays*, p. 9; and "*The Knights of the Square Table*: The Boy Scouts and Thomas Edison Make an Arthurian Film," *Arthuriana* 4 (Winter 1994): 313–23. See also Bert Olton, *Arthurian Legends on Film and Television* (Jefferson, NC: McFarland, 2000), p. 156.
6. For brief discussions of the other versions of the Connecticut Yankee story for adult audiences, including various made-for-television versions, see the following: Kevin J. Harty, "Cinema Arthuriana: An Overview," pp. 10–13

[7–33] and "Cinematic American Camelots Lost and Found: The Film Versions of Mark Twain's *A Connecticut Yankee in King Arthur's Court* and George Romero's *Knightriders*," pp. 96–109, in *Cinema Arthuriana: Twenty Essays*. See also Alan Lupack and Barbara Tepa Lupack, *King Arthur in America* (Cambridge, UK: D. S. Brewer, 1999), especially pp. 308–14. For further details on these productions, see also Kevin J. Harty, *The Reel Middle Ages* (Jefferson, NC: McFarland, 1999) and Bert Olton, *Arthurian Legends on Film and Television*.

7. For an excellent analysis of the character of Hank, see Donald L. Hoffman, "Mark's Merlin: Magic vs. Technology in *A Connecticut Yankee in King Arthur's Court*," in Sally K. Slocum, ed., *Popular Arthurian Traditions* (Bowling Green, OH: Bowling Green State University Popular Press, 1992), pp. 46–55.

8. As Elizabeth S. Sklar demonstrates in her essay, "Twain for Teens: Young Yankees in Camelot," in Harty, ed., *King Arthur on Film: New Essays on Arthurian Cinema* (Jefferson, NC: McFarland, 1999), pp. 97–108, a number of the youth-oriented versions of *Connecticut Yankee* were "cookie-cutter films: except for some multihued sprinkles here and a dab of icing there, they have few distinctive features, and all taste pretty much alike" (pp. 97–98). Sklar examines three films in detail, and she notes that all "serve up, in one form or another, a microwavable version of the original Yankee's solar eclipse ploy, and all mint (or perhaps milk) ideological capital from the episode of Arthur's slumming amongst the not-so-happy peasants" (p. 99). For an excellent discussion of the various literary adaptations of Twain's *Connecticut Yankee* for children, see Professor Sklar's essay, chapter 3 in this volume.

9. R. Kent Rasmussen, "Dramatic Adaptations of *Connecticut Yankee*," in *Mark Twain: A to Z: The Essential Reference to His Life and Works* (New York: Facts on File, Inc., 1995), p. 98.

10. See Barbara Tepa Lupack, "King Arthur and Black American Popular Culture," in Alan Lupack, ed., *New Directions in Arthurian Studies* (Cambridge, UK: D. S. Brewer, 2002), pp. 105–21.

11. There is a passing reference to Arthur's sword Excalibur and to Merlin's fondness for hiding things in stone; but there is no direct mention of King Arthur. ("Fingall's staff" is also embedded in stone, from which Ben retrieves it.)

12. There is some question about the actual "release" date of the film. The copyright on the film itself is 1998; the Internet Movie database lists the date as 1999; but many film scholars suggest the most accurate date is 2000. (The film went straight to video and was never commercially released.)

13. Kevin J. Harty discusses this motif of healing in several Arthurian films in his essay " 'Arthur? Arthur? Arthur?'—Where Exactly Is the Cinematic Arthur to Be Found?" in Alan Lupack, ed., *New Directions in Arthurian Studies* (Cambridge, UK: D. S. Brewer, 2002), pp. 135–48.

14. Kevin J. Harty, Rev. of *Four Diamonds*, *Arthuriana* 6.2 (Summer 1996), p. 117 [115–18].

15. Raymond H. Thompson, "The Ironic Tradition in Arthurian Films Since 1950," in Harty, ed., *Cinema Arthuriana*, p. 95 [93–104].

16. Alice Grellner, "Two Films That Sparkle: *The Sword in the Stone* and *Camelot*," in Harty, ed., *Cinema Arthuriana*, p. 71 [71–81].

17. I am grateful to Dan Nastali, coauthor (with Phil Boardman) of the forthcoming *Arthurian Annals*, for first acquainting me with this film and with another children's production, *The Legend of Percival* (also discussed in the text), and for providing me with copies of both.

18. Olton, *Arthurian Legends on Film and Television*, pp. 163–65.

19. See entry on "Television" by Raymond H. Thompson and Roger Simpson, in Norris J. Lacy, ed., *The New Arthurian Encyclopedia* (New York: Garland, 1996), p. 608 [607–08].

20. For a list of the episode titles and good descriptions of episodes 1–3, see Olton, *Arthurian Legends on Film and Television*, pp. 164–66.

21. The conflation of these motifs occurs in various earlier literary works, such as Babs Deal's *The Grail* (1963) and Bernard Malamud's *The Natural* (1952).

22. Michael N. Salda, " 'What's Up, Duke?' A Brief History of Arthurian Animation," in Harty, ed., *King Arthur on Film*, pp. 206–07 [203–32]. Salda notes: "what would have been the first Arthurian cartoon was never completed" (p. 203). Hugh Harman and Mel Shaw, two veteran animators, quit their jobs at MGM and Disney to start an independent company; one of their first projects was to be a King Arthur cartoon. The animators never got beyond preparing storyboards before America entered World War II, and afterward they were never able to restart the project.

    I am grateful to Michael Salda not only for his research on the subject of Arthurian animation, which has opened up a new area of study in Arthurian popular culture to me and many others, but also for sharing copies of a number of the cartoons discussed in this essay.

23. Salda, " 'What's Up, Duke?', " pp. 207–08.

24. Salda, " 'What's Up, Duke?', " pp. 209–11.

25. Bert Olton (*Arthurian Legends on Film and Television*, p. 252) offers a synopsis of several of the Scooby-Doo Arthurian cartoons; he also lists another Scooby-Doo Arthurian cartoon adventure, "The Curse of Camelot" (n.d.).

26. Salda discusses these and other cartoons at length in " 'What's Up, Duke?' " and also in "Arthurian Animation at Century's End," in Elizabeth S. Sklar and Donald L. Hoffman, eds., *King Arthur in Popular Culture* (Jefferson, NC: McFarland, 2002), pp. 111–21.

27. Salda, " 'What's Up, Duke?', " p. 219.

28. Interestingly, perhaps in keeping with Lancelot's French origins, the producers have subtly incorporated the music of the "Marseillaise" at several points in the film, including the beginning and the ending.

29. Salda, in "Arthurian Animation at Century's End," p. 113, observed that the film oscillates between serious themes such as adultery and murder and awkward gambits at humor. "We find," he concludes, "a film that at base can't decide whether it is a drama or comedy and whether its audience is old or young."

30. Olton, *Arthurian Legends on Film and Television*, pp. 47–48.

31. Salda, "Arthurian Animation at Century's End," p. 117.

32. Harty, *Cinema Arthuriana: Twenty Essays*, p. 14, notes that this episode was remade, in 1954, with additional footage, under the title *Knutzy Knights*.

33. Bert Olton, *Arthurian Legends on Film and Television*, pp. 11–16. Along with cast lists and other production information, Olton provides excellent summaries of each of the ten episodes that are available on videotape. As he observes, the episodes appear to be randomly selected from the original television series. Moreover, as presented on the five videotapes, they are completely out of order. Olton, however, establishes their chronology as well as the chronology of the twenty additional episodes that are not currently available commercially.

34. Harty, *Cinema Arthuriana: Twenty Essays*, p. 20. Harty writes that the video film version, which was never commercially released, consisted of three episodes taken directly from the series. Olton, who writes that the film version was "an interesting attempt at a plausible interpretation of what the King Arthur of legend might have really been like" (*Arthurian Legends on Television and Film*, p. 142), suggests that the film actually used five of the series' original episodes.

35. Harty, *Cinema Arthuriana: Twenty Essays*, p. 22. In his filmography on p. 256 of the volume, Harty notes that the production (alternatively titled *Shadows*) was directed by Vic Hughes, with a screenplay by Anne Carlton and Stewart Farrar, and starred Cassandra Harris, Donald Houston, Margaret John, Ian Rowlands, Archie Tew, and Rachel Thomas.

36. Robert J. Blanch and Julian N. Wasserman, in "Gawain on Film (The Remake)," in Harty, ed., *Cinema Arthuriana: Twenty Essays*, p. 193 [185–98]. There were also two earlier versions of the Gawain and Green Knight story, both directed by Stephen Weeks. The first, *Gawain and the Green Knight* (United Artists/Sancrest Films, 1973), faithfully reproduced—according to Blanch and Wasserman—some elements of the original poem, such as "the use of a narrator, gamelike atmosphere, and play rules," although it reflected too heavily the influence of Jessie L. Weston's *From Ritual to Romance*. Weeks's second adaptation, *Sword of the Valiant* (Cannon Films, 1983) toned down some of the Weston material but, like its predecessor, excluded the temptation scenes, "the very embodiments of internal tension in the original text, in order to accommodate the material from Chrétien" (pp. 189–90). For a fuller discussion of the particulars of these productions, see Blanch and Wasserman's essay and Olton's synopses. For an excellent analysis of literary versions of *Sir Gawain and the Green Knight* for children, see the essay by Cindy L. Vitto, chapter 4 in this volume. Perhaps of most interest to younger audiences was the casting of the Gawain character: in the 1973 version, it was popular British entertainer Murray Head; in the 1983 version, it was Miles O'Keefe, who had recently appeared on screen as Tarzan.

37. *Merlin of the Crystal Cave* (1991; dir. Michael Darlow) is available on video.

38. "Battlefield," the four-part episode of *Doctor Who*, is available on video (20th Century-Fox Home Entertainment, 1998). For a further analysis of this

episode, see Kristina Hildebrand, "Knights in Space: The Arthur of *Babylon 5* and *Dr. Who*," in Sklar and Hoffman, eds., *King Arthur and Popular Culture*, pp. 101–110.

39. *A Connecticut Yankee in King Arthur's Court* (1952; dir. Franklin Schaffner) was an original made-for-television Westinghouse Studio One production starring Boris Karloff as King Arthur and Tom Mitchell as a middle-aged Hank Martin. A nineteenth-century inventor, avid reader of almanacs, and superintendent of an arms factory, Hank is hit in the head by one of his angry workers, a blow that sends him back to Camelot. The Westinghouse production, which was made only three years after the release of the Bing Crosby film directed by Tay Garnett, was soon followed by *A Connecticut Yankee* (1954; dir. Fiedler Cook), with Edgar Bergen and Carl Reiner, and *A Connecticut Yankee* (1955; dir. Max Liebman), a restaging of the 1927 musical by Rodgers and Hart, with Eddie Albert as Martin Barrett and Boris Karloff reprising his earlier role as King Arthur. And, in 1960, Tennessee Ernie Ford got trapped in a time machine in *Tennessee Ernie Ford Meets King Arthur* (dir. Lee J. Cobb). For more information on these productions, see Lupack and Lupack, *King Arthur in America*; Harty, *Cinema Arthuriana* and *Cinema Arthuriana: Twenty Essays*; and Olton, *Arthurian Legends on Film and Television*.

40. Olton, *Arthurian Legends on Film and Television*, pp. 195–96. Olton offers useful cast and production information.

41. Several episodes of *Between the Lions* are now available on video. I am grateful to Michael A. Torregrossa for bringing the video version to my attention.

42. See, e.g., Adam Sherwin, "Spielberg to Retell Legend of Arthur," in *The Times* (London), July 16, 2002 ("Home News"), p. 6, and Louise Jury, "Spielberg Turns His Talents to Mini-Series on the Life of King Arthur," in *The Independent* (London), July 16, 2002 ("News"), p. 7. Sherwin writes that the miniseries "will depict the battle for Guinevere's affections, Merlin's wizardry and the search for Excalibur. It will also recreate violent battles against the Saxons in the 6th-century AD, in which historians record that a fierce warrior leader called Arthur played a key role."

43. Olton, in *Arthurian Legends on Film and Television*, pp. 200–201, makes reference to other Merlin videos apparently intended for young viewers. He lists, e.g., *Merlin's Magical Message* (from the 1970s), which used Arthurian characters to promote dental health, and *Merlin's Magic of Learning* (1979).

CONTRIBUTORS

JUDITH L. KELLOGG has been teaching in the Department of English at the University of Hawaii since receiving her Ph.D. in Comparative Literature and Medieval Studies from the University of California at Berkeley. She has had a long-time association with the biennial Conference on Literature and Hawaii's Children (and has codirected three of the conferences). She has also given numerous public lectures on such topics as King Arthur in text and image, Merlin, quest literature, *Star Wars*, and dragons. Since the publication of *Medieval Artistry and Exchange: Economic Institutions, Society, and Literary Form in Old French Narrative* (1989), her research has focused on two areas: the influence of the Arthurian tradition on recent fantasy and children's literature, and the works of Christine de Pizan. She recently guest-edited a special issue of *Arthuriana* on "Arthurian Tradition in Children's Literature."

ALAN LUPACK, immediate Past President of the International Arthurian Society/North American Branch, is Director of the Robbins Library and Adjunct Professor of English at the University of Rochester. Creator of the award-winning database *The Camelot Project*, he is author or editor of numerous essays and books on Arthurian topics, including *The Dream of Camelot*, a volume of poetry; *Sir Lancelot of the Laik and Sir Tristrem*, an edition for TEAMS; *Retelling Tales*; *"Arthur, the Greatest King": An Anthology of Modern Arthurian Poetry*; *Arthurian Drama*; *Modern Arthurian Literature*; *New Directions in Arthurian Studies*; and—with Barbara Tepa Lupack—*Arthurian Literature by Women* and *King Arthur in America*, winner of the 2001 Mythopoeic Society Scholarship Award.

BARBARA TEPA LUPACK has written extensively on literature, film, and culture. Her most recent books include *Insanity as Redemption in Contemporary American Fiction: Inmates Running the Asylum*, named an "Outstanding Scholarly Book" by *CHOICE* in 1996; *Critical Essays on Jerzy Kosinski*; *Vision/Re-Vision: Adapting Contemporary American Fiction by Women to Film*; *Nineteenth-Century Women at the Movies*; *Literary Adaptations in Black American Cinema: From Micheaux to Morrison*; and—with Alan Lupack—*Arthurian Literature by Women* and *King Arthur in America*.

ANDREW LYNCH is Associate Professor in English, Communication and Cultural Studies at the University of Western Australia and a member of the Editorial Board of *Arthuriana*. His publications include *Malory's Book of Arms* (D. S. Brewer, 1997) and several articles on Malory. He also writes on medievalism in the modern period.

DAN NASTALI is an independent scholar and the current bibliographer of the North American Branch of the International Arthurian Society. He is coauthor, with Phillip C. Boardman, of *The Arthurian Annals*, a chronological bibliography of all Arthurian works in English from the beginning to 2000.

JEROME V. REEL, JR. is a medieval historian whose Ph.D. is from Emory University. He and his wife Edmee, a librarian and a first-rate researcher, have been involved in the Clemson University community for forty years. Currently, he is Senior Vice Provost and Dean of Undergraduate Studies. The two of them have been active in the field of Arthurian Studies for twelve years.

ELIZABETH S. SKLAR is on the English faculty at Wayne State University, where she teaches Old and Middle English language and literature. She has published on a variety of Arthurian subjects, medieval and modern, and has served on the Executive Advisory Council of the International Arthurian Society/North American Branch and the executive council of the Popular Culture Association, for which she currently serves as area chair for Arthurian Legend. She recently coedited (with Donald L. Hoffman) a volume of essays on *King Arthur in Popular Culture*.

CHARLOTTE SPIVACK is Professor of English at the University of Massachusetts. Her numerous publications include books—*George Chapman, The Comedy of Shakespeare's Stage, Ursula K. Le Guin*, and *Merlin's Daughters: Contemporary Women Writers of Fantasy*—as well as essays in such publications as *Centennial Review, Journal of Women's Studies in Literature*, and *Critical Survey of Poetry*.

RAYMOND H. THOMPSON has recently retired as Professor of English at Acadia University in Nova Scotia. He is the author of *The Return from Avalon: A Study of the Arthurian Legend in Modern Fiction* (1985); an Associate Editor of *The New Arthurian Encyclopedia* (1991) and its supplements; Coeditor of *Merlin: A Casebook* (2003); and consulting editor of Pendragon Fiction, published by Green Knight. He has also conducted a series of interviews, *Taliesin's Successors: Interviews with Authors of Modern Arthurian Literature* <http://www.lib.rochester.edu/camelot/intrvws/contents.htm>

MICHAEL A. TORREGROSSA is a graduate student in English at the University of Connecticut (Storrs). His published work includes two essays on Arthurian film, a bibliography of Arthurian comic books, and entries in the supplement to *The New Arthurian Encyclopedia*. He has also presented papers on the Arthurian tradition at regional, national, and international conferences.

CINDY L.VITTO is Professor of English at Rowan University. She earned her Ph.D. from Rice University, where her dissertation, "The Virtuous Pagan in Middle English Literature," won the John W. Gardner Award for the Best Dissertation in the Humanities and Social Sciences in 1985 and was subsequently published by the American Philosophical Society (1989). She is coeditor of the forthcoming collection of essays *New Perspectives on Criseyde* and author of *Grammar by Diagram: Understanding English Grammar Through Traditional Sentence Diagramming* (2003). She has also authored notes to accompany the Modern Library's 2002 reissue of George Philip Krapp's translation of *Troilus and Criseyde* and coedited *The Rusted Hauberk: Feudal Ideals of Order and Their Decline*. She has presented several papers on *Sir Gawain and the Green Knight*; her article "*Sir Gawain and the Green Knight* as Adolescent Literature: Essential Lessons" appeared in *Children's Literature Quarterly* (1998).

INDEX